Contents

Acknowledgments

I AM INDEBTED TO William Carroll, Lena Orlin, Garrett Sullivan, and several anonymous press readers, who read the whole manuscript, and to Heather Dubrow and Laura Knoppers, who read substantial chunks of it; all of these fine scholars gave me detailed and enormously helpful suggestions.

I delivered portions of the book as papers at the West Virginia Shakespeare and Renaissance Association and to groups at the University of Massachusetts at Amherst, Pennsylvania State University, the Hudson Strode Center for Renaissance Studies at the University of Alabama, and the Center for Literary and Cultural Studies at Harvard University. Thank you to those who gave me many valuable suggestions on those occasions.

I benefited from a three-year grant from the Social Science and Humanities Council of Canada, which afforded me the aid of a fine research assistant, Dr. Faith Nostbakken. I also enjoyed the help (courtesy of the English Department at Pennsylvania State University) of five excellent research assistants: Jane Baston, Richard Cunningham, Nhu Vu, Ryan Netzley, and Elizabeth Gross.

I am happy to acknowledge a good working relationship over the past sixteen years with the University of Illinois Press, which has published four of my books, and I give special thanks to the patient, efficient, and intelligent Ann Lowry, my longtime editor.

Thanks also are due to my two daughters, Dana and Rachel, grown up now but still supportive; and, most of all, thanks are due to Roland Anderson, who read parts of the manuscript and listened to the rest, as it unfolded, over meals. He was the man I thanked as "my respected colleague and dear co-vivant" in the acknowledgments of my first book in 1984. Reader, I married him.

Note on Spelling

EXCEPT IN QUOTATIONS from Geoffrey Chaucer and Edmund Spenser, all spelling has been modernized.

*Vagrancy, Homelessness, and
English Renaissance Literature*

Introduction

The voices of the wretched, the miserable and the alienated, weak and
plaintive, have never found citizenship in the beautiful palace that is
literary history.

—Piero Camporesi

SO INSISTENTLY DID Renaissance writers hammer at the issue of vagrancy,
so frenetically did the Tudors legislate against vagrancy, that R. H. Tawney
once famously concluded that "the sixteenth century lived in terror of the
tramp" (*Agrarian Problem* 268). In 1547, four vagrancy bills were introduced
in the House of Lords, resulting in legislation so harsh that it specified a
penalty of two years' enslavement for a first vagrancy offense and life enslavement if the slave ran away. This suggests governmental panic at an emergency
situation; and yet as C. S. L. Davies shows, "there seems to be no reason why
vagrancy should be an exceptionally acute problem in 1547" (536–38). To hear
early modern pronouncements about vagrants, A. L. Beier notes, one would
think that "governments lived under veritable siege from them" (*Masterless
Men* 12). J. Thomas Kelly's chronology of Tudor and Stuart statutes, proclamations, and prosecutions relating to vagrancy runs to thirteen pages of small
print (*Thorns on the Tudor Rose,* appendix 3). But contemporary reactions
seem persistently to exceed the situation.

Considering the lack of evidence that people living on the streets really
were a major public menace, "the inescapable conclusion," writes William
Carroll, "is that Tudor authorities feared vagrants far out of proportion to
their actual menace" (*Fat King* 36). Bronislaw Geremek calls "excessive" the
"preoccupation with the problem of beggars on the part of the leading reformers, political figures and eminent literary men of the time: it was perceived as the chief evil of their age" (190).

But "excessive" to whom? Surely the spectacles of poverty were shocking
enough to elicit strong responses. In 1583, Phillip Stubbes reported that "the
poor lie in the streets upon pallets of straw, and well if they have that too, or

else in the mire and dirt, . . . having neither house to put in their heads, covering to keep them from the cold, nor yet to hide their shame withal, penny to buy them sustenance, nor anything else, but are permitted to die in the streets like dogs, or beasts, without any mercy or compassion showed to them at all" (59–60). (For debates over revisionist claims that poverty in this period was not as serious as has been thought, see appendix A.) No, it was not the horror of poverty that the Tudors exaggerated. It seems clear from hindsight that early modern opinion-setters exaggerated—not the social problems of poverty, which were certainly serious to those who suffered them, but the threat that vagrancy and beggary posed to everyone else. A few Renaissance authors recognized the disproportion: the pseudonymous Cuthbert Cony-Catcher, genially defending small-time con artists in *The Defense of Cony-Catching* (1592), advised Robert Greene to abandon his attacks on rogues and petty swindlers and focus instead on more damaging social nuisances such as usurers and lawyers. But most contemporaries saw vagrants as a serious threat.

Not only was the response to vagrancy excessive, but it was also weirdly off-target. A number of beliefs about vagrants current in early modern England have been shrewdly questioned and even wholly discredited by modern historians: the belief that vagrants were organized in highly disciplined societies or fraternities with kings and hierarchies of the underworld; that they schooled each other in a number of intricately graded criminal specializations; that they were politically seditious and economically radical, a true threat to the stability of the state; that they were witty scam artists or fiendishly clever masters of disguise, capable of infiltrating decent society; that they were sexually rampant and promiscuous, keeping women as sex slaves; that they were unemployed by choice, preferring to live in idleness off the labors of others; that they wandered aimlessly, with no clear destinations; that they spoke their own language, thieves' cant.

Why did the period pay so much attention to this group, and why did it so misrepresent them? Historians have uncovered much information about vagrancy in this period, and what interests me here is the discrepancy between the historical record, on the one hand, and contemporary representations of vagrancy, on the other. The distinctive contribution of my study, I hope, lies in its exploration of the cultural implications of that bizarre lack of fit.

One mythmaking engine was the literary genre that has come to be called "rogue literature," flourishing all over Europe but especially rich in England, with Robert Copland's *Highway to the Spital-house* (1536[?]), Gilbert Walker's *Manifest Detection of the Most Vile and Detestable Use of Dice-Play* (1555), John Awdeley's *Fraternity of Vagabonds* (ca. 1561), Thomas Harman's *Cave-*

at for Common Cursetors, Vulgarly Called Vagabonds (1566–67), and cony-catching pamphlets of the 1590s and the early seventeenth century by Robert Greene and his imitators. In such pieces, the down-and-out homeless, often rural, rub shoulders with sophisticated urban con artists. The scams of the former comprise mainly feigned disability, while the tricks of the latter involve disguise, mastery of genteel behavior and language, infiltration of polite society, and devilishly clever tricks. It is important that the period called both these types "rogues": partly just because they inhabited the same literary genre, destitute vagrants became guilty by association with criminal scam artists. In this genre one finds full-blown many conceptions about vagrancy that historians now judge to be erroneous: the existence of rogue hierarchies with chiefs, rogue society's organization into minutely differentiated criminal specializations, its members' sexual profligacy and merry idleness. This is hardly "high literature." To give a rough idea of the desirability of its street address within the suburbs of the literary canon, rogue literature courts a readership that would now go in for tabloids.

Rogue literature was pan-European. In Spain, Matheo Aleman's four-volume *The Life of Guzman de Alfarache* (1599), translated into English as *The Rogue* (1623) with an admiring commendatory poem by Ben Jonson, is kin to Greene's rogue pieces in featuring a hero who becomes a rogue through his mother's profligacy, remains a rogue by choice even when he has a chance for a respectable trade, joins up with an organized society of rogues with a set of laws, begs for alms by feigning hunger even though he has been gourmandizing, loves begging as a life of liberty, is acquainted with a beggar who maims his own child as an aid to begging, and periodically indicts respectable society as no more than a well-dressed fraternity of thieves—all features familiar in English rogue literature. However, the hero of the founding Spanish rogue novel, *Lazarillo de Tormes* (1553), takes no delight in the vagrant life into which he is thrust as a child when his father dies and his mother cannot support him. The emphasis is on his chronic state of near-starvation and the shifts to which he is put to stay alive. When finally he scrapes together a little money, the first thing he does is buy a decent suit of secondhand clothes so that he can look for a legitimate job; and once he gets a job (as the story ends, he is the town crier), he never considers returning to a life of begging—giving the lie to common stereotypes about the homeless as idle, work-shy, and wedded to a life of beggary. English rogue literature, however, is more like *The Life of Guzman de Alfarache* than *Lazarillo de Tormes*.

Set against what historians have learned about the actual lives of the early modern vagrant poor, English rogue literature appears as a major site of misrepresentation. As J. A. Sharpe summarizes:

The first impression to strike anyone turning from the statutes and the rogue literature to court archives . . . is that the vagrant emerges as a much tamer phenomenon from the second than from the first. The large bands of vagrants . . . are absent; there is little evidence of a "fraternity of vagabonds"; and the justices examining vagabonds seem not to have been in any way concerned about such matters. Most of those apprehended do not seem to have been the professional rogues legislated against in Parliament, but were usually unremarkable representatives of the lower, and hence more vulnerable, strata of society. . . . This stratum of mobile poor must have irritated many contemporaries, but it is difficult to see it as a universally subversive threat. (*Crime* 143–44)

Note that Sharpe groups together "the statutes and the rogue literature" as twin sources of the erroneous impression that vagrants constituted a "universally subversive threat." As I will argue, the similarities here between official law and trashy popular literature comprise more than an odd coincidence: rogue literature (the tabloids of its day) *influenced* statutes. The word "rogue" itself seems to have migrated from rogue literature into the Poor Laws; and in more general ways, the myths generated by rogue literature were the yeast acting upon a dough of public anxieties to produce the bitter bread of repressive legislation. From her studies of the enforcement of criminal law in early modern Sussex, Cynthia Herrup concludes that "convicts from outside of eastern Sussex, or those who wandered without any settled residence, were less likely to receive mercy than were local convicts." She attributes this to popular beliefs of the sort fostered by rogue literature: "as defendants, strangers were particularly vulnerable because they had no local family or neighbors to vouch for them and because the popular belief in a criminal underworld sabotaged their credibility" (178).

It is arguable, in turn, that repressive legislation itself manufactured the vagrant class. Criminalizing vagrancy singles out a group for scapegoating. As Paul Slack notes, "Vagrants were not in any other respect proven criminals at the time of their punishment. If they had been, they would have been indicted and convicted for the more serious offence. . . . People who were convicted and punished for vagrancy alone, and not for any other crime, . . . were the people for whom the offence was invented: suspicious persons in the middle ground between the deserving poor and the criminal fraternity" (*Poverty and Policy* 92–93). Indeed, Slack argues, this class of people was called into existence by the laws enacted against it: "Vagrancy legislation . . . helped to create the conditions it was directed against. It was self-confirming" (*Poverty and Policy* 100). Thus, it was circular. Why should there be laws against vagrancy? Because vagrants are criminals. How do we know they are criminals? Because vagrancy is a crime.

Why, then, did early modern England manufacture this public enemy? Political and economic explanations have so far predominated. Fear of disorder, many have argued, was deliberately fueled by authorities, especially the Crown, to justify the growth in power of a centralized state—subversion generated in order to be contained. Marx held that it was in exactly this period and exactly this nation, England, that the preconditions for capitalism came together and that the existence of a vagrant class was one of those preconditions. What the sixteenth century branded as immoral, feckless wanderers, Marx regarded as a class of propertyless workers, the sine qua non of capitalism. Many of the causes of poverty and vagrancy that I discuss in this study—enclosures that expropriated agricultural land, the dissolution of the monasteries, the Poor Laws' prosecution of vagrants—feature in *Das Kapital* as formative events for capitalism. Marx drew directly on Sir Thomas More's discussion of enclosures in *Utopia,* which I discuss in chapter 3. C. S. L. Davies suspects that unemployed vagrants "were a useful excuse to make palatable a policy of enforced employment, and, by implication at least, to reduce still further the worker's limited ability to bargain" (536); and although the 1547 vagrancy act permitting the enslavement of anyone who refused labor at any wage was "not systematically used, as it could have been used, by employers to force down wages" (546), the period did see the proliferation of many forms of enforced labor, from public works projects to houses of correction, and its legislation laid the groundwork for transportation to penal colonies (541). Patricia Fumerton, in a book in progress, argues that newly evolving patterns of labor in a more fluid labor market, including "multiple jobs, frequent job-switching, and above all geographical mobility," rather than a lifelong trade in a single locale, were misunderstood as aimless vagrancy.

These political and economic explanations make sense as far as they go, but I want to enrich the cultural mix. I will argue that many groups in society and several intellectual movements had a stake in exaggerating the threat vagrants posed, that many were constructing their own identities against what vagrants represented.

To some extent the modern scholar's hindsighted impression of the period's preoccupation with vagrancy is an artifact of the sheer number of writers from various social groups who at least mentioned vagrancy and homelessness, in however minor a way: even if vagrancy had been a major concern for nobody, it was a minor concern for so many that, from this historical distance, it looms large. Before I lay out this argument, however, I will rehearse some of the evidence against common early modern beliefs about vagrants. This is worth spending a few pages on, because I want it to be clear how very distorted the representations of vagrants are in rogue literature and other early modern texts; and because, despite compelling evidence of their unreliability, Renaissance literary portraits of rogues still get used as windows onto social history. Some of the assumptions about vagrant life long discredited by historians keep cropping up in unexpected places in scholarly writing—even in historical writing. I will, then, begin by clearing the air and setting down the early modern items of belief that one can now be reasonably sure were false or at least seriously distorted. Like a veritable Harman or Greene, I here unmask imposture.

Myths Unmasked

First, the common belief that vagrants were organized in highly disciplined societies (evinced, for example, in John Awdeley's title *The Fraternity of Vagabonds*) has been discredited by historians. Beier notes, "There is limited evidence of hierarchies among vagrants. A London vagabond told Kent officials in 1597 that he was the 'Lord of Rogues,' but what that meant is unclear. To people living in a society obsessed with hierarchy, it was natural to assume that criminals had leaders and followers. Evidence of solidarity among vagrants is also scarce" (*Masterless Men* 125). Catharina Lis and Hugo Soly write, "Research indicates that the stories of secret associations of rogues with their own hierarchies and vocabulary sprang mostly from the vivid imagery of contemporaries. . . . The 'subculture' of beggars and vagabonds was in great measure [an] imaginative creation" (83).[1] Ian Archer summarizes the findings of historians of crime: "Anxieties about gangs of thieves . . . bore little relationship to the reality of small groups of poor migrants engaged in casual theft for subsistence purposes" (*Pursuit* 206).

   Second, the belief in an intricate system of criminal specializations, prominent in works by Harman, Awdeley, and later Greene, is a stark contrast to the improvisational, hand-to-mouth subsistence of real vagrants as established by nearly all historians of vagrancy. This distortion is particularly significant because it creates a shadow structure mimicking legitimate Elizabethan trade specializations, thus helping to erase the unemployment problem by creating the impression that vagrants *did* have employment, gainful if not lawful, in their own world and obscuring for readers the fact that vagrants lacked a "world" in any real sense. The ease with which the Renaissance assimilated criminal specialties to artisan specialties appears in texts such as *Cock Lorel's Boat* (ca. 1518–19), in which a three-page list of highly specialized trades (such as mustard makers and buckle smiths) modulates, toward the end, into a list in which criminal specialists mingle freely with actors and other entertainers; the latter part of the list includes players, purse-cutters, tumblers, jugglers, thieves, whores, bawds, and "dissimuling beggars" (sig. [B5]ᵛ–Ci).

Third, although vagrants were feared as fomenters of sedition and potential overthrowers of the state,[2] it was not wandering beggars who rose in riots and political rebellions. In 1549 Sir John Cheke feared Norfolk rebels would "stir up . . . hurly burlies [i.e., uprisings] of vagabonds" (sig. hii–iii), and a letter of the same year ascribed danger in a time of rebellion to "many idle vagabonds and other lewd and seditious persons" (C. S. L. Davies 546). The word "seditious" is crucial: "sedition" now means "conduct or language inciting to rebellion against the constituted authority in a state"—a serious enough charge—but in the sixteenth century the term was even stronger, connoting "a concerted movement to overthrow an established government" (*OED*); as "concerted" suggests, the concept of sedition assumed an *organized* body of dissidents. The word appears again in a letter from the Privy Council to the Shrewsbury Corporation in 1571, demanding vigorous prosecution of "vagrant persons"; it firmly links petty pilfering with sedition: "There is no greater disorder nor no greater root of thefts, murders, picking, stealing, debate, *and sedition* than is these vagabonds" (qtd. in Ayledotte 157; emphasis added). Roger B. Manning believes that "it may have been alarm at the number of vagrants swept up after the 1569 rebellion that prompted the enactment of the Vagrancy and Poor Relief Act of 1572 . . . , the most repressive vagrancy law of the Elizabethan period" (165).

But the vagrants apprehended that year were hardly a political threat. As Slack writes, "The Rising in the North in 1569 scared many local authorities, . . . but the searches for vagrants after it turned up only one potential source of sedition, a beggar . . . who claimed to have been a soldier. . . . The Midland Rising of 1607 attracted apprentices, artisans and labourers. . . . But riots did not justify the fear of the wandering rogue. Although a vagrant was said to have spread information about a projected corn riot in Kent in 1587, at root popular disturbances were community affairs, not the work of strangers" (*Poverty and Policy* 101). After food riots over the price of fish and butter in 1595, martial law was declared, a provost martial was appointed to round up vagrants, and "a special commission was set up to coordinate action against vagrants in the city and suburbs"; but the actual rioters had been apprentices, not vagrants (Archer, *Pursuit* 1–2). Rebels in Kent in 1528 were led not by vagrants but by settled tradesmen—a cutler, several clothmakers, a shoemaker, a smith; the leader of Kett's Rebellion in Norfolk in 1549 was a tanner (J. T. Kelly 59, 63). Piero Camporesi notes in a European context that "the turbulence of the very poor, while capable of causing anxiety and dread,

never went beyond a bit of unorganized looting, incapable of being transformed into anything more than a furious but short-lived rebellion" (35).
Archer argues suggestively that "riot was a negotiating strategy" by which
apprentices and other interest groups reminded magistrates of their duties
toward various sectors of society (6); lacking the requisite social solidarity
that apprentices conspicuously possessed, vagrants remained (despite popular misconceptions of their underworld organizations) outside such loops
of influence.

Misidentification of vagrants as political agitators resulted in social and
economic programs of far-reaching influence. Manning concludes that "the
vagrancy and labour statutes, the statutes known collectively as the Elizabethan Poor Law, and the Books of Orders were enacted and promulgated
during the mid-Tudor, late-Elizabethan, and early-Stuart crises because the
governors of England attributed the origins of public disturbances to the
problem of masterless men" (185). The Poor Laws remained active through
the nineteenth century: several centuries of public policy toward the poor
were founded on an erroneous belief in vagrant sedition.

Fourth, although some writers suspected vagrants as radical communists—Henry Smith preached in 1593 that vagrants "were of the opinion of
the Anabaptists, that every man's goods must be common" (111)—there is
no evidence that the truly down-and-out articulated *any* economic doctrines.
The abolition of private property and the holding of goods in common were
discussed by some intellectuals, as this study will demonstrate; but where
vagrants were concerned the charge of communism seems to have stemmed
from general fears of unrest and disorder and from myths about vagrant
"fraternities," which were imagined to provide a mechanism for the pool-
ing of goods.

Fifth, vagrants were not jobless by choice. Paul Slack writes, "The picture
which the instigators of the Norwich census drew—of idle, filthy beggars,
wasting their income on drink, sleeping in doorways, and producing bas-
tards—bore little relation to the facts revealed by the census," which shows
"people desperately striving to maintain respectability" (*Poverty and Policy*
85). Those who failed might have to go on the road, but this was hardly the
same as genial idleness. On the issue of the jobless as violators of the work
ethic, Slack finds

> a fundamental and damaging lack of fit between Puritan perceptions of pov-
> erty and the facts. Censuses of the poor like that in Norwich did not uncover
> idle rogues, drunk and disorderly thieves and bastard-bearers, but whole house-
> holds reduced to poverty by depression in the town's worsted industry. Some
> characteristically Puritan medicines for poverty were therefore misplaced. Ef-

forts to deter the poor from wasteful patterns of consumption and to accustom a few of them to moral and work-discipline did little for the mass of the underemployed and unemployed in the declining textile towns. (*Poverty and Policy* 153)

Sixth, tales of vagrants' sexual orgies and their keeping of women as sex slaves are almost certainly what they sound like: tabloid-style fantasies. If orgies occurred, they probably were not heterosexual orgies, since women were scarce. As Beier and others show, women were greatly in the minority among early modern English vagrants (*Masterless Men* 52, table 3). Diane Willen shows that although women outnumbered men among the settled "deserving" poor, for a variety of reasons they were much less likely to take to the road.[3] And existing evidence points to vagrancy as a lonely path: most traveled alone or in groups of two or three—not the scenario of which orgies are made. Some historians have argued that the lack of evidence means nothing, for battalions of beggars could have split up to avoid incurring suspicion upon entering a town, and the dearth of documentation on sexual orgies is to be expected. But surely one has a right to demand that allegations of group sex and female slavery be backed up with evidence, not supposition—and not the tabloid-style evidence of rogue literature.

Seventh, there is very little evidence that vagrants spoke thieves' cant, a myth fostered particularly by rogue literature. D. B. Thomas traces the notion of thieves' cant to German medieval literature: "The Constance *Ratsbuch* of 1381 gives the first inventory of individual rogues in the manner that Harman was later to immortalize. Vintner uses a few Rotwelsch words in his *Blume der Tugend* (1411), and others occur in the anonymous *Des Teufels Netz* (ca. 1420). About 1425 the Lübeck Dominican Herman Korner relates in his *Chronica Novella* a story of a band of murderers with a peculiar language of their own" (9–10). Sebastian Brant's *Narrenschiff,* adapted into English as *The Ship of Fools* (1509), offers a list of cant terms. In the preface to the late fifteenth-century *Liber Vagatorum* (Book of vagabonds and beggars) (1528), which included an influential glossary of thieves' cant, Martin Luther took an interest in beggars' lingo, claiming that "such Beggar's Cant has come from the Jews, for many Hebrew words occur in the vocabulary" (65). D. B. Thomas concurs that "Latin and Hebrew supply most of the strange outlandish words in the German beggars lingo" (55) and attributes this to the presence, among the ranks of medieval secular beggars, of students and clerics in minor orders who begged as they moved around Europe or slipped by imperceptible degrees out of the clergy and into the ranks of thieving vagrants (55). But if the Latin and Hebrew vocabulary of thieves' cant is seemingly more appropriate to educated people than to the dregs of society who allegedly spoke it, another explanation is that the educated writers who described it simply invented it.

A. L. Beier's "Anti-language or Jargon? Canting in the English Underworld in the Sixteenth and Seventeenth Centuries" reports only six cases in England in which references to thieves' cant occur in court depositions rather than in imaginative literature, and all six occur after the publication of Awdeley's and Harman's cant lexicons, raising the possibility—which Beier denies rather unpersuasively (73)—of literary influence on the judicial testimony. Slack harbors a shrewd suspicion that thieves' cant was simply made up by writers of rogue pamphlets, noting that "references to ['Pedlar's French'] outside literary contexts are extremely rare" and suggesting that though "it is impossible to say whether vagabonds ever . . . borrowed terms and styles of life from literary art, the possibility cannot be ruled out" (*Poverty and Policy* 96, 105; see also Sharpe, *Crime* 145). Noting that the first recorded use of thieves' cant in English occurs not in a court deposition but in rogue literature (Robert Copland's *Highway to the Spital-house*), Beier acknowledges that evidence for real-life canting is slim, "largely anecdotal," and "second-hand" ("Anti-language" 70). Though he cautiously concludes that "there is probably sufficient documentation to support the view of literary sources that canting existed" (71), it looks as if independent evidence, indisputably uncontaminated by rogue literature, is practically nonexistent.

Students of canting, including Beier, John L. McMullan, and M. A. K. Halliday, often accept the Tudor explanation that canting was meant to enable secret communication without arousing suspicion. Gilbert Walker explains in *A Manifest Detection of . . . Dice-Play* that card sharks used canting "to the intent that ever in all companies they may talk familiarly in all appearance, and so covertly indeed that their purpose may not be espied" (35). But this makes no sense. If modern-day poker players suddenly started conversing in pig Latin, even people who could not understand their cant would surely suspect that something was up, that these two players knew each other better than they were pretending to, and that they were signaling each other in ways they did not want other players to understand. This would hardly make for inconspicuousness. Given the publicity attending thieves' cant, mentioning a "bousing ken" or "stalling to the rogue" in the midst of a scam would have been a dead giveaway. It would not have mattered if people understood the words: they would have known that thieves' cant was being spoken and have been on their guard. Only a numskull thief would have used such slang in public. The "inconspicuous" explanation is absurd enough to comprise in itself evidence that "cant" was largely a literary fabrication.[4]

Many common beliefs about vagrants, then, do not stand up to scrutiny.

As Beier summarizes, "If vagrants' movements in time and place were not random but guided by identifiable economic forces; if they were not in the main wilfully idle criminals organized in gangs; if they did not pose much real threat to the state: then the repressive policies directed against them hardly seem justified" ("Vagrants" 26). Despite the contrary findings of historians, however, the image of rogues as promulgated by rogue literature has proved remarkably resilient: the very phrase the "Elizabethan Underworld" still conjures up for many people a realm of canny rogues, too idle to work, organized into hierarchical bands of thieves, streetwise practitioners of criminal specializations who spoke in thieves' cant, kept women as sex slaves, and were constitutionally merry. Ironically, some historians have helped perpetuate these highly colored images by using rogue literature as a historical source. As I will show in chapter 1, the historians J. S. Cockburn, David Palliser, Peter Burke, Roger B. Manning, Robert Jütte, A. L. Beier ("Anti-language"), and Johannes Fabricius all base historical conclusions on a piece of rogue literature, Thomas Harman's *Caveat for Common Cursetors.* The very historians whose findings have done so much to undermine beliefs about vagrants that grew out of rogue literature will sometimes turn around and use rogue literature as historical evidence. Manning, who skeptically ascribes fear of outlaw bands to the currency of Robin Hood stories (162–63), is still persuaded that "there did exist a small hard core of 'sturdy beggars' and 'lusty rogues' whom no law could compel to do honest labour" (160); the sole source on which he bases this opinion is Harman's *Caveat.*

As a literary scholar, I will argue that rogue literature creates a fanciful world drawing fulsomely on comic storytelling and jest books and that this creation of imaginative writers ought to be inadmissible as historical evidence of social conditions in the real world. But then, what kinds of evidence *should* be admissible? Knowing that sometimes historians have relied on such suspect "information" as Harman's, how far can one rely on what they have established about vagrants? Especially recalling that in the case of negative conclusions one must always (after four centuries) make some allowances for lost records, it *does* behoove scholars to treat historical data with caution; but one need not opt for complete skepticism. Some things can be known with fair certainty: the names of leaders of political insurrections (none of whom were vagrants); assize archives that indicate that vagrants traveled mostly alone or in small groups rather than in large, threatening bands; court records of interrogated vagrants that often reveal that they were moving on a regular beat, from harvest work to large fairs, or were on their way to London to seek work, rather than wandering aimlessly; censuses that tell a story of people thrown out of work against their will rather than taking to the vagrant life for ease and merriment. Scholars do not have as many hard facts as they would like, but what one does have points in the same direction—to a sharp disjunction between the real material conditions under which vagrants lived and the ways they were represented in literature and the visual arts.

Some misrepresentations of vagrancy were purely opportunistic—much rogue literature, for example, looks like an effort to turn a penny in the literary marketplace. But some misrepresentation appears to have an agenda. And even market-oriented rogue literature was at the very least convenient to those whose ends were served by scapegoating vagrants.

Preoccupation, Scapegoating, Misperception

With regard to Renaissance representations of vagrancy, I see three separable though overlapping questions. First, why did so many different early modern writers and thinkers concern themselves with vagrants? Second, why did contemporary social theories cordon off the vagrant poor from the settled poor? And third, why did writers so seriously misperceive and misdescribe the vagrant poor?

First, why did so many write about vagrancy? It is true that vagrancy and homelessness made poverty highly visible in many people's neighborhoods. Beier reports that vagrants "were ubiquitous, present all the year round in towns, and spilling into the countryside in summer. They camped almost everywhere—in fields and farm buildings; in city streets and suburban hovels; even on the doorsteps of Parliament and the monarch's court" (*Masterless Men* 85). They accosted even Queen Elizabeth:

> Early in January 1582, towards the end of Christmastide, the Queen was riding through Islington when her carriage was surrounded by a great crowd of beggars. The incident must have alarmed her, because William Fleetwood, recorder of London, was ordered to begin a sweep of masterless men the same day. The campaign lasted about ten days and netted several hundred vagrants—100 being taken in a single day. The beggars in Islington were easily located because they were wont to huddle together for warmth among the brick kilns in the village. (Manning 169)

The sixteenth century witnessed recurrent spasms, lasting for a decade or more, of desperate poverty, and the mobility of the desperately poor brought them to the attention of many thinkers, who had many reasons for finding vagrancy appalling. Why, though, did they write about it? One might have expected, as a coping mechanism, some version of denial, some head-in-the-sand pretense that the desperately poor were not there. Why not just ignore them? But—and this is in many ways to their credit—that was not the route Renaissance thinkers took. They did not ignore vagrant poverty but insisted on addressing it.

I suggest that the presence of the desperately poor—the placeless, illiterate, and hungry—was an embarrassment to various upbeat Renaissance publicists, and at some level of consciousness they knew it. Humanists trumpeting the dignity of man had some explaining to do when faced with human refuse limping around the streets, running sores disfiguring their half-naked bodies. (As Natalie Zemon Davis says, humanists' "aesthetic commitment to classical ideals of beauty, order, and harmony made them especially unable to tolerate the noise, disorder, and human 'ugliness' on the city streets" [61]). Protestant reformers advocating the interpretation of the Scriptures by one's own inner light were brought up short by those who could not read their own names. The new nationalists found the presence of starving people a public relations problem that, without serious propagandizing, could put a real damper on national pride. Those singing the praises of home found homelessness and overcrowded slums a difficulty. A society much occupied with disease control saw vagrants as diseased; a culture steeped in semimagical beliefs about pollution denounced the poor as dirty; an intelligentsia espousing codes of civility sniffed at the poor as uncivil. The vagrant poor became such bogeymen not because they were *big* bogeymen so much as because they were *everybody*'s bogeymen. What seems a preoccupation with vagrancy ("the sixteenth century lived in terror of the tramp") is to some extent an artifact of vagrancy's having become a plank in most party platforms—and though not always a big plank, it was everyone's plank. The different reasons for this, depending on whether one is talking about humanism, religious reform, nationalism, or domesticity, will be teased out in separate chapters of this study. But I believe that the impression of a cultural preoccupation results from a confluence of interests: many different groups had a stake in the issue.

Second, why did contemporary social theories cordon off the vagrant from the settled poor? Pronouncements on the poor, in documents from sermons to the Poor Laws, split the poor into two groups, recommending compassion for one group—the deserving poor—and heaping abuse on the other, the undeserving. I will focus on representations of the "undeserving," the vagrant homeless. Why did the educated upper echelons of society excoriate these dregs of society, a harsh response that seems gratuitous? When it comes to the settled, respectable poor, we find considerable good will, good intentions, and sincerity on the part of humanists, religious reformers, and nation builders; they passionately declared their desire to improve the lot of humanity, and I believe they meant it. In important ways, they *did* improve the lot of their contemporaries. But instead of extending their humane principles to the lowliest poor, humanists and reformers excluded and even persecuted them. Relief was dispensed under the Poor Laws or sympathy extended according to Christian precept mainly to the settled poor, while the homeless were perceived as almost nonhuman. As Keith Wrightson says, "The settled poor [were] relatively fortunate in that they had a recognised place in society and were eligible for parish relief under the Elizabethan Poor Law. . . . Beyond them and well outside the charitable consideration of the authorities, were the vagrant poor" (141). Nothing should be done about them, counseled preacher Henry Arthington; they should just be "punished for example sake" (sig. [B4]ᵛ).

Even the most humane of treatises and sermons on poor relief grow harsh and ungenerous when downright vagrants are at issue. The otherwise generous preacher John Downame, for example, finds one class of persons to whom alms should *not* be given: "sturdy beggars, and vagrant rogues, the blemish of our government, who have nothing in propriety but their licentious life and lawless condition; no known father or mother, wife or children, but a promiscuous generation, who are all kin, and yet know no kindred, no house or home, no law but their sensual lust; . . . men . . . who like idle drones, feed upon the common spoil, and live by the sweat of other men's brows: which kind of poor are not to be maintained in their wicked courses" (38). The poor man to give to, Downame counsels, is "the poor householder" (39).

It was partly to *enable* social programs for the settled poor that persecuting the nonsettled poor seemed advisable. Scapegoating vagrants, a readily definable class of undeserving poor, allowed such authors to promote generous giving to other poor people. Such a scapegoated class was necessary because givers had become afraid of being seen as gulls who could not distinguish between the deserving and the undeserving, a fear fostered by a variety of writers, from preachers to legislators. The political theorist Sir Thomas Elyot advised that being "moved with compassion" for "every little occasion" is a "sickness of the mind" (2.81; see also chap. 3); writers of rogue literature showed victims duped by beggars feigning disabilities (in a favorite phrase of Thomas Harman) as worthy of being "laughed to scorn" King Edward VI in 1551 attributed "slack execution of the laws" against vagrancy to "foolish pity" (C. S. L. Davies 546). Partly because of changing concepts of poverty (see appendix A), authors had become afraid of being dismissed as soft-hearted for counseling generosity, especially if they did not demonstrate tough-mindedness toward at least one type of poor. Thus the preacher Robert Allen, in a humane plea for increased charity to the poor, finds it necessary to exempt vagrants from charity and denounce "the vagabond life of a most wicked and unprofitable, yea a most dangerous and harmful sort of people; the which . . . were of late years so mightily increased, that by their licentious and unjust, yea very sturdy and shameless vagring and begging all mercy of alms-giving was so violently catched up and devoured at every rich man's gate, and also at every poor man's door, that mercy was degenerated"; such people were "altogether unworthy of any alms" because they "utterly refused to work" (sig. A2). Scapegoating vagrants helped other kinds of poor people: by legitimizing compassion, it encouraged the charitable to open their purses to the settled poor. But it was hard on vagrants themselves.

At the legislative level, persecuting the vagrant poor became, by around mid-century, a precondition for benefiting the settled poor. C. S. L. Davies dates to the vagrancy law of 1547—the harshest in English history—"the doctrine that increased penalties for vagabonds were an act of charity, a necessary concomitant to increased poor relief, [which] remained important into the next century and beyond" (540). It was from 1547 on that poor laws came in pairs, one setting down penalties for the vagrant poor, the other providing relief for the settled poor. In 1543 the King's Book had condemned "all idle vagabonds and sturdy beggars which being able to get their living by labor, take such alms wherewith the poor and impotent folk should be relieved and sustained" (C. S. L. Davies 539); and four years later the 1547 statute translated alms into a government welfare program on the same underlying principle: suppressing the vagrant poor would free up funds for the settled, impotent poor.

It is not as paradoxical as it seems that Robert Crowley, a mid-sixteenth-century champion of the penurious and an advocate of private and governmental measures to narrow the gap between rich and poor, wrote harshly about idle beggars. In 1550, the same year in which Crowley's *Way to Wealth* blamed uprisings of the poor on rack renting and enclosures by the rich, Crowley's *One and Thirty Epigrams* pilloried able-bodied beggars who "ought to be constrained / To work" and proffered an anecdote of two beggars carefully nourishing sores on their legs; one confesses: "I would not have it healed / . . . For were it once whole / My living were gone" (sig. Bii–Biii^v). An important political and economic writer, Crowley recognizes that the rich fear that the poor harbor leveling tendencies ("they would have no gentlemen") and communistic aspirations (they "would have all things common")—fears that he finds overblown (sig. [B7]). The rich, he writes, have brought uprisings on themselves, and he counsels them to give their own dinners to the needy: "So shall you both feel and know their disease" (*Way to Wealth* sig. [B7]). Harshness toward beggars does not contradict this compassionate stance but complements it, even enables it, legitimizing Crowley as a tough-minded, realistic social commentator rather than a sentimental dreamer. This is why even his book of epigrams, which like rogue literature unmasks beggars' fakery, can plausibly close with a call for openhanded generosity to the poor in general:

> Yet cease not to give to all
> Without any regard,
> Though the beggars be wicked
> Thou shalt have thy reward. (*Epigrams* Bii–Biiiᵛ)

Desire to help the settled poor, then, paradoxically contributed to persecution of the vagrant poor. That so much cultural energy went into redirecting pity and compassion to the deserving rather than the undeserving is a measure of how much pity and compassion were at large in society, how great was the temptation to indiscriminate charity and clemency. In 1596, after nearly a century of public polemics on the necessity of harshness toward the undeserving, Justice of the Peace Edward Hext still reported that thieves escaped punishment because "the simple countryman and woman . . . are of opinion that they would not procure a man's death for all the goods in the world" (Tawney and Power 2:341).[5]

Third, why did the period *misrepresent* vagrants? The burning gaze trained on the dregs of society by so many respectable people suggests that the placeless were more than simply a bad blemish on the Renaissance self-image. They were also to some degree necessary to that image. At a more general level, I will argue that anxiety about rogues who were guilty of geographic mobility was fueled by anxiety over social mobility. At a more specific level, I think that religious reformers, humanists, central governments, and promoters of domesticity defined their own identities in opposition to the identity of vagrants, whose image became distorted because rather than being based on observation it was often constituted by projection.[6] The respectable projected onto vagrants qualities they disowned in themselves—social mobility, linguistic innovation, sexual misconduct, sedition, idleness. This image-making went all in one direction, the vagrants having left no writings.

The "Othering" process, well described in reference to Elizabethan prejudice against foreign cultures or foreign workers in England, has not been much recognized as operating in the case of domestic vagrancy. Claire McEachern, for example, while recognizing that among the "pernicious effects of the nation is the seemingly inevitable reliance of community on the creation (and frequent persecution) of an Other" (25), does not take note of the nationalist's casting of vagrants as Others. Yet the Othering process is plainly visible in the fact that it was the demonization of wandering beggars that gave Renaissance attitudes toward poverty their distinctive coloration. Grappling with the difficult question of what exactly was new in Renaissance policy toward the poor, Elsie Anne McKee considers, in turn, centralization of authority for poverty legislation, communities' responsibility for their own poor, lay rather than clerical control over social policy toward the poor, compulsory versus voluntary support of poor relief, and the distinction between deserving and undeserving poor; but all these phenomena had some medieval roots. The one unique feature of Renaissance policy that McKee finally fixes on is the *prohibition against begging:* it is this that gives Renaissance treatment of the poor its distinctive character (96–98; see also Geremek 164–65).[7] Though begging was never wholly outlawed in England (licenses to beg were issued), begging was very strongly discouraged, and it is noteworthy that all the other measures McKee discusses concerned mainly the settled, deserving poor—the prohibition against begging alone bore heavily on the vagrants, who were singled out as a scapegoated class.

To illustrate the way the respectable projected onto vagrants qualities they disowned in themselves, in chapter 2 I argue that Protestant theologians demonized *bad* dependency in friars or vagrants to justify *good* dependency consequent on Protestant theology. Jeffrey Knapp, citing Catholic rhetoric depicting the Church of England's break with Rome as a "wandering" away from European Christendom, suggests that this Protestant "nation accused of vagrancy" engaged in "shifting the blame for English vagrancy to the vagrants themselves" (138–42), a scapegoating of "bad vagrancy" to justify the English Reformation's "good vagrancy."

Jest Books and Rogue Literature: Vagrancy and the Comic Spirit

Another lack of fit between reality and representation is the gap between the miseries of vagrants' lives and the persistently comic aura surrounding them in literature and other arts. As Suzanne Stratton shows, most northern European depictions of beggars in the visual arts tended toward the comic and satiric; and in Italy, Il Ruzzante's Menego, counting up five and a half months to go until harvest and fearing that the peasants will starve before then, though appearing in a dialogue written during the terrible famine of 1528, is meant to be a comic figure, as indicated by the work's tone and its title, *Dialogo Facetissimo* ("most facetious dialogue") (Camporesi 36–37).

Tudor England witnessed several strange cohabitings of starvation and comedy. The terrible famine years of the 1520s and 1530s coincided with a literary craze for jest books, including (in England) such pieces as *A Hundred Merry Tales*, Walter Smith's *Twelve Merry Jests of the Widow Edith*, and *Tales and Quick Answers, Very Merry, and Pleasant to Read*. In the 1590s a fresh wave of jest books reached print, including *Scoggin's Jests*, *The Merry Tales of the Mad Men of Gotham*, and *Tarlton's Jests*, and Shakespeare alone wrote ten comedies during that decade, which seems a little odd, considering that these were among the worst famine years of the century.[8] London aldermen reported to the Privy Council in the famine year 1596, "the great dearth of victual which hath been continued now these three years, besides three years' plague before, . . . so hath impoverished the general estate of this whole city, that many persons, before known to be of good wealth, are greatly decayed and utterly disabled for all public service, being hardly able by their uttermost endeavours to maintain the charges of their private families in very mean sort: divers of them being enforced to relinquish their trades, and to dissolve their households" (Archer, *Pursuit* 10–11). It is thought-provoking to juxtapose *Tarlton's Jests* or Shakespeare's *Twelfth Night* with another kind of document from the same decade: observing that "London's burial records abound with references to vagrants dying in the streets and near-by fields," Beier culls a list from the burials registered in St. Botolph's without Aldgate between 1593 and 1598:

> Edward Ellis a vagrant who died in the street.
> A young man not known who died in a hay-loft.
> A cripple that died in the street before John Awsten's door.
> A poor woman, being vagrant, whose name was not known, she died in the street under the seat before Mr. Christian Shipman's house called the Crown . . . in the High Street.
> A maid, a vagrant, unknown, who died in the street near the Postern [i.e., Gate].
> Margaret, a deaf woman, who died in the street.
> A young man in a white canvas doublet . . . being vagrant and died in the street near Sparrow's corner being in the precinct near the Tower.
> A young man vagrant having no abiding place . . . who died in the street before the door of Joseph Hayes, a brazier dwelling at the sign of Robin Hood in the High Street. . . . He was about 18 years old. I could not learn his name. (*Masterless Men* 46)

It is not as if those who enjoyed jest books and comedies were entirely insulated from the specter of people dying alone, shelterless and nameless, or that these phenomena were irrelevant to each other: in some texts of the period, vagrancy and even vagrant deaths were in themselves presented as funny. I will be emphasizing the weirdly comic nature of much Renaissance writing about vagrancy and the poor.

Vagrants often star in jest books, such as *A Merry Jest of a Man That Was Called Howlglas* (by the pseudonymous Till Eulenspiegel) and Smith's *Widow Edith*. Although social historians have mined it for information on historical conditions, rogue literature, I will argue, has more in common with jest books than with historical reality. Rogue literature is basically a comic genre. Its flippancy and weirdly inappropriate jokiness are easily missed when searching such texts for information about the Elizabethan Underworld. What startles the modern reader as inappropriate smirking when Harman is talking about capital punishment of beggars for petty thievery is really a genre trademark that gives away the parentage of works like Harman's: they are descended, I believe, from jest books. The jesting tone is crucial to understanding how vagrants got exempted from the social projects of those who willingly lent a helping hand to the settled poor: as "rogues," vagrants were sometimes dismissed from serious social concern as laughable butts of jokes, sometimes anathematized as a social threat when regarded as tricksters, whose witty self-reliance relieved the public of the promptings either of pity or responsibility. Like jest books, rogue literature coincided with some terrible times: consider the fact that major pandemics of plague in 1535, 1563, and 1592 were contemporary with rogue pieces such as Robert Copland's *Highway to the Spital-house* (1536[?]), John Awdeley's *Fraternity of Vagabonds* (early 1560s), and Robert Greene's cony-catching pieces (early 1590s). That pieces couched as comic warnings occurred in periods of deep public anxiety suggests serious purposes underneath the laughter.

Rogue literature and jest books have always been viewed as effusions of popular culture, positively oozing the heady nectar of Merrie Olde England. But rogue literature was not written by rogues, and jest books were not penned by clowns. These texts are products of the educated and often the propertied classes, and they should be read as such. Tessa Watt has shown why "popular culture" must be used inclusively during this period. The cheapness of ballads and chapbooks did not mean that the highest echelons of society failed to buy them: "Ballads were hawked in the alehouses and markets, but in the same period they were sung by minstrels in the households of the nobility and gentry, who copied them carefully into manuscripts" (1). Sheer expense would have prevented a vagrant from buying Sir Thomas More's *Utopia;* but no constraint operated in the opposite direction: the most stellar intellectuals could buy ballads. "Chapbooks which sold for twopence, and appealed to 'honest folks that have no lands,' were also bought by a Staffordshire lady and carefully left in her will to her clergyman son" (Watt

1–2). University-educated writers seem to have got real enjoyment out of the humblest of jest books: in 1578, Edmund Spenser lent to Gabriel Harvey his own copies of *Howlglas, Scoggin's Jests,* and *Skelton's Jests* (along with the Spanish rogue novel *Lazarillo de Tormes*), stipulating that if Harvey failed to return them by January 1, he would forfeit the four volumes of Lucian he had loaned to Spenser (Furnivall xlviii)—an exchange of authors that offends the modern reader's sense of "educated" tastes but seemed unremarkable to Harvey. And as the jest book genre shows, the elite went farther than consuming what is today regarded as cheap popular literature: intellectuals like Thomas More were involved in its *production.*

More himself wrote and published a jest book, *A Merry Jest How a Sergeant Would Learn to Be a Friar,* which did not make the splash in literary history that *Utopia* made: the few who mention it dismiss it as a minor curiosity in a great writer's career. But just as scatological filth and invective, seemingly suited to a fraternity of vagabonds, were basic rhetorical tools for religious reformers, so vulgar jest books appear as early in the humanist tradition as does recovery of classical texts. This is not simply a strange gallimawfry: jest underlay modes of social differentiation that helped maintain privilege. I hope to persuade readers that we should listen to what Renaissance jests say and the tone in which they say it.

The discourse of vagrancy adopted into merry, happy-ending genres (comedies, jest books, rogue literature, trickster tales) material sad enough for tragedy—death by hanging, loss of home, destruction of community. But in Renaissance literary theory, mere sadness did not make a tragedy: you needed greatness too, and that meant noble birth. The low social position of vagrants disqualified them from starring in tragedies. Renaissance social hierarchies influenced the pecking order of literary genres: Sidney placed on top of his generic ladder genres with high-caste personae—epic and tragedy—and at the bottom he situated a genre with low-caste personae—pastoral. Jest books and trickster tales were so far off the generic map as to have sunk from view. But literary theory influenced social realities too: the habit of giving serious literary treatment and dignity to the wellborn while laughing in comic contexts at the lowborn reinforced attitudes that prevented real-life poor people from being taken seriously. The only way homeless people could get into a tragedy was as fortune-fallen aristocrats and royalty, as in *King Lear,* where Edgar, Kent, Gloucester, and Lear himself become "shamefaced poor." Most poor people stayed in comic genres, in which lightheartedness erased their misery. Situating vagrants in comic genres, in line with long-standing literary conventions involving the social hierarchy, promoted what I will call the "funnification" of poverty. Low social rank relegates beggars to a generic landscape in which jokes and tricks, not soliloquies or eulogies, are appropriate. Beggars behave with earthy merriment rather than tragic dignity partly because of the *literary* context dictated by their low degree. As real vagrants were put into places that denied them dignity—the stocks, Bridewell—so the poor were consigned to undignified literary genres.

The pretense that vagrants formed organized societies is a comedic move: comedy famously brings people together. Beggars' banding together in merry groups recalls happy-ending literary antecedents like the Robin Hood tales. In real life, vagrancy split families apart, and historians such as Peter Clark ("Migrant in Kentish Towns") maintain that vagrants typically traveled alone—more like the isolating movement of tragedy.

Related to the comic tone of much vagrancy literature is the idealization of the vagabond life. I will suggest that vagrants became associated with the freedom that ordinary citizens felt they lacked, that romanticizing their freewheeling life was a vicarious escape from a world of religious strictness, moral probity, humanistic moderation, civil manners, homekeeping domesticity— all of which a citizen could assent to in theory but which in practice must often have felt confining. Also, several texts suggest that the very publicity attending the vagrancy problem made people afraid to go outside for fear the vagrants would get them. Fashioning vagrants as monsters could make people feel like prisoners in their own homes, inclining them to romanticize the supposed freedom of those not locked up, namely, the vagrants themselves. To real vagrants, such a false view of happiness, freedom, and self-reliance was no better than demonization: it relieved the consciences of those who might otherwise have felt obliged to help them.

Many in England were chuckling at recent jest books like *Widow Edith* and *A Hundred Merry Tales,* while others were dying of hunger in the streets in the winter of 1527–28, which—capping a series of poor harvests across Europe—was harsh everywhere. London's poor, weakened by hunger, were shaken by sweating sickness, and there were food riots in Kent. In the great university city of Padua, Italy, in 1528, recalled Giovan Battista Segni, "every morning throughout the city twenty-five or thirty dead from hunger were found on dung heaps in the streets. These paupers did not even resemble men. . . . One sees almost everyone reduced to the formless thinness of a mummy, so much that . . . the skin hides nothing supported by the skeleton with very little flesh" (Camporesi 26). But merriment lived on—at least for some. In the great trading city of Venice, the chronicler Marino Sanudo created an eerie, ghastly picture of revelers at Christmas, and again at Carnival, gaily abroad in Venetian holiday masks, finding their paths blocked by starving people. "Every evening on the Piazza San Marco, on the Rialto, in all the city streets, crowds of children would cry out to passers-by: 'Give us bread! We're dying of hunger and cold.' It was terrible to behold. And in the morning there were corpses under the palace porticoes." By February, Sanudo continues, "in addition to the Venetian poor . . . wailing in the streets, there are also the poor from Burano, with their scarves wrapped around their heads and their children in their arms, begging for alms. Many also come from as far as Vincenze and Brescia. . . . Impossible to listen to mass in peace, for at least a dozen beggars will surround you; impossible to open your purse without an immediate plea for money. They are still there late in the evening, knocking on doors and crying, 'I'm dying of hunger'" (qtd. in Geremek 132).[9] The macabre juxtaposition of holiday merriment with starvation captures the strange spirit of the early sixteenth century. To consider the discourse of vagrancy means confronting both death and merriment—both the terror of the age and its sometimes terrible laughter.

Historical Contexts

Because this is a literary study, and because historical contexts have been rehearsed in other books and essays, I have relegated much of the historical context material to appendix A, which contains information on the question of how many vagrants traveled England during the period; the extent and the causes of vagrancy and poverty; contemporary attitudes toward unemployment as a moral failing rather than an economic condition; and the Poor Laws and other major administrative changes affecting the poor. Most importantly, see this appendix on changing concepts of poverty; on the fact that between the twelfth and sixteenth centuries the concept of almsgiving as redemptive and nondiscriminate charity as a spiritual good modulated into a concept of charity as a duty to be carried out circumspectly, distinguishing carefully between deserving and undeserving poor. Lest one idealize medieval concepts of poverty, one should recognize that they were often self-serving and complacent. One cannot help agreeing that "the sanctification of poverty justified the status quo: the poor were nailed to a cross at the bottom of society" (Lis and Soly 22). However, desanctified poverty was, if anything, even worse.

Since the treatment of vagrants depended on their status as undeserving poor, I will set forth here the grounds on which the Renaissance drew the distinction between deserving and undeserving: the deserving were hardworking, the undeserving idle; the deserving were often disabled; the undeserving feigned disability; the deserving were local people, the undeserving aliens—foreign to one's parish or even to England; the deserving were house-holders, the undeserving homeless; the deserving were settled and stayed home, while the undeserving were mobile and wandered. I will now flesh out these criteria.

First, the deserving were industrious. The workhouse, which was invented in sixteenth-century England and spread across Europe, reflected contempt for vagrant idleness: labor "had strong religious-moral connotations as a remedy against sinful idleness" and workhouses fought "the supposedly main cause of poverty, viz. idleness" (Jütte 177). Thomas Harman doggedly disregards the possibility that the jobless are anything but idle, though when he rebuked a vagrant woman her for her "lewd life," she demanded, "'How should I live? None will take me into service. But I labour in harvest-time honestly'" (100)—she has *tried* to find work and works seasonally when possible. Elizabethan employment schemes often failed to place vagrants in jobs—owing in part, no doubt, to the bad press vagrants got in works like Harman's. One of Harman's rogues "runneth about the country to seek work, with a big boy his son carrying his tools as a dauber or plasterer"; but, Harman sneers, "little work serveth him" (112). Even when confronted by jobless people seeking work, Harman cannot stop himself from denouncing their idleness, and his reaction was typical: "there was no recognition . . . that people wandering or loitering might be trying to find work, not to avoid it" (Slack, *Poverty and Policy* 29).

Second, the deserving were disabled. Writers on poverty always made an exception for the disabled: disability was the only legitimate alternative to hard work. In a sample tally of the parish poor in *An Ease for Overseers of the Poor*, the column headed "Defects" lists "palsy," "idiot," "lame," "deaf," "diseased," "dumb," "bedrid," and "blind" as sample defects and recommends as a basic principle of poor relief "that they may have a proportional allowance according to the continuation and measure of their maladies and miseries" (7). The emphasis on disability rests on the underlying assumption that anyone physically capable of work will be able to find work—which simply made the unemployment problem disappear by blaming it on idleness.

In the translator's preface to Martin Bucer's treatise on alms, faked disability is a pretext for the secularization of poor relief; the specter of such fakery loomed large in Renaissance imaginations (see appendix A; see also Mowat, "Rogues, Shepherds, and the Counterfeit Distressed"). Counterfeit disability, the very foundation of bureaucratic control of poor relief in that it provided a pretext for taking charity out of individual hands, was one of vagrants' main deceits in rogue exposés, from the *Liber Vagatorum* to Awdeley and Harman, which did crucial cultural work in teaching people to distrust their own judgment about who deserved alms and to leave it all to experts.

The deserving poor included only the "real" disabled. Texts from Harman's *Caveat* to Shakespeare's *2 Henry VI* feature tests to unmask fakery, implying that faked disability is a widespread problem. (A modern equivalent would be complaints about welfare recipients ripping off the system.) To Harman, most beggarly disability is faked. Robert Allen argued in *A Treatise of Christian Beneficence* (1600) that suppressing vagrancy would free up money to relieve "many poor labouring householders" and "uncounterfeit impotent" (sig. [A3])—his use of "uncounterfeit" in preference to "genuine" or "authentic" casts the "uncounterfeit" as a minority and assumes "counterfeit" as the default setting for impotence. *An Ease for Overseers* warns that "to inquire after poor is the next [i.e., easiest] way to procure poor; for such is the impudency of this age, that many will dissemble their estates, to have relief" (29).

Third, the deserving were local rather than beggars recently arrived from out of town: all over Europe, alien beggars were periodically expelled from cities, and it was Elizabethan policy to ship the indigent back to their "home parishes," although many had maintained no connection with the parish of their birth for years. Discussing which poor folk should be relieved first, if a community could not afford to relieve all, John Downame specified that "we are to relieve the inhabitants of the same city, shire, and country, before those who are of other nations" (136). Here the animus against vagrants rubs shoulders with resentment of foreign workers—another cluster of attitudes familiar in modern times. Also, as the sixteenth century wore on, vagrants were banished not just from parishes but also from England, marking the beginning of the long practice of transporting undesirables to the colonies. In an age of increasing nationalism, vagrants became not just local nuisances but national enemies. Treating vagrancy as a foreign threat and vagrants as aliens looks like a mental evasion, effacing the failures of economic systems and social programs at home. As J. A. Sharpe notes, "It is difficult to draw any real distinction between the vagrant and the unstable poor of the parish, the migrant workers, servants or poor labourers who had no real stake in the community, and who were terribly vulnerable to the economic crises of the period" (*Crime* 146).

Fourth, the deserving were housed: that they were supposed to stay home in their houses (as well as their parishes) presupposed that they *had* houses. In *A Treatise of Christian Beneficence*, Allen reports with unrealistic optimism that with vagabonds having now been suppressed (for which he praises the Lord Chief Justice), public money is left over to relieve the deserving—"poor labouring householders" (sig. [A3]). Harman too, as I will show, draws the deserving/undeserving line between the householding poor and the houseless. On purely financial grounds, the need of the unhoused is normally greater than that of down-at-the-heels homeowners, but Allen and Harman judge by standards other than need: poor householders deserve support because they are the social betters of the unhoused. To those who have, more shall be given. The Renaissance continued the medieval distinction between the "shamefaced poor" and other paupers, the "shamefaced" being "members of the middle or even upper classes who have lost their social status and been reduced to poverty; it is never applied to the mass of working poor for whom indigence was a normal condition. For [the working poor], the acceptance of charity involved no loss of dignity" (Geremek 40). In practice the "shamefaced" were often treated as deserving, while the others were dealt with as undeserving. During a great crisis of hunger in France in 1535, for example, "the argument was that aid should be given first to the 'shamefaced poor,' those who had a place of their own to live and did not beg in the streets, but were unable to earn their own living. Social morality and collective solidarity demanded that this group should be the first to receive support" (Geremek 153). Though here the nonshamefaced are not pushed firmly into the category of undeserving, they slide perceptibly in that direction. The moral category "deserving" could become coextensive with a social category similar to "decayed gentry"; those without social status slide toward "undeserving." Such slippage between moral and social categories helps make sense of the limiting of "deserving poor" to householders.

Fifth, the deserving stayed home in their houses and in their parishes rather than roaming aimlessly abroad like the undeserving. A. L. Beier sketches vagrant life in early modern England:

> Tramping the roads was a permanent condition for most vagrants. They reported having "small dwelling" and "no abiding place." One told Montgomeryshire justices in 1568 that he "dwells nowhere, nor has no abiding but there as he may have work"; another, seized in Leicester in 1594, said that he "has no dwelling, but is a traveller abroad for his living." When pressed by magistrates, they might produce places of birth or previous residence, but in reality few had regular abodes. In Warwick in the 1580s just fifty of the 130 vagrants could claim a home, and few had had households of their own. Many had been cut loose for years, some for periods exceeding a decade. A woman apprehended in Cheshire in 1574 states that "she has used the art of begging from her cradle," while Anne Morris told Chester officials in 1629 that she had left her home sixteen years earlier, since when she had "had no place of abiding." (*Masterless Men* 70)

Some lived in alehouses, some in and out of jail, some in outbuildings—barns, brick-kilns, or cellars; many slept in haystacks or under hedges (*Mas-*

terless Men 83–85). Alehouses crop up most often in rogue literature; Harman, insisting that only disreputable alehouses accept vagrants, lists a few of these sordid establishments, including one poignantly named "The House of Pity" (109).

Mobility also seemed to characterize vagrants' speech. As Manning notes, "vagrants were thought to be incorrigible rumour-mongers" (163), and the political dangerousness of rogues often comes down to their being accused of having spread rumors of riots and revolts. In an age of political censorship before the advent of electronic media or even newspapers, those who were mobile became almost a figure of News, sought out by some and rooted out by others. Rogue literature often features a printer, and rogues themselves seemed like print, with its uncanny properties of swift replication (rogues seemed to be everywhere) and its ability to travel across the land, spreading news.

I will argue that fulminations against vagrants' geographical mobility project or displace fear of other kinds of change and mobility: religious and intellectual change, social mobility.[10] The use of the word "place" to mean both social rank and geographical location gives away the game: in the synecdochic thinking of the age, those with no fixed place to live came to represent other cultural dislocations occasioned by the Reformation, humanism, or new bureaucracies. Anxieties about unstable social gradations or about changes in the English language, I will argue, came to rest on the shoulders of the placeless. If the idea of projection and displacement has a Freudian and hence anachronistic ring, the mental habits involved are distinctly early modern. As I argue in *The Scythe of Saturn: Shakespeare and Magical Thinking,* Renaissance minds still harbored residues of belief in magical forces, which facilitated leaps between the material and the immaterial. Scapegoating conflated the material and the immaterial—as a load can be transferred from one person's shoulders to another's, so guilt can be transferred. To this kind of thinking—in which modern-day firm distinctions between material and immaterial are themselves anachronistic—transactions between material and immaterial came naturally, and it is not surprising that real geographical wanderers came to represent something immaterial—change and mobility in the social, political, and intellectual life of the age.

Disability and homekeeping were connected: since the Renaissance sometimes identified home with the body (see chap. 6), those recommending cloistered homekeeping thought naturally in terms of disabled bodies. The way writers harped on disability suggests that not only were they willing to make allowances for disability but that to some extent they even hoped for it, as an immobilizer of undesirables. It was the blind and lame beggars who most consistently elicited sympathy—those whose disability most effectively prevented speedy, purposeful motion. Renaissance insistence on householding, valorization of settled life, underwriting of disability, and demonization of vagrancy reflect, I think, deep-seated unease about mobility.

Terminology

My main terms of choice are "vagrant" and "vagrant poor." I would prefer "homeless," since it is the unhoused condition on which I want particularly to focus, but "vagrant" was a sixteenth-century noun whereas "homeless" was not. "Vagrant" can serve as a synonym for "homeless" insofar as the Poor Laws made it hard to be homeless without being vagrant. Those with no homes *could not* settle in one spot, even under one hedge: the law kept them moving. The problem is that "vagrant" carries (as it were) a certain amount of ideological baggage. In foregrounding mobility rather than lack (as "homeless" points only to lack), "vagrant" had in its own day a menacing quality reflecting the age's deep-rooted suspicion of mobility. (Even now, I think, "vagrant" sounds more menacing and faintly murderous than does "homeless person.") "Homeless" would stress lack rather than self-sufficient agency, and I am attracted to its homely Anglo-Saxon roots in contrast to the Latinate air of repressive officialdom clinging to "vagrant." But since the embeddedness of "homeless" in the landscape of modern-day experience may get in the way of what I am trying to say about the Renaissance, I have reluctantly opted for "vagrant."

I use "discourse of vagrancy," in Foucault's sense of "discourse," to refer to the ideology governing representation of the vagrant poor as undeserving, idle, feckless, irresponsible, unrooted, sexually profligate, dangerous, seditious, criminal, tricky, deceitful, impressively histrionic—able to feign disability on the one hand, respectability on the other. The discourse includes the idea of vagrant societies, organized in hierarchies with criminal specializations and with chiefs; of a foreign tongue, thieves' cant; of ragged clothes and diseased bodies. Defined entirely by opponents of the vagrant poor, this discourse comprised a tissue of stereotypes perpetuating contempt for vagrants.

I use "discourse" in the singular. To use a near-obligatory plural to assure readers that I am aware of complexities and not indulging in totalizing or hegemonic assumptions would suppress a signal feature of Renaissance beliefs about vagrants—their weird homogeneity from one field to the next. Some widely divergent groups cast vagrants as their opposite number—Reformation theologians, humanists, preachers, monarchists, nationalists, writers on civility and domesticity, writers of rogue literature and jest books—yet their pronouncements have a ritual sameness. Since it was not true that vagrants were organized into societies or conversed in thieves' cant, it is remarkable how many different kinds of writers said it was true. Boundaries between rogue literature and Poor Laws, between humanist treatises and popular jest books, dissolve as each contributes to the discourse of vagrancy, often in uncannily similar terms. To pluralize these into separate discourses would risk missing the common cultural work these different groups, and different genres, are performing. This is not to say that I will never draw distinctions among the genres that participate in the discourse of vagrancy: there are, for example, important differences of tone, with the comic treatments located more frequently (though not exclusively) in rogue literature, jest books, comedies, and comic subplots of more serious plays. Even within a single genre, some works will give more play to urban rogues and some to disabled beggars. But the frame of reference the different works share is more conspicuous than their differences. Whether he is the subject of laughter or of serious invective, the sturdy vagrant is someone to be warned against; whether he is an urban cardsharp or a country woman pretending to have lost her cottage to a fire, the rogue is deceitful, preying on the public.

Though vagrants often begged, and the term "beggar" is unavoidable, so thoroughly desacralized is begging that at present the term is loaded with menace, conjuring filthy panhandlers accosting people who are afraid of them. The "holy beggar" was a mystical figure in the Middle Ages; but the Renaissance used the term "beggar" as an insult. "Beggar" stresses agency and activity; I want rather to emphasize the lack of a basic necessity, namely, a home. "Professional beggar" insidiously implies that the beggar has secreted a cache of money somewhere—the charge Harman levels against Nicholas Jennings (see my chap. 1). "Professional beggar" may denote only the gaining of one's whole income from begging, but it connotes skill, training, professional standing, and wealth. It hints at the discredited idea of a subculture of organized rogues.

As an alternative to "vagrant," I would certainly not choose "rogue," a word born in the rogue literature of Awdeley and Harman and then enshrined in Elizabethan criminal codes. In the word's post-Renaissance afterlife, A. V. Judges and others have created the genre "literature of roguery" as that which depicts the Elizabethan Underworld. Sweeping homeless wanderers in with the criminal underworld has helped make them all seem criminal. Although many vagrants did turn to crime, it seems to me prejudicial to classify them first as criminals and only secondarily as the hopeless social casualties that many of them were—particularly since the crime many were guilty of was merely vagrancy.[11] And the word's connotations are problematic. The idea of a "genial rogue"—that playful, piratical type with a twinkle in his eye—imparts a sense of the fun of those roguish times in Merrie Olde England, thus reproducing the Renaissance ploy of using humor and playfulness to alchemize the miseries of the poor into merriment. "Gallery" in the title of Arthur Kinney's anthology *Rogues, Vagabonds, and Sturdy Beggars: A New Gallery of Tudor and Early Stuart Rogue Literature* clearly alludes to that endearing notion of the "rogues' gallery." (Roguery is touted as fun in any number of present-day "Renaissance Fayres.") The wonderful word "rogue" speaks volumes for how modern readers have viewed poverty in this period, but it is highly prejudicial.

"Vagabond," fairly interchangeable with "vagrant," was usually negative in coloration (often used more viciously than now, I think), though it occasionally figured in an idealization of vagabondage and as such is the grandfather of our "vagabond," meaning the blithely footloose, given as a brand name to recreational vehicles to conjure the freewheeling, carefree life. "Vagabond" has too rakish an air.

The indiscriminate Renaissance use of "rogue" (and sometimes "conycatcher") occludes important distinctions between destitute rural migrants and urban down-and-outs on the one hand, clever con artists on the other. The latter are seldom represented as homeless. Gilbert Walker's description of the fine London house of some crooked dice-players in *A Manifest Detection of . . . Dice-Play* reads like a parody of Erasmus's *Convivium Religiosum* (The godly feast) in the elegance of its "well-trimmed chambers, the worst of them appareled with verdures, some with rich cloth of arras, all with beds, chairs, and cushions of silk and gold" (68). A far cry from the vagrants sheltering in barns in Harman's *Caveat,* who burrow naked into filthy straw to keep away from the lice. And yet early modern usage applied "rogue" to both. It is important to my project not to fall back on terms that effect that conflation; I want to separate out homelessness and vagrancy as discrete conditions. This is why I give more space to Awdeley, Harman, and writers who focus on genuinely *poor* rogues than to Greene, Dekker, and the other cony-catching writers who focus more on prosperous con artists—although there are many important links between them, not least the fact that generically they have long been lumped together as rogue literature.

"Masterless men," a phrase given wide currency by A. L. Beier, was an early modern term; it is a favorite too with New Historicist literary scholars since it stresses the power relation of masters and servants and is politically oriented in hinting at fears about sedition. It is not a bad term: contemporaries did stress the breakup of traditional master/servant arrangements and often identified dismissed or runaway servants as a significant component of the vagrant population. As Palliser notes, "many nobles and gentry did gradually reduce the size of their households, whether as a voluntary measure of economy or because of the statutes limiting numbers of retainers" (119). But using this term risks buying into the Renaissance belief that the vagrant poor were seditious. Encoded in "masterless men" is the assumption that one not under his master's thumb will evade the magistrate's thumb too, if he does not actively plot the monarch's overthrow.

Sometimes, despite its slight anachronism, I will use the term "homeless." It was an adjective in the early seventeenth century but has been in common use as a noun—as in "the homeless"—only in the last few decades of our own time. (It does sometimes occur earlier, however—for example, in Emma Lazarus's poem inscribed on the Statue of Liberty.) "Homelessness" is a nineteenth-century coinage. Shakespeare uses "houseless" (though not "homeless") as an adjective. When I use "homeless," it will be partly *because* it is anachronistic, an instance of what Kim Hall helpfully calls the "strategically anachronistic" (261). Modern attitudes toward the homeless often uncannily resemble early modern attitudes, and I want a word that will occasionally remind readers of that. One hears today that the homeless are lazy, shiftless, malingering, uninterested in getting jobs. It is easy to miss the resemblance, if one refers separately to early modern "masterless men" and modern-day "homeless people"; by sometimes using the same term for both, I hope to bring the similarities occasionally before readers' eyes. Of course, one should not collapse obvious differences between early modern and modern homelessness. The mix of economic and social causes is different, as are available social programs and safety nets. Legal penalties for vagrancy have changed, as have urban landscapes. But at the very least, the sixteenth century laid the groundwork for some modern attitudes.

Tudor England itself singled out the homeless for special treatment: they were the only class of person ineligible for public relief (see appendix A). Because those of no fixed abode were kept moving by local authorities, to be homeless was also to be parishless, and poor relief was administered by parishes. For this reason, "placeless" is useful, suggesting not only lack of domicile but everything else that implied: lack of a parish, of eligibility for government poor relief programs, of a station ("place") in life, of employment, of embeddedness in a web of master/servant or master/apprentice relations. "Placeless" *was* a sixteenth-century word: its meanings included "without a fixed place or home," "not local," and "out of office or remunerative employment" (*OED*). I will sometimes use "placeless" to evoke all these complex lacks.

It may be that to be without a home meant something different in the Renaissance from what it means now, insofar as "home" had different connotations. But while "home" in a modern context may have warm and cozy emotional associations compounded of the Victorian "angel in the house," Dickensian firesides, "live better electrically" commercials from the 1950s, and television familial utopias, from "Father Knows Best" to "The Waltons"—a world bound to seem foreign to a Tudor time-traveler—still, the groundwork for such nest-worship was laid in Tudor times. Erasmus's *Convivium Religiosum* idealizes a home with cozy, womblike enclosed gardens, fine art, and excellent food; two of Sir Thomas More's early biographers sing the praises of his Chelsea house, with its library and garden house for withdrawing from the world (Roper 14; Harpsfield 90, 107). For Mistress Page in *The Merry Wives of Windsor,* "home" means laughing with family and friends "by a country fire" (5.5.235–36). In *The Taming of the Shrew,* Katherine idealizes the housewife's life as one of lying "warm at home, secure and safe" (5.2.155). In *The Winter's Tale,* Polixenes associates "home" with the "mirth" of playing with his little son, whose "varying childness" cures all evil thoughts (1.2.165–71). In such passages, elements of an idealized "home" (which modern readers might consider Victorian) are already fully in evidence—home as a warm, cozy, firelit, family place, a refuge. It is true that Tudor domestic arrangements differed from those of the present day—people often lived in the building where they worked, and servants and apprentices were part of the family; but that hardly suggests that with hindsight modern readers are tempted to overemphasize homelessness. If anything, Tudor domestic arrangements must have given home a *stronger* emotional charge as the center of one's world than one experiences today, and therefore homelessness might have been even more traumatic for its victims and homeless people even more frighteningly alien than in today's experience. It is true that Tudor households offered individuals much less privacy than do modern households; but for the discourse of vagrancy, a more pertinent consideration than privacy is *security,* protection against a threat allegedly posed by vagrants themselves. This preoccupation with security—relatively new in Tudor times—is again visible in our time. I cannot see discarding the word "homeless" because of changes in the emotional coloration of "home."

Did Vagrants Have a Renaissance?

To adapt Joan Kelly's famous question about women, one might ask whether the vagrant poor had a Renaissance. Certainly they were, for the most part, left out of the Reformation. What was it to them if Luther nailed his Ninety-five Theses to a church door, penned "A Mighty Fortress Is Our God," and dauntlessly avowed "Here I stand"? What did they care that legions of Reformers championed the right of every Christian, no matter how humble, to read the Scriptures by himself or herself, without benefit of priestcraft and in his or her own language, to approach on his or her own two feet the throne of God? The vagrant poor mostly could not read, could not afford books, were too ragged and dirty to be welcomed by decent congregations, were too distracted by hunger and misery to care. And what was the new humanism to a ragged beggar? In 1487 Pico della Mirandola had imagined God informing humankind, "In conformity with thy free judgment, in whose hands I have placed thee, thou art confined by no bounds"; Pico proclaimed that a human being, "winnowing out all things by right reason, . . . is a heavenly not an earthly animal" (4–6). Even a depressive Hamlet conceded, "What a piece of work is a man! How noble in reason, how infinite in faculties, in form and moving how express and admirable, in action how like an angel, in apprehension how like a god!" (2.2.304–8). But while many were marching under the banner of humanity, some grubbed for roots to stay alive: "Many sixteenth-century chronicles relate that turnips, rape, roots, flowerbulbs, leaves, and grass were the only foodstuffs available in time of dearth" (Lis and Soly 74). Was this root-grubber the creature that winnowed out all things by right reason, a heavenly not an earthly animal? The rise of nation-states, too, had little to offer a vagrant. As France, Spain, the Holy Roman Empire, and England emerged from feudalism and came to resemble modern states, England led the way in forging a new rhetoric of nationalism; and yet large blocs of people had little reason to share in the new national pride. Although Spain may have ruled the high seas and plundered the New World for gold,

> workers in New Castile lived like animals: they were chronically underfed and lived in rickety huts of earth or wood, without furniture; men, women, and children slept crowded together on stamped earth. The moment seasonal employment began, thousands of hungry *jornaleros,* often with their families, trekked from village to village offering their labour. Since they had at most three or four successive months of full-time work, they had to try during most of the year to get by on odd jobs. The life of this pitiful mass was hence a daily struggle for mere existence—a struggle whose outcome was extremely uncertain. (Lis and Soly 73)

These unhoused people (or people housed in rabbit warrens of slums) could hardly partake of the newly coalescing ideology of home and domesticity. Witold Rybczynski shows new concepts of home taking shape first in Holland, where the boundary between a home's immaculate interior and the untidiness of the street was a new idea: "the order and tidiness of the household were evidence neither of fastidiousness nor of a particular cleanliness, but instead of a desire to define the home as a separate, special place" (66). Home acquired new meanings in early Tudor England, as the Tudors enlisted the individual household as a unit of social control. In "Renaissance National Husbandry," Wendy Wall shows how domesticity went hand in hand with patriotic notions of Englishness in domestic handbooks of the day. In an age when home was increasingly valued and the idea of home pumped up with ideological rhetoric, vagrants were without homes. The untidiness of the street was their world. Gervase Markham's handbook *The English Housewife* gloried in that national treasure, the "complete woman" with her "skill in physic, cookery, banqueting-stuff, distillation, perfumes, wool, hemp, flax, dairies, brewing, baking, and all other things belong to a household" (title page); but while this paragon was creating a domestic symphony out of plenteous material goods, many Englishwomen lacked both goods and a house to put them in.

Vagrants, John Downame says, "have nothing in propriety"—meaning, primarily, no material property. Margreta de Grazia discusses the ways in which early modern identity was "contingent upon possessions" (24–27). But Downame's contrasting "propriety" with "licentious life" suggests that "propriety" also has the sense of behavior suitable to a time and place, modulating perhaps toward its later meaning of conformity with polite manners. "Propriety" is the first of many words in this study that, by combining discourses (here, the discourses of property ownership, decent morals, and proper etiquette), suggest economically (and insidiously) that all these things are connected. One who lacks property also lacks manners and morals. But this word is even richer, and its implications more frightening: "propriety" also suggested personal identity, selfhood, "belonging to oneself" (*OED*). To lack a home, to lack property, was to lack a self.[12]

In his book on destitution, the economist Partha Dasgupta writes that "in asking the question what sorts of lives are well-lived, we at once ask what things are necessary for persons to be able to live such lives. When we inquire into a person's state of destitution we simultaneously seek to know what precisely he be bereft of" (8). Therefore, Dasgupta continues, "by studying an extreme form of ill-being we can obtain an understanding of well-being itself" (9). Similarly, I believe much light can be shed on the normative mentalities of the well-off in the Renaissance by observing what they thought about those who had nothing. In what early modern writers said about vagrants appears as if in a photographic negative what they wanted the Renaissance to be. Scholars from Burckhardt and Michelet to Douglas Bush to Joan Kelly have skirmished about the Renaissance: when and where it started, what it was all about, who it included, even if it existed. Though scholars may never agree about what the Renaissance was, they can discern what those who lived in it thought it was not: the Renaissance wanted to be everything vagrants were not.

Plunging into this topic in medias res, I begin in the mid-sixteenth century, with a work that crystallizes many motifs of the discourse of vagrancy and employs one of its salient modes, the comic: Harman's *Caveat*. Harman provides a door into the later period: his word "rogue" leads into the Elizabethan Poor Laws, his abram-man into *King Lear*. But before turning to the later century, I devote four chapters to the roots of the discourse of vagrancy in the Henrician era, especially the 1520s and 1530s. In his introduction to *Rethinking the Henrician Era* (1994), Peter C. Herman writes to redress what he sees as neglect of an era by focusing heavily on courtly writers; I doubt that in calling for more attention to Henrician texts Herman had in mind texts that interest me—*Twelve Merry Jests of the Widow Edith* or *A Man Called Howlglas*. Still, I agree that this period has been too long neglected. For my topic, the 1520s and 1530s are a watershed era, absolutely essential to understanding texts of the High Renaissance.

I conclude with *King Lear*. Though Shakespeare may not be an obvious candidate for inclusion in a book dealing otherwise with rogue literature, jest books, and much nondramatic literature, Shakespeare was familiar with the discourse of vagrancy and with attitudes toward the poor and homeless that permeated it. He drew on rogue literature not only in *King Lear* but also in the Autolycus scenes of *The Winter's Tale*, with their canting terms, and two Shakespearean texts appear to allude to Robert Copland's early contribution to the discourse of vagrancy, *The Highway to the Spital-house*. *Macbeth*'s Porter, imagining himself the porter of Hell, welcoming "all professions that go the primrose way to th' everlasting bonfire" (2.3.18–19), is reminiscent of Copland's Porter, who equates the Spital-house for the poor with Hell. In *1 Henry IV*, Falstaff too "remembers the Porter": he situates Hal's truancy amid the mighty beggars and vagabonds that Copland asks the Porter about. Falstaff's demand "Shall the blessed son of heaven prove a micher and eat blackberries?" (2.4.404–5), combining the rare word "micher" with blackberry-eating, echoes Copland's question to the Porter:

> How [do] they live all day, to lie here [i.e., at the Spital-house] at night?
> As losels, mighty beggars and vagabonds,
> And truants that walk over the lands,
> *Michers*, hedge-creepers, fillocks and lusks,
> That all the summer keep ditches and busks,
> Loitering and wandering from place to place,

And will not work, but the bypaths trace,
And live with haws, and hunt *the blackberry,*
And with hedge-breaking make themselves merry. (4)

All this bespeaks the discourse of vagrancy: "mighty beggars" would later be called "sturdy beggars"; the vagabonds are unemployed not because of economic conditions but because they "will not work"; the emotional condition of vagrant beggars is, as usual, "merry." Copland's language rejoices in what would become vintage terms in the discourse of vagrancy: "loitering," "lusks," and "losels" would later be echoed by Harman in the *Caveat:* "loitering lusks and lazy lorels" (113). ("Lorel" is a variant of "losel," meaning "worthless rogue"; "Cock Lorel" means "chief rogue.")

When Falstaff calls Hal a blackberry-eating micher, Shakespeare locates Hal's tavern truancy within the discourse of vagrancy: "micher" meant not only a simple truant but specifically one who pretends to poverty (and is also a petty thief). Slumming for his own purposes, Hal comes to resemble the literary legion of counterfeiting beggars who feign poverty and disability to advance their own interests.

Shakespeare's familiarity with the discourse of vagrancy included perhaps the Poor Laws: Richard Wilson thinks the "piercing statutes" that "chain up and restrain the poor" in *Coriolanus* (1.1.81–82) "clearly allude to the Elizabethan vagrancy acts" (85). I will argue that *King Lear,* with its Poor Tom—the signature figure of rogue literature—is deeply committed to issues of poverty and homelessness.

The majority of texts I treat in any detail are in one way or another comic. It is not until *King Lear* (1608) that one finds the issue of homelessness accorded the dignity of tragedy. The homesick Touchstone in *As You Like It,* stumbling exhausted through the woods, cries out: "When I was at home, I was in a better place" (2.4.15). Touchstone is a court jester who lives in a comedy; and like many another homeless wanderer in the literature of the day, he is meant to be funny. Other wanderers who were laughed at in the Renaissance did not, like Touchstone, have a home to which they could return. One of my aims is to give serious treatment to some at whom Renaissance literature invites us to snicker; to give some critical attention, if not downright "cherishing" (to use Harman's word), to those who never were at home, who never knew a better place.

Notes

1. The "fraternity" stereotype is durable: four centuries later, the anthropologist Mark S. Fleisher still combats the common belief that all homeless street criminals belong to organized gangs: "Years of street ethnography exploring the life trajectory of street crim-

inals show that these men and women aren't members of criminal organizations such as the Aryan Brotherhood, Mafia, Medellín Cartel, Mexican Mafia, or other major drug cartels. These folk are 'rabble,' the ordinary street criminals who cycle between jails and prisons" (245).

2. This is one theme sounded more often in directly political literature than in rogue literature.

3. Carroll's suggestion that more women than men were involved (*Fat King* 2n.1) apparently refers to poverty levels in general and not to vagrancy rates.

4. Stephen Greenblatt compares rogue literature's vocabulary lists of thieves' cant to Thomas Harriot's word list of Algonquian terms in his *Brief and True Report of the New Found Land of Virginia* (1588) and to Prince Hal's learning the lingo of tapsters the better to manipulate his future subjects, noting the element of alienness in both cases: "Hal's remark about drinking with any tinker in his own language suggests, if only jocularly, that for him the lower classes are virtually another people, an alien tribe" (*Shakespearean Negotiations* 49).

5. Similarly on the Continent, stubborn public sympathy for the disfranchised poor sparked legislation aimed at toughening public attitudes. In Amsterdam, "an ordinance of 1614 accused 'many people' of sabotaging the repression of unlicensed begging 'from misplaced compassion'"; crowds sometimes shouted at or threw objects at provosts arresting vagrants, or even snatched arrested people from provosts' hands; in Paris, crowds comprising kitchen servants, poor artisans, and workers "beat and outraged" the police, "saying it was an offense to God to chase away the poor" (Spierenburg, *Prison Experience* 77–78).

6. In her book-in-progress "Spacious Voices/Vagrant Subjects in Early Modern England," Patricia Fumerton laudably tries to get beyond seeing vagrants projectively, through the eyes of the respectable, and seeks a vagrant's-eye view—for example, through the autobiography of a seaman, Edward Barlow, whose experience, though not literally vagrant, enacts the unsettled, serial employment typical of vagrants. Barlow's memoir covers his life from 1659 to 1703, considerably after the period I am exploring; no such materials exist, to my knowledge, for the sixteenth century. Down-and-out vagrants left no surviving writings at all for this earlier period, for which a true vagrant's-eye view would be exceedingly difficult to come by. Sometimes I do try to tease out a vagrant's worldview from the ventriloquizing of the voices of the poor in writings of the well-off (for example, Harman's vagrant woman [see my chap. 1]). But this is not the main thrust of my own project.

7. Surveying the visual arts, Suzanne Stratton shows that although "beggars had an established place in religious art until the Reformation, . . . about 1500 the position of the beggar in Northern painting began to change, reflecting a new moral condemnation" (78). Sixteenth- and early seventeenth-century images of beggars by Pieter Brueghel the Elder, Bartel Beham, Jacques Callot, Joris van Vliet, Pieter Quast, Adriaen van de Venne, and the young Rembrandt show "antipathy toward the subject. Their beggars are deformed and querulous brutes, inspiring revulsion rather than sympathy" (79). See also Lucinda Kate Reinold's Ph.D. dissertation, "The Representation of the Beggar as Rogue in Dutch Seventeenth-Century Art."

8. "There had been two disastrous harvests in 1586 and 1587, but after that adequate harvests had resumed. . . . However, the four harvests from 1594 to 1597 were terrible, the worst consecutive run of the century" (Palliser 26).

9. Though generalization is tricky, my impression is that continental European texts on poverty in this period emphasize hunger most heavily, while English texts focus more on homelessness. But there was plenty of hunger in England during the period's numerous harvest failures: "when the harvest failed, as it did in 1555 and 1556, it produced the mass starvation recorded by the Venetian ambassador" (Palliser 6).

10. On the new social mobilities of the age, see Palliser 83–94. As Palliser shows, King Edward VI expressed dismay at this increasing social mobility, complaining that "the grazier, the farmer, the merchant become landed men, and call themselves gentlemen, though they be churls" (qtd. in Palliser 83). Palliser also notes that social movement became evident in a religious context: "the tiresomely frequent disputes over church pews, to take only one trivial example, occurred because men and women rising in wealth and respect demanded better seats" (83–84).

11. This process seems to have begun already in the sixteenth century: J. A. Sharpe shows that "one crucial innovation was the criminalization of the poor, or at least a reconceptualization of 'crime' in such a way that it came mainly to consist of forms of behaviour in which the poor were most likely to indulge. In the middle ages occasional members of the nobility turned criminal, while the more mundane offenders were characteristically drawn from the village elite. . . . The middling sort and even the aristocracy in the early modern period were not as tame as has sometimes been suggested. Nevertheless, by the end of our period crime was regarded primarily as an activity of the poor" (*Crime* 251). And Spierenburg adds that "the undifferentiated phrase 'the criminalization of the poor' is a misleading concept. It was beggars and vagrants who bore the main burden of the intensification of repression" (*Prison Experience* 86).

12. Fumerton, adducing several legal records of vagrants—which included the charges "not giving any account or reason of her wandering," "not able to give account of her life," "not able to yield any account of his idle course of life"—concludes that "it is as if, in the minds of early modern authorities, an account of one's life, or what we might call 'autobiography,' could belong only to the settled; not to be able to give such an account labeled one as criminal." Fumerton speculates stimulatingly about the effect on personal identity and subjectivity of living a life that was unmoored to a stable occupation and property. (I wonder whether this Renaissance sense of a life without a tellable story is a remote origin of the modern slang application, to the ne'er-do-well, of "no account" as an adjective meaning worthless.)

1. Vagrancy and the Work of Thomas Harman

THE EARLY MODERN vagrant poor inhabit many documents—texts often considered the purview of historians (Poor Laws, parish registers, censuses), and texts claimed by literary scholars (Erasmian colloquies, Shakespeare plays). Some liminal texts like rogue literature, not quite good enough to be canonical literature and not quite true enough to be history, awkwardly straddle the line. A foundational text of English rogue literature, Thomas Harman's *Caveat for Common Cursetors, Vulgarly Called Vagabonds,* which describes vagrant life purportedly on the basis of personal interviews with vagrants, has long served as a source for the social history of vagrancy. But historicist readings of this text have ignored its comic tone, and I will argue that it makes less sense to read it as protosocial history than as a subspecies of the Tudor jest book.[1] This is not to say, however, that Harman's *Caveat* lacked serious consequences: it appears to have influenced not only later authors of rogue literature but also the nation's lawmakers. The fortunes of this text bespeak the political and social power of what readers often consign—with affectionate contempt—to the category "popular literature."

The social historian A. V. Judges wrote in *The Elizabethan Underworld* (1930) that "Harman has all the deftness of the trained sociologist; . . . [he] had no axe to grind in the composition of his work; his account may be accepted as genuine and in most particulars correct" (495), an astonishing view of *A Caveat* as a transparent window onto social history. When Judges reprinted his work with a new preface in 1965, he let this statement stand. Frank Ayledotte had set the tone in 1913 by accepting Harman's work as credible history: he called his *Elizabethan Rogues and Vagabonds* "the first book to treat Elizabethan rogues and vagabonds from the point of view here taken, piecing together historical and literary material so as to make as complete a picture as possible of their life" (v). Ayledotte proudly admits to having used Harman, primarily, "as a basis for a detailed account of rogue customs" (27).

Practitioners of social history are still drawing on Ayledotte, and recent scholars are still using Harman as historical evidence. In 1972 Arthur Kinney reported that "for years Harman has been considered an early but most successful sociologist, . . . [whose] keen eye for significant detail of dress, food, origin, training, and the sexual life of his subjects . . . [align him] with modern sociology" (105). In 1977 J. S. Cockburn used Harman's *Caveat* alongside records of court assizes as valid sources of historical information on "vagrant criminals and their methods" (62). In 1983, David M. Palliser adduced Harman's information about rogues when attempting to gauge the number of vagrants on the roads in the sixteenth century and the extent of their criminal involvement (120–21, 312–13); the same year, Peter Burke wrote that Harman was "moved by a curiosity not unlike that of modern anthropologists" (179); and in *Poverty and Deviance in Early Modern Europe* (1994), Robert Jütte—in nearly identical words—concurred. In 1988 the sole source Roger B. Manning gave for the information that "there did exist a small hard core of 'sturdy beggars' and 'lusty rogues' whom no law could compel to do honest labour" (160) was Harman's *Caveat*. A *Times Literary Supplement* reviewer in 1995 gave high marks to Johannes Fabricius's medical history *Syphilis in Shakespeare's England* for finding information in John Awdeley and Harman on "the subculture formed by the travellers of the period—" 'upright men,' . . . 'doxies,' etc.—whose antisocial and criminal behaviour could only encourage the spread of diseases like plague, smallpox, syphilis and gonorrhoea" (Flood 12). In 1994, A. L. Beier could still describe Harman as "traditionally . . . the most credible of observers of the canting underworld" ("Anti-language" 68).

I suggest, however, that far from being a credible source for social history, Harman *was* an axe-grinder, in a class with Sir Bercilak. His every syllable bespeaks an antivagrant agenda, unsettlingly prophetic of a modern American idiom of law and order, of getting tough with "welfare bums." Harman addresses his antipoverty tract to one of England's richest women, Bess of Hardwick, whose life, says her biographer Ethel Carleton Williams, was one "of unbridled greed and an insatiable lust for property" (60). Hardwick, already a substantial landowner herself, had recently married the Earl of Shrewsbury, who possessed "vast areas of land in Yorkshire, Derbyshire, Nottinghamshire, Shropshire and Staffordshire," including Sheffield Manor, Sheffield Castle, South Wingfield Manor, Rufford Abbey, Welbeck Abbey, Worksop Manor, Buxton Hall, Tutbury Castle, and other houses and minor manors (Durant 54). As a well-to-do landowner himself, Harman forthrightly allied himself with these interests and attacked vagrancy accordingly.

Paul Slack suggests that "the pamphlets of Harman and his successors, . . . along with continental literature in the same vein, . . . have been treated seriously by . . . historians because they seem to hint at the existence of a distinct culture of poverty, not unlike that which some sociologists have detected in twentieth-century societies" (*Poverty and Policy* 104). The notion of a culture of poverty is, however, not ideologically innocent. As Catharina Lis and Hugo Soly note, "Many sociologists take as an article of faith the concept of a 'culture of poverty,' but, in contrast to Oscar Lewis, who coined the term, they portray the living conditions and patterns of behaviour of the poor as the outcome of the personal inadequacy or inferiority of families locked into the poverty trap. Some exceptions aside, more attention has been paid to the specific system of values of the poor than to the economic and political structures which lie at the roots of social inequality and cultural segregation" (xi). (On the "culture of poverty," see also Burke; Lloyd.) Does Harman get treated seriously by historians and sociologists who buy into a view of the poor as responsible for their own condition—a view that resembles Harman's own?[2] For whatever reasons, historians mining *A Caveat* for information on vagrancy have often treated it as ideologically neutral, a window onto the sixteenth century; only rather recently have readers begun to recognize that the virulent attacks on the poor in this rogue literature may themselves, as Mark Koch suggests, "have played a more direct role in desacralizing mendicancy than did the theological writings of the Protestant reformers" ("Desanctification" 96). If so, rogue literature was a crucial intervention in society: the waning of the medieval ideal of the sanctity of poverty and the spiritual benefits of charity, while opening the door to more secular, government-oriented concepts of charity and poor relief (see appendix A), also spawned harsh attitudes toward the poor that were rampant during the early modern period and are also widespread today.

A Caveat may have influenced high echelons of Elizabethan officialdom, and it left its mark on important social legislation. The landmark Poor Law *An Act for the Punishment of Vagabonds, and for the Relief of the Poor and Impotent* (1572) set forth the legal definition of a "rogue" (sig. [A6]^{v}-Bi) and repeatedly used the words "rogue" and "roguish," beginning with its opening sentence: "Where all the parts of this realm of England and Wales, be presently with rogues, vagabonds, and sturdy beggars exceedingly pestered, by means whereof daily happeneth in the same realm horrible murders, thefts, and other great outrages, to the high displeasure of almighty God, and the great annoy of the commonweal" (sig. [A5]). Indeed, the word "rogue" would persist as a technical term in successive Poor Laws right through the nineteenth century. (It also passed into Stow's *Summary of the Chronicles* [1573] "and from there directly into Holinshed's *Chronicles* [1577]—and even into the *Chronicles'* index" [Mowat 65; see also Pories 37–39]). Yet the word has not been noted in print before the mid-sixteenth century. The terms "vagabond," "sturdy vagabond," "beggar," and "mighty beggar" had been the terms of choice in earlier vagrancy legislation: in Henry VII's statutes against vagabonds and beggars of 1495 and of 1503–4, in Henry VIII's of 1531 and 1536, in Edward VI's of 1547 and 1552, in Mary I's of 1555, in the City of London's orders suppressing beggars of 1517 and the City of Southampton's orders of 1536. In all of these documents the word "rogue" does not appear. (See reprints in C. H. Williams's *English Historical Documents, 1485–1558.*) Significantly, the word "rogue" was first introduced, as thieves' cant, by Awdeley and Harman in the early to middle 1560s; and by 1572 it had become elevated to the status of a legally defined technical term in a statute.

Though "rogue" could have gained currency through oral parlance, nonprinted written communications, or printed materials that have been lost or that the *Oxford English Dictionary* simply missed, the correspondence of date (Harman and Awdeley using the word in popular works of the mid-1560s, Poor Laws using it for the first time in 1572) seems more than coincidental, especially since the 1572 statute explicitly inveighs against two of Harman's categories of feigning vagabonds, "counterfeitors of licenses passports" and "shipmen pretending losses by sea" (sig. Bi). I cannot prove that drafters of the 1572 Poor Law had personally read *A Caveat,* but the likelihood of their having encountered *A Caveat* at least at secondhand seems good, given its currency, its popularity, and the evidence of its influence on a number of kinds of texts. *A Caveat* was popular when printed in 1566–67: an expanded edition appeared within a year; and before that, the Stationers Company fined two separate malefactors, Gerrard Dewes and Henry Bynneham, for marketing pirated editions.[3] Reprinted in 1573 and 1592, *A Caveat* was generously plagiarized by Thomas Dekker in *The Bellman of London* (1608), *Lantern and Candlelight* (1608), and *O Per Se O* (1612), and by Samuel Rid in *Martin Markall, Beadle of Bridewell* (1610). Harman's work sparked decades of rogue literature, most famously Robert Greene's cony-catching pamphlets of the 1590s, which racily detailed life in the criminal underworld. William Harrison borrowed freely from Harman for book 2, chapter 10 of his *Description of England,* which was prefixed to Holinshed's *Chronicles,* thus enshrining Harman's work within establishment historiography. Harman's description of an "abram-man" or "poor Tom," which he shares with a contemporary work on vagrancy by Awdeley, *The Fraternity of Vagabonds,*[4] was taken up by

Shakespeare in *King Lear,* and Harman's vocabulary lists of thieves' cant formed the basis of later slang dictionaries. (Given Harman's residence in Kent, it is interesting that the records of Knole House in Kent include a vocabulary of thieves' cant, which appears on the back of a document dated 1690 [Sackville-West 135–37]; of its eighty-five terms, thirty-two are in Harman.)

If rogue literature *did* create categories that became codified in the Poor Laws, its terms were even inscribed on the bodies of the poor: whereas the Poor Law of 1547—before Harman and Awdeley wrote—dictated that vagabonds be branded with the letter "V," escaped slaves with the letter "S," the Poor Law of 1604, expanding on those of 1572 and 1592, dictated that incorrigible rogues should "be branded in the left shoulder with a great Roman R," which would "remain for a perpetual mark upon such rogue during his or her life" (*Act for the Continuance* sig. C3–C3ᵛ).[5] It appears, then, that some in high authority had been influenced by Harman's *Caveat.* The exotic word "rogue" thus helps one track an idea from rogue literature into legislation, suggesting that the people who wrote laws in early modern England also read—or at least were influenced at second hand by—rogue literature.

Awdeley devotes only three lines to "a wild rogue"; Harman elevates "rogue" to a major term, and the word gains momentum as *A Caveat* goes on: it is expanded into two categories, "A Rogue" and "A Wild Rogue," upon which Harman dilates with extended anecdotes for six pages. Later, "rogue" retroactively becomes one of two umbrella categories including all other kinds of vagrants (109–10); and Harman, reviewing his work, describes it as "this book of Rogues" in the woodcut caption of the penultimate page of the 1567 edition. Thus it was probably Harman who stamped the word onto public awareness. I am not arguing that the word "rogue" in itself has any deep significance[6] but that because it was newly coined, it serves as an important clue to the influence of rogue literature.

At just the time *A Caveat* was published, 1566–67, the House of Commons was debating a bill on punishment of vagabonds (Leonard 68); the bill that eventually came out in 1572, just five years later, shows signs of having been influenced not only by Harman's use of "rogue" but by the prominence he gave to the danger and ubiquity of vagabonds. As E. M. Leonard points out, in the 1572 bill "the regulations concerning vagrants are severe, more severe than in any other Act except the [unenforceable] slavery statute of 1547. For a first offence, a vagabond was to be whipped and bored through the ear"; a third offence merited death, and many were hanged—for vagrancy alone—under this statute (70–71).[7] It is in the decade preceding this formative period for the Poor Laws that a literature proliferated that stigmatized the vagrant poor and introduced terms for categorizing them. Slack contends that "the image of the vagrant rogue produced laws which manufactured a vagrant class out of an amorphous group of poor migrants. The system made paupers and delinquents by labelling them" (*Poverty and Policy* 107). Slack also asserts that "the very process of labelling a man a vagrant helped to make him one. The first punishment was the decisive stage in the downward social spiral which produced a dangerous and incorrigible rogue. When the constables happened to catch people at the respectable end of the vagrant spectrum, they gave them a firm push towards the opposite extreme" (*Poverty and Policy* 99). In this crucial social process, an influential role seems to have been played by rogue literature.

The Workings of the Comic Mode

In one of *A Caveat*'s most memorable scenes, Harman offers a poignant description of vagrants bedding down for the night in a barn:

> The men never trouble themselves with [making of beds], but [take] the same to be the duty of the wife. And she shuffles up a quantity of straw or hay into some pretty corner of the barn where she may conveniently lie, and well shaketh the same, making the head somewhat high, and drives the same upon the sides and feet like a bed: then she layeth her wallet, or some other little pack of rags or scrip under her head in the straw, to bear up the same, and layeth her petticoat or cloak upon and over the straw, so made like a bed, and that serveth for the blanket. Then she layeth her slate (which is her sheet) upon that. And she have no sheet, as few of them go without, then she spreadeth some large clouts or rags over the same, and maketh her ready, and layeth her drowsily down. Many will pluck off their smocks, and lay the same upon them instead of their upper sheet, and all her other pelt and trash upon her also; and many lyeth in their smocks. And if the rest of her clothes in cold weather be not sufficient to keep her warm, then she taketh straw or hay to perform the matter. The other sort, that have not slates, but tumble down and couch a hogshead in their clothes, these be still [i.e., always] lousy, and shall never be without vermin, unless they put off their clothes, and lie as is above said. If the upright-man come in where they lie, he hath his choice, and creepeth in close by his doxy. The rogue hath his leavings. (108)

I called the passage "poignant," for so it is to me; but to Harman it is just an example of such people's shiftlessness and immorality. Here he first calls the vagrant woman a "wife," and the conventional division of labor (bedmaking is "women's work") and mention of "duty" recall the "particular duties" sections of marriage sermons. The wife's pitiful parody of domesticity is for Harman a reasonable facsimile of true comfort: his "pretty corner of the barn" conjures a snug and cozy spot, even though the idea of cozy comfort is soon belied by Harman's account of the elaborate techniques of burrowing naked into the straw and piling rags on top that the vagrants must practice to keep from freezing and to discourage lice. And the "wife's" domestic bustling and nestmaking soon dissolve into brutality with the entrance of an "upright-man," a bullying vagrant of whom other vagrants go in fear. The women, now no longer "wives," are the leftovers of a sordid meal, as the rogue takes his pick of the upright-man's "leavings." Female vagrants, then, are seen by Harman as sex slaves: "These doxies be broken and spoiled of their maidenhead by the upright-men, and then they have their name of doxies. . . . And afterward she is common and indifferent for any that will use her" (105). (Belief in vagrants' promiscuity was widespread in the period; for example, the preacher Robert Allen accused vagrants of practicing "filthiness of adultery and fornication" in "all places of their confused lodging together, at every fair and market throughout the land" [A2ᵛ].)

This is certainly a bleak scene; but such a judgment of the heavens, though it at times makes Harman tremble, touches him not with pity. For Harman the wanderers are lazy, malicious, immoral—to pity their misery is to be duped by their deceits. Most of the men, he thinks, have a bundle salted away and are merely feigning poverty; most live "merrily," a favored term of Harman's (76, 77, 78, 83). The women are less well-off, since upright-men despoil them of whatever they get (100); but they deserve wretched lives because they are sexually loose. At no time does Harman display any recognition of the social conditions that made people homeless. He simply and unabashedly blames the victim.

Harman maintains that there have been a lot of beggars around for a long time; he cites an eighty-year-old acquaintance who recalls hordes of beggars assembling for handouts after a funeral in 1521;[8] but he thinks that what is new among present-day beggars in 1566 is the prevalence of thievery and the use (new within these thirty years, he thinks) of a special language known as "pedlars' French or canting" (64). Like many contemporaries, he sees vagrancy as a large and worsening social problem.

One explanation for the concern about vagrancy at this particular historical moment is that Awdeley's and Harman's works came on the heels of what Slack describes as "the greatest mortality crisis of the [early modern] period, between 1557 and 1559, when 11 per cent of the population of England may have died" from famine and influenza (*Poverty and Policy* 48–49). Such epidemics often spawned harsh attitudes toward vagrants, as the "growing realization that disease was not caused by corruption of the air or conjunctions of the stars but spread from one person to another focused suspicion on vagabonds and wandering beggars during an epidemic" (Lis and Soly 79). The popularity attested by *A Caveat*'s printing history suggests that Harman's harsh attitudes met a receptive audience, and the harsh conditions of the time suggest why.

A fascinating feature of this text, though, is that harshness often issues in laughter, as Harman's moral outrage at vagrants' wicked lives modulates with callous ease into a flippant giggle. Several of *A Caveat*'s many anecdotes end with neighbors laughing at victims of vagrants: an old man accosted by highway robbers (69), a parson tricked by two pretended nephews who grab his arm out a window (76–78). An ostler beaten up by a vagrant while trying to recover some pilfered property just wants the whole thing hushed up: "I shall be mocked and laughed to scorn in all places when they hear how I have been served" (98). Like jest books, *A Caveat* treats humiliations and beatings as hilarious and admires trickster figures. The whole genre of warnings against rogues owes much to early Tudor jest books. For example, chapter titles of Robert Greene's cony-catching pamphlets feature the jest book "How" formula. Greene's "How a Cook's Wife in London Did Lately Serve a Collier for His Cozenage" or "A Merry Tale; How a Miller Had His Purse Cut in Newgate Market" recall many Henrician-era jests—Sir Thomas More's *Merry Jest How a Sergeant Would Learn to Be a Friar, How Howlglas Set His Hostess upon the Hot Ashes with Her Bare Arse*. I propose that rogue literature, long treated as social or cultural history, is instead a subspecies of the Tudor jest book. (On jest books, see appendix B.)

In Henrician literature, "merry jest" is almost a technical term, distinguishing broadly humorous tales rejoicing in untimely farts, picturesque petty revenges, and buffetings about the pate from older "jests" or "gests," which were simply narratives with no connotations of joking. (The word "joke," from Latin *jocus*, came into use in the seventeenth century.) While verse jests, characteristic of the genre's pre-1525 phase, appear to be homegrown, the prose jest collection had many continental forebears (see chapter 3), and a specialized collection tracking the career of one Howlglas was ushered into English by a German original by the pseudonymous Till Eulenspiegel, first printed in English as *A Merry Jest of a Man That Was Called Howlglas* (ca. 1519). This was followed by the "career" of Widow Edith in Walter Smith's *Twelve Merry Jests of the Widow Edith* (1525), the only collection in verse rather than prose, and later by English prose collections including *A Hundred Merry Tales* (1526), *Tales and Quick Answers, Very Merry, and Pleasant to Read* (1532), and *The Merry Tales of the Mad Men of Gotham* (1565 [earlier edition lost]), attributed to Andrew Borde. This was a cohesive genre with set conventions. Though some of the tales are quite old, the format in which they were packaged became standard—the "How" formula; the predominance of tetrameter, dimeter, or ballad stanza in verse jests; the slapstick; the repertoire of vulgarities; and the repetitive diction (such as oaths by real and invented saints).

Rogue literature fits seamlessly into this genre: Harman's and Greene's works are basically prose jest collections. Harman's *Caveat* is a collection of trickster tales, with practical jokes and victims laughed to scorn. His labeling of the tales with vagrancy categories makes the work at first appear sociologically organized; but I suggest that it is really an old-fashioned tale collection with a narrative frame, like Henrician jest collections. During a second jest book craze, in the 1560s, most of the early jests came out in fresh editions, and this was exactly when Harman's *Caveat* first appeared. A third jest book boom in the 1590s coincided with the publication of Greene's cony-catching works, frankly employing the term "merry tale." In *Pierce's Supererogation; or, A New Praise of the Old Ass* (1593), Gabriel Harvey mentions jest books and cony-catching pamphlets together, as if they were the same (17).[9] It is in this literary environment of jest books, and not some hypothetical milieu of protosocial history, that I think rogue literature should be read. In 1573 fresh editions of Smith's *Widow Edith* and Harman's *Caveat* appeared, and I think both should be read as jest books about vagrants. It would be pointless to wax rigid about what counts as a jest book or to draw firm lines around the genre—jest books often pilfered tales from other genres or the oral tradition, and jests migrated into other genres as vagrants migrated around England. But I am arguing that the collection of funny stories, often with a narrative frame, was a familiar enough feature of the cultural landscape when Harman and Greene wrote to make it natural for readers to place Harman's or Greene's works against this generic backdrop.

Those who read *A Caveat* as protosociology emphasize Harman's descriptions of vagrant types and ignore or play down the anecdotes that follow them. But why not regard the anecdotes as tales and *A Caveat* as a framed story collection? Harman in fact calls his anecdotes "tales": after the first impression he "added five or six more tales" (67). Rather than reading the anecdotes as illustrations of types, one could regard the type descriptions as links between tales, similar to Chaucer's tale prologues. Far from comprising a serious treatise on criminal types, the type descriptions are just the glue that holds the tales together. Consider the weight given to the stories compared to the type descriptions: of the work's main body (excluding prefaces and appendixes), 31 percent of the space is devoted to type descriptions, 69 percent to stories. The dedicatory epistle to Bess of Hardwick functions as a narrative frame, introducing Harman as a collector of tales, comfortably ensconced in a country mansion where he hears stories—Harman's equivalent of "In Southwerk at the Tabard as I lay." Reading *A Caveat* this way obliges readers to consider the extent to which Harman as narrator is himself a fiction: just as one distinguishes between Chaucer the poet and Chaucer the pilgrim, should one not try to separate Harman the magistrate from Harman the jest book narrator?

Or one could see this work as marrying the framed jest collection to the genre of warning-against-rogues-by-categorizing-them (e.g., Awdeley's *Fraternity of Vagabonds* or the *Liber Vagatorum* [The Book of Vagabonds]), which in turn belongs to a late medieval literary form, the list of social categories or of tradesmen and artisans. Alexander Barclay's *Ship of Fools* (1509) is such a listing, as is its imitator *Cock Lorel's Boat* (ca. 1518–19) and *its* imitator, Robert Copland's *Highway to the Spital-house* (1536[?]). Awdeley apparently placed his *Fraternity of Vagabonds* in this genre: the title page boasts, "confirmed forever by Cock Lorel." *Cock Lorel's Boat* refers to its list of trades as a "fraternity" (sig. [B4]–[B5]ᵛ), and it contains a three-page list of "all crafts" (sig. B5]ᵛ): tallow chandlers, cord-wainers, quilt makers, buckle smiths, book printers, harp makers, mustard makers, rat-takers, "dissimuling beggars." (This literary form recalls the list as an ancient, widespread oral form, from the orally transmitted genealogies of Africa or the South Pacific to Homer's lists of ships.) This plotless listing genre is wedded by Harman to a narrative tradition, the framed tale collection, with category descriptions replacing earlier connecting devices such as Chaucer's interactions among storytellers.[10] But the tales still preponderate.

Henrician listing texts were closely contemporary with the blossoming of jest books; indeed, they were written in the same ragged verse and with similar diction—*Cock Lorel's Boat*, for example, uses the familiar jest book tag "by Saint Joan." They allude to a world of jesting in calling their characters fools or sometimes making them literal jesters—*The Ship of Fools* makes erring humanity out to be fools, as does *Cock Lorel's Boat*, all of whose woodcuts feature people in fool's caps. One of the craft guilds in *Cock Lorel's Boat* is "borders," or jesters. Awdeley, author of *The Fraternity of Vagabonds*, was oriented toward jest books: as a printer, he owned the rights to *A Little Jest How the Plowman Learned His Paternoster*, *A Sackful of News*, and *A Hundred Merry Tales* (see Hazlitt, *Shakespeare Jest-Books* 1:iv). Other evidence indicates that works like Awdeley's and Harman's occupied similar categories to jest books in printers' minds: Henry Bynneham, prosecuted in 1567 for pirating Harman's *Caveat*, entered in the Stationers' Register in 1576 the jest book *Tales and Quick Answers*. The climate was hospitable to prose tales: the short-story collection *Painter's Palace of Pleasure* appeared in 1565, and part 2 was published in 1567—contemporary with Awdeley and Harman.

Most of Harman's tales are comic, involving trickery, comic table-turnings, whippings, and buffetings—the staples of Tudor jesting. If Harman's comic treatment of vagrant-whipping seems callous to us, comic beatings were the very stuff of late medieval and early Renaissance jesting. Fabliaux rejoice in comic beatings: trickster wives cause their jealous husbands to be beaten with sticks; a gambling priest is beaten by rascals so "they almost mutilated him" (Eichman and Duval 13) but gets even with them through "trickery and deception" (29); a fair sample of the quality of fabliau hilarity is this:

> They beat him so much, both high and low,
> That they broke his back.
> With their sticks and feet and hands
> They gave him more than thirty wounds
> And made him shit in his pants. (Eichmann and Duval 61)

Marks of such comic storytelling are all over *A Caveat*. An old man's neighbors laugh heartily when he is held up by highwaymen, since he has absentmindedly forgotten how much money he has about him. Bumpkins are bemused when their bedclothes are hooked off at night without waking them. After robbing a parson, two scoundrels force him to drink their health. A traveler obligingly asks a habitual horse thief to walk his horse while he transacts some business. Some shifty operators of a "hospital" are stung when, at a midnight revel they are hosting for great lubbers who are feigning disability, some neighbors steal a roast pig off the fire while the hosts are mediating between their disorderly guests and a constable; the constable laughs up his sleeve. A gaggle of local wives ambush a lecher with his pants down, thrashing him soundly. This is sociology? This is a jest book.

I am not arguing that because texts about vagrants were situated as jest books, they should not be taken seriously. The act of positioning the miserable and the suffering as objects of laughter or as self-sufficient tricksters had serious consequences for them. As has been shown, the very word "rogue," as legally defined in Elizabethan Poor Laws, likely came from comic works on vagrancy. Real-life vagrants branded with the letter "R" for "rogue" were reaping the serious legacy of jest books.

An analogous group, women, provides a model of how jests affected the vagrant poor. My *Women and the English Renaissance: Literature and the Nature of Womankind, 1540–1620,* which devotes much space to antifeminist jesting, asks that readers recognize the power of jest "to color, often permanently, our attitudes toward the objects of jest" (6). Noting that "almost all formal misogynistic attacks of the period represent themselves as jest" and that humor looms very large in Western misogyny, I argue:

> Literary jest has not been without its effect on real women. If women are not taken seriously, it is partly because they have been viewed for so many centuries through the eyes of jesters. Husbands can evade serious discussion of marital difficulties because jesters have taught them to dismiss even legitimate wifely complaints as shrewishness or female hysteria. Employers are reluctant to hire women to do physical labor because of jokes about women's weakness and timidity. . . . A woman cannot debate an issue without fearing criticism for female illogicality, cannot take a moral stand without suspecting that her auditors consider her a scold, cannot hold a simple conversation without wondering whether she is talking too much. Women have internalized all the old jokes: was that the jokes' purpose all along? . . . Many theorists of jest have recognized in laughter a tool for asserting and maintaining superiority. . . . Humor is difficult to combat because he who protests even against a cruel jest can always be accused of not being able to take a joke. . . . Many of the damaging stereotypes which hamper us all in our daily lives have been built up gradually, piece by piece like great mosaics. And the pieces are jokes. (31–32)

A recent serious misreading of my work exemplifies how jest's insidious power can be underestimated: from my report that "many stage misogynists are basically comic figures," Brian Vickers concludes that I have "conclusively shown" that "there is not much misogyny in the supposedly patriarchal Renaissance" (*Appropriating* 341). To the contrary: I think the Renaissance—actually and not "supposedly" patriarchal—seethed with misogyny and that its jesting was far from harmless.[11] What happened to women through antifeminist jesting happened to vagrants and other powerless groups—they were laughed into corners from which they could not escape. Marcus Fabius Quintilianus (Quintilian), whose rhetoric text was widely used, advised that "though laughter may appear a light thing, as it is often excited by buffoons, mimics, and even fools, yet it has power perhaps more despotic than any thing else" (1.432). Jest's despotic power appears in its ability, across centuries, to erase real misery by making it appear an artifact of jesting. Vickers's belief that Renaissance women were not oppressed, since those who joked about them were only kidding, reveals how joking about a group can block recognition of their oppression. For the classical jest theorist Cicero, whose influence on the Renaissance was incalculable, "so potent a resource is joking" that he allots it "twice the space devoted to all the passions together"; jest's primary use is for "direct personal attacks. . . . The mood is openly hostile.

. . . The chief interest of jokes is their power to discredit and humiliate" (Lipking 274–77).[12]

To position a book about homeless people as a jest book was to identify the poor as funny, worthy of contemptuous laughter rather than social concern—the same impulse that relegated the lowborn to comic subplots in the drama. The prospect of being "mocked and laughed to scorn," which Harman keeps mentioning in *A Caveat,* reminds of us the constant dread of belittlement fostered by educated writers: the early modern rhetorician Thomas Wilson, for example, advises in his *Art of Rhetoric* that to get the better of an opponent, one should "laugh him to scorn" (138).[13] And when vagrants are figured as wits rather than butts, as tricksters preying on a hapless public, witty self-sufficiency erases their helpless misery and heightens their menace.

Where this can lead appears in a Jacobean comedy that incorporates the cony-catching underworld, Ben Jonson's *Bartholomew Fair.* Its underworld characters are so much shrewder and more interesting than its slumming bourgeoisie that admiration for their witty trickery disables any audience pity for the lower social orders, rendering superfluous any public assistance programs for the poor or policies to change the economic system. When the joke is on the propertied classes, when trickster underworld characters seem to have the upper hand, the camaraderie between trickster and audience ironically erodes fellow feeling between theatergoers and *real* city proletarians: does a wizard at pursecutting, like Jonson's Edgeworth, need the audience's sympathy? Though audiences must to some extent have distinguished between such theatrical representations and real London life (Jonson, after all, draws on the venerable Roman comedy tradition of the witty slave making a fool of his master), the barrage of depictions of the poor as canny rogues, over many years and in many genres, must have fostered a climate in which the tenderhearted and charitable felt like gulls if they pitied or relieved beggars. The Renaissance adoption of the dispossessed (not only the poor but also the insane and the deformed) into a *comic* world had noncomic consequences.

Roguery and Soldiering: The Issue of Faked Disability

Harman reconfigures need into greed. He knows vagrants are ragged, that they need to use clothing even in lieu of blankets, and he notes several times that what they most often steal is clothing, but he never entertains the possibility that they are stealing it to wear it. He instead posits a more commercial motive: when linen is stolen off clotheslines or hooked out of windows, "the marks shall be picked out clean, and conveyed craftily far off to sell" (71), suggesting an organized fencing network. Clothing theft is a persistent motif in rogue literature: an early appearance of a derivative of "rogue" occurs in the context of stealing clothing from hedges: Awdeley reports that the thieves' cant for such hedge thievery is "storing of the Rogeman" (3), and Harman describes the use of what appears to be a variant of this cant term, "stalling to the rogue" (72), in a kind of initiation rite for rogues. In Shakespeare, Falstaff recognizes the down-and-out as natural clothing thieves. Among his "pitiful rascals" there is "not a shirt and a half in all my company, and the half shirt is two napkins tacked together, . . . and the shirt, . . . stolen from my host at Saint Albans" (*1H4* 4.2.44–45); he knows they will steal clothing as they march ("They'll find linen enough on every hedge" [4.2.46–47]), but he does not imagine them picking out the marks and selling the shirts for profit.

Many of the "dishonorable-ragged" that Falstaff recruits have been soldiers—"ancients, corporals, lieutenants, gentlemen of companies" (4.2.23–24). Scholars of early modern poverty recognize demobilized—and often disabled—soldiers as a persistent, significant element of the destitute homeless, and disorder from hungry disbanded soldiers was feared with good reason—in 1589, for example, troops were called out and martial law imposed when hundreds of Drake's disbanded soldiers threatened the peace in London (J. Thomas Kelly 64). But Harman views such soldiers as merry vagabond tricksters. His list of types of vagrants begins with the former soldier, the "ruffler": after the war, "shaking off all pain, [he] doth choose him this idle life, and wretchedly wanders about the most shires of this realm" (67). This wretchedness is painless because it has been voluntarily chosen, out of idleness. (As Garrett A. Sullivan Jr. points out, travel—given the road conditions of the period—was hardly an idle activity, as its etymological connection with "travail" suggests [personal communication].) Harman considers soldiers' disabilities faked: war wounds are made to be lied about, were probably received in a drunken brawl rather than in battle, and are to be boasted about in one's cups and to serve as an aid to begging. Though war-inflicted disabilities were very common in the period, popular stereotype often dismissed them as drunken lies. In Shakespeare, such stereotypes intrude sourly even on Henry V's great rallying speech on the threshold of Agincourt, where combatants are invited to look forward to their old age, when each will "strip his sleeve and show his scars," and reminisce boozily about the war while "in their flowing cups" (*H5* 4.3.47), an uneasy foreshadowing of the American Legion hall. Pistol plans to return home, live by thievery, and lie about a wound inflicted ignominiously by a soldier on his own side: "To England will I steal, and there I'll steal; / And patches will I get unto these cudgeled scars, / And swear I got them in the Gallia wars" (*H5* 5.1.86–88). Do Pistol's phony war wounds undercut the heroic injuries of English soldiers at Agincourt? Or is Shakespeare inviting careful distinctions between the real war wounds of worthy demobilized soldiers and the faked war wounds of the idle? It is hard to tell in *Henry V,* but it is not so with Harman: to him, all combat wounds are faked, all homeless soldiers are idle knaves seeking a beggar's merry life of ease.

To Harman, fake war wounds are only one example of rampant pretended disability. One of his most fulsome anecdotes relates his exposure of Nicholas Jennings, a phony epileptic who had been growing rich on ill-gotten gains. To Harman, there *are* legitimately ill people, but we do not see much of them because they stay home (more will be said on this presently). All the sick vagrants Harman describes appear to be faking. (Many do die of illness by his report, but since they nearly always succumb to venereal disease, they had it coming to them. He does not dwell on sexually transmitted diseases as a cause of disability, and hence of begging, but instead positions death by the pox only as an abrupt conclusion, like hanging.) So healthy a life does begging, going naked, and sleeping in freezing barns appear to be that vagrants have to fake illness to inspire pity.

And they *do* inspire pity, at least among the ordinary people that Harman encounters. Seeing the alleged epileptic, smeared with the Renaissance equivalent of ketchup to make him appear bloody, an "honest poor woman that dwelt thereby brought him a fair linen cloth, and bid him wipe his face therewith; and there being a tub standing full of rain-water, offered to give him some in a dish that he might make himself clean" (86). The boys whom Harman hires to tail the beggar see him renew "his face again with fresh blood, which he carried about him in a bladder, and [daub] on fresh dirt upon his jerkin, hat and hosen"; they see that "some gave groats, some sixpence, some gave more. For he looked so ugly and irksomely, that every one pitied his miserable case that beheld him" (87). Such indiscriminate compassion is exactly what Harman wants to put a stop to: those who pity and relieve beggars are easily gulled fools. This soft-hearted public is to some extent a rhetorical device: as in more modern times, if one pens a hardhitting warning against deceitful welfare recipients, it is useful to posit a vulnerable, bleeding-heart public wholly at their mercy. Nonetheless, England was not entirely populated by such flinty-hearted souls as Harman: the distress even of downright beggars *was* pitied and relieved, against the advice of Harman and many other writers.

As Harman would have it, the compassionate have simply been deceived, frequently by faked disability. The fact that Elizabethan legislation included actors among rogues and vagabonds grows more understandable in light of Harman's assumption, shared by many of his contemporaries, that vagrants were constantly acting, pretending to disability, pretending to illness, pretending to be poor when in fact they had a tidy packet salted away.[14] Nicholas Jennings, the feigned epileptic, even pretends to be homeless when he actually has a comfortable house and a wife. As I shall show, the histrionic talents of vagrants were thought to extend to mimicking gentility as well. One elaborate cony-catching scam involving four rogues is described by Thomas Dekker as a play: "Two of them . . . have clothes of purpose to fit the play, carrying the shew of gentlemen; the others act their parts in blue coats" (*Lantern and Candlelight* 240).

Disguises, to Harman, demand unmasking. Mark Koch argues that "skepticism, so much the epistemological foundation of the Reformation and the Enlightenment, is crucial to the desanctification and demystification of the beggar" ("Desanctification" 99); yet Harman's skepticism is selective: he is skeptical of beggars' claims to be disabled but accepts unquestioningly every assertion about their evil lives—a constable's secondhand story about a sledge-throwing orgy, the unlikely blanket-hooking tale. What he is willing to believe is anything showing beggars in a poor light: not so much skepticism—though it masquerades as such disinterested observation—as the witch-hunter's determination to unmask hidden practices, of which faked disability remained one of the most prominent.

The Criminalization of Poverty

By labeling all his categories with terms from thieves' cant—though not all vagrants were thieves—Harman assimilates all to the criminal underworld, a move that A. V. Judges replicated, in our own era, lumping together works on vagrancy with works on crime, under the heading *The Elizabethan Underworld*. Other anthologies and studies that reproduce Judges's assimilation of the literature of poverty to the literature of crime include Frank Wadleigh Chandler's *Literature of Roguery* (1907), Ronald Fuller's *Beggars' Brotherhood* (1936), Gāmini Salgādo's *Cony-Catchers and Bawdy Baskets* (1972), and Arthur F. Kinney's *Rogues, Vagabonds, and Sturdy Beggars: A New Gallery of Tudor and Early Stuart Rogue Literature* (1972). (This move is made in modern sociological contexts, too: even such a highly sympathetic account as Mark S. Fleisher's *Beggars and Thieves: Lives of Urban Street Criminals* [1995] foregrounds its subjects' criminality rather than their homelessness.) Such works often treat rogue literature with a mixture of sociological seriousness and high-spirited enjoyment of wickedness past, of the sheer fun of contemplating a "rogue's gallery." Frank Ayledotte smiles in genial amusement at the way begging licenses made life easy for rogues, and he praises as "excellent and entertaining" Jusserand's account of medieval vagrants (21–23). This combination of moral seriousness with a sense of good fun uncannily reproduces Harman's tone.

Even if thieves' cant were real rather than just a figment of the imagination of rogue literature's authors (and I think its reality is pretty dubious), surely not all homeless people would have used cant. Typical vagrants on the road, as described by A. L. Beier in *Masterless Men*—a woman following her deserting husband, a pregnant girl fleeing from home—would hardly describe themselves as "autem morts" or "doxies." Using this language criminalizes all vagrants. Harman furnishes an early modern example of what David Matza describes in modern times as a "public tendency, echoed by certain sociologists, to gratuitously extend the features of the inner circle—the hard core [who *are* criminal] to the wider but next removed circle of the welfare poor, and then to the furthest removed circle of the poor altogether" (606). Thus all poor people are suspected to be criminal. Most Elizabethan works dealing with vagrancy also deal with crime; but not all crime literature deals with vagrancy—Greene's cony-catching pamphlets, for example, offer no comment on his criminals' living quarters (or lack thereof) and do not represent criminals as poor or hungry. These works are very different from Harman's text, which, however callously, recognizes a link between crime and poverty and glimpses the miseries of the poor. Yet modern editors nearly always anthologize Harman's work along with crime pamphlets. Then and now, subsuming poverty under crime both erases poverty and homelessness as prominent concerns and tars poverty with the brush of crime.

Suspicion of Mobility

Nicholas Jennings being put in the stocks, Harman calls "condign punishment" (illustration facing p. 97). Why were the stocks considered punishment befitting vagrants? Because, I suggest, the crime of vagrants was mobility. They wandered in an age whose official ideologies prized settled domesticity; they shifted roles and identities in an age that was officially committed to rigid occupational categories and was starting to be concerned about the stability of identity. The harsh judicial punishment of Jonson's title character in *Volpone* (1606), a *rich* man who plays the vagrant's supposed game of feigned disability, embodies the period's desperate need to pin down any kind of slipperiness with punishments producing immobility:

> Since the most was gotten by imposture,
> By feigning lame, gout, palsy, and such diseases,
> Thou art to lie in prison, cramped with irons,
> Till thou bee'st sick and lame indeed. (5.12.121–24)

Harman defines "cursetors" as "runners . . . about the country" (66) suggesting frenetic, disorganized, aimless rushing about. His denouncing them as "the wickedest walkers" (109) is likely just for alliteration: he more typically sees them as runners, dashing energetically about the countryside doing mischief: Irish rogues "run about the country with a counterfeit licence" (84); the rogue William Jinks "runneth about the country to seek work, . . . but little work serveth him" (112). Such roving is to Harman illegitimate in itself, and he harps continually on the forged documents that allow vagrants to wander at large. He neatly draws the line between the deserving and the undeserving poor. The undeserving are the "rowsey, ragged rabblement of rakehells, that—under pretence of great misery, diseases, and other innumerable calamities which they feign—through great hypocrisy do win and gain great alms in all places where they wilily wander, to the utter deluding of the good givers"; they funnel money away from the deserving poor, "deceiving and impoverishing of all such poor householders, both sick and sore, as neither can nor may walk abroad for relief and comfort (where, indeed, most mercy is to be showed)" (61). The deserving poor are immobile—they do not wander but are householders (which for Harman does not disqualify them as "poor"), and they are also too sick and sore to go out. All the mobile, wandering homeless he discusses—those who "wilily wander"—fall among the undeserving. Harman's attitudes, far from being eccentrically harsh, reflect attitudes also embodied in social legislation.

Harman's fear of mobility was not groundless—he lived on a main route into London and would have seen plenty of vagrants. But does the aura of *threat* in wandering to some degree project a fear of early modern social mobility? Harman himself exhibits some such mobility: he is basically a member of the wealthy gentry; magistrates were solid, respected members of the community. But he has also become an author, and he is on good enough terms with a London printer to send him forth as a crimefighter to make citizens' arrests of phony epileptics.[15] The Harman who travels enthusiastically to London to oversee the printing of his book has a foot in the new commercial world of print culture, and anxiety over genteel folk dirtying their hands in print has been well documented for this period. (See, for example, Saunders's "Stigma of Print" and "From Manuscript to Print," Wall's *Imprint of Gender,* and Elsky's *Authorizing Words.*) Harman's dread of vagrants' mobility seems to project uneasiness about the rapid changes that society was undergoing; his scapegoating of vagrants simplifies complex cultural changes by blaming them on a visible group, vagrants.

Given these anxieties about mobility, it is unsurprising that when Elizabethans encountered nomadic aboriginal people overseas, they identified them with English vagrants—"as savage slaves be in great Britaine here, / As any one that you can shew me there" (Drayton, "To the Virginian Voyage" 363)—and ascribed to them character defects stereotypic of English vagrants: as Karen Kupperman notes, they accused Native Americans of "many character defects and vices— . . . improvidence, vengefulness, treachery, thievery, sexual promiscuity. . . . The men are often said to be lazy" (121). As Greenblatt notes, Columbus also had justified his appropriation of Indian territory by disbarring Indians from full humanity on grounds of their mobility, their nomadism, and the fact of their "having no settled dwellings" (*Marvelous Possessions* 66). Colonies that seemed to offer great promise of mobility were from the outset marked by repressive structures of confinement and immobility—in America, slavery, indentured servitude, and Indian reservations; in Africa, slavery; in Australia, penal colonies. The Renaissance passion for immobilizing and imprisoning cast its shadow over many English colonies. Vagrants, and sometimes the kidnapped children of beggars, were sent to the colonies, and early New England social policy included a typically Elizabethan solution to the problem of noxious mobility: houses of correction (Kupperman 123). In a sermon advocating the transportation of vagrants to the colonies, John Donne compared the whole New World to the most notorious workhouse/prison in England: "if the whole country were but such a *Bridewell,* to force idle persons to work, it had a good use" (4:272).

Neighborhood Watch Comes to Kent

Harman, a country magistrate with estates in Kent, dedicated *A Caveat* to Bess of Hardwick, then Countess of Shrewsbury, to warn her (and presumably other immensely rich property owners) against the dangers of unwise, indiscriminate charity. Though posterity may regard the toughminded Hardwick as aptly named, Harman's depiction of her as perilously softhearted enlists for his purposes a stereotypic association of women with unwise mercy and pity; this indeed may account for his dedicating the work to her rather than to her husband, the Earl of Shrewsbury. Harman's self-description as a "poor gentleman" (62) is not a declaration of poverty but a gesture of self-deprecation; he was "poor" mainly by comparison with the likes of Bess of Hardwick. As various passages of *A Caveat* attest, he was a member of the landed gentry, with tenants, servants, a field full of fine geldings, and the title "Esquire." He kept a hospitable house even after he ceased to keep a charitable house: there was always plenty of money for meals—and for bribery—when he wanted to invite vagrants in for his information-gathering sessions. He was the grandson of Henry Harman, the clerk of the crown under Henry VII, who around 1480 obtained the estates of Ellam and Maystreet in Kent (*Dictionary of National Biography*, s.v. "Harman, Henry"). Thomas's father, William, added another manor to the estate. Inheriting all this, Harman lived at Crayford in Kent from 1547. As Arthur Kinney notes, "that he bore arms of heraldry and had them stamped on his pewter dishes suggests he was well aware of his family's position" (105). Though once a charitable man, Harman came, as he tells his readers, to realize how vagrants had duped him:

> I . . . , a poor gentleman, have kept a house these twenty years, whereunto poverty [i.e., poor people] daily hath and doth repair, not without some relief, as my poor calling and hability may and doth extend, I have of late years gathered a great suspicion that all should not be well. . . . For I, having more occasion, through sickness, to tarry and remain at home than I have been accustomed, do, by my there abiding, talk and confer daily with many of these wily wanderers of both sorts, as well men and women, as boys and girls, by whom I have gathered and understand their deep dissimulation and detestable dealing, being marvellous subtle and crafty in their kind, for not one amongst twenty will discover, either declare their scelerous [i.e., wicked] secrets. Yet with fair glittering words, money, and good cheer [that is, provision of free meals], I have attained to the type by such as [i.e., learned the manner in which] the meanest of them hath wandered these thirteen years, and most sixteen and some twenty and upward, and not without faithful promise made unto them never to discover [i.e., disclose] their names or anything they showed me. For they would all say, if the upright-men should understand thereof, they should not be only grievously beaten, but put in danger of their lives, by the said upright-men. (62)

Now, who exactly is being wily here? Harman has wormed his way into the vagrants' confidence with deceitful words, bribes, and food, has discovered their secrets, and then betrayed them—at the end of *A Caveat*, despite his "faithful promise . . . never to discover their names," he publishes all their names in alphabetical order, in many cases including distinguishing physical characteristics to make them further identifiable, positively inviting retribution by homicidal upright-men and, more to the point, by the law. Although Greenblatt argues that Harman is typical of his age and class in regarding his "broken promises [as] acts of civility" that are beneficial to society at large (*Shakespearean Negotiations* 52),[16] even John Awdeley's conscience toward vagrants was somewhat tenderer: *The Fraternity of Vagabonds'* enabling fiction is that information about vagrants was obtained through a plea bargain by a vagrant brought before a justice of the peace; to avoid retribution from fellow vagrants, the informer demanded that his name not be revealed, and Awdeley's text does not identify him; nor does it name any other individuals. Harman's text is quite exceptional in this regard. Frank Ayledotte, combing contemporary records of criminal prosecutions from areas surrounding Harman's residence, discovered eighteen names from Harman's list that appear in the lists of those prosecuted; in all eighteen cases, the crime for which they were punished is simply listed as "vagabondage" (122, 150–51). Indeed, a court document dated January 13, 1597, verifies the prosecution of Nicholas Jennings for feigned epilepsy (Carroll, *Fat King* 82–83). Throughout his work, Harman accuses vagrants of deceit and trickery; yet it would be hard to outdo the deceit and trickery that he confesses to.

Harman's deceit includes just the kind of deception that Harman is determined to smoke out: feigned disability. Despite his stance as an invalid confined to his country residence for many years, he is presently found in lodgings in London, overseeing the publication of two editions of *A Caveat* and showing no signs of longterm illness: indeed, upon overhearing out a window the begging activities of an alleged epileptic, he strides into the street "at a sudden," interrogates the man, then sends to Bethlehem Hospital to interrogate the warden about the man's story; he then gets apprentices to shadow the beggar and employs a printer friend to set him up and betray him into confessing how much money he has made at begging (85–90). The next day Harman dashes off to Newington to follow the progress of the case. The immobility and seeming illness that allowed Harman to get these stories in the first place, contrasted with his later robust health, suggest that he himself is a phony invalid, using feigned illness to deceive, trick, and betray—exactly what he accuses vagrants of.

A further piece of duplicity appears: while Harman presents himself as a private citizen, householder, charitable man, and author, he plays down his position as a magistrate. That Harman was a commissioner of the peace, responsible for punishing offenders against the Poor Laws, he reveals about two-thirds of the way through *A Caveat*: "I have had some of them brought before me, when I was in Commission of the Peace, as malefactors, for bribering and stealing" (93); he has "taken away from them their [forged begging] licences, . . . with such money as they have gathered" (84). Paul Slack notes how much power over vagrants the Poor Laws granted to justices of the peace, power that could be exercised with a high degree of arbitrariness: "Vagrancy legislation was discretionary. It cast a broad net which quite intentionally left opportunity for selective enforcement. It compelled justices and constables to discriminate when confronted by the large mass who might be caught by it" (*Poverty and Policy* 92). Those into whose confidence Harman insinuates himself over a meal may tomorrow appear before him on a vagrancy charge. His jollying them into revealing, in private conversation, crimes and deceits for which he has power to prosecute them is a serious abuse of power. Justices of the peace could sentence vagrants to banishment, the galleys, or death. In *A Caveat,* Harman has a "dumb" man tortured until he speaks. As bullies with power over vagrants, upright-men hardly outdid Harman. Indeed, noting that Nicholas Jennings, the feigned epileptic, like Harman possesses a collection of pewter,[17] William C. Carroll suggests that Jennings's "fundamental doubleness . . . mirrors the doubleness of Harman himself. . . . The center and the margins are not so different" (*Fat King* 86).

The issue of a vagrant's supposed life of leisure raises questions about Harman too. The echo effect between vices of the poor and vices of the rich has been noted in later social theory. David Matza, reflecting on Thorstein Veblen's "spurious leisure class" where "at the very bottom of the class system, as at the very top, there developed a stratum that lived in leisure and was given to predatory sentiments and behavior" notes that George Dowling wrote in 1893, "The opulent who are not rich by the results of their own industry . . . suffer atrophy of virile and moral powers, and like paupers live on the world's surplus without adding to it or giving any fair equivalent for their maintenance" (628). Can the Thomas Harman who inherited from his father and grandfather three manor houses with extensive lands possibly be considered one of those who "live on the world's surplus without . . . giving any fair equivalent for their maintenance"? Has the condition of living off others' labor caused any "atrophy of . . . [his] moral powers"? The harshness of his dealings with the vagrant poor, along with his utter lack of self-reflection, make one wonder.

When it comes to deceit, to false presentation of self, which Harman finds fundamental to the vagrant character, the author of *A Caveat* again exposes himself as a target. Harman may not even have been a justice of the peace: A. L. Beier tells me, in a personal communication, that the Pipe Rolls in the Public Record Office, which record justices' per diems, contain in the years 1539–66 no trace of Harman; and an index of Patent Rolls in the Public Record Office lists Harman not as justice of the peace but as commissioner of sewers in Kent.

(More will be said on this in chapter 4.) Be this as it may, Harman's posture as the worldly-wise investigator of vagrants' deceits, his stance as a reporter on the underworld scene with direct, firsthand knowledge, is also undercut by the fact that most of his evidence comes from literary tradition.

Data Collection or Literary Borrowing?

In the 1567 edition of *A Caveat,* Harman italicizes his conviction that *"some thing lurk and lay hid that did not plainly appear"* (sig. Aii), an English version of the Latin tag *aliquod latent quod non patent* (Something is hidden which is not obvious), cited by the rogue Jack Wilton as he proceeds to unveil his occulted history in Thomas Nashe's *Unfortunate Traveller* (255). Another version of the saying, *multa latent quae non patent* (Many things lie hidden which are not exposed), appears at the end of a cant decoding in Robert Greene's *Notable Discovery of Cozenage* (177). The repetition of this phrase indicates the centrality to rogue literature of the conceit of bringing hidden practices to light. In later rogue literature, the lantern shedding light on dark practices was to become a controlling image, as in Dekker's *Lantern and Candlelight.* The lantern carried by the ancient Greek truth-seeker Diogenes came to symbolize the rogue writer's relentless spotlight on hidden evils. Despite the posture of investigative reporting, however, most of the roguish practices supposedly unmasked by rogue literature are gleaned from earlier literary exposés of vagrancy. Harman borrows from Awdeley's *Fraternity of Vagabonds* and ultimately the *Liber Vagatorum.* And since the *Liber Vagatorum* was a late fifteenth-century text, Harman's claims to up-to-the-minute reporting ring false; even in its own time, the *Liber Vagatorum's* air of being an exposé of tricks "nowadays" was an artifice—many of its rogue scams were copied from an early fifteenth-century work (Davis 277n.29). Knowing that some of his anecdotes originate in a literary tradition, can one believe *anything* that Harman says? What if he simply stole some of his information and made up the rest, rather than interviewing vagrants at all? Modern readers will never know how much of *A Caveat* to believe; but enough of it is borrowed from other texts, rather than based on experience, as Harman claims, to suggest that he is living a lie as much as the vagrants are.

But this is true of much rogue literature; for example, Greene's exposés of the niceties of cheating at cards and dice, published in the 1590s as gleanings of his own firsthand experience, are heavily plagiarized from Gilbert Walker's *Manifest Detection of . . . Dice-Play* (1552). The world of rogue literature is not at all what it claims to be or what some social historians have taken it to be—a world of tough investigative reporting by fearless crime-fighters infiltrating a dangerous underworld. Instead, it is a literary world where texts spawn other texts.[18] As a source of information for historians, it ought to be highly suspect.

But even the language of the Poor Laws, which typically justifies harsh punishments of vagrants on grounds of a crime wave currently sweeping the nation, far from reflecting current crime statistics, is simply copied from earlier statutes. Compare, for example, the opening of *An Act for the Punishment of Vagabonds, and for the Relief of the Poor and Impotent* (1572), which alleges that "all the parts of this realm of England and Wales, be presently with rogues, vagabonds, and sturdy beggars exceedingly pestered, by means of which daily happeneth in the same realm horrible murders, thefts, and other outrages" (sig. [A5]), with the allegation in the earlier *An Act Concerning Punishment of Beggars and Vagabonds* (1531): "In all places throughout this realm of England vagabonds and beggars have of long time increased and daily do increase, . . . whereby . . . daily insurgeth and springeth continued thefts, murders, and other heinous offences and great enormities" (qtd. in C. H. Williams 1025). Such influence from text to text makes it hard to judge how far the public perception of increasing crime was merely an artifact of a litany of official condemnations of increasing crime, passed on from one generation to the next. The phenomenon resembles the persistence of modern politicians' laments over the prevalence of crime, even in years when the national crime rate decreases.

Readers have often been misled by the hard-hitting language of investigation and exposé into mistaking for sociological data collection what is actually literary borrowing. Scientific-sounding language can be deceptive. As Thomas Kuhn and others have shown, early modern science was often piggybacked on magical beliefs, and it is not uncommon to find early modern natural philosophers—forerunners of our "scientists"—applying the same language to the uncovering of nature's "secrets" as their contemporary witch-hunters applied to the unmasking of occult practices of sorcery, and as writers of rogue literature applied to the unmasking of underworld practices. When William Gilbert, for example, in his pioneering work on the protoscience of magnetic philosophy, writes that "the occult and hidden cause" of magnetic variance has "to be brought to light" (229), readers may be mistaken if they assume that "occult" refers neutrally to the as-yet-undiscovered. It is easy for the modern, science-immersed age to misread as thoroughly rational and scientific the writings of early scientists whose own mentalities were often steeped in the *magically* occult. For example, William Harvey, discoverer of the circulation of the blood, treated tumors by laying the hand of a corpse on them.[19] How different in kind from the occult powers of witchcraft *did* the secret forces of magnetism seem to an early modern mind like Gilbert's? The fact that he performed experiments and used a language of empirical observation may obscure the extent to which his mentality still partook of much that a modern observer would call superstition. Harman, like Gilbert, makes empirical claims: he and other writers of rogue literature claim information on vagrants to be based on direct personal observation; but just as in science an empirical-sounding language often *preceded* a fully scientific mentality, so in rogue literature a prototype of the empirical, direct-observation rhetoric of crime reporting seems to have preceded any real investigative reporting. The period was developing—perhaps through the influence of natural philosophers like Gilbert—the rhetorical habit of appealing to direct observation; for example, as Annabel Patterson points out, there is the Holinshed chroniclers' devotion to eyewitness testimony (*Reading Holinshed's Chronicles* 38). But rogue literature's "empirical" language is little but rhetorical window dressing. The sixteenth century did not distinguish firmly between discovery and invention—indeed, several discourses used the two words interchangeably. Rogue literature's extensive plagiarism suggests that most of its discoveries were in fact inventions, as was the case with witchcraft. What has long misled scholars is the modern-sounding empirical language in which it is couched.

Exploring the period's fascination with bringing secret things to light, Patricia Parker sees a link between "the anatomist's opening and exposing to the eye the secrets or 'privities' of women and the 'discovery' or bringing to light of what were from a Eurocentric perspective previously hidden worlds" in the age of exploration (240). Both had elements of prurience and voyeurism. Their "shared language of opening, uncovering or bringing to light" also involves monster literature, to which the literature of exploration was often related; a 1600 geographical history of Africa contained "a map of Africa folded and closed upon itself, which, when opened up, brings before the reader's gaze the land of monsters, of Amazons, of prodigious sexuality and of peoples who expose those parts which should be hid" (240–41). The relevance to the discourse of vagrancy of such texts on newly discovered foreign monstrosities declares itself: Harman and his fellows also bring hidden practices to light; they too find (among vagrants) monstrous human beings, prodigious sexuality, and ragged, naked immodesty; and they often exoticize vagrants as not English. Parker further relates this cluster of ideas to the age's passion for eyewitness accounts and to the growth of informing and spying: "This shared language of 'discovery' as informing or spying on something hid . . . [gives] many of these exotic histories their affinities with the ocular preoccupations of the growing domestic network of . . . informers and spies, charged with reporting on the secret or hid" (240–41). Harman and later cony-catching writers did position themselves as "spies charged with reporting on the secret or hid." But again, modern readers should be wary of reading this rhetorical posture as a herald of modern empirical methods. Even contemporaries were highly skeptical of the "eyewitness" accounts of monstrosities by foreign explorers, which they sensibly enough equated with storytelling; and the whole enterprise of spying into abuses was epistemologically tainted from the start by the very belief in exotic monsters.

Thieves' Cant and Magistrates' Cant

Harman treats vagrants' lingo as a self-contained language and not just a peppering of slang; he appends a glossary and a dialogue in thieves' cant, complete with a translation. Giving vagrants their own language makes them seem foreign and non-English; indeed, Harman says many are Irish, Welsh, and gypsies (see 64, 80, 81, 84, 91, 113). Yet Harman too speaks a special language, excessive and eccentric. His huge sentences wander like vagabonds (*A Caveat*'s opening sentence is 280 words long). His alliterations are downright manic: "peevish, pelting, and picking practices" (62); "I many times musing with myself as these mischievous mislivers, marvelled" (63); "lewd, lecherous loiterings" (69); "lewd, lousy language of these loitering lusks and lazy lorels" (113); "bold, beastly, bawdy beggars and vain vagabonds" (114). If vagrants coin words, so does Harman: he defends his Latin coinage "cursetor" as not much more newfangled than "vagabond": cursetors are "runners or ranters about the country, derived of this Latin word, *curro*" (66). Other examples of Harman's recent Latinate imports include "scelerous" (62) and "caveat" itself, newly naturalized in English at the time he wrote. Barry Taylor suggests that for Harman to have admitted that he coined "cursetor" to alliterate with "caveat" would have meant acknowledging "a rhetorical dimension of discourse which has no place in Harman's ideology of plain style and transparent meaning"; thus, to admit "his departure from the community of plain-speakers into the company of verbal contrivers and double-talkers . . . would be to erode the categorical distinction between his own discourse and that of the cony-catcher" (16–17). If vagrants had a language, educated males had long spoken and written their own language, with Latin and Latinate English coinages, which helped keep them an exclusive class. David Cressy shows that "the gentry, clergy and members of the professions were so similar in their literacy that they can be regarded as inhabiting a single cluster at the accomplished end of the literacy scale" (124), and it is membership in this educated caste to which Harman's language lays claim. As if to buttress the educated against the social mobilities of the age, inkhorn terms were being coined as fast as millwheels strike. Educational opportunity promoted social mobility, and in the face of new arrivals to their level of society the educated produced outlandish new words; as in Norbert Elias's formulation, the upper classes grew increasingly refined to distinguish themselves from upwardly mobile classes thrusting up from below. Vagrants here appear as a parody of the educated, both madly minting strange new words. In *The Alchemist,* Jonson suggests that cant is not different in kind from more pretentious technical vocabularies: Surly finds the "brave language" of alchemy, stuffed full of Latinate terms such as "infuse," "volatile," and "tincture," to be "next to canting" (2.3.37–42). Richard Halpern, inquiring into "why Tudor society would allocate a substantial part of its resources to an educational program that so heavily emphasized the teaching of classical rhetoric, letters, and style" (21), argues that a "mysterious addiction to style" (20), however irrelevant to the practical concerns of most citizens, lay at the heart of the Tudor educational system because such education constituted "a mechanism of class distinction. . . . Latinity was . . . a mark of gentility and hence a support for class distinctions" (25), allied in the classroom with an attempt to extirpate "narrative forms of popular culture" (25). Harman claims educational value for *A Caveat,* but his embedded anecdotes suspiciously resemble "narrative forms of popular culture": his stake in emphasizing his respectable, educated Latinity is clear.

It is too simple to dismiss as mere hypocrisy Harman's committing of offenses that he castigates in others: practicing deceit, pretending disability, coining words, rushing about. While the text's internal contradictions hint that the whole thing is ironic, that *A Caveat*'s first-person speaker is playing Gulliver to Harman's Swift in a clever exposé of the heartlessness of wealthy magistrates, I cannot ultimately read the text that way.[20] For such irony to be detectable, the speaker's opinions would need to be conspicuously more extreme than those of his contemporaries, as when the speaker of *A Modest Proposal* advocates cannibalism; but Harman's opinions jibe with official Elizabethan policy utterances, which *did* blame the poor for their poverty and *did* provide whipping, stocking, and even hanging for the crime of being unemployed. And is not castigating in others what one distrusts in oneself precisely how "Othering" works? One purges oneself of vices by projecting onto some hated group the qualities most disturbing in oneself. Harman is saying, "I am not deceitful, and *my* language does not insulate my social group—*they* are doing those things; *vile vagrants,* not my sort, are damaging society."

A similar projection from one social group onto another seems involved in Harman's keen interest in vagrants' sexuality: "they couch comely together, and [i.e., as if] it were dog and bitch" (70); "to one [i.e., for every one] man that goeth abroad, there are at the least two women,[21] which never make it strange when they be called, although she never knew him before" (78); "not one amongst a hundred of them are married; for they take lechery for no sin, but natural fellowship and good liking, love" (94); "these autem-morts be married women, as there be but a few. For autem in their language is a church. So she is a wife married at the church. And they be as chaste as a cow I have, that goeth to bull every moon, with what bull she careth not" (99). (Harman's frequent shifting from singular to plural when discussing vagrants tracks the effacement of their individuality in his generalizing discourse.) Harman damns vagrants' freely bestowed sexual acts while implicitly approving the aristocratic practice of selling oneself in mercenary marriage deals, prominent in the life of *A Caveat*'s much-married dedicatee, Bess of Hardwick. (Of Bess's marriage to the Earl of Shrewsbury, her biographer David N. Durant judges, "Their marriage must not be looked upon as anything other than an amalgamation of assets from which both sides would benefit" [54]). And Harman recognizes perfectly well the sexual improprieties of the propertied classes. The longest and most developed of his anecdotes features a wealthy farmer who tries to extort sex from a vagrant woman and is also infamous for importuning and threatening to rape local wives. The vagrant woman, true to Harman's usual attitude, is no better than she should be, being pregnant with a child of uncertain paternity. But she avoids (by trickery) sleeping with this faithless husband and sees him severely punished, significantly, by whipping, the typical punishment for beggars; she does this out of a sense of solidarity with his wife (100–105). The farmer's behavior severely erodes Harman's distinction between settled, moral householders and mobile, immoral vagrants, but Harman seems unaware of this inconsistency, even though he reports that the farmer's wife, because of her husband's fondness for harlots, goes in constant fear of contracting that hallmark of vagrancy, venereal disease. As Slack says of Elizabethan crime and punishment, "the crimes being punished were not just those of the poor. To think that they were is . . . to swallow contemporary propaganda whole. . . . Of 320 people presented for a variety of disorders in one year, 1629–30, only 34 were vagrants or strangers. . . . The stigma of drunkenness and disorder was attached to the poor because they were the easiest target, not because they were the only one" (*Poverty and Policy* 104).

A Caveat Deconstructs

In the anecdote just discussed, the friendship between a vagrant woman and a settled farm wife gives the lie to Harman's view of vagrants as living totally outside society. (Later he reports that vagrant women try to prevent being robbed by leaving their money with honest housewives, which also suggests friendship crossing the boundary between settled and vagrant [110].) This discrepancy is far from anomalous: throughout *A Caveat,* at least from a modern reader's historical distance, one feels a strain that nearly pulls the text apart. It is a text divided against itself. As I have shown, jest book humor subverts serious intent, and prurience undermines moralizing. Also symptomatic of the text's internal division is the chaotic disorder that erupts amid neat categories. Adapting the listing techniques of medieval forebears, Harman tries to assert control over vagrancy by reducing the wanderers to tidy categories. But as his text unfolds, his categories keep overlapping, interpenetrating, shifting. Harman shares a number of categories with Awdeley's *Fraternity of Vagabonds:* Awdeley offers twenty-two types of vagabond, Harman twenty-four, and the two share sixteen categories. However, Awdeley's list lacks order, mingling thieves, bullies, and beggars, men and women, the employed and unemployed. Harman seems to have sorted his vagrants, as Chaucer makes groups of clergy or aristocracy in the General Prologue to *The Canterbury Tales;* like Chaucer, Harman does not label the groups but leaves readers to discern them. In the first group of six able-bodied, dangerous criminal types—the ruffler, upright-man, hooker or angler, rogue, wild rogue, and prigger of prancers—the emphasis is mostly on thievery or bold highway robbery. These beg only with an ulterior motive: the hooker begs by day to case the houses from which he hooks clothing and valuables through windows by night; the prigger of prancers, a horse thief, begs in order to present himself as a prospective farmhand—and thus to get close to the horses. The next group—again, a group of six—is not criminal, except insofar as Harman considers faked disability a crime. They do not steal or bully but merely beg, usually employing a fake disability or counterfeit begging license: the palliard, frater, abram-man, counterfeit crank (pretended epileptic), the dummerer (pretended dumb man), and freshwater mariner or whipjack—a type singled out by later legislation (the 1572, 1597, and 1604 Poor Laws, for example, legislate against those who deceitfully pretend to have been shipwrecked as an aid to begging). The next group of four types are not, like the previous twelve, unemployed. Rather, they are itinerant tradesmen: tinkers, pedlars, jarkmen, and patricos. Any itinerant worker could be caught by Elizabethan vagrancy laws, which were now criminalizing even such time-honored figures of oral tradition as wandering minstrels and ballad singers. Harman is confused by the tradesmen—being gainfully employed, they cannot so easily be accused of idleness; but they *are* itinerant, and mobility itself was frightening. He decides that tinkers *are* idle, mostly drunkards, and deceitful—they make extra holes in pots so that they will need more mending. Jarkmen are not idle, but they *are* criminal: these literate vagrants do a thriving business in forged begging licenses. Patricos, wandering priests specializing in marriage ceremonies, are idle since underemployed: as Harman says, few of the randy vagrants are actually married. Pedlars, he admits, "be not all evil, but of an indifferent behaviour" (93). His unease about them hints that pedlars were an uncomfortable parody of merchants in this era of commercial mobility and that society assuaged its unease about merchant mobility by demonizing lower-class merchants such as pedlars.

Next come six categories of women: the demander for glimmer who pretends her house has burned down (the vagrancy statute of 1597 legislated against those who beg by "pretending losses by fire" [sig. B6^v]), the bawdy-basket, autem-mort, walking mort, doxy, and dell. Finally, there are two categories of children: the kinchin mort and kinchin co, a little girl and a little boy. All is very neat and tidy, except that in the appended lists of vagrants' names, which Harman sorts by category, the categories interpenetrate considerably: on the list of upright-men are two itinerant tradesmen, a well-driller and a faucet-maker; some listed as upright-men, the stoutest of the criminal types, have disabilities—a lame hand, a shaking head. On the list of rogues appear two counterfeit epileptics, an itinerant tradesman (plasterer), and two with disabilities (stammerers). And Harman suddenly collapses his twenty-four categories into three—upright-men, rogues, and palliards—claiming retroactively that two of these are umbrella categories including all the others: "Although I set and place here but three orders, yet, good reader, understand that all the others abovenamed are derived and come out from the upright-men and rogues" (110). Vagrants also shift easily from one category to another: when Nicholas Jennings is exposed as a counterfeit epileptic, he sets up as a freshwater mariner, claiming to have been shipwrecked. If assigning vagrants to categories was Harman's way of trying to fix them, to arrest their alarming mobility (just as Elizabethan statutes sought to arrest the mobility of real vagrants), his own text keeps deconstructing the categories.[22]

Did Harman and his contemporaries see that this text keeps pulling itself apart? I doubt it. Comic tone seemed appropriate to this subject matter in Harman's day, as it does not (or may not) today. And the mania for categorization into minute subheadings was such an ingrained rhetorical habit of the period that the oddities and internal contradictions of Harman's system would scarcely have been noticed—not to mention that the rogue catalog was an accepted convention. But I think that although the fracture lines within Christianity, on the subject of charity and the treatment of the poor, were not very visible this early in the Reformation, *A Caveat*'s internal contradictions signal irreducible conflicts in a society that promulgated both Christian and anti-Christian doctrines about the poor. The opening operates like repentance literature: Harman casts his former generosity to wandering beggars as profligacy, an indiscriminate outpouring of money. His frequent theme of vagrants' impenitence ("Repentance is never thought upon until they climb three trees with a ladder" [69]) forms a neat contrast with his own repentance for the sin of overgenerosity. Works on almsgiving—such as John Downame's *Plea of the Poor; or, A Treatise of Beneficence and Alms-Deeds*— typically devoted significant space to urging a golden mean between niggardliness and profligacy in giving. Later vagrancy texts would also use the repentance trope—Greene rationalizes his intimate knowledge of beggars' tricks by claiming to have lived in the criminal underworld; now, repenting, he has chosen to publish all. But Harman's "repentance" is oddly topsy-turvy: repenting of unconditional generosity is quite out of step with the values of the grandfather of all repentance stories, that of the Prodigal Son. Reducing himself to poverty through high living, the prodigal son was clearly a member of the undeserving poor; yet the story's Christian moral emphasizes the father's unconditional forgiveness of the penitent. Love is love, however abused, and misery is misery, however deserved. Love with no strings attached is the essence of biblical Christianity, and distinguishing between the deserving and undeserving poor might well be considered—if not unchristian—then at least alien to the spirit of foundational Christianity. *A Caveat,* a very secular text, seldom glances at Christianity; indeed, in a professedly Christian age it did not do to put Christian notions into too close a relation with developing social policies toward vagrancy. One committed Christian reader, C. S. Lewis, later pronounced Harman "a hard, inquisitive man. . . . For the misery behind the roguery he shows no more pity than a stone; though he claims (as such men always do) to have reached his present state of mind after having often given and been often deceived" (296). Harman's change of heart, his new toughness with the vagrant poor, seems confused because the behavior he repents of was Christian behavior. But his topsy-turvy repentance reproduces an upside-down world, which over several centuries had replaced Christian advocacy of unconditional charity with charity as a calculated transaction: Harman no longer gives the poor free meals—he trades meals for information. Or the meals are a kind of investment, which eventually pays off in sales of *A Caveat,* almsgiving yielding to entrepreneurship.

Death by Lack of Cherishing

A Caveat deconstructs itself by its humor, which undermines seriousness; its prurience, which subverts morality; its fixed categories, which disintegrate; and by Harman's replication of the vices that he condemns. But the most important deconstruction is that Harman's own hard-nosed mercilessness keeps unraveling, as the text is fractured by eruptions of what looks like pity. Harman is quite a good storyteller, rejoicing in his anecdotes, and Arthur Kinney has observed that one cause of the text's tonal disjunctions is that Harman gets caught up in the funniness of his comic stories: "he loses himself," Kinney says, "in the telling of them" (106). I think Harman gets caught up, too, in the sadness of his sad stories; and it is here that Christian compassion threatens, if only momentarily, to burst the dike of his ruthless, antivagrant social conservatism. Although, as I will argue in chapter 2, one cannot attribute all changes in attitudes toward begging to the Reformation, one might cautiously conjecture that Harman, whose exact dates are not known but who had inherited his father's estates by 1547, might well have been born a Catholic and have experienced the Reformation of the 1520s and 1530s as a child or young man, which may shed light on his split consciousness on the question of how much sympathy to feel for beggars.

Near the end of *A Caveat* there occurs a wrenching story, which (with due allowance for the problem of how far one can rely on any account Harman proffers) may lend support to Annabel Patterson's belief that the voices of oppressed common people *can* come through to modern readers from the dark recesses of the sixteenth century, "by way of ventriloquism, in the texts of the dominant culture, . . . in the trope of reported speech" (*Shakespeare and the Popular Voice* 41).[23] By giving her a meal and promising her money, Harman wangles a conversation with a "doxy" who has been on the road for eighteen years. Whether he ever met such a woman or spun her out of his imagination with the aid of popular stereotype and the stories he heard while on the bench as a commissioner of the peace,[24] the woman's story sheds light on the culturally generated tensions that caused such figures to be imagined. As Lena Orlin has pointed out to me in a personal communication, Harman's betrayal of the vagrants' confidence is disturbing whether or not it is true or fabricated, "simply because Harman does not scruple to portray himself as a man who has betrayed vagrants; this suggests that vagrants have no honor worth honoring."

To his credit, Harman does emphasize long-term homelessness as his predecessors do not. Awdeley's only mention of this, for example, comes in reference to the wild rogue who "hath no abiding place" (5). But other aspects
of his talk with this woman are less appealing. "Before I would grope her
mind," he smirks, "I made her both to eat and drink well" (106). His diction
suggests prurient interest in the details of her sex life ("grope her mind") and
a personality habituated to control and command ("I made her").

Before I recount this conversation, or rather interrogation, it might do well
to consider what—if the story had any contact with reality at all—might have
been its physical setting. Though Harman "made her both to eat and drink
well," she surely would not have been invited into the dining area or great
hall of his manor house; a person like her would be lucky to get as far as the
kitchen, and she might have been fed in the yard. Harman would not have
broken bread with a vagrant woman; one pictures him standing over her, his
country gentleman's good clothes a vivid contrast to her rags, waiting for her
to finish while she bolts down the given food hungrily, uneasily. He speaks
in the cultivated, assured accents of a justice of the peace and proprietor of
three manor houses; her rough accent announces her humble station. Lynda Mugglestone shows how the fifteenth and sixteenth centuries witnessed
a transition, "especially marked after the emergence of printing in the 1470s"
(9), wherein the language of London's educated classes emerged as standard
English, set against the speech of non-Londoners (now decried as rustic) and
against members of the lower classes—plowmen, servants, and porters (9–
14). Though a full-blown semiotics of accent and class was not firmly fixed
in England until a later period, vocabulary and accent as class markers are
already clearly visible in rhetoric manuals such as Richard Sherry's *Treatise
on Schemes and Tropes* (1550), which showed how mastery of language placed
an educated speaker "above the common manner of speaking of the people"
(37), or George Puttenham's *Art of English Poesie* (1589), which set the standard English of the educated against "the speech of a craftsman or carter"
(144). Harman's diction would have differed noticeably from the beggar
woman's, further eroding any sense of neighborly hospitality.

Harman does not note how demeaning it must be for a woman forced by
hunger to be subjected to an interrogation about her sex life. Writing about
"welfare" neighborhoods in the modern United States and Great Britain, the
sociologist David Matza notes that social workers are always in and out of
the houses of the poor: "Their habits are seen as a suitable topic for inquiry,
their paths as warranting redirection, and their lives as requiring intervention" (654). "Welfare functionaries," he notes, "possess a license to scrutinize"
(655). Matza also discusses "the stigmatizing consequences of such scrutiny.
[Welfare] recipients are obliged, as a condition of assistance, to partly for-

feit their privacy and partly surrender key symbols of maturity" (655–56), such as control of their money. These modern practices continue the institutionalized surveillance that churchwardens and overseers of the poor had practiced in Harman's day. Even so, Harman's censorious preachiness would not necessarily have sat well with some Christians of his own time: the Puritan John Downame, for example, disapproved of the way some rich people "browbeat the poor with proud, sour, and severe looks" while others "turn away their eyes and faces from them, as though they were such an eyesore as might not be endured" (29); he advocated "kind and loving language" to the poor, "contrary whereunto is the practice of those who join with their alms proud expostulations, harsh words, and upbraiding speeches" (31), a fair description of Harman's stance.

If being constantly under the baleful eye of the authorities is stigmatizing and demoralizing now, it could be downright terrifying in the sixteenth century, when many believed in the evil eye, thinking that a gaze directed in anger or violent disapproval had power to harm its object. The administrative manual *An Ease for Overseers of the Poor* (1601) providing detailed instructions to men of substance on administering parish poor relief, hints at the residually magical way in which such "overseers" were regarded; the text connects "overseer" with "seer," which is "a special title of inspiration. . . . By divine inspiration [an ancient seer] had foresight and prescience of future things; hereof the prophets were afterward called seers" (7). The overseer's surveillance is a surrogate for the all-seeing eye of God, who is "called *Pantoculus,*" the manual avers, "because he seeth all things" (13). The overseer is also "an eye to the magistrate" (12). Harman, however, preferred to act as his own "eye"; and one can well imagine the discomfort of a ragged, hungry vagrant woman as this grand personage fixed his eye on her. Harman's opening question clearly uses the verb "know" in the biblical sense of carnal knowledge. Here is the conversation:

> "Tell me," quoth I, "how many upright-men and rogues dost thou know, or hast thou known and been conversant with, and what their names be?"
>
> She paused awhile, and said, "Why do you ask me, or wherefore?"
>
> "For nothing else," as I said, "but that I would know them when they came to my gate."
>
> "Now, by my troth," quoth she, "then are ye never the near, for all mine acquaintance for the most part are dead."
>
> "Dead!" quoth I, "how died they? For want of cherishing, or of painful diseases?"
>
> Then she sighed, and said they were hanged.
>
> "What, all?" quoth I, "And so many walk abroad, as I daily see! . . . When were they hanged?" quoth I.

"Some seven years agone, some three years, and some within this fort-
night.". . .

"Why," quoth I, "did not this sorrowful and fearful sight much grieve thee,
and for thy time long and evil spent?"

"I was sorry," quoth she, "by the mass. For some of them were good loving
men. For I lacked not when they had it, and they wanted not when I had it, and
divers of them I never did forsake, until the gallows departed us."

"O merciful God!" quoth I, and began to bless me.

"Why bless ye?" quoth she. "Alas! good gentleman, every one must have a
living."

Other matters I talked of. But this now may suffice to show the reader, as it
were in a glass, the bold beastly life of these doxies. (106–7)

In Harman's question "'how died they? For want of cherishing, or of painful diseases?'" the "diseases" are unsurprising: Harman maintains throughout the text that most vagrant men die young, of the pox or of hanging. What
is surprising is that he does not suspect hanging, and it is even more surprising that he comes out instead with the poignant "want of cherishing." "Cherish" meant "to treat with tenderness and affection, to make much of; to take
affectionate care of" (*OED*), having overtones of parental care. Biblical uses
of "cherish" carried connotations of a loving sexual relationship.[25] Surpris-
ingly humane in his diction, Harman suggests that from a lack of parental
or wifely care and nourishing, these homeless men died. "Cherishing" casts
them as the world's orphans, the world's unloved widowers, and suggests that
falling through a crack out of the range of human affection can prove fatal.
Readers are jerked out of this compassionate mood, however, by the grim
tidings that these men have not died from want of cherishing but have been
hanged. Harman's flippant little joke seems brutal: "'What, all? . . . And so
many walk abroad, as I daily see!'" So legion are her lovers, he implies, that
if all were hanged, the vagrant population would be noticeably depleted if
not annihilated—rather a rude thing to say to a woman. Then arises the issue of grieving: "'did not this sorrowful and fearful sight much grieve thee,
and for thy time long and evil spent?'" She agrees that she is grieving but
refuses to accept his definition of grief as penitence induced by the spectacle
of death. She mourns, she insists, not out of guilt but out of love and compassion: she cared about the men. "'I was sorry,' quoth she, 'for some of them
were good loving men. For I lacked not when they had it, and they wanted
not when I had it, and divers of them I never did forsake, until the gallows
departed us.'" Here is love at its most basic, forged on the road, in stolen
moments, between people who are society's dregs, expressing itself in the
sharing of a little food when one or the other of the couple has it. In seem-

ing defiance of Harman's views, she deliberately casts these relationships in the language of the Anglican marriage service: "'them I never did forsake, until the gallows departed us'" echoes the service of holy matrimony: "for better for worse, for richer for poorer, in sickness and in health, till death us depart" ("depart," meaning "separate," was used in the Anglican service until 1662).[26] In taking a man "for worse," "for poorer," "in sickness," and "till death," the homeless woman, one feels, would know whereof she spoke. Her tender regard for the "good loving men" paints a very different picture from the brutal scene in the barn cited earlier in the chapter, which Harman finds typical of the sex lives of women vagrants. But her desperate assertion that "'every one must have a living,'" a cri de coeur on behalf of the vagrant poor, opens no doors to social consciousness for Harman: abruptly recoiling from his own sympathetic portrait, he brusquely damns all "doxies" for their "'bold beastly life.'"

As Patterson suggests, when a dominant text ventriloquizes the voices of the poor, unexpected echoes may reverberate: "the ventriloquist must himself utter, in order to refute them, ethical and pathetic claims whose force may linger beyond his powers of persuasion" (*Shakespeare and the Popular Voice* 42). In Harman's story, it is the voice of the homeless woman, rather than the censorious pronouncement of the moralist, that remains to haunt the modern reader's ears. One is left feeling that whatever else her homeless companions died of, it was not at least from *her* want of cherishing.

Notes

1. John Philip Timpane Jr. discusses rogue literature's debt to jest books, and also to early Tudor plays such as *Youth* and *Hick Scorner,* in his Ph.D. dissertation "The Romance of the Rogue: The History of a Character in English Literature, 1497–1632" (see especially chap. 4).

2. And do I question how seriously one should take Harman because I adhere to a contrary ideological position? It is possible, certainly. Readers who doubt the disinterestedness of my analysis should read Harman, court archives, and jest books and decide for themselves what category Harman belongs in and whether his stories should be used in support of historical conclusions.

3. The first edition is not extant; in the 1566–67 edition (STC 12787), which Harman calls the second impression, he says that the first edition was partly printed by November 1, 1566. There is an entry in the Stationers' Register on January 8, 1567. The dedication to Bess of Hardwick postdates the first edition, since she did not become Countess of Shrewsbury until 1567. A third edition came out in 1567 (1568 by the modern calendar [STC 12787.5]), then two pirated editions (not extant), a fourth edition in 1573 (STC 12788), and a fifth in 1592 (STC 12789), thus totaling seven editions, six of them within seven years of the first edition. Except where otherwise stated, I use the version reprinted in the sec-

ond edition of A. V. Judges's *Elizabethan Underworld.* The 1592 edition, retitled *Ground-work of Cony-Catching* (STC 12789), was published anonymously with its title page approximating one of Greene's cony-catching pamphlets, which were much in vogue at that time. See Ruth Samson Lubarsky, "Telling a Book by Its Cover; or, How Harman Masquerades as Greene." For a discussion of early editions, see Carroll, *Fat King* (70).

4. Allan G. Chester doubts Furnivall's attribution of this piece to its printer, Awdeley, and doubts the existence of a 1561 edition, the evidence for which is a reference in the Stationers' Register to a "ballett called the Descriptions of Vakabondes," which Chester thinks was actually a ballad, now lost; Awdeley printed many broadside ballads in 1561. Awdeley signed a number of pieces that he did write, while *The Fraternity of Vagabonds* was published anonymously. Harman mentions a previous work on vagabonds a couple of times, and Chester does not doubt that this was *The Fraternity of Vagabonds.* Since in his dedicatory epistle Harman reports seeing "a small brief" about vagrancy, presumably *The Fraternity of Vagabonds,* "a few years since," the publication date of Awdeley's work cannot be very much later than 1561, for Harman published his work in 1566. Since Chester's essay was published, another publication has come to light: the second section of *The Fraternity of Vagabonds* in the 1565 edition, *The Twenty-three Orders of Knaves,* was published separately about 1561; the single extant copy, in the Pierpont Morgan Library, is bound with Harman's *Caveat.* Though the emphasis in *The Twenty-three Orders of Knaves* is on idle servants, the work mentions vagabonds, though it does not use "rogue," and it was possibly this work that Harman had in mind when he spoke of a "small brief" on vagabonds; if so, it was Harman rather than Awdeley who introduced the word "rogue" into English. (Idle servants were conceptually linked with vagabonds: in contemporary belief, the one regularly became the other.) Since only the title page of the 1565 edition of *The Fraternity of Vagabonds* is extant, modern scholars really have no evidence of the word "rogue" having been in print anywhere before *A Caveat.* But even if *The Fraternity of Vagabonds* is antecedent to *A Caveat*—and even if it did introduce the important word "rogue"—*The Fraternity of Vagabonds* is a slim, insubstantial work, lacking the development and memorable anecdotes that made *A Caveat* influential. *The Fraternity of Vagabonds* describes vagabond types in brief cameos only a few lines long; it was possibly under the influence of Harman's developed anecdotes that the 1575 edition of *The Fraternity of Vagabonds* added a section of three such anecdotes on "cozeners and shifters" (6–11).

5. Harman himself takes an interest in the Poor Laws and their terminology: defending the neologism "cursetors" (but not—presumably because it is no Latin coinage but mere thieves' cant—the neologism "rogue," which was to prove infinitely more influential), Harman declares in his epistle to the reader that he intends to make his work accessible to modern readers by using modern terms for vagabonds. The term "vagabond" itself is reasonably new, as Harman has determined by perusing Poor Laws in old statute books. He writes that laws made in the time of Henry III or Edward I used now-archaic terms such as "faitours," "roberdsmen," "draw-latches," and "valiant beggars" (60). He notes that the word "ruffler" appears in "a statute made for the punishment of vagabonds" during Henry VIII's reign (67). The dedication to Bess of Hardwick positions his work as a kind of imaginative extension of the Poor Laws, which he describes accurately in their double-edged function: to promote "the relief, succour, comfort, and sustentation of the

poor needy impotent and miserable creatures" and to provide "most wholesome statutes, ordinances and necessary laws . . . for the extreme punishment of all vagrants and sturdy vagabonds" (61).

6. The *OED* describes "rogue" as thieves' cant of unknown origin. It entertains but finally rejects the possibility of a connection with the French adjective "rogue," meaning "arrogant"; but given the gradual shift in spelling, from "roge" (and occasionally "roag") to "rogue," there was possibly some orthographic interference from the French "rogue," which suggests an identification in people's minds between vagrancy and arrogance. Many vagrants such as "upright-men" and "courtesy men" *were* considered arrogant and bullying, rather than humble and down-and-out. The notion that vagrants were not really helpless at all, but actually presumptuous, was basic to rogue literature. The *OED* also suggests a relation to the noun "roger," another piece of thieves' cant, meaning a beggar who pretended to be a poor scholar from Oxford or Cambridge; the word is used twice in Robert Copland's *Highway to the Spital-house*, which suggests a link between Harman's and Awdeley's work and the earlier Tudor discourse of vagrancy. *The Highway to the Spital-house* incorporates a short passage of thieves' cant that Thomas Dekker later reproduced in his cony-catching piece *Lantern and Candlelight* (Copland, *Highway* 24).

7. An alternate explanation, mentioned earlier, was that "it may have been alarm at the number of vagrants swept up after the 1569 rebellion that prompted the enactment of the Vagrancy and Poor Relief Act of 1572" (Manning 165). But one might also suspect that the publicity generated by Awdeley's and Harman's antivagrant literature of the mid-1560s contributed to the decision to single out vagrants after a rebellion in which there is no evidence that vagrants played a role.

8. As Eamon Duffy shows, funeral doles had long been one way through which the poor were supported: "alms were given as a matter of course at every funeral" on the assumption that the poor would pray for the soul of the deceased (362). Harman thinks of an occasion when some 140 beggars congregated at a rich man's funeral to receive a dole of tuppence and food (64). However, the trend to include only local poor and deserving poor eroded such doles; some wealthy testators of late medieval London wanted to "exclude beggars and 'runners about town' from their doles. By the beginning of the sixteenth century a growing number of testators sought to ensure that a closer control was exercised over their funeral doles; . . . a common restriction was to 'poor men of my parish'" (Duffy 363).

9. As noted in this study's introduction, Harvey also borrowed from Spenser a batch of three jest books and a rogue novel (*Howlglas, Scoggin's Jests, Skelton's Jests,* and *Lazarillo de Tormes*), suggesting that these book-lending friends considered jest books and rogue literature to be similar sorts of reading—Harvey calls them "foolish books" in a marginal note (Furnivall xlviii).

10. Chaucer too weds the craft-list to the tale collection, though in a different way from Harman: he first makes his descriptive list in the General Prologue and then begins his tale collection. Where Chaucer makes the listed characters *tellers* of tales, Harman makes his the *subjects* of tales.

11. Though it may seem churlish to reject the views of one who consistently praises my work, praise based on near-total misunderstanding is an ambiguous asset; nor am I happy with Vickers's (mis)use of my work against my fellow feminists.

12. For theorists of jest and joking, and essay collections on jest, see Freud, Bergson, Corrigan, Enck et al., Feibleman, Lauter, Wyndham Lewis, Farnham, Ornstein, Carl Hill, Oring, Attardo and Chabanne, Berger, Greenhill et al., Palmenfelt, Carnes, Pratt, and Christie Davies.

13. Pamela Brown discusses the role of women in rogue literature as mockers of "caught conies": by serving as "performers and interpreters of events and texts," women, whose laughter "could be scathing and was greatly feared," sometimes enforced repressive community standards through the laughing mockery of skimmington rides; but they could also turn their laughter against the gouging wealthy in times of economic scarcity, as in the two "female rogue" pieces Brown discusses (203–4).

14. Patricia Fumerton, adapting Jean-Christophe Agnew's ideas on theatricality and the market, views the period's connecting of vagrants with actors in terms of the "serial selves" taken up out of necessity by vagrants as they switched jobs and also as they altered their identities through aliases to avoid prosecution.

15. It is not just any printer but the printer of *A Caveat* itself whom Harman enlists in his campaign to expose the phony epileptic: the printer seems a surrogate for the text itself, as Harman envisions an active role for *A Caveat* in exposing and arresting the pseudo-disabled. In his chapter on fraters, Harman warns that these often possess phony licenses to collect money on behalf of hospitals, but he assures readers that a license "in print" possesses "authority": "For the printers will see and well understand, before it come in press, that the same is lawful" (81). Thus Harman positions printers as agents of law and order, even agents of the Crown, in combating criminal vagrancy. Stephen Greenblatt notes that "in much of the cony-catching literature of the period in England and France, printing is represented in the text itself as a force for social order and the detection of criminal fraud" (*Shakespearean Negotiations* 50–51). It may be no accident that other printers besides Harman's were involved in bringing to light vagrants' supposed deceits: John Awdeley printed and may have authored *The Fraternity of Vagabonds;* Robert Copland wrote and printed *The Highway to the Spital-house.* Considering the three attempted piracies (one successful) of *A Caveat* and the shameless repetitiveness with which the presses poured out cony-catching pieces, it looks as if a major impetus driving rogue literature was the wish to capitalize on the new commercial possibilities of print. Thomas Dekker even describes a cony-catching scam whereby itinerant printers solicit patronage on the basis of dedication pages hastily printed up and attached to old, discarded books: they "travel up and down most shires in England, and live by this hawking" (*Lantern and Candlelight* 238).

16. Greenblatt explains the betrayal as a rhetorical strategy to heighten the sense of verisimilitude: "Harman is concerned to convey at least the impression of accurate observation and recording—clearly, this was among the book's selling points—and one of the principal rhetorical devices he uses to do so is the spice of betrayal: he repeatedly calls attention to his solemn promises never to reveal anything he has been told, for his breaking of his word assures the accuracy and importance of what he reveals" (50). He also notes that "the danger of such accounts is that the ethical charge will reverse itself, with the forces of order . . . revealed as themselves dependent on dissembling and betrayal and the vagabonds revealed either as less fortunate and well-protected imitators of their betters or, alternatively, as primitive rebels against the hypocrisy of a cruel society" (*Shakespearean Negotiations* 51).

17. It is interesting that it is pewter, too: "Among a large sample of 441 inventories, taken between 1532 and 1601, including many estates of £5 or less, 95 per cent included pewter. It is a striking case of a former luxury which had spread right down the social scale" (Palliser 115). Hence the pewter is an obvious emblem of the erosion of social distinction, an emblem of the social instability and mobility that, I am arguing, fueled anxieties leading to the demonization of the geographically mobile. Harman's outrage at Jennings's pewter is a cry from a threatened class.

18. Some generic trappings of rogue literature appear even in modern social science writings about urban street crime. For example, Mark S. Fleisher's *Beggars and Thieves: Lives of Urban Street Criminals,* like sixteenth-century rogue pamphlets, brims with anecdotes and brief biographies of criminals, concludes with a glossary of thieves' slang, identifies criminal specializations by nicknames resembling thieves' cant ("a skeezer is a woman who trades sex and companionship for drugs" [63]), deduces a criminal past by decoding tattoos (just as sixteenth-century authorities read a history of crime in vagrants' brand marks), bases its knowledge of street crime on personal interviews which yield information concerning secret slang and criminal practices. Indeed, Fleisher's "eventually, after years on the street, I understood hustlers' words and wanderings" (7) sounds disarmingly like Robert Greene's self-descriptions, and its "w" alliteration harks back to Harman. Like Greene, Fleisher assures readers (in the section "Fieldwork and Ethics," 69–77) that he is *in* the criminal world without being *of* it.

19. I discuss the residue of magical thinking in early modern English culture in *The Scythe of Saturn: Shakespeare and Magical Thinking.* See also Brian Vickers's *Occult and Scientific Mentalities in the Renaissance.* My thinking about William Gilbert's two-edged rhetoric has been sparked by a chapter on Gilbert in Richard Cunningham's Ph.D. dissertation "The Attraction of the Truth: Navigating Experience in Early Modern Literature."

20. One curious feature of the text that might support the idea of a speaker set up to be undercut by the author is the fact that "the harmans" and "harman-beck," which look like plays with the author's name, make their first appearance in English in Harman's appended list of thieves' cant, where they are said to mean "the stocks" and "the constable," respectively (115). If the author had chosen "Harman" as a pseudonym, knowing it meant "the stocks," one might very well suspect that the speaker was himself the target of some satire. However, Thomas Harman was a historical figure, and what is known of his material circumstances and career seems to jibe with the autobiographical facts the speaker drops into *A Caveat* (66–68, 70, 72, 74, 79, 80, 89, 93). Unfortunately, no other published works by Harman survive for comparison. It is also possible that Thomas Harman invented the alleged thieves' cant "the harmans" and "harman-beck," playing on his own name.

21. This is one of several details that show Harman's information to be deeply unreliable as social history: historians have shown that women were greatly in the minority among early modern English vagrants (see the introduction).

22. Modern social scientists are still trying to create an orderly world out of disorganized batches of homeless criminals. For example, as Fleisher notes, they have created "the concept of crime career, the notion that criminals' offenses become more serious with time" (11). Fleisher objects that this "reification of street deviance as a career shields outsiders from seeing the disorder, dysfunction, and irrationality of deviant behavior. The

concept of career projects a sense of order, planning, and design, which applies to physicians, businessmen, professors. But in the daily lives of hustlers, order and planning and design are absent" (11). To posit the crime career is to try "to understand behavior in one culture (unlawful society) with a concept appropriate in a distinctly different culture (lawful society)" (11). Similarly, sixteenth-century rogue literature tried to perceive order in a riot of vagrant disorder by imposing on it a neat scheme of specialist categories, probably modeled on the legitimate world of trade specializations.

23. Greenblatt, who calls such ventriloquism "recording," is less sanguine than Patterson about "the recording of alien voices—the voices of those who have no power to leave literate traces of their existence" (*Shakespearean Negotiations* 48)—because "the subversive voices are produced by and within affirmations of order; they are powerfully registered, but they do not undermine that order" (52). The extent to which subversive forces are contained by the establishment is of course a major point of debate in recent historicist studies.

24. As Palliser shows, "Minor offences could be despatched by a justice sitting alone in his own house" (305), which disturbingly unsettles the boundary between law court and site of domestic hospitality.

25. Harman uses the same expression at another point where pity erupts, his proto-Dickensian description of corrupt poorhouse officials who starve the poor and eat well themselves: "the impotent and miserable creatures committed to their charge . . . die for want of cherishing" (81).

26. Harman also alludes to these words from the marriage service in speaking of patricos, who "make marriages till death did depart" (94). Awdeley alludes to the same words, also in the context of patricos, and is more cynical about the matter than Harman: "A Patriarke Co doth make marriages, and that is, until death depart the married folk, which is after this sort: when they come to a dead horse or any dead cattle, then they shake hands and so depart every one of them a several way" (6).

2.   Joke Books and the English Reformation

I shall for the time being become a court jester.
—Martin Luther

To say that something was a joke is not to say that it was not serious.
—Patrick Collinson

IN TRACKING, over the next four chapters, the formation of the discourse of vagrancy in the 1520s and 1530s, a period when beggary and vagrancy were identified as major social problems and important social policies were formulated to deal with them, I have allotted religious writers, humanists, and apologists for the monarchy separate chapters purely for convenience. In fact, there was much overlap, and a figure like Erasmus can no more easily be categorized "humanist" or "theologian" than Harman can neatly distinguish among upright-men and wild rogues. Sir Thomas More is a central figure in the Reformation (the subject of this chapter), the new humanism (chapter 3), and Henry VIII's consolidation of power (chapter 4). As an opponent of the Reformation, he challenged rhetoric that cast the Catholic clergy as sturdy beggars; as a humanist, he created a central text on beggary, *Utopia;* as Henry VIII's Lord Chancellor, he fostered a monarchy justified by a discourse of home and family. More wrote a jest book and drew on collections of jest for his theological writing; and the jest book about a vagrant woman that will be explored in chapter 5, Walter Smith's *Twelve Merry Jests of the Widow Edith,* is closely linked with More in its setting, authorship, and printing.

Mindful of the dangers of separating out Reformation phenomena from others, I will suggest in this present chapter the multiple ways in which the Reformation and the emergence of beggary/vagrancy as a prominent public policy issue existed in a symbiotic relationship.

A Supplication for the Beggars: A Literary Trope Makes History

The English Reformation got under way with a resounding shot across the bows: an incendiary tract by Simon Fish, *A Supplication for the Beggars,* applied the terms "beggars and vagabonds," "sturdy," and "idle" to the Roman Catholic clergy. Anyone skeptical about my claim that the discourse of vagrancy was integral to the Protestant project in England should read this essay.

From late medieval times, lay beggary had sometimes been associated in the popular imagination with clerical mendicancy, and as the Reformation caught fire, theologians began equating the two. Luther often conflates secular beggars with mendicant brothers and preaches against both; in Germany, *Der Betler-orden* (The Mendicant brotherhood) was applied to both (D. B. Thomas 13). Thus the Reformers' passion against institutional Catholicism rubbed off on secular beggars. Just as Queen Elizabeth I would appropriate the cult of the Virgin Mary, so (by their common link with mendicancy) vagrants absorbed official resentment of monastic orders and of Catholicism itself. Religion and rogue literature reinforced each other when writers such as Thomas Harman and John Awdeley posited the existence of *fraternal* orders of beggars. Out of this general milieu of demonized begging emerged a very specific document, *A Supplication for the Beggars,* which trained the language of the discourse of vagrancy on the Catholic Church.

This crucial text conflating sturdy beggary with Catholicism appeared in 1529, when England was a dry tinder box. A powerful Lutheran faction was attached to Anne Boleyn; Henry VIII was craving (and the Pope blocking) a divorce, to marry Anne; the king needed funds and was casting an eye on Church lands; public anticlericalism was fueled by Cardinal Wolsey's unpopularity; civil lawyers resented the power of ecclesiastical courts. According to John Foxe, the match that ignited the tinder was *A Supplication for the Beggars,* which was written by a Lutheran sympathizer, Simon Fish. Anne Boleyn presented it to the King. Given wide currency by being reprinted in Foxe's *Book of Martyrs,* this essay, which touched off the English Reformation, takes as its central motif the issue of beggary.

In Fish's scheme, the deserving poor are "wretched hideous monsters (on whom scarcely for horror any dare look), the foul, unhappy sort of lepers, and other sore people, needy, impotent, blind, lame, and sick, that live only by alms," so numerous that "all the alms of all the welldisposed people of this your realm is not half enough for to sustain them, but . . . they die for hunger" (1). But the undeserving are *not* the usual sturdy, able-bodied beggars feigning disability—they are the Catholic clergy, whose parasitism on society casts them as "beggars" taking bread from the deserving. Over the years, Fish writes to the king, there have "craftily crept into this your realm another sort (not of impotent, but) of strong, puissant, and counterfeit holy, and idle, beggars and vagabonds," namely "the bishops, abbots, priors, deacons, archdeacons, . . . priests, monks, canons, friars, pardoners, and summoners" (1), who have "gotten into their hands" more than a third of the kingdom (2). This "greedy sort of sturdy, idle, holy thieves" (4) extort money under the threat of heresy charges. Fish's specialized categories of clergy resemble specialized classes of rogues in Awdeley or Harman. In later "supplications" modeled on Fish's the resemblance is even stronger: in the anonymous *Supplication to Our most Sovereign Lord, King Henry VIII* (1544), England brims with "chantry priests, soul priests, canons, residentaries in cathedral churches, prebendaries, monk pension[er]s, morrow mass priests, unlearned curates, priests of guilds and of fraternities, or brotherhoods, riding chaplains" (42). The clergy-as-sturdy-beggars trope later aided writers attacking chantries, including the anonymous author of *A Supplication of the Poor Commons*, who alleged that "sturdy beggars" are "not yet weeded out":

> Piteously complaineth the poor commons of this your Majesty's realm, greatly lamenting their own miserable poverty. . . . Not many years tofore, your Highness' poor subjects, the lame, and impotent creatures of this realm, presented your Highness with a pitiful and lamentable complaint, imputing the . . . chief cause of their penury and lack of relief, unto the . . . infinite number of valiant and sturdy beggars which had, by their subtle and crafty demeanour in begging, gotten into their hands more than the third part of the yearly revenues and possessions of this your Highness' realm. (61–63)

Like other Reformers (Luther, Zwingli, Tyndale) Fish assails the notion of Purgatory on economic grounds: the need to pray for souls in Purgatory justifies financial exactions to maintain monastic foundations such as chantries: "to gather these yearly exactions, . . . they say they pray for us to God, to deliver our souls out of the pains of purgatory; without whose prayer, they say, or at least without the pope's pardon, we could never be delivered thence" (11). But, Fish proclaims, "there is no purgatory: . . . it is a thing invented by the covetousness of [churchmen]. . . . If that the pope with his pardons for money may deliver one soul thence; he may deliver him as well without money; if he may deliver one, he may deliver a thousand; if he may deliver a thousand, he may deliver them all, and so destroy purgatory" (11).

As Germain Marc'hadour writes, "the cutting edge of the issue of purgatory was the money which belief in it brought to the priests. [This] . . . became increasingly apparent during the 1520s because of the calamities afflicting Western Europe: droughts, epidemics, . . . wars" (lxxii). The issue of Purgatory linked theological reform with economic crisis, and Fish exploits pity for the deserving poor (in whose voice he speaks) to pillory monastics, whom he casts as the undeserving. The penalty he decrees for monastics is what the law dictated for beggars: "Tie these holy idle thieves to the carts, to be whipped naked about every market town till they will fall to labor, that they, by their importunate begging, take not away the alms that the good christian people would give unto us sore, impotent, miserable people" (14). Thus the Henrician Reformation was conflated with the discourse of vagrancy.

Fish's incendiary essay drew a response ten times its length from no less a worthy than Sir Thomas More, soon to be Lord Chancellor. More's *Supplication of Souls* adopts the persona of souls in Purgatory, recalling the centrality of the Purgatory issue. In a playful moment, More has these souls explain their knowledge of Fish's book: some of their colleagues in Purgatory who had died shortly after Fish's work was published conveyed its purport to fellow sufferers. Admirers of More in his "humanist" phase (1500–1520)—the More of *Utopia* and the friendship with Erasmus—often find appalling his "theological" phase (1520–35), when he prosecuted heretics and poured out anti-Reformation polemics, increasingly harsh and intolerant (see Schuster 1144 and passim). But the anti-Reformation More scores a number of excellent points against Fish's reforming polemic. Fish, he charges, oversimplifies the complex problem of poverty with an easy scapegoating: the poverty of beggars Fish "layeth to the only feet of the clergy" (115). Fish also ignores the church's role as the main poor relief agency. Fearing priestly corruption, Fish wants no hospitals built: "What remedy then for the poor beggars?" (117; see also 137–38). More finds naïve Fish's belief that proceeds from seizure of church property would go to the poor (142), which proved prophetic. David Knowles summarizes the actual result of the Reformation's confiscations: "the transference of property at the Dissolution did not to any significant extent benefit other religious, educational or charitable institutes, or assist impoverished classes; no social injustice was in fact remedied" (459). These vast revenues, Knowles continues, were frittered away: "Even before the end of the reign, the recurring regular revenue from the spoils was less than half the original monastic income, and the capital of land and precious objects had been repeatedly raided for needs that were purely passing, without being used at all to endow the Crown with a permanent revenue, or the country with religious, educational or social assets" (401). Though loyal to the Crown, More astutely foresaw that confiscated church money would not reach the poor. Accurate too was his prediction that turning clergy out of their livings would swell the ranks of beggars (147–48).

Fish, More thinks, has no real interest in the poor; he uses them to pull on the heartstrings while his real motives lie elsewhere. More argues that the "great face of charity" Fish puts on by speaking "in the name of the poor beggars" is "the devil's drift, alway covering his poison under some taste of sugar" (118). He was probably right. Marc'hadour details the high-level power plays surrounding the essay that Fish presents as a simple plea from the poor. The Dukes of Suffolk and Norfolk, the latter being Anne Boleyn's uncle, who urged the confiscation of abbey lands, used Henry's infatuation with Anne to further their cause. In bringing up heavy rhetorical guns against Fish, "More is not answering one pamphlet; he is aiming . . . to stem a widespread movement headed by a now powerful faction with direct and intimate access to the king" (lxviii).

More faults Fish's lack of evidence—on the extent of beggary or of the church's holdings, on the intimate details of friars' lives (124 and passim). Yet More provides no evidence when denying that there are more poor nowadays or that they are starving—he just asserts that though corn is short, people are charitable (118–19). This was rather insensitive in an age of harvest failures; but his skepticism about the seizure of church property proved justified, as appears in another "supplication," *A Supplication of the Poor Commons,* published after the Dissolution, which still called the clergy "sturdy beggars" and beseeched the King:

> Restore to the poor members of Christ their due portion, which they trusted to have received, when they saw your Highness turn out the other sturdy beggars. But alas! they failed of their expectation, and are now in more penury than ever they were. For, although the sturdy beggars got all the devotion of the good charitable people from them, yet had the poor impotent creatures some relief of their scraps, whereas now they have nothing. Then had they hospitals, and almshouses to be lodged in, but now they lie and starve in the streets. Then was their number great, but now much greater. . . . Many thousands of us, which herebefore lived honestly upon our sore labour and travail, bringing up our children in the exercise of honest labour, are now constrained some to beg, some to borrow, and some to rob and steal, to get food. (79–80)

Alleging that cottagers who once leased abbey lands have been charged increased rent by the abbeys' new secular owners, the writer pleads, "Endanger not your soul by the suffering of us, your poor commons, to be brought all to the names of beggars and most miserable wretches" (81).

Charges of Sexual Profligacy and the Comic Literary Tradition

Fish's polemic offers a salient example of a *literary* move having wide-reaching social consequences: by casting the Catholic clergy as despised "sturdy beggars" lacking the respectability of disability, Reformation rhetoric increased public contempt for the vagrant unemployed, now guilty by association with Catholicism. But vagrants also absorbed sexual charges against the clergy, and I will argue that these, too, were *literary* in their origins.

Harman's lurid sketches of vagrants wallowing in promiscuity may well owe something to the link that had been forged between sturdy beggars and the clergy, for the clergy too were accused of lechery—especially reprehensible given their vows of chastity. Luther charged that priests and monks "have disgraced our mothers, wives, daughters, and sisters, and made harlots of them" ("Exposition of Psalm 127" 319). Fish's *Supplication for the Beggars* associates lechery with idleness, recommending manual labor as a cure: "Set these sturdy loobies [i.e., lubbers] abroad in the world, . . . to get their living with their labor in the sweat of their faces" (14),[1] since monks and friars assail "every man's wife, every man's daughter, and every man's maid" (6).

Charges of sexual misconduct had severe consequences for fraternal orders in England, a nation that (nearly alone in Europe) carried the Reformation to the extreme of completely abolishing the monastic system: clerical immorality served as one of the main pretexts for this abolition. In hearings leading to the dissolution of the monasteries, the chief evidence comprised the findings of a royal commission of "visitors" who descended on monasteries; these *comperta* (or discoveries) "achieve their effect by a pitiless enumeration of what seems an unending list of sexual offences, with only an occasional reference to other charges" (Knowles 297). This official "evidence" resembled some venerable comic storytelling—everyone had heard tales of naughty doings in monasteries, sometimes in anticlerical satires. Chaucer's Friar Huberd, "a wantoune and a merye" has made "many a mariage / Of yonge wommen at his owene cost," presumably to dispose of women he has got pregnant (*Canterbury Tales*, general prologue, ll.208, 212–13). Among other hijinks in that finest literary flowering of the sex-crazed monastery, Boccaccio's *Decameron*, a young monk evades punishment for having sex by spying through a peephole the abbot copulating with the same woman (first day, fourth story); a man feigns dumbness and destitution (like one of Harman's "dummerers") to get a job as handyman in a nunnery, where (handy indeed) he copulates his way through the convent, including the abbess (third day, first story). Fabliaux, too, feature wife-seducing heroes who are often priests or university students bound for religious orders. By Tudor times, tales of sexy monasteries must have been known, not least through the oral tradition, to almost everybody.

Satire turns the powerful tool of laughter to serious social criticism, and comic antimonasticism and antifraternalism ran alongside serious theological opposition to mendicancy in the late Middle Ages and early Renaissance.[2] Such satire had the appeal of the antiauthoritarian in an age when the church was the voice of authority; and it was antiauthoritarian in the most delicious way, showing pompous religious personages, prating about the claims of the spirit, as themselves the slaves of undignified bodily appetites.[3] The triumph of the body over a pretentious spirit is always funny, and Boccaccio and Chaucer were loved for their glorious comedy. But in the Reformation, this marvelous comedy was to have serious results.

Among the most influential state comedians in history was one of the "visitors" who reported on the moral state of monasteries. Richard Layton sent back regular dispatches from his lightning tour of a remarkable number of monasteries, addressed to that architect of the Dissolution, Thomas Cromwell. The letters, witty and salacious, and other alleged findings became quarries for the *comperta,* the official evidence against monastic orders. (Another visitor was Thomas Legh. The names Layton and Legh are not, of course, allegorical, but under the circumstances they are easy to remember.) Knowles thinks that Layton's primary aim was to collect "serious matter for the *comperta,* and to keep Cromwell amused by scandal" (283). Independent checks do not corroborate Layton's scandalmongering tales. The extensive documentation of regular visits of bishops to monasteries all over England were rigorous in noting (if not always acting on) sexual incontinence among monastics, but they did not turn up anything like the massive sexual mischief Layton alleged. And if bishops were not disinterested observers, one might expect more objectivity—or even bias in the opposite direction—in reports of the commissioners for the suppression, who surveyed monasteries just before the Dissolution; yet they, too, failed to note sexual misdeeds on anything like the scale Layton reported. Where direct comparisons can be made, it is apparent that Layton distorts and even invents sexual strayings. Knowles notes remarkable discrepancies between the Layton/Legh letters and commissioners' reports:

> At the Cistercian abbey of Garendon, Layton and Legh report five addicted to "sodomy," one of them with ten boys, and note that three seek release from their vows. The commissioners state that all are "of good conversation, and God's service well maintained; all desire to continue in their religion or be assigned

to some other house." . . . At Gracedieu, . . . the visitors charged two nuns with incontinence and of having borne children; the commissioners note that they are "fifteen with the prioress, of good and virtuous conversation and living." . . . At Handale and Yedingham (Yorks) the visitors noted that Alice Brampton and Agnes Butt had each given birth to a child. The commissioners reported all as "of good living," and had occasion to note that the two ladies were aged respectively seventy and forty-nine. (300–301)[4]

Of alleged monastic sexual depravity, Knowles concludes, "The statistics . . . cannot be accepted as reliable evidence of what at first they seem to assert, viz. the universal depravity of more than half the religious houses" (302–3). Christopher Haigh summarizes, "There is very little evidence that the conduct of the clergy was worse than it had been in earlier centuries, and a good deal to suggest that it was much better" (*English Reformations* 9; see also 41–42). If evidence points toward Thomas Harman's having gleaned most of his "knowledge" of vagrants from literary pieces rather than from the firsthand experience he claims, I think the same is true of Layton: what he claims to have observed comes instead, I propose, from the tradition of salacious, jokey stories about sexual high times in the monasteries.

Layton's heavily ironic description of the "holy father prior" of Maiden Bradley seems to echo Chaucer's wry encomium to Friar Huberd, who married off his cast-off women: the prior "hath but six children, and but one daughter married yet of the goods of the monastery, trusting shortly to marry the rest. His sons be tall men waiting upon him, and he thanks God he never meddled with married women, but all with maidens the fairest could be got, and always married them right well. The pope considering his fragility, gave him licence to keep an whore" (Cook 40). Layton shares a smirk with Thomas Cromwell over a powerfully preaching bishop; Layton sniffs out fabliau-like trickery and sneakings about by night, as the bishop has a smith make a key to let in wenches at night "and specially a wife of Uxbridge" (Cook 71). The bishop also seduces a nun by promising that after each copulation she can confess to him and be absolved, and he has a smith remove an iron bar from the abbess's window so that he can "go in to her by night" (Cook 72). Layton's tale of his raid on an abbey full of secret passages for the clandestine conveyance of prostitutes, and of surprising the abbot's mistress, who tries to escape naked through a secret passage (the abbot apparently having decamped, leaving her behind), has the aroma of a high-spirited Boccaccio tale:

On Friday 22nd October I rode back with speed to take an inventory of Folke-stone [Priory]. . . . Immediately descending from my horse, I sent Bartelot your servant, with all my servants to circumcept the abbey, and surely to keep all back doors and starting holes [i.e., private entrances—literally, refuge holes for hunt-

ed animals such as rabbits], etc. I myself went alone to the abbot's lodging joining upon the fields and wood, even like a cony clapper [i.e., a rabbit warren]
full of private ways; a good space knocking at the abbot's door, neither sound
nor sign of life appearing, saving the abbot's little dog, that within his door fast
locked, bayed and barked. I found a short pole-axe standing behind the door,
and with it I dashed the abbot's door in pieces, and set one of my men to keep
that door, and about [the] house I go with the pole-axe in my hand, for the
abbot is a dangerous desperate knave and a hardy. But for a conclusion, his
whore alias his gentlewoman bestirred her stumps towards her starting holes,
and there Bartelot watching the pursuit took the tender damsel, and after I had
examined her, to Dover there to the mayor to set her in some cage or prison
for eight days, and I brought holy father abbot to Canterbury, and there in
Christ Church [Priory] I will leave him in prison. . . . At last I found her apparel in the abbot's coffer. (Cook 56–57)

Tellingly, Layton sees his narrative in literary terms—as comedy with touches
of the tragic: "To tell you all this comedy, but for the abbot a tragedy, it were
too long" (57). His chuckle over the superstitious false relics he finds suggests
that he has been reading Chaucer's Pardoner's Prologue, and presently he
mentions exactly the sort of reading he goes in for—comic anticlerical satire: "Ye shall receive a book of Our Lady's miracles, well able to match the
Canterbury Tales" (38). And the reading tastes of Layton's correspondent,
Thomas Cromwell, also ran to the comic: between 1530 and 1532, he acquired
a copy of *The Jests of Skelton* (Nelson 109). The link with comic literary anticlericalism could not be clearer. Legh, too, conceived of his sexual findings
as comic; at one point he forwarded to Cromwell a love letter from a friar to
a prioress "to make you laugh" (62). What gives away the roots in comic tales
of such "evidence" is the air of high-spirited comedy in this sexual skullduggery and the persistent trickiness: secret passages, sophistical juggling with
promises of absolution, aliases on love letters.

The antimonasticism of jest books and other comic tales did cultural work
similar to that of Reformation polemics. As a staunch opponent of religious
reform, More showed himself aware of the way reformers used comic tradition when, in *A Dialogue Concerning Heresies,* he put into the mouth of his
Lutheran-leaning speaker a series of venerable comic tales about clerical lechery—the one about a poor man who finds a priest in bed with his wife, and
so forth. The reforming Bishop John Bale, trying to root out belief in English
saints, adopted the same heavily ironic tone toward monastic salaciousness
as had Thomas Layton. In his *Acts of English Votaries, Comprehending their
Unchaste Practices and Example By All Ages, From the World's Beginning to this
Present Year* (1548[?]), Bale exhaustively "documents" the sexual depravity

of "the Pope's clergy," nearly all of them being "whoremongers, bawds, . . . Gomorrems," a "sodomitical swarm," "sodomites and devils," since the dawn of time (8). Though denizens of early medieval English monasteries were often canonized and were still popularly venerated in 1546, Bale declares that they have "brent in their lusts, and done abominations without number" (8). His account, dripping with sarcasm, of a bishop who kept a "fair damsel" in a monastery (33) could have come from Layton's letters to Cromwell, *A Hundred Merry Tales,* or a popular book like *Cock Lorel's Boat,* whose narrator meets on the road a merry company of friars with "many white nuns with white vails / That was full wanton of their tails" (sig. Ciii). Out of context, it is hard to tell whether some passages come from the comic literary tradition or a Reformation polemic: their tone is indistinguishable.

And when anticlerical satire and polemic got entwined with the discourse of vagrancy, what happened, paradoxically, was that literary satire once in the service of antiestablishment critique was turned instead against the dispossessed—the vagrant poor, who now shared with the discredited clergy the stereotype of sexual incontinence. Comic anticlericalism was to the Reformation what rogue literature was to the Poor Laws, and the hinge uniting comic anticlericalism with rogue literature was the early Reformation rhetoric equating the Catholic clergy with sturdy beggars.

Liber Vagatorum: Rogue Literature's Gift to the Reformation

In one crucially revealing instance, a patriarch of the Reformation, Martin Luther, drew directly on rogue literature to buttress an antimendicant, antivagrant polemic. A founding document of continental rogue literature, the anonymous *Book of Vagabonds and Beggars* (*Liber Vagatorum*) equated alleged beggar societies with mendicant religious orders: it was subtitled *Der Betler Orden* (The mendicant brotherhood). First printed about 1509, it had run through some thirty editions before Luther wrote a preface for it in 1528.[5] The grandfather of Awdeley's *Fraternity of Vagabonds* and Harman's *Caveat for Common Cursetors*[6] and the great-grandfather of Greene's cony-catching pamphlets, the *Liber Vagatorum* warns against thirty-four specialized beggar categories, labeled with terms from *rotwelsch* (Beggars' Welsh)—thieves' cant. One category, *bregers* ("honest paupers with young children" [76]) are deserving poor; thirty-three are undeserving. The author briefly recognizes the possibility of unwilling beggary through unemployment; *bregers* are also less threatening than others because these family people stay in their villages rather than roaming. They are the shamefaced poor, fallen from former respectability. *Bregers* are "known in the town or village wherein they beg, and . . . would, I doubt not, leave off begging if they could only thrive by their handicraft or other honest means, for there is many a godly man who begs unwillingly, and feels ashamed before those who knew him formerly when he was better off, and before he was compelled to beg. Could he but proceed without he would soon leave begging behind him. *Conclusion:* To these beggars it is proper to give, for such alms are well laid out" (76). The rest of the *Liber Vagatorum* concentrates on fake disability. *Klenckners* "sit at the church-doors, and attend fairs and church gatherings with sore and broken legs; one has no foot, another no shank, a third no hand or arm. . . . The people who give alms to him are cheated—inasmuch as his thigh or his foot has rotted away in prison or in the stocks for wicked deeds. *Item,* one's hands has been chopped off in battle, at cards, or for the sake of a harlot. *Item,* many a one ties a leg up or besmears an arm with salves, or walks on crutches, and all the while as little ails him as other men" (77). *Grantners* practice false epilepsy: "Some fall down before the churches, . . . with a piece of soap in their mouths, whereby the foam rises as big as a fist, and they prick their nostrils with a straw, causing them to bleed, as though they had the falling sickness" (89);[7] one recalls the "counterfeit cranks" of Harman's *Caveat,* who have "a piece of white soap about them, . . . [which they] privily convey . . . into their mouth, . . . [and] foam as it were a boar" (85). Disability in the *Liber Vaga-torum* is highly specialized: *seffers* "besmear themselves all over with salve, . . . looking as though they had been ill a long time, and as if their mouth and face had broken out in sores; but if they go to a bath, . . . these go away again" (119). *Schweigers* "smear themselves with horse dung, thereby appearing as if they had the yellow sickness, or other dreadful disease" (121); *voppers* are phony madwomen (105).

The *Liber Vagatorum*'s tricksters come out of a comic storytelling tradition. One ingeniously counterfeits a ghastly leg by stealing a dead thief's leg and tying up his own; in good jest book fashion, he is exposed and runs off on his good legs (78–79); a similar episode occurs to general merriment in *2 Henry VI* (2.1.66–165). Autolycus's trick of pretending a "rogue" has stolen his clothing in *The Winter's Tale* (4.3), also a scam in the closely contemporary *Puss in Boots,* is a regular practice among *Liber Vagatorum* tricksters called *schwan-felders* or *blickschlahers,* who "when they come to a town, leave their clothes at the hostelry, and sit down against the churches naked, and shiver terri-bly . . . . Some say they have been robbed by wicked men; some that they have lain ill and for this reason were compelled to sell their clothes" (103).

Like later rogue literature the *Liber Vagatorum* has a mixed tone—jokey relishing of trickiness shifts to sober warnings to a vulnerable public. Readers may emphasize the jokiness or the sobriety, as they wish. I read these texts as aiming mainly at entertainment, with a veneer of "warning as a public service" either as a sop to respectability or as part of the joke, since repressive seriousness can make a trickster tale even funnier. (I do not often find Renaissance jests funny—they are often heartless, lean heavily on slapstick, and are sometimes downright incomprehensible—but one can tell what was *meant* to be funny by markers such as "they laughed him to scorn.") I suspect that few sixteenth-century readers took these works seriously as public service announcements. But that is *my* reading of rogue literature.

Martin Luther read quite otherwise. In his preface (1528) to the *Liber Vagatorum,* he reports, "I have thought it a good thing that such a book should not only be printed, but that it should become known everywhere, in order that men may see and understand how mightily the Devil rules in this world; . . . such a book may help mankind to be wise, and on the look out for . . . the Devil" (65). Some Renaissance theorists opposed the idea of a single right way to read a text; but Luther was not one of them. He knew the right way to read this text, and heeding its playful jokiness was not that way:

> The right understanding and true meaning of the book is . . . this, viz. that princes, lords, counsellors of state, and everybody should be prudent, and cautious in dealing with beggars, and learn that, whereas people will not give and help honest paupers and needy neighbours, as ordained by God, *they give, by persuasion of the devil, and contrary to God's judgment, ten times as much to vagabonds and desperate rogues—in like manner as we have hitherto done to monasteries, cloisters, churches, chapels, and mendicant friars,* forsaking all the time the truly poor. For this reason every town and village should know their own paupers, as written down in the Register, and assist them. But as to outlandish and strange beggars they ought not to be borne with, unless they have proper licences and passports; for all the great rogueries mentioned in this book are done by these. If each town would only keep an eye upon their paupers, such knaveries would soon be at an end. I have myself of late years been cheated and befooled by such tramps and liars more than I wish to confess. (65; emphasis added)

Like Harman and Greene after him, Luther is quick to assert that he has not gleaned *all* his knowledge of vagrants from what amount to jest books—he has had personal experience, and it has been bitter. His report of being cheated is intriguing. Are we to imagine that in attempting to nail his Ninety-five Theses to the church door, Luther was brought to a standstill by some *grantners* foaming at the mouth after surreptitiously chewing soap or by shivering *schwanfelders* and *blickschlahers,* who "sit down against the churches naked," and that he was taken in by these tricks? Was the Reformation almost stopped in its tracks by a bar of soap? Be that as it may, here is another instance of religious reform being directly affected by a comic literary tradition.

Other serious texts reveal the *Liber Vagatorum*'s influence. Alexander Barclay's *Ship of Fools* (1509), a 600-page rant on society's evils based on Sebastian Brant's *Narrenschiff* but double its size, judges vagrants harshly: "Few of them I find of good intent" (cxxvi). His section "Of Foolish Beggars and Their Vanities" makes the same points Luther makes in his "Preface" to the *Liber Vagatorum:*

> Alms is ordained by god our creator
> For men that live in need and wretchedness
>
> . . . .
> But yet such caitiffs boldly in dare press
> For their lewd life without all manner dread
> This alms taking from them that have most need. (cxxvii)

Like Luther, Barclay links secular beggars with mendicant friars: beggars feign disability, friars fake miracles. But had Barclay directly observed beggars? His charges suspiciously resemble details in the *Liber Vagatorum.* Some beggars feign lameness and bloody themselves, Barclay charges—a ploy in the *Liber Vagatorum.* Others, he says, mangle their children to gain pity; the *Liber Vagatorum* says some beggars "treat their children badly in order that they may become lame—and . . . would be sorry if they should grow straight-legged—for thereby they are more able to cheat people" (129). Both Barclay and the *Liber Vagatorum* claim that if beggars get good clothes they still wear rags so people will give them clothes (cxxviii).

Just as comic rogue literature, filiated with jest books, seems to have influenced the Poor Laws, and through them to have influenced real poor people, so comic tales about monks, nuns, and friars were pressed into service in the campaign to oust the Catholic Church from England. In the *Liber Vagatorum,* rogue literature and comic anticlericalism meet: the *Liber Vagatorum*'s roster of specialized beggars includes such religious hangers-on and/ or pretenders as dobissers, vagierers, pardoners, *reliquarii* (relic vendors), dallingers, suntvegers, and curtalls. And this double-genre popular work influenced (by his own account) the thinking of the one continental reformer who above all others left his stamp on the English Reformation: Luther. Lest modern readers be tempted to underestimate the power of jest and comic literature, they should recall that in the case of the dissolution of monasteries, jest and the comic ultimately brought down stone buildings.

The Dissolution of the Monasteries

No anemic affair of dry theological disputation, no mere bureaucratic reorganization substituting an archbishop of Canterbury for a pope, Protestantism in England involved massive physical destruction of material culture. Parish church after parish church was razed to the ground. "Lesser masonry and columns they could undercut, shoring up with timber as they went, till all was ready to set light to the wood and bring everything down, but some of the piers needed gunpowder to shift them" (Knowles 384). The Dissolution was a calculated destruction of what had been home to monastics: by destroying buildings, commissioners meant "to ensure that there should be no return for the monks. As a new owner put it after he had pulled down the church, the nest had been destroyed lest the birds should build there again" (Knowles 386). Reformers recognized home as essential to identity—with no monastic home for monks and nuns, Catholicism would wither.

Some former monastics accepted government pensions; some turned Protestant. Many became vagrants. Of these, some preserved vestiges of religious vocation by performing weddings for other vagrants (a disheartening task, Harman claims, given vagrants' habitual free love). "Patricos," Harman calls them; Awdeley's spelling "patriarcho" or "patriarke co" makes clear the word's link with "patriarch" or "pater," suggesting that these vagrants are former priests or monastics. The patrico became a stock figure in plays dealing with beggary; a character named Patrico appears in Richard Brome's *Jovial Crew.* The definition of "frater" as one who begs on behalf of a hospital, the monastery's successor in poor relief, dates to Awdeley's *Fraternity of Vagabonds (OED)*; that it also meant "friar" suggests that this category of vagrant comprised ex-friars. Early in the Henrician Reformation, monastics were charged with roaming abroad and seducing rather than staying home in their monasteries and praying. Later, many roamed abroad permanently.

When the monastic lands that had separated London's surrounding towns were opened up to development, it allowed London to coalesce rapidly into a major city (Rasmussen 35). Ironically the Reformation, whose writers so often fulminated against vagrancy, helped through its massive confiscations of church property to create the city that vagrants headed for: London, where wages were higher than in the country, beckoned to the unemployed.

Closing the monasteries, which had dispensed poor relief, also created a gap in social services, making the poverty problem suddenly much worse, especially in the years before secular relief became sufficiently organized. A commissioner's letter reported that one nunnery supported many "artificers, labourers, and victuallers," who provided services to the "gentlemen's children" educated there and to sojourners: "the town and nunnery standeth in a hard soil and barren ground, and . . . if the nunnery be suppressed, the town will shortly after fall to ruin and decay, and the people therein . . . are not unlike to have to wander and to seek for their living" (Cook 116). Leaders of the Northern Rising, a revolt in opposition to dissolving the monasteries, "were convinced that monasteries gave considerable help to the poor and needy" (Knowles 327); Robert Aske "grudged" against the suppression, "because the abbeys in the north parts gave great alms to poor men" (Knowles 328).[8] As Slack summarizes,

> The dissolution of monasteries, chantries, religious guilds and fraternities in the 1530s and 1540s radically reduced existing sources of charity. The real aid which they had provided for the poor was no doubt concentrated geographically, but it was more substantial than has often been supposed, and its destruction left a real vacuum. . . . Monasteries alone provided £6500 a year in alms before 1537; and that sum was not made good by private benefactions until after 1580. . . . Contemporaries were quick to bemoan the loss, to demand new endowments to fill the gap, and to complain of the failure of the Chantries Act of 1547 to guarantee in practice the continuation of charitable works. (*Poverty and Policy* 13)

The seizure of church lands had an indirect effect on revenues available for charity in that before the Dissolution, "the bulk of ordinary parish income came from the rents of property bequeathed in the past" (Haigh, *English Reformations* 29).

Did the brutalizing effects of such wholesale cultural destruction increase callousness toward the mobile poor? Facing death for his part in the Northern Rising, the intrepid Robert Aske declared that "the abbeys were one of the beauties of this realm to all men and strangers passing through the same" (Knowles 328); can such wanton destruction of buildings and artworks that had been sources of aesthetic pleasure and local pride have been without psychological ramifications? As Knowles writes, "Especially in the numberless small houses in field, forest and dale, the work of destruction was swift, and the church and cloister of yesterday were left a stripped and gutted ruin, . . . [but] not without the protests of those who were shocked at the spectacle of the desecration of buildings solemnly dedicated to God by previous generations. . . . It was the swift, callous irreverence of the Augmentations men, . . . and the not unnatural fear that everything venerable and sacred might soon likewise be snatched away, that precipitated the explosion of wrath in the northern risings" (387). Eamon Duffy writes that "stripping away externals of Catholic worship . . . must often have had a profound if not always conscious effect. . . . The removal of the images of the saints, of the altars, and perhaps most of all the brasses and obit inscriptions calling for prayers for the dead, which were ripped up from gravestones and sold by the hundredweight from 1548 onwards, were ritual acts of deep significance. . . . The removal of the images and petitions of the dead was an act of oblivion, a casting out of the dead from the community of the living" (494). "We can only guess," Duffy continues, "at the impact on [parishioners'] sense of the sacred when they saw their priest feed his swine from a trough which had once been the parish holy-water stoup, or heard Thomas Carter jingle about the parish with a bell on his horse's harness which had once summoned them to adoration at the sacring" (585–86). It would be surprising if such a tremendous, sudden, and brutal upheaval did not affect significantly the middle-Tudor psyche. The callousness of a man like Thomas Harman, capable of shrugging off with a laugh the promptings of conscience concerning the poor, is perhaps to be expected of a man who had witnessed, in his youth, the destruction of monasteries and the miserable exodus onto the roads of so many of those who had looked after the poor.

The Reformation, then, influenced the emergence of beggary/vagrancy as a prominent public policy issue: rhetorically, in the welding of anticlericalism to the discourse of vagrancy; and materially, in the destruction of the Catholic Church as the agency responsible for the poor. But the coming of Protestantism had other important effects on the poor, especially the vagrant poor, and it is to these that I now turn.

Protestant Theology and the Poor

All major Protestant theologians addressed poor relief: "In 1523 Luther helped in the reorganization of poor relief in the Saxon town of Leisnig; three years later, Zwingli directed a plan for the reform of public welfare in Zürich; in 1541 Calvin established the precise working of poor relief in Geneva"; their principles "followed the same general lines: prohibition of begging, forced labour, and centralization of poor relief providing minimum benefits" (Lis and Soly 87). Such continental thinking entered England primarily through the enormous influence of Luther. The reformers acted in good faith, sincerely concerned about poverty, honestly dedicated to improving conditions. Since they really believed that a will to work would prevent a fall into poverty, it made sense to discourage idleness by legislating against relief for the able-bodied. New conditions that rendered jobless even those willing and able to work were not readily decipherable at the time—indeed, though hindsight gives modern viewers a rather different perspective, economic forces are often mysterious, and present-day public policy experts are often no better predictors than Renaissance pundits of what harm their well-intended policies may do. My focus inevitably requires discussing the harm that befell the vagrant poor, but I do not deny that reformers' policies did real good for other groups, especially the settled poor. As I argued in the introduction, to some degree helping the settled poor was conditional on harsh treatment of vagrants. I am trying not to *blame* religious reformers. Though I will indicate the harm their policies did, I take them at their word that they sincerely wanted to improve the quality of life in Christian commonwealths.

Luther's influence was seminal (see McKee's summary of the spread across Europe of ideas on policy toward the poor), and his statements merit a close look. Called in to advise the parish of Leisnig on reorganizing its poor relief, Luther wrote the preface to a parish constitution, "Ordinance of a Common Chest" (1523), whose twin villains are mendicant monks and the idle poor: "no monks, of whatever order, . . . shall henceforth have any sort of begging concession within our parish," and Leisnig is not to accept the burden of "nonresident, fictitious poor and idlers who are not really in need" (185). The principle is clear: "No men or women beggars shall be tolerated in our parish, either in the city or in the villages, since anyone not incapacitated by reason of age or illness shall work or . . . be expelled" (186).

In both "Treatise on Good Works" (1520) and "Trade and Usury" (1524) Luther cites Psalms 37:25, "I [have] never seen a man of faith who trusts God (that is, a righteous man) forsaken, or his child begging bread," ostensibly to assuage fear that alms might impoverish the giver. But the text has a sting in its tail: anyone whose child is begging bread must be unrighteous. Like English Protestant preachers after him, Luther encourages charity while harshly exempting vagrants from its benefits: "What kind of good deed is it if we are kind only to our friends? . . . A Christian man must rise higher, letting his kindness serve even those who do not deserve it: evil-doers, enemies, and the ungrateful. . . . St. Ambrose says, 'Feed the hungry: if you do not feed him, then as far as you are concerned, you have killed him.' . . . Nonetheless, the authorities and cities ought to see to it that vagabonds, Jacob's brethren, and whatever strange beggars there may be should be barred" ("Treatise" 109–10). ("Jacob's brethren" were pilgrims to the tomb of St. James of Compostela. Note the suspicion of anyone on the road—of mobility itself—a significant change from medieval redemptive pilgrimages.) In "To the Christian Nobility of the German Nation Concerning the Reform of the Christian Estate" (1520), Luther inveighs, "One of the greatest necessities is the abolition of all begging throughout Christendom. . . . [Nations should make laws] that every city should look after its own poor. . . . No beggar from outside should be allowed into the city whether he might call himself pilgrim or mendicant monk" (189). The shape of sixteenth-century European laws governing poverty attests to the success of such thinking. Here Luther conflates clerical mendicants with lay beggars: "many vagabonds and evil rogues . . . call themselves mendicants. . . . There is no other business in which so much skullduggery and deceit are practiced as in begging" (190). Luther continues that the jobless are to be kept just barely alive: "It is enough if the poor are decently cared for so that they do not die of hunger or cold. It is not fitting that one man should live in idleness on another's labor" (190).

Reformers' practical policies for dealing with the poor were a logical extension of what is often called the desacralization of poverty. In medieval thinking, the poor were "a natural part of God's plan of salvation. . . . God could have made all men rich, but He wanted there to be poor people in this world, that the rich might be able to redeem their sins. . . . The exaltation of charity not only offered the rich the opportunity of buying their salvation; it effectively sanctioned wealth and justified it on ideological grounds" (Geremek 20). Mark Koch discusses "medieval belief in what Marcel Mauss, in his [essay on] . . . gift exchange, refers to as 'economic theology.' Alms are given with the belief that they will be repaid with interest in this world, and, failing that, will surely be repaid in heaven" ("Desanctification" 91). As Murray Kempton notes with brutal clarity, "the poor have been placed among us for the primary purpose of affording the comfortable a chance to discover how virtuous they are" (4). But at least medieval doctrine promoted care of the poor, for whatever selfish motives; Renaissance ideologies, however unintentionally, provided excuses to neglect them.

Though Puritanism's emphasis on work had some adverse effect on beggars, who were assumed to decline labor out of idleness, historians no longer attribute shifting attitudes towards beggary primarily to Puritans, as did earlier historians such as Weber and Tawney. In fact, many Puritans advocated charity.[9] In 1583 Phillip Stubbes complained,

> God commandeth in his law, that there be no miserable poor man, nor beggar amongst us, but that every one be provided for and maintained of that abundance which God hath blessed us withal. But we think it a great matter if we give them an old ragged coat, doublet, or a pair of hosen, or else a penny or two. . . . If we give them a piece of brown bread, a mess of porridge (nay, the stocks and prison, with whipping cheer now and then is the best portion of alms which many gentleman give) at our doors, it is counted meritorious. (59)

John Downame charged in 1616 that charity "in this frozen age of the world is much neglected" (45). Pleas for unconditional charity rather than distinctions between deserving and undeserving, though rare, did occur among both Catholics and Protestants. In 1545 the Spanish Dominican Domingo de Soto argued, in Bronislaw Geremek's words, that "the poor may sometimes resort to dishonest methods of evoking our sympathy and compassion, but they do this from necessity, in order to conquer indifference and soften hardened hearts" (198). Continuing his paraphrase of de Soto, Geremek writes, "It is far better to give alms to twenty vagrants than to repulse them and risk depriving the four genuine paupers among them of much-needed support. The policy of distinguishing between genuine and false paupers entailed too many moral risks to be acceptable to the Christian conscience" (198). The English Protestant Henry Bedel preached, "Be merciful to the poor indifferently without respect of persons. . . . Let the beggar be wicked, thou shalt have thy praise. Though some make an occupation of it [i.e., become professional beggars through idleness], . . . yet Paul . . . doth not deny thee to do good to all" (Sig [C4]^v). A good man, Downame said, "chooseth rather to offend on the safer side; because it is better the poor man should take a slight surfeit, . . . than to be pinched and famished for want of necessaries" (26). Downame goes on to declare: "Poverty and want dejecteth the mind" (29). Medieval economic theology might have been expected to appeal to Puritans. Indeed, Downame takes literally Psalm 112:9, showing that the individual who gives liberally will enjoy "a most prosperous and flourishing estate in this world and in the world to come" (229). Natalie Zemon Davis notes that new poor relief policies were very similar in a Catholic city such as Lyon and a Protestant city such as Nuremberg. She also shows how Lyon created a new secular poor relief system in the 1530s by a coalition of Protestants and Catholics.[10]

Despite such complexities, however, Protestant theology did abet the crucial shift away from a concept of alms as redemptive: moving from good works toward faith as the basis for redemption weakened that premier good work, almsgiving: as late as *Everyman* (ca. 1485), good works are synonymous with "alms deeds." As Mark Koch says, the "belief that almsdeeds would be repaid by God was undermined considerably by the doctrine of justification by faith" ("Desanctification" 94). Symptomatic of the change is Tyndale's substitution, in his New Testament translation, of "love" for "charity" (Schuster 1255). A speaker in Robert Greene's *Quip for an Upstart Courtier* complains that Puritans "preach faith, faith, and say that doing of alms is papistry, but they have taught so long *Fides solam justificat* [faith alone justifies] that they have preached good works quite out of our parish; a poor man shall as soon break his neck as his fast at a rich man's door" (sig. G2^v). Though Elsie Anne McKee rightly opposes oversimplified ascriptions of declining charity to justification by faith (99), reforming writers persistently found the doctrine troublesome. Bedel, in *A Sermon Exhorting to Pity the Poor* (1571), cites the second chapter of the biblical book of James, "Faith if it have not her exercises in her self, she is dead," and adopts the theologically high-handed expedient of declaring almsgiving an act of faith, not a good work, an "exercise of faith to give to the poor" (sig. A2ᵛ, [A3]). As Paul Slack notes, though Catholic charity was impelled by "a quest for salvation . . . through the practice of mercy," yet "preachers in England were nervously anxious to counteract any inclination among Protestants to let doctrines of grace and justification by faith discourage good works: rather, they argued that 'charitable generosity [was] . . . proof' that a man was a 'true and not a false Christian'" (*Poverty and Policy* 10). Such anxiety bespeaks strong temptation to neglect good works. Compared to alms, faith is cheap.

Protestantism has always wrestled with the moral irresponsibility inherent in de-emphasizing good works. (The problem still loomed large in Lutheran confirmation class in my youth.) A heavy emphasis on faith encourages passivity, a trust in the Lord that tempts a Christian to neglect action. The Protestant work ethic grew in part out of a theological solution to this problem: re-encouraging good works as the outward sign of faith. Christians work hard to show how faithful they are, especially if the doctrine of election is involved. Logically, predestination ought to encourage passivity if not fatalism—no quantity of good works, no neglect of works, can change God's mind about whether one is saved; but in practice, since good works were a sign of election, Calvinists worked hard to prove to themselves and others that they were saved. That this did not operate to reinstate alms deeds may reflect the slippage between good works and hard work that affected Protestant attitudes toward the unemployed. As "good works" were detached from "alms deeds," the former increasingly meant secular work. "Vocation" (from Latin *vocare*, to call) earlier meant a calling by God—to salvation or a religious life—but by the mid-sixteenth century it had come to mean primarily "one's ordinary occupation, business, or profession" (*OED*). It is this expansion of "vocation" to embrace secular activities that Falstaff burlesques when claiming of highway robbery, "'Tis my vocation, Hal; 'tis no sin for a man to labour in his vocation" (*1H4* 1.2.116). But when working hard in a secular vocation became a duty to God, the unemployed were ungodly. If work was salvation, idleness was damnation; and the poor were called idle.

It is difficult to know how much headway the notion of justification by faith made during the sixteenth century in England. As Patrick Collinson notes, "Puritan writers reported that mere conformists, whom they dismissed as 'neuters,' 'cold statute protestants,' comprised a majority of the population; . . . few had heard of justification by faith alone" (*English Puritanism*

19). But a good deal of energy went into enlightening the masses on this point. Lewis Wager's secular morality play *The Life and Repentance of Mary Magdalene,* for example, laid out the concept in simple terms:

> There was never man born yet that was able,
> To perform these precepts just, holy and stable,
> Save only Jesus Christ.
> So by faith in Christ you have Justification
> Freely of his grace and beyond man's operation. (64)

Though the doctrine alone is clearly not sufficient, in isolation from the many other pressures I discuss in this book, to account for the waning impulse to give handouts to beggars, it seems to me very suggestive that Protestant theologians and other Reformation writers were so defensive about it and strove so mightily to instill the idea that good works were still necessary. The fact is that a religion based on faith, on the notion of an individual's helpless depravity apart from divine grace, is conducive to moral laziness. Theorists of "Othering" posit that in enlisting Others against whom to define themselves, dominant groups heap onto a scapegoated group qualities that they themselves wish to disown. And the two groups that Protestant theologians attacked most violently—secular beggars and members of monastic orders—were accused of laziness. Mendicant friars, dependent on handouts, and beggars, jobless and dependent on the kindness of strangers, uncomfortably parodied humankind as imagined by Protestant theologians—depraved by nature, stripped of agency when it came to good works, dependent on the grace of a higher being. I think it was in part unwillingness to face squarely the disturbing consequences of their own theology that led Protestant theologians to demonize—and to be preoccupied with—beggary.

Christopher Haigh maintains that "the negative, mocking aspects of the Reformation message had far more impact than the new slogans of justification by faith and election" (*English Reformations* 200); unsurprisingly, obscene images of the pope or tales of lecherous friars made more of an impression than did abstractions about faith. But it was precisely the "negative, mocking aspects of the Reformation message" that rubbed off on vagrants, whose begging was identified with despised clerical mendicancy, whose vagrancy was linked with the wanderings of friars, and whose supposed sexual profligacy was conflated with that of the comically lecherous clergy. To show that intellectual notions like justification by faith had not taken firm root in England even by the end of the sixteenth century is not to undermine the idea that poverty was desacralized: the practice of almsgiving to vagrant beggars was weakened not only by declining belief in "economic theology" but also by the fact that almsgiving was discouraged by law and ridiculed by satirical mocking that conflated beggars with Catholics.

The Comic Mode in Reformation Rhetoric

Though Protestant theological doctrines played a crucial role in disempowering vagrant beggars, Haigh's contention that "mockery" as a Reformation tactic is more powerful than abstract theological doctrines jibes with what I have been arguing about the power of the comic mode. I have shown that vagrants and the Catholic clergy were subject to similar hostile representation and that both groups suffered from being tarred with the same brush. It is important that the hostile representation was in both cases often comic in its workings. If it is true, as I argue, that comic literary anticlericalism influenced the Henrician Reformation, it matters that the exact period of the break with Rome, dissolution of the monasteries, and the coalescence of the English discourse of vagrancy—the 1520s and 1530s—also saw the first flowering of the jest book genre, in which clerical and especially monastic figures (as well as vagrants) loom large.

A "young and lusty" monk, the title figure of *A Merry Jest of Dane Hew, Monk of Leicester, and How He Was Four Times Slain and Once Hanged,* is double-crossed by a tailor's wife with whom he has an assignation—after he gives her money, her husband jumps out of a chest and brains him. *A Little Jest How the Plowman Learned his Paternoster* features a trickster-priest. The friar in *A Merry Jest of the Friar and the Boy* suffers supernatural trickery, as a boy with a magical panpipe forces him to dance through a briar patch after causing his stepmother to emit mighty farts. In Sir Thomas More's *A Merry Jest How a Sergeant Would Learn to Be a Friar,* a sergeant adopts a friar's disguise to make an arrest and instead is beaten up, to general hilarity. The hero of Johan Splinter's *Merry Jest and a True How Johan Splinter Made His Testament* has worked for two nunneries all his life, but when the nuns desert him in his aged poverty, he tricks them into supporting him in style by pretending to count up vast monies in his room; the nuns, as he expects, secretly watch him. (Clearly they are Boccaccio-type nuns, habituated to watching male guests through peepholes.) Several tales in [Till Eulenspiegel's] *Merry Jest of a Man That Was Called Howlglas* deal with a priest's one-eyed mistress. Lecherous monks and friars abound in other jest books, too, such as *A Hundred Merry Tales.*

One of the earliest texts of the English discourse of vagrancy, Robert Copland's *Highway to the Spital-house* (1536[?]), is contemporary with the heyday of Henrician jest books, and two classic Henrician jest books, Walter Smith's *Widow Edith* (1525) and [Eulenspiegel's] *Howlglas* (ca. 1519), deal with vagrants. I have been proposing that the whole genre of rogue literature that made a joke out of vagrancy should be considered a subspecies of the Tudor jest book.

Jest was a carefully cultivated rhetorical device for polemics and preaching; indeed, a number of jokes collected in Renaissance jest books can be traced to medieval sermons, particularly those written by friars. Fighting fire with fire, Reformation polemicist Henri Estienne uses comic stories to stigmatize friars as frivolous jesters. In one of his antimonastic anecdotes, a Franciscan preacher, having wagered that he can make half of his congregation laugh and half of it weep at the same instant, dresses in a short clerical gown with nothing underneath and then makes a sober speech to the congregation (who weep); leaning earnestly toward them and crossing his arms, he pulls up his gown to expose his bare backside to those behind him (who laugh), thus winning the bet and bringing a whole new meaning to the Christian ideal of turning the other cheek (281). This anecdote, appearing in a serious Reformation theological work, bears a suspicious resemblance to a tale in *Howlglas,* one of the texts in which rogue literature shakes hands with the jest book. Even as a child the trickster Howlglas achieves a reputation as a "mocker"—a title that he assures his father is wholly undeserved. One day, riding through town seated behind his father on a horse, Howlglas pulls up his gown and moons the townsfolk. They revile him, but Howlglas persuades his father, unaware of the mooning, that the people are unjust (sig. Aiiᵛ–Aiii). These two stories of tricksters who present one face to those before them, another to those behind, together offer a wonderful example of the way both rogue literature and Reformation polemic drew upon jest books.

Reformers knew that jesting could be serious. In "To the Christian Nobility of the German Nation Concerning the Reform of the Christian Estate" (1520), Luther presented himself as a court jester (*Hofnarr*): "Perhaps I owe my God and the world another work of folly. I intend to pay my debt honestly. And if I succeed, I shall for the time being become a court jester. And if I fail, I still have one advantage, no one need buy me a cap or put scissors to my head" (123). The image of the dyspeptic reformer in cap and bells is arresting; perhaps it is only self-deprecation. But in another "work of folly," Luther's adversary Erasmus, in a brilliant rhetorical paradox, turns a *Ship of Fools*–like attack on universal folly into an advocacy of humility: in *The Praise of Folly,* all Christians are, in St. Paul's words, "fools for Christ's sake" (Corinthians 4:10). As do Barclay's *Ship of Fools* or *Cock Lorel's Boat,* Erasmus saw all people as fools; but he also knew (like King Lear after him) that serious

matter could be uttered by one wearing cap and bells. Reformation contro-
versialists often made serious points in the guise of jesting. The desanctification of poverty, like the disinheriting of the Catholic Church, was accomplished not only by sermons, statutes, and commissions but also by jest and
laughter.

The Vagrant Poor in Reformation Times:
Concluding Observations

The Judeo-Christian tradition had once heavily emphasized charitableness
to the poor. The Old Testament offers such forceful pronouncements as
"What mean ye that ye beat my people to pieces, and grind the faces of the
poor? saith the Lord God of Hosts" (Isaiah 3:15); in the New Testament Jesus
counsels a rich man to "sell all that thou hast, and distribute unto the poor"
(Luke 18:22). However, early modern harshness toward the vagrant poor did
not seem unchristian to contemporaries. Henry Arthington, though he counsels charity, is so harsh in his attitudes toward the poorest people as to undermine severely this advice: the poor have brought poverty on themselves
through idleness, roguery, wastefulness, and reluctance to repent; vagrant
beggars should thus be punished severely. Yet he also quotes approvingly a
number of biblical texts advising respect and compassion for the poor, as do
many of his Christian contemporaries: "Whoso mocketh the poor reproach-
eth his Maker" (Proverbs 17:5); "He that hath pity on the poor lendeth unto
the Lord; and that which he hath given will he pay him again" (19:1); "He that
giveth unto the poor shall not lack: but he that hideth his eyes shall have many
a curse" (19:17); "Whoso stoppeth his ears at the cry of the poor, he also shall
cry himself, but shall not be heard" (21:13); "Blessed is he that considereth the
poor: the Lord will deliver him in time of trouble" (28:27); "For the oppression of the poor, for the sighing of the needy, now will I arise, saith the Lord"
(Psalms 12:5); "He hath dispersed, he hath given to the poor; his righteous-
ness endureth forever" (112:9); "The poor shall never cease out of the land:
therefore I command thee, saying, Thou shalt open thine hand wide unto thy
brother, to thy poor, and to thy needy, in thy land" (Deuteronomy 15:11);
"When thou makest a feast, call the poor, the maimed, the lame, the blind"
(Luke 14:12); "Whoso hath this world's good, and seeth his brother have need,
and shutteth up his bowels of compassion from him, how dwelleth the love
of God in him?" (1 John 3:17); "God loveth a cheerful giver" (2 Corinthians
9:7); "I was an hungred, and ye gave me no meat: I was thirsty, and ye gave
me no drink: I was a stranger, and ye took me not in: naked, and ye clothed

me not: sick, and in prison, and ye visited me not. . . . Inasmuch as ye did it not to one of the least of these, ye did it not to me" (Matthew 25:42–45).

As many Reformation texts attest, acceptance of Judeo-Christian precepts about the poor in general coexisted with harsh personal and institutional attitudes toward the vagrant poor in particular, just as in more recent times fundamentalist Christianity has coexisted with "get-tough-on-welfare-bums" conservatism. The doctrine that reconciles them is that of the deserving and undeserving poor. Many modern beliefs about the poor resemble Renaissance beliefs. The modern belief that the poor *could* find work but are lazy and prefer to live off welfare closely replicates the Renaissance belief in idleness as the cause of poverty. Moves in 1995 to strike unwed mothers from welfare rolls recall the Renaissance doctrine that the sexually immoral forfeit all claim to compassion; modern willingness to let such women go hungry replays the frequent citation by early modern moralists of the biblical text "If any should not work, neither should he eat" (2 Thessalonians 3:10). The modern conviction that the poor breed like rabbits was visible in the Renaissance in texts like *An Ease for Overseers of the Poor:* "In this age, the poorest sort of men are straight inclined to marry without any respect how to live: hereof it is that the world grows so populous and poor; for commonly the poor do most of all multiply children" (26). Would moralists literally have countenanced such draconian measures as letting someone die who did not work? Certainly, says the textual evidence. "If Draco that famous law-maker were alive," writes the anonymous author of *An Ease for Overseers,* "he would not suffer him to live who doth refuse to labor" (20). Renaissance thoughts on the unhoused poor are of more than antiquarian interest: this period forged views that resemble attitudes visible today, and the analogy may help modern readers to think through their own stances toward the homeless.

Patrick Collinson, Christopher Haigh, and others have stressed the incompleteness of religious reforms in the sixteenth and early seventeenth centuries: far from permeating the consciousness of all Englishmen, such Reformation notions as justification by faith or the irrelevance of almsgiving to salvation were in some cases ignored out of apathy and in other cases hotly contested out of a wish to return to old Catholic ways. Ordinary people sometimes persisted in giving money directly to filthy beggars rather than adopting the recommended procedure of putting money into church charity boxes, and it may well be that sympathy for the pitifully poor and unhoused contributed to some people's resistance to Protestant social doctrines and ultimately to Protestant reform itself. The embattled state of Christianity in sixteenth-century England, with the repeated reforms, repeals of reform, and reassertions of reform, in itself militated against any orderly or uniform influence of Protestantism on vagrancy. I have tried to suggest the complexity of English Protestantism's impact on the vagrant poor—some of it coming from carefully reasoned theological positions such as justification by faith, some of it arising as a side effect of inflammatory anti-Catholic rhetoric that appropriated a language designed for sturdy beggars, and some of it incidentally resulting from political moves such as the dissolution of the monasteries. No one strand of sixteenth-century religious reform, or even all strands together, can account for the declining fortunes of the vagrant poor; and religious developments are in turn but one thread in the intricate fabric into which vagrants' destinies were woven.

Before I turn to some of the other strands, such as humanism, nationalism, or the valorization of domesticity, I want to close this chapter with one intangible effect on vagrants of the period's religious turmoil: fighting Reformation battles and carrying out Reformation policies diverted national energy away from major social problems and into the arena of religious strife. Many projects of reform and counterreform were inordinately costly. Eamon Duffy's *Stripping of the Altars: Traditional Religion in England, 1400–1580* and Christopher Haigh's *English Reformations: Religion, Politics, and Society under the Tudors* document the enormous resources in money, time, and energy that went into the Henrician and Edwardine Reformations, the Marian restoration of Catholicism, and the Elizabethan restoration of Protestantism: investigating and prosecuting heresy and dissent, plundering church holdings, tearing down altars, rebuilding altars, confiscating relics, hiding relics, legislating prayer books, debating policies on the sacraments, regulating parish religious practices. No wonder that little time, energy, and resources were left for the problems of poverty and vagrancy. Some of the energy that went into efforts to police public morality seems a wasteful diversion, and in the zeal to root out prostitution can be glimpsed residues of the Reformation's crusading passion against monastic sexual offenses. In 1582 John Howes deplored the diversion of attention from poverty to prostitution: "God cannot but be angry with us, that will suffer our Christian brethren to die in the street for want of relief, and we spend and consume our wealth and our wit in searching out of harlots, and leave the works of faith and mercy undone" (in Tawney and Power 3:442).

During Edward VI's reign, notable for energetic altar-strippings and the destruction of superstitious relics, Robert Crowley called the homeless poor "most miserable creatures, lying and dying in the streets full of all plagues and penury!" (*Way to Wealth* 166). Carefully advising the poor to "be obedient, and suffer patiently" (137), Crowley also pointedly raises the specter of uprisings if poverty is not alleviated: his *Way to Wealth* is subtitled *By What*

Means Sedition May Be Put Away, and What Destruction Will Follow If It Be Not Put Away Speedily. He implies that rich people's suspicion that the poor want "all things common" is paranoid and denies advocating communism (142, 156); but his urgent tone suggests that radical measures may be necessary, and he roundly condemns the rich for fostering vagrancy by rack-renting, turning people out of cottages, and violating antienclosure laws. Crowley's *Information and Petition against the Oppressors of the Poor Commons of This Realm* opens with a demand that Parliament get national priorities right:

> Among the manifold and most weighty matters . . . to be debated and communed of in this present Parliament, . . . no one thing [is] more needful to be spoken of than the great oppression of the poor commons. . . . No doubt it is needful, and there ought to be a speedy redress of many matters of religion, as are these:—The use of the sacraments and ceremonies; . . . the superfluous, unlearned, undiscreet, and vicious ministers of the church, and their superstitious and idolatrous administrations. . . . But as for the oppression of the poor, which is no less needful to be communed of and reformed than the other, I fear me will be passed over with silence. (153–56)

This is a devastatingly clear statement of what must finally be said about the poor in Reformation times, and it can be said of *all* the movements Haigh has called "English Reformations"—Catholic counterreform movements as well as Protestant reform movements. The mania for reforming and counterreforming the church, which occupied the whole sixteenth century, ultimately distracted the English nation from the task of curing poverty and vagrancy. With a voice ringing like that of a biblical prophet, Robert Crowley spoke out: "Unless you make the poor to cease from crying, God will not prosper your reformations" (*Information and Petition* 169).

Notes

1. In *Supplication of Souls,* More objects to Fish's assumption that the only real work is manual labor (147–48), and one can only wonder whether the legions of theologians, humanists, reform clergymen, lawyers, and others who spent their time penning lengthy treatises on the idleness of monks and secular beggars had themselves much experience of manual labor, of working by the sweat of their brows.

2. On Chaucer and anticlericalism, see Jill Mann's *Chaucer and Medieval Estates Satire,* and essays by Carolly Erickson, Charles Dahlberg, Arnold Williams, and John Fleming ("Antifraternalism"). Stressing the continuum between antifraternalism in comic poetry and that in serious poetry, theological writings, and public disputes, Penn R. Szittya, in *The Antifraternal Tradition in Medieval Literature,* includes a chapter on Chaucer alongside chapters dealing with French and English theological disputes about the role and status of friars.

3. Aretino, too, trained powerful sexual satire upon a corrupt church: as Ian Moulton shows, "the explicit and graphic description of sex which made the *Ragionamenti* infamous is . . . almost entirely in the service of a powerful attack on clerical corruption" (130).

4. The charge of sodomy was a characteristic move; see Bruce Smith's account of the way homoeroticism was demonized as a pretext for the dissolution of the monasteries (44–46). As Stephen Orgel and others point out, sodomy was a vague charge covering a multitude of practices that were not necessarily homoerotic; but the specific demonization of homoeroticism is a move that could easily be predicted in that homoeroticism, like vagrancy, was almost by definition a threat to the emerging ideology of domesticity and settled, nuclear family life; see chapter 4 of this study.

5. Thirty-two editions of the *Liber Vagatorum* have been identified before 1530, and numerous others appeared throughout the sixteenth century; Pieter Spierenburg identifies the period of its composition, probably the 1490s, as a crisis period for the clash between older ideas about sanctified poverty and newer conceptions about the undeserving poor, fraudulently disabled beggars, and so forth (*Prison Experience* 21–22). The *Liber Vagatorum*'s continental imitators and cousins include *La Vie Genereuse* (The generous life) in France, *La Desordenada Codicia de los Bienes Agenes* (The inordinate greed of two rogues) in Spain, and Teseo Pini's *Il Libro dei Vagabondi* (The book of vagabonds) in Italy.

6. Some items in the *Liber Vagatorum* occur almost word-for-word in Harman; with the *Liber Vagatorum*'s "tinkers who travel about the country . . . have women who go before them. . . . One of them mayhap will break a hole in thy kettle to give work to a multitude of others" (135), compare *A Caveat*'s "tinkers . . . never go without their doxies. . . . If [a wife] have three or four holes in a pan, he will make as many more for speedy gain" (92).

7. Nostril-pricking is a Falstaff trick (*1 Henry IV* 2.4.341). To what extent does Falstaff's trickiness draw on the discourse of faked disability in the vagrancy texts? His strategies do include at one point the ultimate phony disability—he fakes his own death.

8. The very dourness of the Reformation damaged funding that might have gone to the poor: at the height of the Edwardine reforms in midcentury, "there was a crisis in parochial religion. As services became plainer, plays and ales were suppressed, guilds and special funds were abolished, so churches attracted less affection—and much less money—from their people. In the north of England, more than 70 per cent of testators had left bequests to a parish church in 1540–46 [a period of Catholic restoration], but only 32 per cent under Edward VI. . . . It was the same everywhere" (Haigh, *English Reformations* 181).

9. Defining Puritanism is of course notoriously difficult, particularly since the word itself arose as "a term of art and stigmatization which became a weapon of some verbal finesse but no philosophical precision" (Collinson, *English Puritanism* 10) at the opposite end of the religious spectrum from terms of satirical abuse against Catholics. For purposes of considering the effects of various kinds of Protestant reform on the vagrant poor, it seems sensible to adopt Collinson's principle that "Puritanism was neither alien to Protestantism nor even distinct from it but was its logical extension, equivalent to its full internalisation" (*Birthpangs* 95). The most important "logical extension" for my

purposes was a purist insistence on justification by faith, a doctrine not accepted by all Protestants (Henry VIII, for example, was staunchly opposed to it).

10. It is true, though, that in Catholic Ypres a "modern" poor relief scheme with centralized and organized alms and penalties for begging was opposed by the mendicant orders. When Charles V proposed to extend such a scheme to his other realms, he was opposed by the church in Spain (C. S. L. Davies 540).

3. Humanism against the Homeless

When all allowances are made, we may ask why the humanist
conscience, with its conviction that education can change character to
some degree, did not envisage better rehabilitation for the healthy
vagabond.
—Natalie Zemon Davis

LIKE THOSE USUALLY classified as theologians, those most often identified
as humanists (Desiderius Erasmus, Sir Thomas More, Juan Luis Vives, Thomas Linacre, Sir Thomas Elyot, Richard Morison, John Colet, Thomas Starkey)
all addressed the issue of poverty, and in general they too exempted vagrants
and beggars from otherwise humane programs of social reform. The existence of the disreputable poor tried the limits of humanism: it tested the
success of humanist theory in creating a just civil society and the validity of
humanist belief in human dignity. Vagrants presented a challenge to the
humanist intellectual program. Though many humanists wrote with compassion about poverty and offered solutions, the humanist identity, like the
Protestant identity, was constructed partly in opposition to what wandering
beggars represented.

Christianity and humanism look in retrospect almost like opposites: Christianity relied on faith, God's grace, and belief in original sin and human
depravity, whereas humanism was founded on reason, education, and belief
in the dignity of man. Yet many early Tudors regarded themselves as that
seeming oxymoron, the Christian humanist. For convenience I have made a
division between Christianity (in the last chapter) and humanism (in this
chapter), but the Tudor period resists such firm distinctions. Erasmus can
be called both theologian and humanist; and More, profoundly devout during his humanist phase, drew heavily during his theological phase on humanist rhetorical techniques and classical learning. On the causes of poverty,
humanists (like theologians) more often advanced moral than economic
explanations. A decade after Thomas Harman's *Caveat for Common Cursetors,* a character apparently modeled on Harman's Nicholas Jennings, a counterfeit crank, starred in a secular morality play, Francis Merbury's *Marriage*

between Wit and Wisdom, as the Vice figure Idleness. Merbury's "counterfeit crank" (line 213) was an enemy of the secular values Wit and Wisdom. Idleness (or sloth) was a sin in Christian terms and a character defect in humanist terms. Christianity attributed poverty to indulgence in deadly sins, while humanism adduced failure to observe balance and order in the conduct of one's ethical life: to both, such character failings led to gambling, drinking, whoring, gluttony, and spendthrift wastage, culminating in poverty and ruin.

Humanists on Poverty and Vagrancy

In one of his widely read colloquies, Erasmus associated secular vagrancy with clerical mendicancy: in "Well-to-do Beggars," an innkeeper asks two Franciscan friars, "What kind of men are you, anyway, to wander like this without packhorse, without purse, without servants, without arms, without provisions?" and growls, "Seems to me a life of vagabonds" (*Colloquies* 208). Like writers of rogue literature, Erasmus in his colloquy "Beggar Talk" (1524) recognizes as similar fraternal orders the Franciscans and the beggars' fraternities, "the order of the down-and-out" (*Colloquies* 250), and he joins in warnings against "impostor" beggars who fake disability: in "Beggar Talk," one who has been "covered all over with sores" confesses, "all that decoration of mine I had put on with paints, turpentine, sulphur, resin, birdlime, linen cloth, and blood. When I felt like doing so, I took off what I had put on" (*Colloquies* 251). Indigence may result from profligacy, as a speaker in "Beggar Talk" admits: "I was rich. I threw the money away. When it was gone, . . . I ran away in disgrace" (*Colloquies* 250). Beggary comes of idleness: one of his beggars' names, Misoponus, means "hater of work." As Harman later considered begging an easy, merry life, Erasmus has a beggar declare, "begging's the nearest thing to possessing a kingdom," since "freedom, than which nothing is sweeter, belongs to no king more than it does to us" (253). First printed in 1524, in the wake of municipal takeovers of poor relief in Nuremberg, Strassburg, and several Dutch cities, "Beggar Talk" approves of such intervention and accurately foresees its extension across Europe: citizens are "muttering that beggars shouldn't be allowed to roam about at will, but that each city should support its own beggars and all the able-bodied ones forced to work, . . . because they find prodigious crimes committed under pretext of begging" (254). A character in the colloquy "The Godly Feast," famous for its humanist battle cry "Saint Socrates, pray for us!" (*Colloquies* 68), opposes giving alms to beggars: "it's robbery to bestow on those who will use it ill" (70). Erasmus disagreed with Luther on many matters; but about policy toward beggary, they spoke as one.

Highly influential on humanist thinking about social reform was Juan Luis Vives's *De Subventione Pauperum* (1526; Concerning the relief of the poor). Vives, who for a time lived in England, advocated secular rather than ecclesiastical responsibility for the poor, schools for paupers' children, and the centralization of relief administration. Despite his own Spanish Catholic background, Vives (like Catholic thinkers in Lyon and other cities) accepts the shift away from ecclesiastical care for the poor, instead insisting on civic and state stewardship: "As it is disgraceful for the head of the household in a luxurious home to allow any one to suffer hunger or go in nakedness or rags, so in a wealthy city it is not meet that the magistrates should suffer any of the citizens to be oppressed by hunger and want" (4). He continues, "Great is the glory of the state in which no beggar is seen; for a great multitude of paupers argues malice and heartlessness in the citizens and neglect of the public weal by the magistrates" (44). Vives also extends his belief in the nation-state's responsibility for the poor beyond Christendom:

> It is not tolerable that in any state—I will not say in any Christian country, but in any nation where men live after the manner of men—that when some of the citizens so abandon themselves to extravagance as to squander thousands of gold pieces on a sepulchre or a palace or a useless edifice or a banquet or a public office, for lack of fifty or a hundred florins the chastity of a virgin or the health and life of an honest man should be in danger, or a man should be forced to desert his wife and little children. (32)

Vives states emphatically the extent of poverty: "It is a shame and disgrace to us Christians, to whom nothing has been more explicitly commanded than charity[,] . . . that we meet everywhere in our cities so many poor men and beggars. Whithersoever you turn you encounter poverty and distress, and those who are compelled to hold out their hands for alms" (10). He also slips into the Henrician-era rhetoric of blaming poverty on those "sturdy beggars," the clergy, who have "diverted to their own purposes what in reality belonged to the poor" (25). Yet for all his compassion for the poor, Vives shows the deep confusion of his age over their plight: was poverty their own fault, or was it outside their control? Even when he displays compassion for those driven to crime, one witnesses a slide from passive verbs suggesting victimization ("are driven," "are not able to keep") to active verbs suggesting willing agency ("stealthily commit," "casting aside," "put it on sale"):

> Since they have not the means of subsistence, [they] are driven to robbery in the city and on the high-roads; others stealthily commit burglary; the women who are of suitable age, casting aside modesty, are not able to keep their chastity, but put it on sale for a trifle, nor can they be persuaded to abandon this vicious practice; the old women straightway take to pandering, and sorcery as

> a furtherance to pandering; the little children of the poor are most viciously
> taught; the poor themselves with their children, . . . wandering from place to
> place begging, do not participate in the sacraments and hear no sermons, and
> we know not according to what law or by what conventions they live, nor what
> are their religious beliefs. (8)

Vives certainly possesses compassion, but he also registers a sense of the
poor's voluntary vice rather than their powerlessness in the face of circumstances beyond their control: prostitution is "vicious" or a moral vice, and
Vives does not say that prostitutes cannot escape this life but that they "cannot be persuaded to abandon it"—implying intransigence rather than des-
peration. Worrying about the morals of the poor, Vives further demonizes
old women: "Let two censors be appointed every year, . . . eminent men and
of tried integrity, to inquire into the life and morals of the poor. . . . Let them
inquire also most carefully concerning the old women, who are master hands
at pandering and sorcery" (22), an attitude reflecting the "gossip's meeting"
tradition, wherein older women teach vicious tricks to the young (see Woodbridge, *Women and the English Renaissance* chap. 9). Once they are linked with
trickery in Vives's mind, the poor begin slipping out of range of his sympathy. No further recognition of a possible job shortage appears in his brisk
declaration, "Let no one among the poor . . . be idle, provided of course he
is fit for work by his age and the condition of his health" (13). Vives soon
conjures feigned disability: "In order that you may not be imposed upon by
a pretense of sickness or infirmity—which not infrequently happens—let the
opinion of physicians be sought, and let impostors be punished" (14); and
"in the hospitals, let the able-bodied who stick there like drones, living by
the sweat of others, depart and be put to work" (16). Like several Reformation writers, he terms "bloodsuckers" (18) those who live off others' labors:
was there some magical thinking in such portrayals of clerical mendicants
and secular beggars as sucking the blood and usurping the sweat of their
fellows? The age *did* harbor belief in demons who sucked out bodily fluids.[1]
Fear of the poor was partly superstitious. And Vives often recoils from their
filth and disease, seeking to quarantine the dubiously human.

Sir Thomas Elyot, *The Book Named the Governor*

One could attribute concern with beggary to the intellectual curiosity that
prompted humanists' interest in topics of all sorts, but I think beggary is more
central to the humanist project than that. It is no accident that a primary
humanist enunciation of political ideology, Elyot's *Book Named the Gover-*

nor (1531), came out contemporaneously with the passing, in Henry VIII's reign, of the *An Act Concerning Punishment of Beggars and Vagabonds* (1530–31). Creating a blueprint for the ideal English society, Elyot was disturbed by the "infinite number of English men and women [who] at this present time wander in all places throughout this realm, as beasts brute and savage, abandoning all occupation, service, and honesty" (2:81). The plight of the poor to some extent provides the impetus for the whole book.

Like Robert Copland in *The Highway to the Spital-house* and Erasmus in "Beggar Talk," Elyot attributes poverty to the profligacy of those who were once rich: "riot, gaming, and excess of apparel" lead to theft, robbery, murder (2:82). His discussion of poverty, beggary, and vagrancy occurs in the context of advice on mercy. Elyot maintains that a nation's ruler should generally be merciful, except to beggars and vagrants; mercy shown to them is "vain pity": "He that for every little occasion is moved with compassion, and beholding a man punished condignly for his offense lamenteth or waileth, is called piteous, which is a sickness of the mind, wherewith at this day the more part of men be diseased" (2:81). According to Elyot, "vain pity"—roughly equivalent to the modern "bleeding heart liberalism"—afflicts most of the population. As Harman tries to root out ill-advised charity, so Elyot counsels hardening of the heart toward those who have brought indigence on themselves. England has perfectly good laws for dealing with vagrants, he says; but judges are soft on crime. (Elyot, who lived a generation before Harman was a justice of the peace, would doubtless have smiled on Harman's toughness.) The soft-on-crime judge familiar to rogue literature appears as well in this humanist treatise:

> Consider semblably what noble statutes, ordinances, and acts of council from time to time have been excogitate, and by grave study and mature consultation enacted and decreed, . . . for the due punishment of the said idle persons and vagabonds. How many proclamations thereof have been divulgate and not obeyed? How many commissions directed and not executed? Mark well here, that disobedient subjects and negligent governors do frustrate good laws. . . . [Justices of the peace] behold at their eye the continual increase of vagabonds into infinite numbers. . . . Yet if any one commissioner, moved with zeal to his country, according to his duty do execute duly and frequently the law or good ordinance, wherein is any sharp punishment, some of his companions thereat reboileth, infaming him to be a man without charity. . . . And this may well be called vain pity. (2:87)

Drawing himself up to the full height of his learning, Elyot crushes soft judges with weighty Latinate words: "semblably," "consultation," "excogitate," "divulgate," "reboileth," "infaming"—mostly recent coinages, with "excogitate" apparently his own neologism. The pitch of moral indignation seems a measure of how endemic "vain pity" was, and the inkhorn terms—trademarks of the educated, whom Elyot regards as fit to rule—link pitilessness for vagrants to the humanist project.

Concern about "vain pity" confirms the impression that ordinary people persisted in being more pitying and charitable than reformers or humanists advised. But people were confused: was it right or wrong, wise or foolish, to give handouts to wandering beggars? *Should* poor relief be left solely to public authorities? Paul Slack notes "a perceived tension between old charity and new beneficence, a tension which some historians have seen as responsible for many of the witchcraft accusations of the period. These arose from the suspicions and feelings of guilt which were inevitable when neighbourly charity was denied to old men and women in a society which no longer held a clear view as to how or by whom its dependent members should be maintained" (*Poverty and Policy* 168). But humanists undertook to articulate that clear view.

Considering occasions when a ruler might decline to punish an offender, Elyot praises Augustus Caesar's clemency in pardoning Lucius Cinna, who had plotted to kill him, and dispraises English justices of the peace who pardon vagrants for petty crimes. Clearly, justifiable clemency is easier to imagine in faraway, classical times than in situations close to Elyot's own; and a lofty gesture of clemency suits the mythic, godlike stature of Caesar more than a humble English justice of the peace. A would-be Roman political assassin of good family differs from an English pilfering vagrant just as modern-day white-collar crime differs from blue-collar crime; lauding the pardon of the one while demanding the punishment of the other is justice based on class. In a chapter on humanity's "principal virtues," benevolence, beneficence, and liberality, Elyot draws on Aristotle and Cicero to underline the dangers of unwise benevolence, as he has just inveighed against unwise mercy: "Liberality, though it proceed of a free and gentle heart, . . . yet may it transgress the bonds of virtue, either in excessive rewards, or expenses, or else employing treasure . . . or other substance on persons unworthy" (2:90). Buttressing a culture of "decision by experts," Elyot both discourages casual gifts to beggars and undermines larger-scale philanthropy. Many Renaissance texts, drawing on Aristotle's *Nichomachean Ethics* and other classical writings on moderation (that mean between extremes), warn against excessive philanthropy, whose extreme is prodigality. Elyot's excursion into this topic dovetails neatly with his analysis of the causes of beggary—too much philanthropy comprises "excessive rewards, or expenses," a wasting of fortune that may reduce a giver to beggary. Humanist ethics, then, demand parsimony or at least great circumspection in giving, refusing handouts to "persons unworthy." (Elyot does not mention as a violation of Aristotelian moderation the contrary extreme of stinginess.) Here the discourse of deserving and undeserving poor shows its humanist philosophic underpinning, as the previous chapter of this study demonstrates its Protestant rationale: "Liberality (as Aristotle saith) is a measure, as well in giving as in taking of money and goods. And he is only liberal, which distributeth according to his substance, and where it is expedient. Therefore he ought to consider to whom he should give, how much, and when. . . . He that is liberal neglecteth not his substance or goods, nor giveth it to all men, but useth it so as he may continually help therewith other" (Elyot 2:113). He who gives and runs away lives to give another day—a doctrine of great conscience-saving potential.

Circumspection in philanthropy *was* an ancient notion that is visible in Aristotle and Cicero. But fear of impoverishment through generosity acquired fresh urgency in the Renaissance. The humanist move of blaming the poor for ruining their own fortunes by profligacy had the consequence of effacing social boundaries—the poor were not a permanent, fixed group but simply displaced persons who had slipped out of prosperity through moral weakness. This effacement caused logical problems for a conception of social order like Elyot's, which depended on God-given fixed social estates, some fit to rule and others fit to be ruled. The logical contradiction here is similar to the period's definition of sodomy as a potentiality, not an identity, and its simultaneous insistence on God-given heterosexual roles; the contradiction is also analogous to the period's essentialist insistence on fixed gender roles and its simultaneous belief that a woman could physically turn into a man through overexertion or that a man could metamorphose psychologically into a woman by engaging in transvestism. In each of these cases, insistence on the fixity and divine sanction of boundaries, in the face of anxiety over slippage across them, is not quite as illogical as it looks: anxiety over whether a heterosexual might slip into the ranks of sodomites, or a man into the status of a woman, or a humanist into the condition of a beggar, actually helps to *produce* essentialist pronouncements about the immutability of such boundaries.

The ever-present possibility that *anyone* might slip into that declassé underworld, a socioeconomic Fall of Man, was crucial psychologically; it helps account for the humanist preoccupation with beggary. One face of Renaissance social mobility was downward mobility. "Sir Christopher Heydon rose in wealth and prestige in Norfolk, enlarging his great house at Baconsthorpe and keeping eighty servants; but twenty years after his death his son had to mortgage the house to meet his debts. Some gentry fell to a point where they would no longer have been socially recognised by fellow-gentry, like 'John Cockeshutt, gent.', licensed as a drover in 1591. . . . Of 651 vagrants arrested in Salisbury between 1598 and 1638, 70 were accredited with trades, and had presumably failed in business and taken to begging" (Palliser 93). When one was surrounded by the visible poor, the prospect of a plunge into indigence produced anxiety: could excessive generosity to the poor reduce one to penury? Robert Copland conjures such a nightmare image in *The Highway to the Spital-house:*

> They that doth to other folks good deed,
> And hath themself of other folk more need,
> And quencheth the fire of another place,
> And leaveth his own, that is in worse case
> When that is brent [burned], and wotteth not where to lie,
> To the spital then must he needs hie. (16)

The philanthropist grown homeless is a recurrent literary figure. A variant of the man impoverished through profligacy—one of whose prototypes, the Prodigal Son, was a Renaissance favorite—appears in Shakespeare's *Timon of Athens* as the man impoverished through unwise generosity. King Lear's giving away his kingdom, an extreme case of such unwise generosity, occurs in a play whose reiterated instances of precipitous descent into the underworld manifest a widespread fear of slipping into indigence through no moral or ethical failure at all. Considering why the rich are greedy, More's Raphael Hythlodaye suggests that having poor people around gratifies in the rich a "pride which glories in putting down others by a superfluous display of possessions"; but an unfortunate consequence of too-highly-visible poverty is that the rich begin to fear impoverishment, and hence grow more greedy and less willing to practice generosity: "Fear of want . . . makes every living creature greedy and avaricious" (*Utopia* 42). So widespread was anxiety about sudden impoverishment that even the Earl of Shrewsbury, one of England's richest men and the owner of seven stately homes, suffered constant, near-pathological fear of losing his wealth (Ethel Carleton Williams 59). Harman shrewdly played on such fear of unwise generosity in dedicating *A Caveat* to the earl's wife, Bess of Hardwick. The fear that keeps surfacing in the Renaissance—that *anyone* might suddenly become poor, whether guilty of moral lapses or not—belies the official Christian humanist theory that poverty results from moral failure: at some level of consciousness, Renaissance thinkers must have found that theory unpersuasive. Since the very anxiety about loss of wealth harbors the germ of recognition that the poor are *not* responsible for their poverty, it is poignantly ironic that the response to that anxiety, sanctioned by educated thinkers, was to avoid giving money to the poor.

Elyot also juxtaposes punishment and giving in his chapter on justice, which he divides into two sorts, "distributive" and "corrective," anticipating the division of Poor Laws into poor relief and rogue-punishing sections. (Later, in semicrazed musings on kingly duties, King Lear would harp on corrective justice—with beadles, whipped whores, and caitiffs "unwhipped of justice" [3.2.53]—but he would also recognize his regime's inadequacy of distributive justice, specifically that producing homelessness [3.4.32–33].) Perhaps because he has already devoted substantial space in his book to such major issues as dancing lessons, Elyot comes up short of time and space to address corrective justice, which he defers for a later work (never written). And on distributive justice, too, he disappoints: *The Governor* is not the place to look for Lear-like recognitions of the social injustice of ill-distributed wealth. Elyot starts promisingly—"All men grant that justice is to give every man his own" (2:190)—and then makes as if to begin with giving God his due and working his way down: "the first and principle part of justice distributive is, and ever was, to do to god that honour which is due to his divine majesty" (2:189). After this "first" part, one expects a second section, probably a progression through the Great Chain of Being to angels and finally to human social strata, so predictable a Tudor trope that one is perplexed to find there *is* no second part: Elyot never goes beyond God. Completely eliding the effect on human beings of distributive justice is a conspicuous evasion, preserving (by turning a blind eye) the status quo regarding the nation's unequal distribution of wealth. That Elyot does not want to talk about this is in line with his keeping beggars and vagrants in the category of undeserving poor to whom only judges afflicted with "vain pity" would show mercy, and to whom circumspect moderate men need not give money. What Elyot casts as a matter for individual private citizens—the danger of impoverishment through excessive philanthropy—is a synecdoche for society as a whole: redistributing wealth to poorer groups would impoverish the richer.

Elyot did not ignore the claims of the underclass on the nation's wealth. *The Governor* begins with the specter of redistributed wealth. The book, he announces, is devoted to the "public weal," a term he prefers (as a rendering of *res publica*) to "common weal," since many think that "common weal" implies "that every thing should be to all men in common, without discrepancy of any estate or condition" (1:2). Indeed, he says, "commonweal" *should* logically mean a communist state, since "communaltie" means "the multitude," or "the base and vulgar inhabitants not advanced to any honour or dignity" (1:2), and therefore "if there should be a commonweal, either the commoners only must be wealthy, and the gentle and noble men needy and miserable, or else excluding gentility, all men must be of one degree and sort, and a new name provided" (1:3). This is not Elyot's ideal society. Immediately following is Elyot's famous exposition of order and degree ("Hath not [God] set degrees and estates in all his glorious works?" [1:4]); his insistence on the socioeconomic status quo sucks fervor out of a fear that the poor *might* assert a claim to the nation's wealth.

That Elyot *begins* with this issue suggests that his whole political project of order and degree was called forth by fear of social unrest and communism. His first chapter harps anxiously on the importance of degree to maintaining order, on the extreme foolishness of those who advocate leveling: "Without order may be nothing stable or permanent; and it may not be called order, except it do contain in it degrees, high and base. . . . God giveth not to every man like gifts . . . , but to some more, some less. . . . Nor they be not in common (as fantastical fools would have all things)" (1:5). Elyot and his wife studied with Sir Thomas More and were regular members of More's circle at Chelsea; was More's Raphael Hythlodaye, that enthusiast of utopian communism, one of the "fantastical fools" Elyot had in mind?

More's flirtation with communism was unusual for a man of his station; Elyot's staunch hierarchism was the mainstream. *The Governor* is the quintessential humanist document, with its reverence for classical authority, freight of classical exempla, cultivation of a moderate personality, devotion to responsible statecraft, belief in nationhood and civility, and faith in education. In the manner of Castiglione's *Courtier*, it addresses "the education of . . . the child of a gentleman, which is to have authority in the public weal" (1:28), in such essentials as prudence, providence, industry, circumspection, modesty, painting, reading, poetry, exercise, hunting, dancing, and longbow shooting. The popularity of this founding text of English humanism "eclipsed that of any other book of the same period, not excepting even the *Utopia*. So great was the demand that the printer could scarcely supply copies fast enough" (Croft lxx). *The Governor* was reprinted three times, under Elyot's personal supervision, and in fifty years eight editions were published. Its literary progeny included the anonymous *Institution of a Gentleman*, Lodowick Bryskett's *Discourse of Civil Life*, Henry Peacham's *Complete Gentleman*, and Roger Ascham's *Schoolmaster*.

Elyot's career was entwined with Henrician national politics: his work in the service of Anne Boleyn, and King Henry VIII's approval of *The Governor*, in all likelihood contributed to Elyot's being given an important emissarial post involving negotiations over Henry's divorce from Catherine of Aragon (Croft lxxi–lxxvi). He wrote during a formative period for both the

Reformation and humanism, which was also an age of poverty, crop failures, and threatened uprisings. Like other Tudor texts, *The Governor* scapegoats beggars, vagrants, and the "undeserving poor" and vibrates with anxiety about demands for redistribution of wealth. Elyot's vision of an England governed by an accomplished ruling class, which preserved hierarchical order by meting out heavy punishments and frugal financial rewards to the "commonalty," crystallized the attitudes of the educated and the powerful in those years, and various editions of the work transmitted these ideas intact into the Elizabethan age. If an aristocracy that can shoot longbows, write poetry, and dance is an essential component of Elyot's vision of England, so are the homeless, whose shadowy presence gives urgency to the rest of his program.

Thomas Starkey, *A Dialogue between Reginald Pole and Thomas Lupset*

Passionately devoted to establishing a just society governed by the humanist ideal of civility (see chap. 4), Thomas Starkey wrote seriously on political topics, advancing such dangerous ideas as replacing hereditary monarchy with elective leadership (an idea he prudently attributed to his former patron Pole). In *A Dialogue between Reginald Pole and Thomas Lupset* (ca. 1533–35), Starkey displays the usual disapproval of idleness: youths seek out the easiest craft, and a deplorable number wish to learn *no* craft (147). The realm is swollen with "idle and unprofitable persons" (79). Like John Awdeley, Starkey attributes vagrancy partly to the large number of dismissed or runaway servants,[2] and his solution is for the nobility not to keep so many servants— idle children aspire to be servants because it is easier than a trade. "Beggars lusty and strong, yea, and thieves also, should be but few or none at all . . . if this multitude of serving-men were plucked away" (160). Starkey, like Awdeley, is glimpsing obscurely a link between current social problems and the breakup of feudalism.

Starkey's advocacy of compulsory trade school reflects his humanist faith in education. Though humanists more typically fostered *classical* learning, Joan Thirsk describes experiments, between 1580 and 1630, in setting up trade schools in the countryside to reduce unemployment ("England's Provinces" 101–5) and also discusses artisanal training under the auspices of various local "projects" such as knitting and weaving of stockings (*Economic Policy*). Starkey advocates education in crafts: "Every man, under a certain pain [legal penalty for noncompliance], after he hath brought his childer to seven year of age, should set them forth either to letters or to a craft" (142).[3] But like Vives, he associates the poor with disease (see chap. 4). And detesting idleness leads him to advocate expelling the jobless from cities and towns, which (like his recommendation to turn out servants) can only increase the vagrancy he is trying to cure.[4]

The trades these writers had in mind were not suspicious mobile trades like tinker or pedlar but settled trades: an apprentice moved into his master's home, where articles of apprenticeship fixed him for five to seven years. The trade-bound apprentice was the runaway servant's polar opposite— immobility was valorized and mobility suspect.

Starkey is keenly aware of poverty: "We have here in our country . . . too many people; . . . vittle and nourishment sufficient for them can scant here be found, but for lack thereof many perish and die, or . . . live very wretchedly" (77). Starkey's "our country" reflects a new sense of nationhood being forged during his time. Starkey humanely urges clemency for those who commit crimes out of desperate need: "Our law . . . in the punishment of theft is over-strait, and faileth much from good civility. For with us, for every little theft a man is by and by hanged without mercy or pity—which, meseemeth, is again[st] nature and humanity, specially when they steal for necessity" (114). But he makes exception for one crime, and it is a crime of mobility: highway robbery should be "with most cruel death punished" (177).

Starkey, then, is another humanist deeply concerned about poverty and beggary, his faith in education potentially helpful, but who in some ways made matters worse: he misidentified the causes of unemployment, branded the jobless as idle, recommended their expulsion and sometimes execution, and identified the poor with disease. As Catharina Lis and Hugo Soly summarize, "Thomas Elyot, Richard Morison (who drew a connection between impoverishment and rebelliousness), Thomas Starkey and other intellectuals were unanimous in their verdict: idleness is an evil; forced labour was the essential requirement for maintenance of the common good" (86). Again and again such civic-minded writers evince concern over the problem of poverty, strenuously proposing solutions; but they are consistently harsh toward vagrants, whom they exempt from social programs.

Richard Halpern thinks the new humanist educational system helped produce "the ideological category of the *willful* poor, those who were 'captivated by a certain sweetness of inertia and idleness,' as Vives so delicately put it, and were therefore subject to the brutalities of the Tudor and Stuart poor laws" (94). This bore indirectly even on those who never attended school, as Halpern writes: "the schools helped create an ideological climate in which economic success and failure were understood through the categories of diligence and laziness, self-discipline and excess, talent and the lack of it. They thus provided a material and institutional support for the tendency to read structural upheavals and class struggles in terms of individualized, ethical differences" (94).

Starkey toys with the idea that God made the "impotent and poor" because "poverty exerciseth well the piteous minds of them which have enough, and putteth them in remembrance of the imbecility of man's nature," and "provoke[s] men to mercy and pity, and to . . . loving charity" (160). But this medieval sentiment is momentary, because Starkey otherwise insists on human dignity and the possibility of establishing a just civil society by human effort. Humanists did not want to be reminded of "the imbecility of man's nature," and the living example of the "impotent and poor" as evidence of human incapacity was no longer welcome. Michel Mollat argues that "with humanism, contempt for the poor took a subtle and perfidious turn, becoming disdainful and philosophical and—height of irony—invoking the dignity of man as justification. The social failure of poverty stood at the opposite extreme from personal self-fulfillment; to those who exalted success and *fortuna* it made no sense" (255). Discussing other humanists who condemned beggars—Lorenzo Valla, Robert Gaguin—Mollat concludes, "For the humanists, poverty was unworthy of man: in the words of Agrippa d'Aubigne, poverty 'makes men ridiculous'" (256).

Sir Thomas More, *Utopia*

Sir Thomas More affords a fine example of how poverty's ridiculousness, its destructiveness of human dignity, eroded the sympathy even of a writer highly sophisticated about poverty's complex causes. The spectacle of desperate poverty called forth the masterpiece of More's humanist period, *Utopia* (1516), the first half of which treats the issue. *Utopia* embraces the radical solution to economic inequality from which other humanists (Sir Thomas Elyot in 1531, Robert Crowley in 1550) recoiled: a thoroughgoing communism. It was precisely the economic mess early Tudor England was in that elicited this drastic solution. More's guide, Raphael Hythlodaye, begins by describing a conversation he once had with an Englishman of standard views about English thieves. Hythlodaye's Englishman "praise[d] the rigid execution of justice then being practiced upon thieves. They were being executed everywhere, he said, with as many as twenty at a time being hanged on a single gallows. . . . He could not understand how so many thieves sprang up everywhere, when so few of them escaped hanging" (9). Hythlodaye answered:

There is no need to wonder: this way of punishing thieves goes beyond the call of justice, and is not, in any case, for the public good. The penalty is too harsh in itself, yet it isn't an effective deterrent. Simple theft is not so great a crime that it ought to cost a man his head, yet no punishment however severe can withhold a man from robbery when he has no other way to eat. . . . Severe and terrible punishments are enacted against theft, when it would be much better to enable every man to earn his own living, instead of being driven to the awful necessity of stealing and then dying for it. (10)

The Englishman views vagrants as idle: "There are the trades and there is farming, by which men may make a living unless they choose deliberately to be rogues" (12).[5] Hythlodaye reminds him about disabled soldiers and dismissed retainers who, after being jobless, are unemployable: who will hire a vagrant? He then recalls those forced off land by sheep enclosures, who

cannot afford to wait for a buyer, [and so] they sell for a pittance all their household goods, which would not bring much in any case. When that little money is gone (and it's soon spent in wandering from place to place), what remains for them but to steal, and so be hanged—justly, you'd say!—or to wander and beg? And yet if they go tramping, they are jailed as sturdy beggars. They would be glad to work, but they can find no one who will hire them. There is no need for farm labor, in which they have been trained, when there is no land left to be plowed. . . . This enclosing has had the effect of raising the price of grain in many places. . . . The price of raw wool has risen so much that poor people who used to make cloth are no longer able to buy it, and so great numbers are forced from work to idleness. . . . The wool trade . . . is concentrated in few hands, . . . so rich, that the owners are never pressed to sell until they have a mind to, and that is only when they can get their price. . . . The high price of grain causes rich men to dismiss as many retainers as they can from their households; and what . . . can these men do, but rob or beg? And a man of courage is more likely to steal than to cringe. . . . Restrict the right of the rich to buy up anything and everything, and then to exercise a kind of monopoly. Let fewer people be brought up in idleness. (13–14)

Ignoring this remarkably sophisticated economic analysis,[6] the Englishman identifies beggars with mendicant clerics: "These are people I'm eager to get out of my sight, having been so often vexed with them and their woeful complaints"; he would "make a law sending all these beggars to Benedictine monasteries, where the men could become lay brothers, . . . and the women could be nuns" (18). When a friar joins in the discussion, the Englishman says, "you friars are the greatest vagabonds of all" (18).

Hythlodaye's views on the death penalty, like Thomas Starkey's, are enlightened: "It's altogether unjust to take away a man's life for the loss of someone's money. Nothing in the world that fortune can bestow is equal in value to a man's life" (14). He continues, "If theft carries the same penalty as murder, the thief will be encouraged to kill the victim whom otherwise he would only have robbed. When the punishment is the same, murder is safer, since one conceals both crimes by killing the witness" (15). But Utopia is not wholly utopian: Hythlodaye praises Utopians for having, instead of the death penalty, life imprisonment without parole—still a very harsh penalty for theft. And Hythlodaye's reassurance that "every year some are pardoned as a reward for their submissive behavior" (17) is bleak, accepting economic equality at the expense of political repression. Stephen Greenblatt finds that repeatedly in *Utopia,* "freedoms are heralded, only to shrink in the course of the description" (*Self-Fashioning* 40–41).

But Utopians are not driven to theft by need: because everyone works and everyone shares, everyone eats. Refreshingly, Hythlodaye blames England's economic problems on the idleness not of the poor but of the rich, who are "rapacious, wicked, and useless, while the poor are unassuming, modest men who work hard. . . . I am wholly convinced that unless private property is entirely done away with, there can be no fair or just distribution of goods, nor can mankind be happily governed" (28). *Utopia* closes by reasserting book 1's main theme:

> What kind of justice is it when a nobleman or a goldsmith or a moneylender . . . who makes his living by doing either nothing at all or something completely useless to the public, gets to live a life of luxury and grandeur? In the meantime, a laborer, a carter, a carpenter, or a farmer works so hard and so constantly that even a beast of burden would perish under the load; and this work of theirs is so necessary that no commonwealth could survive a year without it. Yet they earn so meager a living and lead such miserable lives that a beast of burden would really be better off. Beasts do not have to work every minute, and their food is not much worse; in fact they like it better. And, besides, they do not have to worry about their future. But workingmen not only have to sweat and suffer without present reward, but agonize over the prospect of a penniless old age. Their daily wage is inadequate even for their present needs, so there is no possible chance of their saving toward the future. (82)

One reason the early sixteenth-century economy was shaky was that over centuries of feudalism peasants could never afford technological improvements, and landlords who could afford improvements did not bother: "50 per cent or more of the gross output of servile peasants was creamed off, and . . . landlords on the average applied only 5 per cent of their incomes for productive purposes. . . . The nobility . . . squandered the vast bulk of the extorted surplus" (Lis and Soly 28). More is one of the few Renaissance writers to ascribe social evils to the irresponsibility of the *rich*. Furthermore, Hythlodaye insists that hunger is more a matter of distribution than of production: "Take a barren year of failed harvests, when many thousands of men have been carried off by hunger. If at the end of the famine the barns of the rich were searched, I dare say positively enough grain would be found in them to have saved the lives of all those who died from starvation and disease, if it had been divided equally among them. Nobody really need have suffered from a bad harvest at all" (83).

More's analysis is the most forward-looking treatment of poverty that this study has seen so far, ascribing poverty to complex social forces rather than simply to idleness. Where other writers attributed vagrancy to the running away of lazy servants, More writes, "the high price of grain causes rich men to dismiss as many retainers as they can from their households" (13). Utopia prevents unemployment through trade schools: "Each person is taught a particular trade . . . , such as wool-working, linen-making, masonry, metalwork, or carpentry" (36). Yet much in Utopia is harshly repressive, and even More makes an exception—as nearly everyone did—for outright beggars. England's idle drones do include "the rich, especially the landlords," but they also include "the sturdy and lusty beggars, who go about feigning some disease as an excuse for their idleness" (38). Here, suddenly, the victims of sheep enclosures, the brave poor eager to work if only they could find a job, disappear in favor of an easy stereotype of lazy beggars feigning disability to escape work—the literary stock-in-trade of writers from Erasmus to Harman. When phony disabled beggars and lazy friars enter the text, it is an eruption of a *comic* tradition, and when Hythlodaye's interlocutor calls the friar a vagabond and the friar takes umbrage, a cardinal counsels the fuming friar not to "set your wit against a fool's wit and try to spar with a professional jester" (18–19). It is a comic atmosphere that mediates the shift by which beggars lose Hythlodaye's sympathy. And again, by comic I do *not* mean insignificant: jesting could have grave consequences. If Renaissance laughter often seems heartless to us—the essence of merriment was to visit the madhouse to laugh at the insane or to watch whores being whipped—Renaissance notions of the comic were grounded in classical theory: Cicero drew upon Aristotle in defining the *ridiculus* as what was repugnant and deserving of ridicule, especially deformity and turpitude. Vagrants, regarded as both deformed (lame, blind, sore-ridden) and turpitudinous (lying, thieving, promiscuous), were obvious candidates for derisive laughter.

In humanism as well as the Reformation, then, the vagrant poor lost their claim on sympathy—a claim the settled poor continued to press with some success—because they were the butts of jokes or were perceived as belonging to a realm of tricksters rather than victims. More himself was a great joker. One of his jests was the pretense, abetted by several fellow humanists, that Utopia was a real place. Erasmus described More as having "something of the air of one who smiles easily, and (to speak frankly) disposed to be merry rather than serious or solemn, but without a hint of the fool or the buffoon" (letter to Ulrich von Hutten 17). Erasmus continues:

> From boyhood he has taken such pleasure in jesting that he might seem born for it, but in this he never goes as far as buffoonery, and he has never liked bitterness. In his youth he both wrote brief comedies and acted in them. Any remark with more wit in it than ordinary always gave him pleasure. . . . There is nothing in human life to which he cannot look for entertainment, even in most serious moments. If he has to do with educated and intelligent people, he enjoys their gifts; if they are ignorant and stupid, he is amused by their absurdity. (18–19)[7]

The jest book heroine Widow Edith is an ignorant and fairly stupid person (she does not always have the wit to cut and run even when her schemes are on the verge of exposure), and More's family certainly finds amusement in her absurdity, if Walter Smith's report (however fictionalized) is true to the spirit of the household. In the tenth of Smith's *Twelve Merry Jests of the Widow Edith*, set in More's Chelsea home, Edith is slipped a violent laxative that gives her chills, fever, and seismic belly rumblings. The whole household mirthfully conspires to keep her from leaving the chamber, until Mistress More takes pity on a fellow woman's sufferings and helps her excuse herself. Running desperately through the halls, Edith makes it only as far as the coalhouse, where she relieves herself with such a great "smoke" that a servant reports (to general household merriment) that the coalhouse is on fire. Edith is then stripped of her gown and sent to prison to sit in chains for three weeks, for the crime of pretending to be wealthy. This too is meant in a lighthearted, comic vein—when Edith gets out of jail she is "glad and merry" [sig. Fiiii]. If this does not seem a particularly humanist moment in English literature, one should recall the tenor of More's own wit. Though "jesting was the main object of his life," as Erasmus had claimed, and a Dutch writer once described More as being "every inch pure jest" (More, *Latin Epigrams* 187), it is harsh jest. As Joanna Lipking notes, More uses jests "to caricature and degrade. . . . His harsh humor reflects the rhetorical strategy of the Ciceronian orator" (360–62). G. R. Elton finds it disturbing that More's wit,

> which so enchanted his friends, nearly always had a sharp edge to it: he often, and knowingly, wounded his targets. We are told that his temper was exceptionally equable and his manner ever courteous; yet through nearly all his life

he displayed restlessly combative moods and in his controversies lost his tem-
per, dealing ruthless and often unfair blows. His famous merry tales pose some
manifest psychological problems. Is it not strange that when this man, who
created such a happy family life, wished to amuse he constantly resorted to strikingly antifeminist tales? I can recall no single story that shows a woman in a
favourable light; that world of parables is peopled by shrews and much-
oppressed males. ("Thomas More?" 197)

Elton interprets this according to More's own psychology; but combative and
cruel vulgarity was pretty much the flavor of Henrician wit. Edith's own wit
is vulgar (her gift to a suitor at More's house is a generous fart), and such
humor is at home in More's household and in contemporary comic pieces
such as Robert Copland's *Jill of Brentford's Testament*, where Jill wills her
beneficiaries one fart each. Jesting antifeminist tales were a staple in many
genres (see Woodbridge, *Women and the English Renaissance*). More retells a
favorite antifeminist jest, the one about the devil, the dumb wife, and the
aspen leaf, while refuting Reformation theology. Laughter, it is said, distances
one from emotion, and it is possible that laughter was one of the main cat-
alysts separating More from his early sympathies for the poor and helping
to bring on his later harsh, intolerant heretic-hunting phase. More had
thought deeply about poverty as a social issue,[8] and in *Utopia*, he wrote more
sensitively and intelligently about it than nearly anyone else in his day. But
as C. S. Lewis notes, "In the *Confutation* (1532) More had come to include
communism among the 'horrible heresies' of the Anabaptists and in the
Dialogue of Comfort he defends private riches" (169); *Utopia*'s idea of curing
poverty through communism was heard no more. Perhaps More had just
changed his mind, Lewis muses: "The times altered; and things that would
once have seemed to him permissible or even salutary audacities came to
seem to him dangerous" (167). Or, Lewis considers, seeing that "Erasmus
speaks of [*Utopia*] as if it were primarily a comic book," maybe in *Utopia*,
More was only joking (171).[9]

I cannot see all of *Utopia* as joking: too much passion animates the passages about the miseries of the poor and the irresponsibility of the rich. But
sharp-edged joking flares up at crucial moments, preparing readers for the
later, less tolerant More. The argument between the friar and the "professional jester" who says that friars are as bad as vagabonds, the inclusion among
society's drones of "sturdy and lusty beggars, who go about feigning some
disease as an excuse for their idleness"—moments like these, which solicit
conventional giggles at friars and vagabonds, are fissures through which beggars slip out of More's sympathies and into the untouchable underworld of
jest books. At exactly the time he published *Utopia*, 1516, More published a

jest book, *A Merry Jest How a Sergeant Would Learn to Be a Friar,* a slapstick romp of thwackings and buffetings precipitated by a young man's habit of running off (like Edith) without repaying borrowed money. I have argued that rogue literature's situating of vagrants in the world of jokes and tricksters has analogues in Reformation rhetoric about beggars and mendicants, which itself drew on comic traditions of jesting about friars and vagabonds. The writings of Erasmus and More show the idea of vagrants as jokey tricksters to have been alive in early Tudor humanism as well. Humanists as well as reformers regarded poverty as a serious problem; but for both, the *vagrant* poor were to be feared as wicked and despised as funny.

The very title *Utopia* is a kind of joke: *Eutopia* would have meant "a place where all is well," but *Utopia* means "no place." The pun perhaps glances at More's little hoax, pretending that Utopia was a real place, as if to give away the secret to those who knew their Greek. In a bleaker sense, "*Utopia*" acknowledges that the place where all is well, where nobody is poor or hungry, and where "place" in the sense of social status is unknown, is in fact nonexistent. "Eutopia" as "Utopia" is but a melancholy jest: More's brave new place is really no place.

Humanists and Jest Books

In 1593, surveying the shining lineage of English humanism from Sir John Cheke to Roger Ascham to Sir Philip Sidney to Edmund Spenser, heirs to ancient Rome and Athens, Gabriel Harvey grew enraged. These golden realms of canonical literature and high culture had now been invaded by the likes of Robert Greene and Thomas Nashe: "The Ciceronian may sleep, 'til the Scogginist hath played his part; one sure cony-catcher, worth twenty philosophers; . . . the less of Cambridge, or Oxford" (*Pierce's Supererogation* 17). The conflation of jest book ("Scogginist") and cony-catching pamphlet (Greene) shows yet again that jest books and rogue literature occupied the same mental space. But the dichotomy between Cicero and *Scoggin's Jests* is false: from early Tudor times, the loftiest humanists had savored *both* Cicero and jest books. Cicero was the major theorist of jest. Jest collections, or facetiae, formed part of the continental humanist program from the beginning. A Latin jest book composed by the father of Italian humanism, Petrarch, the *Rerum Memorandarum Libri* (Book of memorable things), included an elephant joke. A century later, an extensive jest book, *The Facetiae,*[10] was assembled by Poggio Bracciolini, whose career was foundational for European humanism: his travels to unearth long-neglected classical texts enabled a revolution in classical learning; his invitation of Chrysoloras to Florence from Constantinople established Greek studies in Italy, a crucial humanist development. When Poggio died in 1459, his jest collection was already famous; the first editions appeared about 1470, and with the coming of print some sixty editions of *The Facetiae* appeared over the next century, in Latin, Italian, and French (Lipking 112; see also Storer). The first Latin collection of Aesopian fables included eight of Poggio's jests, felicitously called *Schimpfreden Poggy* (Lipking 114); Caxton's *Aesop* included some of Poggio's jests too. Poggio inaugurated a craze among continental humanists for increasingly massive jest compilations, resulting in works by the Italians Antonio Beccadelli (Panormita), Piccolomini, Lodovico Carbone, Paolo Cortesi, Ludovico Domenichi, Piovano Arlotto, and Giovanni Pontano; by the Germans Heinrich Bebel, Sebastian Brant, Nicodemus Frischlin, Johann Gast, and Luscinius (Otmar Nachtgall or Nachtigall); and by the Belgian Adrian Barlandus (or von Baarland). Leonardo da Vinci jotted down jests among scientific, artistic, and literary observations in his notebooks. Erasmus's jest collection is a colloquy, "Convivium Fabulosum" (1524; Feast of fables), with jest-tellers named Polymythus ("teller of many tales"), Gelasinus ("laughter"), Eutrapelus ("witty"), Philythlus ("lover of nonsense"), Philogelos ("laughter-loving"), and Lerochares ("joker"). Again, these jokesters were serious humanists: Nachtgall wrote on theology, canon law, and music, published a Greek grammar, and promoted Greek studies; Barlandus was professor of eloquence at Louvain, and his jest book is "a work of humanist learning" (Lipking 144) complete with scholia "glossing the texts and citing parallels from other authors" (Lipking 149; see also Barbara C. Bowen).

Baldassare Castiglione, whose wit and urbanity dazzled the court of Henry VII when he visited in 1506, devoted the whole of book 2 of *The Courtier* to the topic of jesting, with many illustrative jokes; he clearly considered jesting second in importance only to the delineation of the ideal male courtier, which occupies book 1, and of more pre-eminence than the ideal female courtier, which waits until book 3. Since jests were essential to a courtier's conversation, and *The Courtier* is cast entirely as such conversation, all four books are peppered with jests. Castiglione drew on classical treatises, especially Cicero's *De Oratore*, as did the English rhetorician Thomas Wilson, who included a section on jest in his *Art of Rhetoric* (1553). As Lipking notes, "Poggio's successors apparently accepted his view of the *facetiae* as a continuation of classical tradition. Their prefaces . . . commonly cite ancient writers and philosophers" (115). Even the humble collection *Tarlton's News out of Purgatory* (1590) claimed kinship with "pleasant *facetiae*" (sig. A2ᵛ) and alluded to *De Oratore*.

Renaissance literati recommended jests as a useful item for orators and an essential aspect of a gentleman's conversation. Anticipating the *Reader's Digest* joke column "Laughter, the Best Medicine," the medical treatise *Mensa Philosophica* (ca. 1500) offered 241 jests to promote good health through relaxing the mind. Such rationalizations may suggest some qualms about the frivolity, vulgarity, or cruelty of these jests. Humanist jest books feature personnel who are socially superior to those in jest books not represented in humanist terms (legates and ambassadors rather than shoemakers and millers). But in individual jests, readers would be hard put to distinguish between the intellectual jesting of Poggio, Erasmus, or Castiglione and the jesting in collections usually dubbed "popular," such as the anonymous *Hundred Merry Tales* or "Till Eulenspiegel's" *Merry Jest of a Man That Was Called Howlglas.* Poggio's collection rejoices in a full complement of fart jokes, and Erasmus's, while less scatological than many, ends with a fart joke that identifies words issuing from the mouth with farts emitted from the anus—a choice between a man's two "faces" that recalls episodes in *Howlglas* and a theological tract by Henri Estienne (see above) and exists in a troubled relation to the humanist celebration of language. The compiler of *Tales and Quick Answers, Very Merry, and Pleasant to Read* retells a joke that was in Petrarch's collection and is classical in origin—it is first found in Macrobius, fifth century A.D. (see Barbara C. Bowen 21); of all English jest books, this is the most thoroughly influenced by continental facetiae: forty-five of its jests are from Poggio, and many others come from other continental collections; most of the "quick answers" come from Erasmus (Lipking 226–27).[11] A numskull tale that appears as jest 69 in the 1526 *A Hundred Merry Tales,* usually considered a humble popular work, had appeared two years earlier in the jest book of the German humanist Luscinius; and jest 60 was borrowed from *A Hundred Merry Tales,* by Thomas More, by the Reformation preacher Hugh Latimer, by the rhetorician Thomas Wilson, and by the polished Elizabethan courtier Sir John Harington—who also borrowed jests 11 and 58 (Lipking 342–50). *A Hundred Merry Tales* was printed by John Rastell, More's brother-in-law; and since tale 9 is borrowed from Rastell's *Nature of the Four Elements,* some think that Rastell actually wrote *A Hundred Merry Tales,* while others suspect More of being the author (Lipking 186–87). Thomas Berthelet, who published Elyot's *Book Named the Governor* in 1531 (and was to publish four more editions), the following year published *Tales and Quick Answers.* Renaissance jests confound notions of neatly demarcated social hierarchies: many such jests may strike us as "shit lit" (in several senses of the modifier); but jests—even crude belly laugh jests reveling in the lower bodily stratum (to use Bakhtin's phrase)—loomed large in the humanist project.

Poggio's jest book displays salient features of the genre. Some of his 270 jests have the flavor of folktales, while others feature characters of higher social standing—papal secretaries (Poggio's own profession), lawyers, generals. Over twenty feature lecherous monks and friars. Such jest book scurrility was later taken seriously as anti-Catholicism: Poggio's *Facetiae* was placed on the *Index Expurgatorius* in 1545 (Poggio 19), supporting my claim that comic anticlericalism was co-opted by the Reformation. Alongside recognizably modern jokes—short pieces with a comic punch line—Poggio includes wonder stories (a rain of blood, a cow giving birth to a dragon, a merman found on the coast of Dalmatia). While these tales may strike us as medieval,[12] other stories display a wry humanist skepticism. Tale 4 lampoons the pre-Reformation belief system that Marcel Mauss calls "economic theology."

> A Jew who had been urged . . . to embrace the Christian faith was not eager to part with his worldly goods. He was advised by many to give them to the poor, since, according to the Gospel, . . . he would be repaid a hundred times over. Convinced at last, he converted, and distributed all his possessions to the poor, the needy, and the mendicants. As a result, for a month, many Christians competed with each other for the privilege of showing him their hospitality. . . . But since he made a precarious living at best, he found himself in a state of perpetual anxiety, hoping for the promised hundred-fold return. Meanwhile, people grew weary of feeding him, and he became so impoverished that he fell ill with diarrhea. . . . He despaired of ever recovering either his health or the hundred-fold of his wealth. One day upon being forced by his discomfort to get some fresh air, he got out of bed and went to a nearby meadow to relieve himself. When he was finished, as he looked for some grass to wipe his bottom, he found a piece of linen rolled up and filled with precious gems. Having again become rich, he consulted a doctor, regained his health, bought a house and property, and lived from then on in the most gracious opulence. Then everyone said to him, "See, did we not tell you that God would repay you a hundred-fold?" "Absolutely," acknowledged the man. "He certainly has, but not before my turds had nearly bled me to death." (Poggio 27–28)

Here is another tale of impoverishment through excessive philanthropy, with affinities to several story groups—the loss of everything and the physical plagues recall the Job story; the fair-weather friends and fortune discovered in a field recall *Timon of Athens*. This story is one of many that Poggio seems to have drawn from exempla, comic anecdotes that spiced medieval sermons (Lipking 104). But the scatological interest in diarrhea and feces is pure jest book.[13] In a Bakhtinian uncrowning, the lower bodily stratum overwhelms the Christian ideal of generosity, exposing such ideals as rather absurd: only the absurdly literal-minded take in a material sense (the hundred-fold reward) what should refer to spiritual reward. The hypocrisy of Christians who counsel generosity and then desert a generous man in his need reflects adversely on their character and on the belief system itself. The tale is humanist, not in any belief in human dignity (which is conspicuously absent), but in its skeptical frame of mind, which surfaces again in the interestingly similar tale 86:

> There lived in Florence an enterprising ne'er-do-well who was very self-confident despite having no profession. After reading in a medical book the name and formula of certain pills that were good for a multitude of illnesses, he conceived the bizarre idea of impersonating a doctor, by the grace of these pills only. After having a large quantity of them compounded, he . . . wandered through villages and towns as a practicing physician. He prescribed the pills for all manner of sicknesses, and haphazardly achieved a few cures. After that the fool's name spread to other fools. One day someone who had lost his ass came and asked the fellow if he had a remedy for missing donkeys. The charlatan said "yes" and prescribed a dose of six pills. The next day, after following his instructions, the peasant set out to find his ass. But along the way the action of the pills forced him to seek immediate relief for his bowels, so dashing from the road into the bushes he accidentally came upon his missing ass grazing there. He praised the physician's art and pills to the heavens. After this peasants flocked to the latter day Aesculapius in droves, for they had heard that here was a doctor who even had a remedy for recovering lost property. (Poggio 84–85)

This member of the idle unemployed prefers charlatanism to honest labor—a familiar trope in the discourse of vagrancy—but the tale otherwise resembles that of the rich Jew: when a man goes into a field to attend to a bout of diarrhea, he accidentally recovers what was lost (the Jew's wealth, the fool's ass—or perhaps one should say donkey). Ignorant fools attribute recovery of property to a charlatan's bogus wisdom—just as common folk applied to village wizards for spells to recover missing property. Poggio's dry skepticism about this "cure" is at least protohumanist. But what is really interesting is the homology with the first story, where ignorant Christians attribute recovery of property to divine grace consequent on charity to the poor. The similarity of the tales invites us to equate quack medicine with sanctification through charity—both are a kind of scam. Poggio might believe in dragons and monsters, but he does not believe in folk medicine/magic or in "economic theology," and he debunks both by reducing them to the level of involuntary bowel movements. Scatology thus becomes a signifier of intellectual skepticism. Over the next several centuries, humanists would combat what they saw as superstition, both in religion (where intellectuals attacked "redemptive" almsgiving) and in protoscience (where intellectuals attacked folk magic and wizardry). Poggio's skepticism in these two tales embodies both intellectual currents, providing more testimony to the serious functions of jest.

The folklorist Lutz Röhrich, who sees the jest genre as rooted in "humanistic facetiae," argues that jest forms arise in magic-permeated folktales when magical belief is yielding to skepticism: "When the magical world loses its hold, jest flourishes and mixes with almost every other genre," including the jest-legend or jest-saint's legend (52). Jest operates "within an earthly realm without magic": in "The Boy Who Left Home to Find Out about the Shivers," the hero, "using his healthy, rational human intellect, laughs off an arsenal of . . . ghosts" (53). "Healthy, rational human intellect" was the stuff of the humanist project. If the tales of the rich Jew helped by divine grace and of the fool with his miracle-cure pills remind us in tone of Layton and Legh's letters to Cromwell, laughing at local beliefs in the curative powers of a saint's comb, that is because jesting belongs to the world of skepticism that drained magic out of both religion and medicine. In jest folktales, "although it seems miracles have occurred, only coincidence and trickery underlie the events" (such as the coincidence of finding the jewels or the ass, the trickery of the pills); "in jest and farcical tales, the belief in miracles benefits only the trickster who uses it to exploit and con backward people" (Röhrich 53). The jest book genre is exactly contemporary with humanism and the Reformation; all three manifest a skeptical, debunking spirit toward the worldview they are replacing.

Most of these jests were old: they came from Cicero, from medieval sermon exempla, from folktales. But it was Renaissance humanists who collected them, isolated them as a genre, printed them, theorized them with intellectual rationales. As Lipking writes, "In classical times, the joke had a subsidiary role within other traditions, not an independent life of its own. It is above all a Renaissance form" (14).

The Male Vagrant as Jest Book Hero: *A Merry Jest of a Man That Was Called Howlglas*

The first prose jest collection in English—apart from the clutch of Poggio's jests appended to Caxton's Aesop—was a translation of the German *Merry Jest of a Man That Was Called Howlglas* (ca. 1519), by the pseudonymous Till Eulenspiegel, whose surname means (as does Howlglas) "owl mirror." Like Poggio's charlatan pill-vendor, Howlglas for a time poses as a doctor. He plays an aromatic prank on another doctor, involving farting and a full chamber pot. Here again, scatology can be a signifier of intellectual skepticism. "How

Howlglas Made a Sick Child Shit That Afore Might Not Shit" (sig. Ciᵛ) exposes a seemingly miraculous cure as a charlatan's scam: Howlglas surreptitiously deposits a colossal turd of his own in the chamber pot of a desperately constipated child. Another episode from Howlglas's phony doctor phase
resembles tales exposing faked disability, like the "dumb" man Harman tor-
tures into speech, or the pretended cripple Simpcox in *2 Henry VI,* who spryly
runs away when whipped by a beadle, to bystanders' derisive cries of "A
miracle!" (2.1.150–56): Howlglas "cures" a hospital full of the sick by telling
them to run outdoors, since the last one out will be burned up to make a
powder to cure the rest (sig. Cii–Ciiᵛ). *Howlglas,* which to modern readers
has the feel of lowly popular culture, was related to the skeptical world of
humanism: the hospital jest is also in Poggio's *Facetiae* (tale 189), as are several other *Howlglas* episodes (Lipking 175).[14] In a popular jesting mode congenial to the debunking spirit of Erasmus and the relic-exposing reform tem-
per of Cromwell, Layton, and Legh, Howlglas manufactures a phony relic out
of a dead man's head and dupes people into making great offerings, which
he pockets. He also debunks superstitious behavior such as wizards selling
concoctions to aid prophecy: still rejoicing in scatological humor (in a tale
resembling Poggio's tale 165), he puts figs up his anus to coat them with excrement, lets them sit several days, and crushes them for musk, claiming that
whoever has them in his mouth will prophesy. Some Jewish merchants buy
this at vast expense to learn when the Messiah will come; when they taste the
foul figs, they know they have been tricked, and Howlglas hastily leaves town.

Our cheerfully blasphemous hero routinely makes a mockery of the
church's solemn rites. In one jest, Howlglas plots to get a parson's fancy horse.
Feigning illness like a good vagrant, he gets the parson to administer last rites,
and during confession he claims to have slept with the parson's maid. When
the parson beats the maid black and blue, Howlglas laughs heartily, then
blackmails the parson out of his horse by threatening to tell the bishop that
the parson has violated the confidentiality of confession. A trick on a wine-
drawer includes a blasphemous parody of episodes from Christ's life: Howlglas inverts a miracle by exchanging wine for water and saves his neck by a
blasphemous trick turning on what will happen to his corpse three days after his death—it has to do not with resurrection but with the kissing of
Howlglas's posterior. When Howlglas *is* dying, he confesses to only two re-
grets: that "when I saw a man pick his teeth with his knife, that I had not
shitten on the end of it" and "that I did not drive a wooden wedge in all
women's arses that were above 50 years, for they be neither cleanly nor
profitable"—old women are always shitting on the ground (sig. [L4]ᵛ). His
confessor, a nun of about fifty, takes umbrage. A priest angling for money

promises to say masses for Howlglas; Howlglas palms off on him a pot of turds with coins on top; plunging his hand in, the priest reaps the fetid reward of his cupidity.

To the late medieval world that lies behind *Howlglas*, the deathbed was the site of a crucial drama: as Eamon Duffy shows, countless treatises and popular block-books on the art of dying "portrayed the deathbed as the centre of an epic struggle for the soul of the Christian, in which the Devil bent all his strength to turn the soul from Christ and His cross to self-loathing or self-reliance. Against these temptations the cross and the armies of the redeemed were marshalled to assist the dying Christian. The bedroom became a crowded battlefield centred on the last agonies of the man or woman in the bed" (317). What then are readers to make of Howlglas's cheerful disregard of last rites, his impudent and scatological "confession" on his very deathbed? Far from suffering "last agonies," Howlglas goes out laughing, making silly jokes with his mother, playing one last practical joke (with the pot of turds), and even arranging—by leaving behind a chest that turns out to be full of stones—for another practical joke to be played after his demise. So much for epic struggles for the Christian soul. The devil hasn't bothered turning up for this one, and even if he had, it would take a better man than Satan to induce self-loathing in Howlglas. The armies of the redeemed are reduced to Howlglas's mother (who has not seen him since childhood but shows up in hope of getting some money out of him), the nun (who lets a personal affront distract her from the holy duty of ministering to the dying), and the priest, so greedy for cash he will promise any number of posthumous prayers, grasp any amount of potted excrement. This skeptical, antiritualist, anticlerical stance occurs not in the work of a Protestant reformer or a reason-venerating humanist but in a jest book.

Throughout, the lecherous, greedy clergy play practical jokes, wager, and are nearly as scatological as Howlglas. When Howlglas signs on as assistant to a priest who keeps a mistress, he farts in church and calls it frankincense, betting the priest that he will not relieve himself in the middle of the church. The priest deposits a large mound in the center aisle, but Howlglas wins the bet by measuring—the turd is not exactly in the church's center. In one jest a bishop, who loves Howlglas for making him laugh, asks him to "do some merry jest" (sig. Hiii); Howlglas wagers that he can get a market woman to break all her pots. Secretly buying the pots, he arranges for her to break them upon a signal; the bishop pays up. When Howlglas reveals the trick, the bishop uses it to win a large wager with some noblemen. Howlglas blackmails the bishop, threatening to reveal the trick; after he gets the money he reveals it anyway. The noblemen decide they cannot do anything because the trickster is a bishop. The anticlerical Howlglas finally becomes an abbey-wrecker. As in Johan Splinter's *Merry Jest and a True How Johan Splinter Made his Testament* (1520[?]), Howlglas gets an abbot, known as a "merry jester" (sig. Kiii^v– Li), to let him spend his old age in the abbey if he leaves them his money. Howlglas soon gets on the abbot's nerves, and when he (rightly) suspects that the abbot is about to turn him out, Howlglas breaks down the stairs. The monks fall into space on their way to matins, one old monk breaking his leg, to Howlglas's hilarity.

Howlglas, popular in England throughout the sixteenth century, jibes with humanism in its skepticism and with the Reformation in its anticlericalism. But it was recognized in its own time as belonging to the discourse of vagrancy; Martin Luther, for example, objected to tales of Till Eulenspiegel and the Parson of Kalenberg on grounds that they glorified roguery (Clemen 23). The first six jests date to Howlglas's youth; during the seventh, he leaves home and never has a fixed abode thereafter: for the rest of the forty-odd episodes, he is on the road, often staying in inns (like real Renaissance vagrants), where he devises various means of beating the check. In the seventeenth jest he cheats an innkeeper out of a big meal by a quibble on words. In the thirty-first Howlglas tricks an innkeeper into providing a big feed for some blind men on the road, returning from a dole at a rich man's funeral. In the thirty-second he plays a practical joke on a mocking, boasting innkeeper. In the thirty-third he gets out of half his bill by skinning the pet bloodhound of the hostess; and since this enrages her, in the thirty-fourth he takes revenge for her unfriendly attitude by picking her up naked out of bed when she is asleep and putting her bare bottom on hot coals he has spread on the floor, so that she is "well burned" (sig. Kii^v), great cause for mirth. At another inn he slips a "strong purgative" ("powder of ginger") to a fellow guest who has laughed at him; the victim vomits so extremely that other guests think he might die; but when Howlglas confesses what he has done, "the guests made good cheer and laughed" (sig. Kiii). This practical joke, a gross reminder of the victim's bodiliness, resembles the one played on Widow Edith—a powerful purgative is slipped to her, too, also in a powder, to general hilarity.

Howlglas is not only a trickster, he is (like Widow Edith) a trickster perpetually on the road. The twenty-eighth jest specifically identifies Howlglas as a vagabond: "At Lunenberg dwelled a flute maker that knew vagabonds by sight. And on a time it fortuned him to spy Howlglas" (sig. [H4]). In the twenty-fifth Howlglas steals wine as a prank and a challenge, since the wine-drawer has boasted of being uncheatable. But this time Howlglas gets caught and imprisoned. Some say he should hang as a thief; others declare that it was only a jest. Sentenced to death, Howlglas asks the city fathers to grant him a boon, a confluence of the world of folktale boons with the grim world where vagrants are sentenced to death for petty theft. The boon, granted on condition that he not ask for a pardon, turns out to be that the city fathers will kiss Howlglas's ass after he has hanged on the gallows for three days. Dubbing this an "unmannerly boon," the city fathers let him off. This episode, like many, ends with Howlglas hitting the road and not looking back.

The tale of how Howlglas became a vagrant is deep-dyed in common conceptions of the idle, irresponsible vagrant character. After his father's death, despite the urgings of his impoverished mother, "he would go to no craft" (sig. Aiii). Unable to face a settled lifetime of hard work, Howlglas marvels that anyone could choose a career that would "abide by him all his life" (sig. Aiii). (One is reminded of Prince Hal's appalled contemplation of the life prospects of Francis, whose very apprenticeship as a wine-drawer sounds numbingly long: "Five year! by 'r lady, a long lease for the clinking of pewter" [*1H4* 2.4.45–46].) Instead, Howlglas gets bread by tricking the baker. His willingness to live by trickery because he does not want to learn a trade is typical of the folk trickster figure and of jest collections organized as "biographies," where, as Harold V. Routh puts it, "contempt for the routine of daily life is unmistakable" (105). In Matheo Aleman's *Rogue; or, The Life of Guzman de Alfarache,* the Spanish rogue praises the sweetness of the beggar's "roguish life" compared with that of a skilled tradesman: "What a fine kind of life was it, what a dainty and delicate thing, without thimble, thread, or needle; without pincers, hammer, or wimble, or any other mechanical instrument whatsoever" (1:253–54). The convention plays into stereotypes about vagrants, stereotypes fostered in part, as Patricia Fumerton argues, by contemporary misconstruing as idle vagrancy of new labor patterns involving frequent job-switching rather than settled apprenticeship followed by life-long practice of a single trade.

Howlglas's embarkation on a life of vagrancy is a masterpiece of feckless dependence on contingency. At the crucial moment, he happens to be sleeping off a drunk in an empty beehive. It is an odd billet, but hives were rich in symbolism—bees' industriousness, their devotion to home and community effort, made them a symbol for the effective society that grew more and more congenial to prevailing ideologies as the Renaissance progressed. Howlglas's usurpation of this strangely empty hive highlights his hostility to all that bees represent: he is idle rather than industrious (they make honey, he sleeps); he has so little devotion to home that he is about to leave forever as a result of a mere accident; and—as appears in his treatment of fellow humans—he is no upholder of the ideal of community. Thomas Starkey might almost have been thinking of Howlglas snoring in his beehive when he penned his harsh prescription for those who refuse to learn a trade: "If any man ha[ve] no craft at all, but, delighting in idleness, as a drone bee doth in a hive, sucketh up the honey, . . . he should be banished and driven out of the city, as a person unprofitable to all good civility" (142). At any rate, two thieves choose this moment to steal the beehive, carting Howlglas away with it: Howlglas starts his career as a vagrant trickster by being himself stolen into involuntary vagabondage. With a folktale trickster's resourcefulness, he capitalizes on accident—from the hive, he pulls the hair of each thief, and when they start fighting, each thinking the other is pulling his hair, Howlglas escapes and begins life on the road. This launching of his career embodies that mélange of predisposition and contingency seen in other accounts of vagrancy, wherein idleness is also a prominent character trait: throughout his career, Howlglas is figuring out "some practice to get money without labor" (sig. [E4]ᵛ), since he "would ever fare [i.e., dine] well, and make good cheer [i.e., have plenty of good food], but he would not work" (sig. [H4ᵛ]).

Howlglas often engages in trickery for practical vagrants' reasons: to get food, clothing, or money. In one jest, he tricks a woman out of a chicken, which he devours. In another, he cheats a man out of cloth, with which he and two accomplices clothe themselves against winter. In another, he sells a horse that he has tricked a parson out of. In another, he turns his scatological bent to account by selling as tallow twelve barrels of turds thinly topped with tallow. But often he tricks tradesmen less for practical gain than, seemingly, out of ingrained opposition to their settled life, which has repelled him since his mother first suggested he try it. He plays the tallow trick on a shoemaker. The flutemaker who recognizes Howlglas as a vagabond deliberately violates hospitality, inviting him to dinner and then locking the house before he arrives: Howlglas takes revenge by luring the wife away, locking himself in the house, and eating all the food—thus depicting the house invasion by vagrants so feared in texts like Harman's *Caveat*.

Like the real-life runaway apprentice Richard Fletcher, who repeatedly averred (as attested in the court record) "I will never serve him" (Fumerton), Howlglas sets his face against his masters. In many jests, he signs on as an assistant to a tradesperson—baker, blacksmith, shoemaker. Fired speedily, usually for making a deliberate mess of his work, he hits the road again. Writers of Awdeley's generation often attributed vagrancy to the idleness of useless servants who quit their jobs to go on the road; one section of the *Fraternity of Vagabonds*, "The 25 Orders of Knaves," is a comic description of lazy, tricksy servants. Howlglas, who when lodging with an apothecary defecates all over his chamber and into twelve boxes of medicine, resembles Awdeley's "Chafe Litter," who "piss[es] in the bedstraw" and "berayeth many

times in the corners of his master's chamber, or other places inconvenient"
(13). Howlglas, blowing the dinner horn at the wrong time so he can steal the
meat, resembles Awdeley's "Rinse Pitcher," always swilling his master's drink
and eating his meat. Howlglas's smart answers and maddening literal-mindedness about instructions ally him with Awdeley's "Chop Logic," who "when
his master rebuke him of his fault he will give him 20 words for one" (13).
Hired as a servant or an assistant, Howlglas is soon fired because he "serves"
his master with some practical joke: to "serve" of course meant to "play a joke
on" as well as "to render service." Servants were considered part of the family, and the decamping of a servant or apprentice could have the same emotional force as if a child of the family ran away, a blow against home and family
values. In his repeated opposition to the world of settled, respectable tradesmen, Howlglas appears less as an unemployed man with practical motives
than as a spirit of opposition to cherished middle-class values.[15]

The continued popularity of *Howlglas* through the sixteenth century suggests disaffection with such values, as if not everybody cherished them. Was
there something stultifying about the code of respectability, the insistence on
homekeeping, sobriety, and piety, the relentless parish-by-parish organization of bureaucratic rules, regulations, and enforcing officers? Did such suffocating good citizenship prompt even the sincerest citizen secretly to admire
Howlglas's unrespectable freedom? Did an overdose of family values make
the respectable long secretly for Howlglas's homelessness? This study's conclusion will take up the phenomenon of idealized vagrancy, the depiction of
beggars' lives as merry because free of society's constraints. Texts of that
subdiscourse sometimes idealize beggary as an escape from the tradesman's
settled life; for example, John Taylor's "Praise, Antiquity, and Commodity of
Beggary, Beggars, and Begging" (1621) glorifies the beggar in part because—
like Howlglas—he "neglect[s] all trades, all occupations, / All functions,
mysteries, arts, and corporations" (98).

Despite the real place names (Bremen, Lubeck), Howlglas is more folktale
trickster than realistic character. As Max Lüthi notes, the European folktale
hero leaves home on a quest, never to return (*Fairytale as an Art Form* 136);
Howlglas, who lives with his poor old mother, like Jack and the Beanstalk,
sets off like many a folktale protagonist to find his fortune. In some ways he
resembles supernatural tricksters like the Native American Coyote, transcending human laws in grand amorality. But one might apply Röhrich's distinction between the moral worlds of true folktales and parodic folktales, which
he calls jests or farcical tales: where traditional folktale heroes win out by
being brave, generous, and good-hearted, "parody . . . alters the folktale's
ethics: only the farcical tale unquestioningly approves of laziness" (53), as does

Howlglas. The jest tale is, in Bakhtin's terms, a "parodic/travestying double" (*Dialogic* 21–22) of the classic folktale. Howlglas is not brave or generous, and he has anything but a good heart. In his day folktales were decaying into parody, because naïve faith in good hearts and magical helpers was bleaching out under the harsh glare of humanist and Reformation rationalism.

Though nonparodic folktales no doubt persisted in oral tradition, *Howlglas* is a text of literacy. It deals with a lower social register than Poggio's jest book, whose noblemen and generals contrast with *Howlglas*'s shoemakers and bakers, but the extant version of *Howlglas* (a compilation of well-worn tales) is the work of someone not only literate but with at least a smattering of education: the thirty-ninth tale is a dispute in verse between Howlglas and a scholar, concerning Venus, Mars, and Bacchus. The genre that *Howlglas* represents parodically assails the naïvete of folktale. Intellectually skeptical, it anticipates the assault by humanists and religious reformers on folk beliefs ranging from village magic to relic veneration. But it is internally conflicted: while the work exposes the simplicity of the folktale mentality, the tales also encode the shrewd skepticism of the folk toward the values of their moralizing tradesmen-masters, and the skeptical figure at the text's center, who unmasks an innkeeper's pomposity or a priest's greed, is himself a hero of the people.

An enthusiast of mooning, Howlglas exposes his bare buttocks to the townsfolk (third jest) and one of his employers, a baker (thirteenth jest). As an insolent gesture, mooning is a milder form of defecating in an employer's mustard pot (seventh jest). Like such defiant defecations, the baring of Howlglas's backside outrages the propriety of the settled, respectable citizenry. Mooning turns the tables on stripping—of a beggar or a prostitute—as a punitive humiliation. Stripping exposes (to the punishing gaze of decently clothed citizens) the naked skin of a vulnerable wretch about to be whipped, a trenchant reminder of the helpless physicality of the powerless. It makes them seem like animals in contrast to the smug intellectuality or spirituality of onlookers safely ensconced in their clothing. But mooning thumbs its nose at onlookers, shifting the shame and embarrassment from the naked person to the observers. Like mirrors as amulets against the evil eye, mooning reflects the shaming gaze back on the voyeur. Its exposure of "shameful" anatomical parts indicts the gazer of the prurient voyeurism that must often have actuated public rituals of humiliation involving stripping. Mooning makes the observer complicit in an exposure of humankind's animal nature. Just as, in Poggio's jest book, scatology becomes a signifier of intellectual skepticism and the debunking of religious superstition, so mooning and farting can be gestures not only of resistance to authority but also of desacralization.

R. W. Scribner discusses an antipapal woodcut of the German Reformation in which "two peasants bare their bottoms and fart at the pope, who is holding out a papal bull of condemnation, identified as such by the fire and brimstone it is emitting. The emission of the bull is thus answered by the emission of wind" (82). As Scribner notes, to treat "objects, persons and actions held to represent the divine order of things in such a manner could vividly demonstrate that they were without supernatural power. The material bodily principle was thus used to desacralise the numinous and withdraw it from the realm of religious veneration. It found expression in polemical literature in injunctions to use indulgences for lavatory paper" (82–83).

Howlglas's use of language against the respectable world is a kind of verbal mooning. Many of his pranks depend on absurd literal-mindedness. Hired by a shoemaker, he is told to cut leather to suit a swineherd, and cuts it to fit a swine's feet. Directed by a tailor to sew a seam so that no one can see it, he sews under a barrel—taking "no one can see the seam" to mean "no one can see you sewing." Told to make a gown called a "wolf," he creates a kind of stuffed animal toy with a wolf's paws and ears (sig. Giii). Ordered to "cast on" sleeves, he throws sleeves at the shirt all night, waiting for them to stick. It is never quite clear whether Howlglas is a folktale numskull or is deliberately forcing his masters to confront the ambiguity of their instructions. Stith Thompson's *Motif-Index of Folk-Literature* lists under the category *"literal fools"* such subcategories as *"disastrous following of misunderstood instructions"* (J2460.1), *"literal following of instructions about actions"* (J2461.1), *"literal numskull throws water on roasting pig"* (J2461.3). Folktales do not always make clear whether disastrous literal-mindedness is owing to stupidity or malice, as in an ambiguous category like *"directions followed literally to the sorrow of the giver"* (J2516). Sometimes the misconstruing is clearly deliberate, as in *"literal misconstruction of order, hero gets revenge"* (J2516.0.1). Considering his hostility to tradesmen, Howlglas's absurd misunderstandings could be read as passive resistance. They resemble familiar stories of military life, such as that of the officer leading a group of enlisted men: they march forward while he moves backward for the sake of issuing orders; when he forgets that directions must be reversed and orders them to turn left when he means right, they literal-mindedly turn left and march off the pier into the harbor. They know he meant "right"; their action makes manifest their duty to obey any order no matter how absurd and subverts the authority of the officer, displaying his mistake to the world. Like many jests, it has its serious point: in desperate war situations as well as harmless exercises, officers' mistakes are writ large on the bodies of their men. This is the kind of resistance Howlglas may be practicing, saying, in a way that costs his employer money by ruining materials, If you're smart enough to be my boss and make more money than I do, you should be smart enough to make instructions crystal clear, or you'll suffer the consequences.

Howlglas's misconstruings are literal-minded insofar as, for example, "casting on" as a sewing term metaphorically extends "casting" as throwing. (Under *"literal fools,"* Thompson's *Motif-Index of Folk-Literature* has a large subcategory on *"metaphors literally interpreted"* [J2470].) Howlglas's misunderstandings resemble what reformers said happened when people worshiped a statue of the Virgin Mary rather than using it simply as a memorial device to evoke biblical episodes or moral values. Image worship involved extreme literalism: in magically venerating an elevated crucifix, one worshiped the signifier (a material object) rather than the signified (Christ, now invisible in heaven). In not making the mental leap from casting as throwing to casting as sewing, Howlglas resembles literal-minded folk who worshiped the image rather than its spiritual signification. In throwing sleeves at a garment in the hope that they will stick, Howlglas enacts a malapropism, and more precisely than being a literal/metaphoric confusion, his mistakes involve taking a word's primary definition rather than its specialized extension. He nearly always construes a word by its default meaning—the meaning now listed first in the *Oxford English Dictionary*. For example, the *OED*'s first meaning for "cast" as a verb is "the simple action: to throw." So specialized is "casting on" as a sewing term that it appears as meaning 80. The *OED*'s first meaning for the noun "wolf" is "a somewhat large canine animal"; as a garment, "wolf" is so specialized that it has escaped the *OED*'s notice altogether. Howlglas adopts as a word's correct meaning what is now (and was probably then) its primary dictionary meaning; he ignores what his boss has in mind, the meaning specialized to the trade at hand. Howlglas's language is that of the unskilled laborer with no notion of the specialized argot of various trades and with no intention of learning it: he is, after all, utterly opposed to acquiring a trade. By enacting malapropisms, he is saying to his bosses, "I cannot be part of your world because I do not speak your language."

The malapropisms of this early text differ from those of high Renaissance texts, where Latin was often misunderstood as English, or some intellectual term was misunderstood as involving the lower bodily stratum. In Nicholas Udall's *Respublica,* a clown hears *respublica* as "rice pudding cake"; in Shakespeare's *Love's Labor's Lost,* a clown hears *ad unguem* as "ad dunghill" (5.1.73–75). As English overwhelms Latin, the lower body associations of puddings and dunghills overwhelm the intellectual meanings of *respublica,* a political entity, and *ad unguem,* a phrase from a scholastic exercise. Clowns' exuberant liberties with language puncture the stuffy pedantries of intellectuals like Holofernes, whose very objection to the clown's malapropisms, "I smell false Latin" (5.1.76) is couched in the language of the senses. In a classic of Renaissance malapropism, Mrs. Quickly's clown-like role in *The Merry Wives of Windsor*'s Latin lesson, *hic, haec, hoc* becomes "'hang-hog' is Latin for bacon" (4.1.38–44), and "genitive,—horum, harum, horum" provokes "vengeance of Jenny's case! Fie on her! Never name her, child, if she be a whore" (4.1.57–58). Though he often behaves like clowns in plays, Howlglas's misconstruings do not involve Latin; they embody tensions not between educated and uneducated but between skilled and unskilled. But they still assert physicality in their blurring of the line between animal and human: Howlglas makes shoes for swine; in place of a garment, he makes a wolf. Humanists like Pico della Mirandola defined humanity against those on the next lower rung on the ladder of being, animals, whom they also identified with the body while identifying humanity with the intellect. Howlglas, with his excretion jests and malapropisms turning people into animals, parodically uncrowns humanistic pretensions, just as he punctures the spiritual pretensions of the religious by his refusal to repent, his cheeky blasphemies, and his evading church rites as handily as he escapes work and settled life.

What looks like a simple, notably crude jest book, then, proves on closer inspection to be a slippery, conflicted text. Though *Howlglas* anticipates reform theology in its comic assaults on clerical lechery, greed, levity, and hypocrisy, Howlglas's literal-mindedness brings him close to the image worshiping mentality that reformers tried to stamp out. The Protestant urge that desacralized the pope and the Catholic clergy also desacralized poverty, and while Howlglas is an anticlerical force, he is also a poor man whose desacralizing gestures therefore rebound upon himself. The skepticism about the hospital full of people apparently feigning illness jibes with the humanist stance on beggary, and the parodic deidealization of the folktale hero bespeaks a skeptical, rational, humanistic stance; yet the text stridently refuses any belief in the dignity of man, and its hero routinely blurs the line between man and animal. *Howlglas* seems to side with lower-class people by glorifying the truculent trickiness of its vagrant hero; but the alternatives the text offers—its hero is either a numskull or dangerously malicious—do not promote tolerance for the lower orders.

"In true numskull tales," says Röhrich, "the dumb hero changes or proves that, contrary to what others think, he is actually not dumb at all. In the farcical tale he *remains* dumb even if he is as successful" (53). Howlglas neither changes nor proves that he is not dumb; the text is ambiguous about whether he is a clever trickster or a stupid numskull. In drama, witty clowns make

puns while stupid clowns (unaware that they are funny) commit malapropisms. But do such distinctions apply here? *Do* Howlglas's misconstruings
comprise resistance? Are his malapropisms deliberate? The text calls him "the
great deceiver" (sig. [E4]), suggesting active intelligence, or a "mocker" (sig.
F and passim), suggesting a satiric spirit. Still, all night is a long time to stand
throwing sleeves at a shirt for the sake of a jest. *Is* he just a numskull?

Howlglas means "owl mirror," and the owl holding a mirror on his tombstone embodies the ambiguity about his intelligence. The owl, sacred to Ath-
ena, was associated with wisdom, but was also a loner, a predator, and an
omen of bad luck. Howlglas is a loner and a predator whose appearance bodes
ill luck to many a tradesman. The owl on his tombstone grips with claws, but
rather than tearing apart a prey she uses the claws like hands to grip a human artifact, a mirror. To whom does she hold up her glass, and what is
reflected? Does she gaze into it herself, a wise and canny hero admiring her
own wit, as Howlglas rejoices in his trickery? Or does she hold it up to the
world, as the satirist holds up his "glass" in works like George Gascoigne's
Steel Glass, so that the world (and the reader) may behold not a wise owl but
a grinning face in a fool's cap, as when the Prince of Arragon in Shakespeare's
Merchant of Venice finds in a casket "the portrait of a blinking idiot, . . . a
fool's head" (2.9.54–59). Is Howlglas himself a mirror for owls, for the wise,
as proverbially the fool was a touchstone to the wise? And then what is a fool?

The fifteenth jest identifies Howlglas with court jesters, as he engages in a
jesting contest with a king's prized jester, an episode anticipating the com-
petitive fooling between two jesters in *Twelfth Night.* Shakespeare uses the
word "fool" for both types of clown—genial idiots like Dogberry or Bottom,
unwittingly employing malapropisms, and consciously witty, intelligent pun-
crafters like Touchstone or Feste. The latter category comprises mostly professional jesters, while the former includes servants, constables, and tradesmen. Yet early modern courts sometimes kept retarded people as court fools,
laughing at them for entertainment, and to some extent the enabling fiction
of the professional court jester is that he *is* mentally deficient, his "fool's license" granted on the understanding that one cannot be accountable for
offensive utterances if he does not know what he is saying. A confusion between wit and butt, jester and mental deficient, was built into the concept of
professional jester. In *As You Like It,* where Touchstone is clearly a professional
court jester in full possession of his wits, Jaques still marvels at Touchstone's
jokes as if he were basically a mental deficient: "He's as good at anything and
yet a fool" (5.4.103–4). Duke Senior has to explain the way that fool's license
works: "He uses his folly like a stalking-horse and under the presentation of
that he shoots his wit" (5.4.105–6). Falstaff, whose complex heritage includes

the clown figure, sees himself as both wit and butt, making fools of others and being made a fool of himself: "I am not only witty in myself, but the cause that wit is in other men" (*2H4* 1.2.9–10). The riddling utterances of Lear's fool are ambiguous—shrewd comments, daft ravings, or something of both? Kent muses, "This is not altogether fool, my lord" (1.4.149). Jest book heroes share jesters' ambiguous status—are they tricksters or numskulls? Elder Olson tries to distinguish between the "lout-comic," featuring characters who, though good natured, are "mad, eccentric, imprudent, or stupid" and the "rogue-comic, with characters "clever but morally deficient" (555). But with Renaissance jest book heroes, this distinction cannot be sustained. In the tale "How Scoggin and His Wife Made an Heir," the eponymous hero of *The Jests of Scoggin* confuses naming an heir with making an heir through copulation, confuses copulation with farting by confounding "heir" with "air," and so forth. The tale entertains both numskull and trickster explanations: "The mis-hearing of a tale maketh misunderstanding. Therefore plain speech is best, although Scoggin knew what was spoken, and turned it to a jest" (94). In a textual world in which we cannot disentangle doltish misunderstanding from self-aware jesting, the term "plain speech" lacks all meaning.

The same ambiguity haunts vagrancy texts. The Middle Ages sometimes identified fools with vagabonds—the Fool in the Tarot deck carries a pack on a stick. It is a useful ambiguity. Not to resolve the question of whether vagrants are stupid unemployables or smart tricksters is to have it both ways: the stupid can be held in contempt, the tricky declared dangerous. Both can be locked up, either in hospitals as mental deficients and hard-core unemployables or in jails as rogues.

Aptly for a world where community is being eroded, Howlglas sets people against each other. He drives villagers into an uproar, fighting over a pile of shoes (sig. Aiii). He sets thieves at each other's throats by pulling their hair. While serving as a priest's assistant, he plays a prank at Easter, when the *Quem Quaeritis* trope is being acted, with the priest's mistress cast as an angel and the three Marys played by village folk whom Howlglas has secretly coached to answer the question "*Quem quaeritis?*" (Whom do you seek?) with "The priest's one-eyed mistress" (sig. Cii). When this occurs, the enraged mistress pops out of the "grave" where she is awaiting her entrance and tries to brain Howlglas but instead hits a Mary by mistake. In the ensuing melee, Howlglas leaves town. His lies foment a feud between an innkeeper and a priest that lasts the rest of their lives; he instigates a row among cream-sellers that ends in all the cream's being dumped in the river. At his death, Howlglas makes two factions fall out, suspecting each other of having replaced his treasure with stones. (He has supplied the stones himself—a welcome variation on turds.) Like Shakespeare's Puck, a spirit with a pedigree in folk magical belief, Howlglas delights in misunderstandings and uproars, in setting people at odds. The motives of neither will yield to psychoanalysis: both are spirits of another sort, embodying the mischief that fosters dissension among neighbors, projections of human cussedness.

Howlglas may have appealed to readers of various social groups. To the working stiff, understrapper to an arrogant and demanding boss, it offered the gratification of watching a cheeky assistant make a monkey of his boss and hit him in the pocketbook. To moralists, it confirmed that servants were lazy, disloyal, and untrustworthy. To humanists—and this text was read by educated men like Spenser and Harvey—it would have confirmed the need for education: one cure for vagrants' fecklessness was to teach them a trade. But although humanists might have enjoyed the tricks in Howlglas and might have reflected on educational needs of the down-and-out, they also (on reading the book) might have felt their hearts hardening, for Howlglas—lazy, irresponsible, brutal, vengeful, dangerous to employ—ratifies humanists' worst stereotypes about vagrants. Religious reformers and humanists, though fervent resisters of the authority of priest or pope, never countenanced worker resistance to lawful masters. Howlglas's gross physicality, his alliance with animals and the lower bodily stratum, undermine the dignity that was a basic tenet of humanism. Again, a seemingly harmless jest fosters harmful attitudes. As an evader of the system of tradesmen, guilds, masters, and apprentices, a truant from settled domesticity, Howlglas would have been a hero mainly to society's lowest, most disaffected segments. For the rest of those who read about his exploits, his funniness must ultimately only have increased readers' contempt for the lower orders, confirming their suspicion that while people like Howlglas might be amusing at times, for respectable people the joke soon wears thin. If hired, people like Howlglas will botch instructions. They cannot stick to a job more than a day. They are always moving around, on the road. They will trick anyone out of food and money. They do not even speak the official language. They shit on the floor of the house, they fart in the church.

As a folktale trickster hero, as Coyote, Howlglas transcends the human—he belongs to the world of marvel, even in his death. When the rope at the foot of the coffin breaks, attendants bury him upright, for "he was a very marvelous man" (sig. Mii^v). But upright posture is here no emblem of indomitable human dignity. In the end, Howlglas's exemption from ordinary human laws mainly removes him from ordinary human sympathy. Like vagrants everywhere, he is not finally human. And like the Reformation, humanism worked against vagrants because, when all is said and done, humanism is for humans.

Notes

1. In his *Anatomy of Abuses in England* (1583), Phillip Stubbes applies to actors the same cluster of insults that were applied to vagrants and the Catholic clergy: they are unclean, irreligious, idle, and live off others' sweat. Plays are performed "to the profanation of the Lord his sabbath, to the alluring and inveigling of the people from the blessed word of God preached to theatres and unclean assemblies, to idleness, unthriftiness, whoredom, wantonness, drunkenness, and what not? and which is more, when they are used to this end to maintain a great sort of idle persons doing nothing but playing and loitering, having their livings of [i.e., from] the sweat of other men's brows" (sig. 6–6ᵛ).

2. For Copland, too, lazy, runaway servants were an important segment of the unemployed: "Such servants as be negligent / In their service, and will not be content / To do their work, but slack their business, / . . . Changing masters, and run from town to town" (18).

3. The attempt to cure beggary through apprenticing impoverished youths to trades eventually caught on as a philanthropic practice among wealthy London tradesmen. The *Last Will and Testament of M[aster] John Kendricke Late Citizen and Draper of London* provided: "I give and bequeath towards the setting on work of forty idle vagrant boys, such as go up and down the streets in the City of London begging and pilfering, the sum of two hundred pounds, to be . . . placed and bound apprentice with a master for the term of seven years at the least, with artmasters, as glovers, pinners, shoemakers, or any other occupation or art which they shall be thought most fit for, . . . whereby in time they may prove good members and live like honest men in the Commonwealth" (Orlin, *Elizabethan Households* 156–57).

4. Mark Fleisher, writing of modern urban down-and-outs, heaps contempt on the idea of education as the cure for such social ills: "Anti-crime programs are based on the education model of social change. This model suggests that behavior depends on knowledge: . . . If criminals were to know about the destructiveness of overusing drugs and alcohol, they would stop overusing them; if criminals were literate and trained in a vocation, they'd get jobs and wouldn't have to rely on crime for money; if criminals were to know how much their offensive behavior hurts people, they would stop doing it; if criminals were to go to prison, they'd learn a lesson and refrain from criminal activities after release; if adolescents and adults on the margin of committing serious crime were to see companions go to prison, they'd learn that crime doesn't pay" (16). To some extent such faith in education, which Fleisher deems ludicrously misplaced, descends directly from the strain of Renaissance humanism that held that evil was the result of ignorance and that if people really understood what was good, they would do it. This notion, however, was already challenged in the Renaissance (Macbeth, for example, faced with a clear-cut choice between good and evil whose implications he fully understands, opts for evil). Also, despite Fleisher's scorn here for the idea that "if criminals were literate and trained in a vocation, they'd get jobs," he elsewhere in the study advocates early childhood intervention and the teaching of basic trades, an option not unlike the humanists' trade school experiments, which do seem to have helped substantial numbers of poor people in their day.

5. The twentieth-century translator's choice of the word "rogues" is of course anachronistic—it first appeared in Awdeley and Harman half a century after More wrote *Utopia*. More's Latin reads *"ni sponte mali esse mallent,"* and Robinson's 1551 translation renders the phrase "if they would not willingly be nought" (sig. Ciiiᵛ).

6. More's analysis, particularly as it concerns enclosures, strongly influenced Karl Marx.
For the Renaissance debate on enclosures and the debate on Marx's views on enclosures,
see my remarks in appendix A.

7. Other contemporaries also remarked on More as a fellow of infinite jest. Richard Pace
wrote in 1517 that More "possesses no common degree of humor and suavity. . . . One
might conclude that Charm itself was his father and Humor his mother. Sometimes,
. . . when the occasion demands, he imitates excellent chefs and sprinkles everything with
the sharp vinegar of his wit" (qtd. in Surtz 42–43). Robert Whittinton referred to More
in 1520 as "a man of an angel's wit and singular learning. . . . A man of marvelous mirth
and pastimes, *vir lepidus salibus, facetis iocis*" (64). Thomas Wilson reported even in 1553
that More's "wit even at this hour, is a wonder to all the world" (147), and toward the end
of the century, Gabriel Harvey jotted down a note that Cicero himself was "as full of his
conceited jests and merriments . . . as our Sir Thomas More. . . . They were born with a
jest in their mouths" (*Marginalia* 113–14). Cast as a character in his own *Dialogue Concerning Heresies*, More says that "a merry tale cometh never amiss to me" (38). Noting that
"More . . . kept a fool, Henry Patenson, who appears in the Holbein study of the More
family group," Joanna Lipking concludes that "from Erasmus's intimate characterization
to Whittinton's formal phrases, these accounts show the beginning of a tradition, a *topos*
of praise for More. . . . It rounds out a portrait of him as an exemplary scholar, rivaling
the continental humanists not only in his learning and skill but in his relaxations as well"
(354–55). Lena Orlin discusses Smith's *Widow Edith* in the context of More's reputation
for jesting ("Chronicles" 258–59).

8. More had some direct contact with the poor too. During his stint in the sheriff's
court, for example, "he did not dispose of great cases, the kind of cases that made lawyers rich, like the one he handled for the Merchants of the Staple. There he saw poor men,
and learned something of what the poor suffered from laws they had not made and scarcely understood" (Hexter xxxvii).

9. Richard Halpern believes that Lewis's emphasis on the jokiness of *Utopia* is an attempt to "depoliticize" the work, to "trivialize the work and stifle debate" (140). He points
to a "conservative tradition of *Utopia* criticism which thrives on ideological delusion" and
"cold-war hysteria" (141). As I have shown, one effective way to disable an issue is to adopt
it into the realm of the comic. In this case, however, *Utopia* to some degree disables its
own seriousness through joking.

10. Poggio was the first Renaissance writer to adopt the term facetiae (from Cicero),
which soon became the standard term for such short, witty narratives. Significantly, the
adjective "facetious" had not yet acquired its present connotations of shallow flippancy
but was wholly laudatory, meaning "witty, humorous, amusing" and also "polished and
agreeable, urbane" (*OED*)—all qualities actively cultivated by the courtly and the humanistic during the Renaissance.

11. Like *Widow Edith* and *A Hundred Merry Tales*, *Tales and Quick Answers* has links with

the More circle: its jest 96 also occurs in More's *Confutation of Tyndale's Answer,* published that same year. The *Confutation* is the first of More's works to show clear signs of familiarity with Poggio (Lipking 244).

12. Of course, humanist skepticism and rationalism never did succeed in eradicating entirely such "medieval" thinking, as the monstrous births and assorted wonders of late sixteenth-century ballads and newsbooks—and of modern supermarket tabloids—attest.

13. Lipking shows how Poggio frequently increased the emphasis on bodily functions, bare bottoms, and excrement over what he found in his sources (107). Heather Dubrow, upon reading the manuscript of this chapter, suggested that the genre of humanist jests be renamed *fecetiae.* Though she urged me to resist this pun, I was unable to, though I did relegate it to the bottom of the chapter.

14. A good example of the migratory career of jests in this period, the hospital tale is also found among the sermon exempla of Jacques de Vitry (no. 154), in a French fabliaux which is the ultimate source of Molière's *Médecin malgré lui,* in the popular Tuscan tale "Il Medico Grillo," in the collection *Mensa Philosophica,* and in the English jest collection *Certain Conceits and Jests.* See Thomas Frederick Crane's "Analysis and Notes" to his edition of Jacques de Vitry's exempla (141–42). By the way, the story of Simpcox's "healing" comes from Sir Thomas More's *Dialogue of the Veneration and Worship of Images,* reflecting the early Reformation debate over the debunking of miracles and relics.

15. The translator's choice of "Howlglas" to render "Eulenspiegel" creates auditory resonances with "galloglass," imported into English from Gaelic about the time *Howlglas* was first printed—the *OED* notes it first in state papers of Henry VIII in 1515. A feudal retainer fiercely loyal to his Irish lord, a galloglass brought to mind the vanishing world of master/retainer relations to which Howlglas stood in opposition. Increasing the resemblance between the words, "Howlglas" was often corrupted to "Holliglass," and "galloglass" was sometimes spelled "gallyglass."

4. Monarchy, Nation Building, and Domesticity

> Positive ideas of home, of a nation and its language, of proper order,
> good behaviour, moral values . . . do more than validate "our" world.
> They also tend to devalue other worlds.
> —Edward Said

OF THE CLUSTER OF PHENOMENA I discuss in this chapter in their effect on the vagrant poor—the Tudor centralization of monarchic power, the articulation of ideologies of nationhood and domesticity—some have a more dispersed agency than others: writers of domestic handbooks, for example, were not directly invested in the project of state consolidation in the way, say, that Henry VIII or Thomas Cromwell were. But the developing ideology of domesticity was very welcome to (and often fostered by) architects of Tudor centralized power. And whether one is talking about identifiable authors of nationhood, like Sir Thomas Elyot or Roger Ascham, or about more nebulous wellings-up of sentiments about domesticity, one can usually recognize the vagrant poor as an enemy.

The Beggar and the King: The Monarchy's Stance on Vagrancy

When Hamlet declares, "your fat king and your lean beggar is but variable service—two dishes, but to one table" (4.3.23–24), his implication is that both are mortal and will be devoured by worms. Hamlet thus means to shock by conflating opposites. As William C. Carroll notes, "The monarch, the top of the social and legal hierarchy, is understood in opposition to the figure at the bottom of the hierarchy, the socially and metaphysically null—the beggar. . . . Some representations of the Wheel of Fortune . . . place the monarch and the beggar on opposite sides of the wheel" (*Fat King, Lean Beggar* 9, 14). As if taking this trope literally, Tudor monarchs defined themselves against beggary, in which (like reformers and humanists) Tudor governments—Crown and Parliament—took a disproportionate interest. Indeed, the reign of every Tudor monarch saw substantial poverty legislation. Henry VII's regime passed Poor Laws in 1495 and 1503–4; Henry VIII's, in 1531 and 1536; Edward VI's, in 1547, 1550, and 1552; Mary's, in 1555; Elizabeth's, in 1563, 1572, 1576, 1593, 1598, and 1601. In the famine year 1598 Parliament passed six poverty acts. Early acts provided simply for punishing vagrants; but from 1547 on laws came in pairs, one for punishing rogues, the other for poor relief, a dichotomy based on notions of the undeserving and deserving poor.[1] Royal proclamations often fulminated against vagrants; one of Elizabeth's earliest aimed at dispersing crowds of vagrants following her court (Hughes and Larkin 2:173).

The concern over vagrancy in Henry VIII's reign partly reflected jumpiness over the possibility of revolt: in 1536, at the height of the Dissolution, a revolt against the destruction of churches, abbeys, and relics engulfed ten northern counties. Its leaders disapproved of Henry's divorce, royal supremacy over the church, and "the aims and methods of Cromwell and his associates," especially Layton and Legh (Knowles 322). This "Pilgrimage of Grace" had little to do with vagrants, but its leaders may have played unwittingly into Henry's fear of vagrants by stressing that suppression of monasteries caused hardship to the poor, that the abbeys in the "desert places" of the north "gave great alms to poor men. . . . None was in these parts denied, . . . so that the people were greatly refreshed by the said abbey" (Knowles 327–28). Henry replied scornfully, "As for their hospitality, for the relief of poor people, we wonder ye be not ashamed to affirm that they have been a great relief to our people"; in fact, they have "spent the substance of the goods of their house in nourishing of vice and abominable living" (329). Henry here is probably under the sway of Layton and Legh's salacious reports (see chap. 2); since these dwelt often on no more than what Knowles calls "solitary sin," one wonders how much the monasteries' substance was wasted by such "vice and abominable living," masturbation requiring little outlay of material resources. It is telling that Henry tars the poor with the same brush as the supposedly depraved Catholic clergy. He also identifies the poor with sedition and revolt—the uprising, on its leaders' testimony, was on their behalf as well the monastics' behalf. In fear of uprisings, governments posited vagrants organized enough to constitute a political threat. As I have noted, historians now believe they were *not* organized, that the fraternity of vagabonds was a literary fiction. But the belief that they were gave authorities a pretext for suppressing them.

How real was the threat of revolts, riots, and uprisings? Appendix 1 of

J. Thomas Kelly's *Thorns on the Tudor Rose: Monks, Rogues, Vagabonds, and Sturdy Beggars* comprises a chronology of all of England's rebellions, conspiracies, riots, disorders, and tumults between the Pilgrimage of Grace in 1536–37 and the riotous assemblies in London in 1641; the total comes to 129. Steve Rappaport, however, argues persuasively that given the harsh conditions prevailing during several decades of the sixteenth century, it is the *lack* of widespread or serious uprisings that is remarkable, especially considering the many extremely violent proletarian revolts that rocked continental cities during the same period: "In general disturbances involved small groups of young men and seldom resulted in destruction of property, let alone loss of life. Rarely were disturbances organised to protest economic or political conditions in London" (10); the only period of frequent urban unrest in London was the 1590s, unsurprisingly since "unemployment, plague, and severe inflation made these the worst years of the sixteenth century for London's people" (13); "disturbances were neither endemic nor, in a city of approximately 150,000 people, very large or threatening" (14). Rappaport also contends that serious, long-term economic depressions in Coventry and York failed to provoke seditious uprisings (20), and he blames twentieth-century historians for exaggerating the extent of sixteenth-century urban disorder. But modern historians have taken their cue from Tudor writers, including writers of rogue literature and of the Poor Laws, who also appear to have exaggerated the threat of disorder and to have blamed existing disorders on vagrants—unfairly, as I have shown in the introduction.

In painting the vagrant poor as seditious, the Crown drew support from humanists. Though some writers of humanistic education, such as Robert Crowley, saw sedition as a predictable result of neglecting the poor and condemned the neglect rather than the neglected, humanism's program committed its writers to an orderly polity, and most responded briskly to the prospect of political uprisings. The anonymous *A Remedy for Sedition* (1536), published during the Pilgrimage of Grace and attributed to Richard Morison, waxes nearly hysterical on the subject of sedition, fearing uprisings of the unemployed (sig. [B4]ᵛ); its cure is unquestioning obedience to the Crown. Demanding "is sedition lawfully defended, where men lay poverty to their excuse?" (sig. Ciiiᵛ), the author lays much at the door of the able-bodied unemployed, the "young and lusty" who will not "learn any honest occupation to get their living, . . . but continuing in idleness, fall to stealing, robbing, murder" (sig. [C4]); he calls them "these bellies that have no hands, these flies that feed upon other men's labours, them that being idle, without any occupation, without lands, fees, wages, do nothing but complain . . . of them that be governors of the realm, and thus . . . sow sedition" (sig. [C4]).

Though humanistically ascribing sedition to bad education, the author does not indicate how the poor might gain a good education. Juan Luis Vives, too, worries about sedition, advising in his work on poor relief that those smoking out the undeserving poor keep an eye out for sedition: "Let the investigators make their examination into the needs of the poor. . . . Let nothing be given if the judgment is unfavorable. Intimidation should not be used unless they deem it necessary in dealing with persons who are refractory and who disparage the government" (*Relief of the Poor* 20). Even this advocate of extensive government relief thought the needs of the poor must take a back seat to law and order, if revolution was a threat: "Tumult and civil discord must be avoided always; . . . this is a greater evil than the misappropriation of the funds of the poor" (25).

The Crown's interest in vagrancy also points to the role of the Poor Laws (in regard to both relief and punishment) in the consolidation of state power. That hallmark of the Tudor century, political centralization, was enabled by a power vacuum—the resources of individual barons had been stretched by the Wars of the Roses; the papacy and the English church were in a historic phase of weakness; the Commons had not yet found the obstreperous strength that would unite them as a political force in the seventeenth century.[2] And the centralizing project was boosted significantly by the practical exigencies of poor relief, in which "both parishes and property-owners were agents of the central government; and that government could communicate a consistent policy to them, and commit them to it. . . . The centre called the tune" (Slack, *Poverty and Policy* 114). In punishment of vagrants, the national government in 1531 assumed legislative control of what had earlier been the "general practice in the early Tudor period for local authorities to punish vagrants, and if they were not native beggars, to order them back to their home" (Palliser 124). From 1585 on, vagrants were dealt with by Crown-appointed provost-marshals, which many in Parliament viewed as "a dangerous extension of the royal prerogative" (Manning 178–79).[3] Another hatchery of centralized bureaucracy was the Reformation, with its Court of Augmentations set up in 1536 to "conduct the business of suppression [of monasteries] and to administer the former monastic property" (Knowles 393). During the suppression, Thomas Cromwell, sitting in London like a spider in a web, getting constant news from various fronts in letters from his peripatetic visitors, provided a model for the federal bureaucrat whose day was dawning. In another policy with long-term centralizing effects, the Crown suppressed local saints' cults in most parish churches (Duffy 409), thus replacing local religious identities with the national uniformity of royally authorized prayer books and homilies. But above all, the bureaucratic mechanisms set up by the Poor Laws helped forge the modern, federal state. As reform of charity "became incorporated into the ideology of the modern State, and accepted as the State's prerogative," a modern state was born out of efforts to "combat vagrancy and ward off the social dangers of poverty" (Geremek 205).

The Crown dictated social policy to parishes but did not fund it, rather like the U.S. government's locally resented unfunded mandates in recent times. "As an ecclesiastical unit the parish had long had a welfare role, and the civil parish, with its origins in the medieval vill, was developing rapidly as Henry VIII and his successors imposed new responsibilities on it: poor relief was only one, though the most important, of them" (Slack 131). The first architect of this policy was Cardinal Wolsey, and from his time through the mid-seventeenth century, "whenever epidemics or bad harvests occurred, councillors followed Wolsey's example, sending instructions to local authorities, . . . and in general trying to mobilize a national response" (Slack 138). The Henrician era was foundational for England as a national state; as G. R. Elton argues, without Henrician administrative reforms "that classical paternal state, the government of Elizabeth, would not have been possible" (*Tudor Revolution* 418). The sixteenth century, then, "saw the creation of the modern sovereign state" (3).[4]

A national relief program, requiring administrative centralization, contributed substantially to the national bureaucracy for which the Tudors are famed and forged links between parishes and the national government in ways basic to the Tudor centralizing project. England was unique in Europe for the *national* level of its poor relief schemes; elsewhere most such programs were municipal. But all this was predicated on the poor staying home and accepting relief in their parishes—how else could bureaucrats sustain channels of responsibility, maintain their bookkeeping? How else could distant parishes be held accountable to a dictating center? Hence the worry about those who left their parishes, who went on the road seeking seasonal work, or who flocked to London. Denying aid to the vagrant poor was meant to starve them into submission, into homekeeping. The Crown had its own reasons for disliking vagrancy: it threatened to derail the Tudor bureaucratic juggernaut. And bureaucracies have their own imperatives of institutional survival: Poor Laws helped justify the very existence of one substantial national bureaucracy.

Conceptualizing vagrancy as a *national* rather than local problem had as a side effect the establishment of a system of prisons. With the advent of national controls arose the idea "that unwanted strangers might be kept off the roads rather than chased away. . . . In earlier times, . . . the problems of the neighboring town or territory that might receive the banished vagrant failed to bother local judges" (Spierenburg, *Prison Experience* 36), but *national* legislation had to take such problems into account. Statutes requiring the return of vagrants to their home parishes seem intended partly to prevent parishes from sloughing off undesirables on neighboring parishes. David M. Palliser suggests that "if the countryside remained free of overwhelming poverty, it was achieved only through exporting its problem to the towns" (123). The ineffectuality of statutes requiring that vagrants return to their original parishes eventually led to centralized immobilization structures for vagrants: bridewells in London, Oxford, Norwich, and elsewhere.

Tudor overestimation of the threat constituted by vagrants may be partly an artifact of the high proportion of vagrants among those punished at the state's hands. As Pieter Spierenburg shows, across Europe an essential component of state formation was the gradual replacement of local by a state criminal justice system: between the twelfth and sixteenth centuries "the power of the courts went up and down with the fluctuations in the power of a central authority. It was the Tudors, finally, who gradually established a monopoly of violence over most of England" (*Spectacle* 10). But the state, endowed only relatively recently with power to initiate prosecutions on its own rather than at the behest of a plaintiff, and lacking a professional police force, could act most effectively against powerless groups; hence, Spierenburg notes, "prosecution was often concentrated on vagrants and other notorious groups" (*Spectacle* 11). The fiction that vagrants were organized and powerful is especially cruel given that it was their very disorganization and powerlessness that rendered them available for the spectacle of public punishment that maintained (largely by smoke and mirrors) the illusion of governmental omnipotence.

The rhetoric of the Poor Laws reveals these statutes to be vehicles of bureaucratic consolidation and exposes the anxiety attending vagrancy—anxiety that was partly real and partly fostered by the Crown to authorize the public punishments so crucial as spectacles of state power. This is revealed through a close look at the rhetoric of the landmark Poor Law of 1597, which, like other Poor Laws, pairs *An Act for the Relief of the Poor* with *An Act for the Punishment of Rogues, Vagabonds, and Sturdy Beggars*. Its poor relief act, statute 3, overawes with visions of authority, of the heavy machinery of state officialdom, before it mentions the puny poor folk who cannot even support their own children:

> Be it enacted by the authority of this present Parliament, that the churchwardens of every parish, and four substantial householders there being subsidy men,[5] or for want of subsidy men, four other substantial householders of the said parish, who shall be nominated yearly in Easter week, under the hand and

seal of two or more justices of the peace in the same county, whereof one to be
of the quorum, dwelling in or near the same parish, shall be called overseers of
the poor of the same parish, and they, or the greater part of them, shall take
order from time to time, by and with the consent of two or more such justices
of the peace, for setting to work the children of all such, whose parents shall
not by the said persons be thought able to keep and maintain their children. . . .
(sig. B2–B2ᵛ)

This opening sentence foregrounds not the poor but the bureaucratic appa-
ratus set up to deal with them—householders, justices of the peace, subsidy
men, and overseers whose imposing presence swells through a stately buildup of clauses and phrases, thudding magisterially upon the ear like a gavel.
The appointment "in Easter week" evokes religious authority underpinning
that of the government. The position of these officials—at the head of the
sentence and of the statute—hints at why the central administration valued
poor relief: not so much because it relieved the poor, whose miseries are not
mentioned, but because it provided the rationale for a vast Tudor bureaucracy. The opening sentence's speech act mainly accomplishes naming—
"shall be called overseers." The adult poor all but disappear in a brief tangle
of confusing syntax—"whose parents" should syntactically (but does not)
mean the children's grandparents—the indigent grown-up generation handily disappears from the sentence. Parliament manifests its will through an
imperative resembling Jehovah's world-creating fiats: "be it enacted." Passive verbs stress the poor people's lack of agency: they are not "thought able
to keep and maintain their children." Bureaucratic officialdom attains pomp
and authority by the stately march of ceremonial phrases: "by the authority," "under the hand and seal," "of the quorum." The sheer length of the
sentence, like a state procession, fosters a sense of authority and control, and
what is quoted is not even the whole sentence—the rest paces forth ceremo-
niously to a length of 561 words.

But statute 4, the rogue-punishing act, is rhetorically very different. Its
opening speech act—"For the suppressing of rogues, vagabonds, and sturdy beggars, be it enacted" (sig. B6)—is a repeal of all previous acts on rogues,
and thus an admission of failure. While in the opening sentence of the poor
relief act the controlling presence of overseers, men of substance, and justices overwhelmed the almost-absent poor, statute 4's opening sentence
swarms with rogues, vagabonds, and sturdy beggars; and rather than being
decently hidden halfway through a long sentence, the threatening social elements are here front-loaded in the very first clause, which nervously uses a
present participle as a noun ("suppressing") as if in hope of turning an on-
going struggle into an accomplished fact. This opening sentence is less than

half the length of that in statute 3—a mere 236 words—and it lacks the other act's majestic, rolling, bureaucratic syntax.

Taken together, these two statutes suggest by their rhetoric the role of the deserving and undeserving poor in the national bureaucracy. The poor relief statute swells with confident pride in the Tudors' successful construction, over the span of the sixteenth century, of a smoothly operating state machinery of poor relief. Its rhetoric does not so much reassure anyone that the poor will be fed as impress on the substantial citizens of every parish in the land their duty to carry out instructions issued from the commanding center. The vagrancy statute posits—and to some extent deliberately provokes—fear. Previous statutes have failed and must be scrapped. The Crown can count on finding in every parish not three kinds of responsible official (churchwardens, subsidy men, and other substantial householders) but three kinds of rogue (rogues, vagabonds, and sturdy beggars). Confidence in a controlling central government, with its intricately functioning poor relief system, is being eaten away by the uncontainability of vagrants. The very language of the Poor Laws gives a sense of what was at stake for the Crown in suppressing vagrancy and in exaggerating the threat it posed.

Vagrancy and the New Sense of Nationhood

That poor relief and vagrancy legislation operated at a *national* level in England linked poverty issues to emerging discourses of nationhood. It was for the good of England that parishes and counties were urged to pull together and provide disaster relief in famine years: "Governors played the 'commonweal' tune for all it was worth in years of dearth. . . . They knew what they were doing" (Slack 145). Disasters can prove a useful glue for national cohesion, as when Henry VIII's government worked to wrest a message of national unity out of crop failures. But too much harping on hunger risked creating an international image problem for England. As Kathleen Pories argues, the highly visible vagrant poor "embodied a symbolic problem because they were taken to represent a malfunctioning country" (18). In his *Dialogue between Reginald Pole and Thomas Lupset* (ca. 1533–35), written in years of harvest failure, Thomas Starkey has Pole declare,

> If you . . . examine the state as it is now, comparing it with the same in ancient time, . . . you shall find, . . . for great riches and liberality in time past, now great wretchedness and poverty, and for great abundance of things necessary, great scarceness and penury; which thing you shall not doubt of at all, if you will first look to the great multitude of beggars here in our country. . . . In no country

of Christendom, for the number of people, you shall find so many beggars as be here in England, and mo[re] now than have been beforetime; which argueth plain great poverty. (89)

Lupset disagrees that beggary reflects badly on the nation: "The multitude of beggars . . . argueth no poverty, but rather much idleness . . . , for it is their own cause and negligence that they so beg; there is sufficient enough here in our country of all things to maintain them without begging" (89). Though he does not deny that people bring beggary on themselves, Pole takes Lupset to task for not recognizing it as a national problem: "You are loath to grant your country to be poor, specially when you compare it with other where you see greater poverty than with us. . . . [But] although peraventure our country be not so poor as many other be, yet this is sure: it is more poor than it hath been in time past, and such poverty reigneth now that in no case may stand with [i.e., be consistent with] a very true and flourishing common weal" (90). The recurrent phrases "your country" and "our country" sound a note of national pride: both speakers worry about beggary on patriotic grounds— Pole wants the problem solved because it is a national disgrace, and Lupset wants not to recognize it at all—allegations of poverty seem unpatriotic.

Authors of rogue literature often position themselves as patriots, depicting rogues as enemies of the nation. Robert Greene, in the dedicatory epistle to his first cony-catching piece, *A Notable Discovery of Cozenage,* declares stoutly, "France, Germany, Poland, Denmark, I know them all . . . ; only I am English-born, and I have English thoughts. . . . Yet in all these countries where I have travelled, I have not seen more excess of vanity than we Englishmen practise. . . . I will only speak of two such notable abuses. . . . The first and chief is called the art of cony-catching" (120). He sounds a nationalist note again at the end: "For the benefit of my country I have briefly discovered the law of cony-catching," concluding, *"Nascimur pro patria"* (134; We are born for our country). A shabby cast of rogues, petty cheats, and drifters were regularly cast as a public evil to be exposed by those who cared about England: Greene somberly warns, "a dangerous enormity groweth by them to the discredit of the estate of England" (120).

Accepting Elton's view of the 1530s as "the crucial moment of change" for English nationhood, since "in that decade parliament declared England 'an empire,' severed the ties that bound the English church to the church of Rome, . . . established the king as 'supreme head' of both church and state," and established "a genuinely national administration,"[6] Richard Helgerson documents "widespread anxiety . . . concerning England's cultural identity. Sovereignty of this new sort put a greater burden on a specifically national sense of self than any existing evidence of national accomplishment could easily sustain. England was now calling itself an empire. Where were the signs of imperial stature?" (*Forms of Nationhood* 4).[7] At this "crucial moment," 1533–35, Starkey's speakers articulate one cause of the anxiety: the damage to national pride of having to confess—or at least entertain the possibility— that England is more beggar-ridden than other European countries or, contrary to humanism's buoyant faith in progress, that England is poorer now than previously. Such a suspicion was especially threatening, since disowning medieval England was an essential nationalistic move:

> Self-definition comes from the not-self, from the alien other. But in the discourses of nationhood, . . . to constitute itself as a nation-state, a political or cultural community must distinguish itself not only from its neighbors but also from its former self. . . . Prompted by the cultural breaks of Renaissance and Reformation, sixteenth-century national self-articulation began with a sense of national barbarism, with a recognition of the self as the despised other, and then moved to repair that damaged self-image. (Helgerson, *Forms of Nationhood* 22)[8]

This disowned medieval self was pre-Reformation and prehumanist. As Roger Ascham put it, in medieval England "papistry as a standing pool covered and overflowed all England," and humanist letters were unknown, people reading only chivalric romances written "in monasteries by idle monks and wanton canons" (230–31). Visions of a new nation, unified and strong after a clean religious and intellectual break from medieval England, might be seriously damaged if England was now materially poorer. But one could argue that poverty had been exacerbated by centuries of initiative-deadening charity. Disowning indiscriminate medieval charity in favor of a modern, up-to-date dogma of deserving and undeserving poor and secularized charity could preserve disdain for the Middle Ages. If the foolishly generous medieval world was still admittedly more prosperous, one could always argue that Tudor times had belatedly reaped an evil harvest of centuries of ill-advised medieval almsgiving.

If the Middle Ages was an alien Other, so too was country as opposed to city life. London's prominence sat well with the values of humanism, always an urban movement. To Starkey, England would remain barbaric until its gentility were firmly centered in the city:

> Our gentlemen must be caused to retire to cities and towns, and to build them houses in the same, and there to see the governance of them, helping ever to set all such thing forward as pertaineth to the ornaments of the city. They may not continually dwell in the country as they do. This is a great rudeness and a barbarous custom used with us in our country. They dwell, with us, sparkled

in the fields and woods, as they did before there was any civil life known or stablished among us; the which surely is a great ground of the lack of all civil order and humanity. (161)

Indeed, European visitors marveled at the way the English nobility lived in country houses rather than in cities. English literary criticism's love/hate relationship with the pastoral[9] owes something to this early Tudor inferiority complex, this fear of being reputed not as an "empire" but as a land of bumpkins, whose very nobility were hayseeds.

The discourse of vagrancy sometimes makes contact with the pastoral. As Heather Dubrow points out, Harman's account of vagrants sleeping and copulating in barns links them with countrified, animal-like sexuality (37). At such moments, the vagrant of popular imaginings is a dark double of the pastoral shepherd, living a spare life close to nature, though without the shepherd's moral authority. But Dubrow also notes that cony-catching pamphlets "portray the rogues' victims as country bumpkins who, having come to the big city, are taken in by its natives" (40). (One thinks also of Autolycus, the city sharper in *The Winter's Tale,* called "a rogue" in the dramatis personae, who attends a sheep-shearing festival to fleece the rustics and uses the thieves' cant "doxy" [4.3.2].) The vulnerability and closeness to nature of these "denizens of a pastoral world [who] enter the city" are "embodied in the label 'cony,'" which of course means "rabbit" (Dubrow 40). As barn-dwellers and travelers through the countryside, vagrants *are* denizens of a pastoral world; as members of a city thieves' underworld, they are urban sophisticates who prey on the inhabitants of a pastoral world. Both kinds appear in Thomas Harman's *Caveat for Common Cursetors, Vulgarly Called Vagabonds:* the vagrants sleeping in barns and the woman who has been on the road for eighteen years are rural vagrants; Nicholas Jennings, a counterfeit epileptic, is an urban sharper. But the one was turning into the other all the time, as displaced rural populations moved to London.[10] In doing so they behaved just as Starkey's dialogue counsels noblemen to behave, so as to enhance England's glory and reputation: they moved to the city and acquired fortune and sophistication. As urban sophisticates who look down on bumpkins, cony-catching urban vagrants are the dark double of Tudor writers on English nationhood. Either way—as bumpkins or urban vagrants—they make handy defining Others for nationalists. If a self is defined by what it does not wish to be, nationalists had reason to disown vagrants: nationalists scorned bumpkins, and if there was anything suspect about moving to the city and disdaining or exploiting the countryside, then vagrants, and not apologists for English nationhood and urban glory, were to blame.

The shape-shifting from cony into cony-catcher bespoke unstable identity. Another frightening aspect of vagrants, as rogue literature represented them, was their status as internal barbarians, for they were nomadic like other barbarians and spoke a barbarous tongue, cant. The problem was that they *were* internal to England; on the whole, it is more comforting when one's defining Others reside elsewhere. As Helgerson shows, "the rhetoric of nationhood is a rhetoric of uniformity and wholeness; the unified self of the Englishman or Frenchman, the Italian or German, is founded on the political and cultural unity of the nation to which each belongs" (22). Rhetoric of nationhood had to condemn vagrants, a disowned part of the national self that embarrassingly had stayed within the national boundaries.

Keeping a shine on the national image meant a shift in the level of vagrant expulsions: early Tudor poor legislation provided for expelling beggars from towns and parishes, but late Tudor beggars were deported from England. The 1597 vagrancy act specified overseas banishment of dangerous rogues, and soon occupants of houses of correction, vagrants rounded up on the streets, and poor children were regularly shipped to North American colonies. Sometimes pressure was brought to bear under the Poor Laws: "in 1620 the Common Council ordered that parents refusing to allow their children to be taken were to have poor relief cut off" (Beier, *Masterless Men* 162–63), or beggars' children were kidnapped and shipped off (Robert C. Johnson; Souden; Breen and Foster; Galenson; A. E. Smith 147–51). Elizabethans, then, helped populate the colonies by kidnapping beggars' children; and a clear case of projecting one's disowned qualities onto a loathed Other was that in rogue literature, beggars steal respectable citizens' children rather than the other way around.

The Rage for Domesticity

This age witnessed "a glorification of the individual household. . . . During the sixteenth century, for example, the phrase 'A man's house is his castle' became proverbial. . . . As Edward Coke put it in a report from the King's Bench, 'the house of every one is to him his castle and fortress, as well for defense against injury and violence, as for his repose'" (Orlin, *Private Matters* 1–2). In Henry Wotton's rosy vision, "Every man's proper mansion house and home [is] the theater of his hospitality, the seat of self-fruition, the comfortablest part of his own life, the noblest of his son's inheritance, a kind of private princedom" (sig. Li^v–L2). And as the state co-opted the parish for its own bureaucratic uses, so it commandeered the home:

The state designated the individual household, in the absence of the old author-itarian church and of a national police, as the primary unit of social control. . . . And it reinforced the preexistent patriarchal hierarchy to further empower the father politically and also to ensure his accountability. . . . Political patriarchalism . . . in the late sixteenth century first analogized the household's structures of authority with those of the state. . . . The political branch canni-balized domestic ideology in order to advance the doctrine of royal absolut-ism. (Orlin, *Private Matters* 3–11)

As Robert Cleaver declared in *A Godly Form of Household Government: For the Ordering of Private Families, According to the Direction of God's Word* (1598), "A household is as it were a little commonwealth" (13). Cleaver con-tinues the household-state analogy: "It is impossible for a man to understand to govern the commonwealth that doth not know to rule his own house" (16).[11] Emphasis on domestic governance was not markedly Protestant: for example, the Henrician best-seller *A Work for Householders; or, For Them That Have the Guiding or Governance of Any Company,* which held each householder accountable for spiritual instruction in his little kingdom the home, was an immediately *pre*-Reformation text, written by a monk, Rob-ert Whitford.

As the poor should stay home in their parishes, householders, especially women, should stay in their houses. Marriage preachers harped on it: "Af-fairs abroad do most appertain to the man. . . . The wife is especially to care for . . . the business of the house" (Gouge 257); "he without door, she with-in: he abroad, she at home" (Whately 84). Surveying domestic handbooks published between 1475 and 1640, Suzanne W. Hull concludes that "the re-spectable middle-class English woman was depicted as a modest lover of home and hearth" (34). Literature routinely deplored "gadding" housewives, with their dodges to get out of the house: "You must to the pawn to buy lawn; to St. Martin's for lace; to the garden; to the glass-house; to your gossip's; to the poulter's; else take out an old ruff, and go to your seamster's. Excuses? Why, they are more ripe than medlars at Christmas" (Dekker and Webster, *Westward Ho* 2.1.214–18). In city comedy, wives sneak out to meet lovers; re-lentless satire on promiscuous citizens' wives does the same ideological work as marriage sermons: promoting immobilized domesticity.

The household was a useful unit of social control since Renaissance house-holds, as Peter Laslett has shown, were self-contained, comprising both home and workplace for most people. Laslett shows how the family lived over the shop, a baker ruling the bakery as senior craftsman and ruling his family as patriarch; apprentices lived in the household and were considered family members. In practice the common distinction between husbands' and wives' roles on grounds of mobility—"the duty of the husband is to travel abroad to seek living, and the wife's duty is to keep the house" (Cleaver 170)—would have applied rather narrowly, mainly to traveling merchants. Most early modern workers did not commute: they worked and lived in the same building. The boss at work was also the father. It made a tidy unit for social control. At stake in the rhetorical overkill attending satire on gadding wives or texts attacking vagrancy was the political importance of preserving that unit.

Ironically, it was the age of Henry VIII, with his six wives and tumultuous, international divorce extravaganzas, that institutionalized family values as an instrument of national policy. Domestic ideology was firmly linked to Englishness, to nationhood. The family connection exists in the very word "nation," whose Latin root means "to be born." Wendy Wall accounts for the "English" in the title of Gervase Markham's housewifery manual *The English Housewife* by exploring links between newly valorized domestic practices and writers' increasing insistence on nation as a category ("Renaissance National Husbandry"). The habit of calling England "Home" produced, by the eighteenth century, a Home Office and home secretary responsible for affairs within England (just as the foreign secretary dealt with foreign affairs) and produced the term "Home Counties" for the four counties around London. This mindset was already in place by the late sixteenth century, when "home" meant both "a dwelling-place, house, abode" and "one's own country, one's native land; used by Britons abroad" (*OED*).

As A. L. Beier writes, "Vagrants were a menace to the social order because they broke the accepted norms of family life. . . . If the normal household of the period contained a married couple, children and servants, then vagrants were a radical departure from it" (*Masterless Men* 51). And since domesticity was a political concern, to be homeless was to evade public policy, to give nationhood the slip. No wonder writers on vagrancy harp on thieves' cant— a foreign language is to be expected of the undomiciled and hence non-English. Rogue literature often represents rogues as enemies of family values in their unrootedness, sexual promiscuity, and turning of kinship loyalties into scams. "Cozen," meaning to execute a trick of the cony-catching variety, first appeared in John Awdeley's *Fraternity of Vagabonds* (ca. 1561) and was regarded as a variant of "cousin": Randle Cotgrave in *A Dictionary of the French and English Tongues* (1611) said the verb meant "to claim kindred for advantage." In Awdeley and other rogue writers, con artists make contact with gulls through claiming distant kinship; in one of Harman's tales, two robbers find out a parson's address by claiming to be his nephews. A rogue in Gilbert Walker's *Manifest Detection of the Most Vile and Detestable Use of Dice-Play* (1555) reveals that "be they young, be they old, that falleth into our laps and be ignorant of our art, we call by the name of a *cousin,* as men that we make as much of as if they were of our kin indeed. . . . [Thus we] make the *cozen* sweat" (76; emphasis added). Families, as historians show, were often split up by the pressures of homelessness. And popular belief credited vagrants with prostituting their daughters, stealing children, using children to tug at the heartstrings of potential almsgivers, deforming their children to render their begging more poignant. Such charges, many of them improbable (why would people who could not support their own children kidnap somebody else's?), suggest that vagrants were envisioned as an antifamily force.

The family is the central political unit in Sir Thomas More's *Utopia,* where every thirty families choose one magistrate. As J. H. Hexter notes, "the businesses of the Medici, the Walsers, the Fuggers, were family firms" (xliii); but "important as the patriarchal family was in early sixteenth-century Europe, it was far more important in *Utopia*" (xliii), which posits a society that was lacking other Renaissance institutions such as guilds and which was structured entirely through the family (lv). More was, with some reluctance, a family man himself: "When I get home," he wrote, "I have to talk with my wife, chatter with my children, and consult with the servants. All these matters I consider part of my business, since they have to be done unless a man wants to be a stranger in his own house" (Letter to Peter Giles 109). Also important as a model for his political familism was monasticism, which provided a potent vision of family.[12] More, for whom "the master trope of the Utopian order turns out to be the great household writ greater still" (Mueller 101), was an architect of the patriarchal family as model for a patriarchal political order.

As Gordon J. Schochet notes, "patriarchal justifications of obedience to political authority were regularly and officially taught by the Church of England; . . . the simple requirement to 'Honour thy father and thy mother' was expanded to include loyalty and obedience to the king and all magistrates" (6). The conjunction of kingship and fatherhood, Schochet continues, "implied that government—and monarchy in particular—was a natural institution" (7). The law classified as petty treason the murder of a husband by a wife or a master by a servant, underlining the analogy between father and king (Dolan 13).

But the new value placed on domesticity went considerably beyond state-sponsored political patriarchalism; it welled up from various sources, religious and secular. Idealizing domesticity *was* integral to the Reformation project (which valorized companionate marriage, attacked celibacy, and abolished monasteries as alternative versions of home); but companionate marriage was increasingly advocated by *both* Catholics and Protestants.[13]

More's piggybacking of familism on monasticism shows such revaluings of the domestic to be perfectly congenial to a committed Catholic. The Catholic Juan Luis Vives wrote on both poor relief and domesticity—his *Instruction of a Christian Woman* outlined a curriculum suitable for producing stay-at-home wives; he also wrote *The Office and Duty of a Husband.* Humanist learning, too, was involved: a classical marriage treatise, Xenophon's *Treatise of the Household,* appeared in English in 1532; its printer, Thomas Berthelet, also printed other important humanist texts including Elyot's *Book Named the Governor.* Edmund Tilney's *Brief and Pleasant Discourse of Duties in Marriage, Called the Flower of Friendship* included Vives and Erasmus as speakers and drew on Castiglione's *Courtier.*

Marriage sermons held forth on parent-child relationships: What were the duties of parents? Should marriages be arranged? Marriage treatises advised on childrearing; Tilney's *Flower of Friendship* exhorted a husband "to be careful in the education of his children; for much better were they unborn, than untaught" (123). To some extent the whole Tudor educational movement—new schools, new curricula, debates over corporal punishment—was an extension of the emphasis on family values. Formal defenses of womankind praised motherhood; Edward Gosynhyll's *Praise of All Women, Called Mulierum Paean* brims with sympathetic comment on the shoulder-aching task of carrying heavy children, the perils of breast-feeding a child with teeth, and the aroma of diapers (sig. Bi^v). Parent-child relationships abound in the period's literature, and no writer was more deeply committed to exploring these than was one playwright who lived apart from his own children: relationships between parents and their children are crucial in the plots of at least twenty-seven of Shakespeare's thirty-seven plays.

A material sign of the new valorization of domesticity was that "much of the increased prosperity of the landowning classes was poured into [house] building" (Palliser 111). William Camden, as Palliser points out, noted that in the 1570s, "more houses of noblemen and private citizens—remarkable for their elegance, size and splendour—began to arise throughout England than in any previous age" (112). Palliser writes:

> A count of 151 Hertfordshire country houses shows that 78 were first built in the sixteenth century, chiefly between 1540 and 1580, and a survey of four widely spread counties (Derbyshire, Essex, Shropshire and Somerset) suggests that more new country houses were built between 1570 and 1620 than in any later half-century. . . . The lesser gentry, and the yeomen farmers, were also rebuilding on an unprecedented scale, as can be seen from the hundreds of small manor houses and large farmhouses of the reigns of Elizabeth and James I that still adorn nearly every part of England. (112)

As Lena Orlin shows, "Elizabethans were house proud" (*Elizabethan Households* 83). In 1529, a new regulation required inventories of the possessions of every deceased person, listed room by room; the surviving invent

ries constitute a huge database that Orlin draws on to conclude that "the sheer quantity of household possessions increased dramatically over the course of the hundred-and-fifty years following the compulsory institution of inventories, . . . at every social register [except among people who had no homes or possessions], at roughly proportionate levels" (83). Tellingly, "household goods assumed pride of place among possessions. While the earliest inventories listed cattle and farm equipment first and household furnishings second, the priority was soon reversed" (Orlin 81). Drawing on a study of the Arden area by Victor Skipp, Orlin shows that in a 1560 farm inventory, house and household goods comprised only a quarter of the value of Edward Kempsale's estate; in 1587 a farmer of comparable station, Thomas Gyll, died leaving household goods amounting to half the value of his estate. "That Kempsale had two rooms and Gyll had four is part of the story of the Great Rebuilding: Gyll had two more bedchambers, or perhaps an extra bedchamber and a parlor. In the Arden area, there was an average of 2.5 rooms in the peasant household in the mid-sixteenth century; one hundred years later, there was an average of 6.5 rooms in the same social stratum" (Orlin 81). Derek Portman offers similar data for the Oxford region. The so-called Great Rebuilding (1570–1640) included a general increase across England in the number of rooms per domestic dwelling. The domestic was becoming more highly valued, more central in the lives of those who had houses. In Thomas Middleton's *Chaste Maid in Cheapside,* the house-proud Allwit revels orgasmically in his household goods:

> We are richly furnished wife, with household stuff.
> . . . We are simply stocked with cloth-of-tissue cushions
> To furnish out bay-windows; pish, what not that's quaint
> And costly, from the top to the bottom?
> Life, for furniture, we may lodge a countess!
> There's a close-stool of tawny velvet too. (5.1.180–85)

If the increase in the number of beggars sparked suspicion that England had declined economically since medieval times, the increase in household goods for the well-off seemed a blow for patriotism and modernity. In his *Description of England* (1587), William Harrison (like an early Allwit) rejoiced in the "great provision of tapestry, Turkey work [i.e., Turkish carpets], pewter, brass, fine linen, and thereto costly cupboards of plate, worth £500 or £600 or £1000" to be seen "in the houses of knights, gentlemen, merchantmen, and some other wealthy citizens" (200). Orlin's finding that "the sheer quantity of household possessions [had] increased dramatically" is borne out by Harrison's observation that in household furnishings, contemporary wealthy folk "far exceed their elders and predecessors" (200). Old men in his village agree that three things are "marvelously altered in England within their sound remembrance" (200)—the increase in household chimneys (no more smoky open fires), vessels of pewter, tin, or silver rather than of wood, and the "great (although not general) amendment of lodging," with featherbeds and pillows replacing the old straw pallets and coarse coverlets (201). That little nagging "although not general," however, opens a fissure in Harrison's consumer utopia, reminding readers of vagrants who would have been glad of an old-fashioned straw pallet. The homeless, antitheses of the commodity-happy homeowner, offered a mute reproach to complacent domestic consumers. And Harrison links the opulently appointed private home with the new sense of national pride: even "inferior artificers and many farmers" now "garnish their cupboards with plate, their joint beds with tapestry and silk hangings, and their tables with carpets and fine napery, whereby the wealth of our country (God be praised therefor and give us grace to employ it well) doth infinitely appear" (200). God wants England to be wealthy and to display its wealth in cupboards and tapestries. How discordant with this vision were the cupboardless, the houseless.

The semiotics of furniture re-enacted an ideology that confined beggars to their parishes and housewives to their homes: even furniture, formerly vagrant within the house, now had to settle down. As some rooms became specialized as bedchambers, beds were no longer rolled out at night into all-purpose rooms. The old trestle table, dismantled after meals, yielded to an immobile table with boards permanently joined. "The size of the cupboards increased and as the tables were joined, these furnishings became progressively less transportable. . . . They participated in the phenomena associated with the Great Rebuilding: like shutters, floorboards, window glazing, and staircases, furnishings came to be thought of as fixtures. Some were even designed with specific household locations in mind. They contributed to the household ethic of stability" (Orlin, *Elizabethan Households* 82). Along with this domestic ossification went an ideal of people themselves—especially women—as fixtures. Children, too, needed immobilizing: as Richard Halpern shows, "the figurative language used by Tudor pedagogues frequently depicted children as innately or potentially vagrant; against this disposition the disciplinary and sedentarizing regime of the school was felt to exert a prophylactic effect" (78). This drive toward fixity only worsened the image of the true vagrant.

Erasmus's *Convivium Religiosum* and the Ideal of Home as a Haven of Safety

In *Coniugium* (Marriage) and other colloquies, Erasmus advised on domestic conduct. In *Convivium Religiosum* (The godly feast), the godly Eusebius entertains friends at his country home. Although his wife, relegated to preparing lunch, is not invited to the colloquium ("she prefers to gossip with women"), the host defends marriage, rejecting medieval misogamy: "I don't agree with those who think a man lucky not to have had a wife. I like rather the Hebrew sage's saying that 'He that hath a good wife hath a good lot'" (*Colloquies* 60). And the home is idealized: in the charmed serenity of enclosed gardens, graceful architecture, fine art, and good food, this *locus amoenus* resembles More's Chelsea house, called by his early biographer Nicholas Harpsfield "right fair," with a library, books, a gallery, a garden, and an orchard. (Both Harpsfield [90, 107] and William Roper [14] mention the garden house More built for withdrawing to for the purpose of meditation, with a chapel, library, and gallery.) Eusebius equates householders with rulers: "If he may be said to reign who lives exactly as he pleases, clearly I reign here" (*Colloquies* 49); and "This whole house is mine; . . . I may have authority in my own realm" (56). (Underscoring this conjunction of domestic ideology and political patriarchalism, the first topic at lunch is the divine sanction of royal authority and the importance of subjects' obedience.) Home is identified with heaven: St. Paul "calls the heavenly mansion . . . οἰχία and οἰκητριου, that is, a home or dwelling" (67). The colloquy attacks the excesses of monasticism, which does not seem digressive if one recalls that monasteries were an alternate form of home—a sumptuous, wasteful sort compared to the one the host here describes as "modest" (71). Tellingly, Eusebius's domestic paradise is set against a world of beggary.

Beggars first enter the colloquy—alongside monastics—within a dozen lines of its opening. Eusebius contrasts country pleasures with the corrupt lives of "priests and monks, . . . who for the sake of gain usually prefer to live in cities," and a "blind beggar who rejoiced in the jostling of a crowd because, he would say, where there were people there was profit" (48)—the preference for a "jostling" crowd, suggesting that he is a pickpocket, casts doubt on his blindness. Defined by what it is not, home is here contrasted with the monastic homes of greedy clerics and with the haunts of thieving beggars with faked disabilities. During a "thin and insipid" lunch—soup, salad, "an excellent shoulder of mutton, a capon, and four partridges," plus dessert (57)—Eusebius remarks, "Enjoying in moderation what the divine goodness has provided, we ought to be mindful of the poor" (69). A guest remarks on the huge beggary problem, evoking the bankrupt philanthropist trope—"Christ commanded us to give to everyone who asks. If I did that, I'd have to beg myself within a month" (70). Eusebius makes the usual distinction between deserving and undeserving—"Christ meant those who ask for necessities"— and conflates beggars with mendicant clergy asking for handouts to beautify luxurious monasteries (70). Presently, a guest returns to the issue of secular beggars:

> Timothy: Many think what is given to public beggars is not well spent.
> Eusebius: Something ought to be given to them, too, at times, yet with discrimination. I should think it wise for each city to look after its own and not to tolerate vagabonds roaming hither and yon—particularly the able-bodied ones, who, I imagine, need a job rather than a dole. (71)

This was the humanist party line; but Timothy probes further, making Eusebius defend his own domestic comfort against the claims of the poor: "You disapprove of spending too much on churches, and yet you could have built this house for much less" (70). The godly host now has to scramble: "Well, I think it's in the modest class. Or call it elegant if you prefer; certainly it's not luxurious. . . . Mendicants build more splendidly. Yet these gardens of mine, such as they are, pay tax to the needy; and every day I economize in something and deny myself and my family in order to be more bountiful toward the poor" (71). Timothy is satisfied with this defense, but should modern readers be satisfied? What Eusebius calls "a little country place" (49) nestles in gardens with artificial streams and fountains, walls covered with painted tiles. Its aviary boasts many species. Its sliding windows have special shutters for coolness. Its many rooms—"the library has its own balcony, overlooking the garden; connected with it is a chapel" (77)—abound in paintings and frescoes depicting nature scenes, the "entire life of Jesus" (53), Old Testament figures, portraits of popes and caesars, and action pictures involving Antony and Cleopatra and Alexander the Great (76–78). As mementos of their lunch, Eusebius gives guests "going away gifts," mere trifles worth "nothing"—gold-embossed books on vellum, a clock "imported from far-off Dalmatia," a lamp, a case full of fine writing pens (75). There is much wealth here, and it is indulged with such becoming *sprezzatura*.

The presence of the poor and hungry was to some degree necessary to complete a wealthy man's assertion of status—the hungry poor both served as a contrast to his plenteous fare and gave an opportunity for the largesse that helped define his status. As Roy Porter notes, Paolo Camporesi has established "the enormous symbolic significance attached to having enough to eat. Eating well was more important than being rich, famous, or of high status—conspicuous food consumption in fact stood as the very proof of all these attributes. The man able to eat handsomely, with a groaning board, with ovens, fires, and cooks, the man able to stand feasts or run soup kitchens for the poor, was recognized to be the grand man" (9). Eusebius, if godly, is also grand.

Should we suspect irony where a character with no visible occupation pontificates, in his sumptuous home, about the greed and idleness of the poor? As with Harman, I cannot read the piece ironically: so idealized is Eusebius's piety as to make unlikely Erasmian awareness of the ironies. But it is possible (as with Harman) that subconscious awareness accounts for the insistence with which the topic of beggary keeps intruding into this rural paradise. In an oblique nod at the hordes of beggars outside the walls—the homelessness that helps define this place as home—Eusebius acknowledges that domestic bliss requires security measures: "Let's go on to those three galleries above the ones you saw, . . . looking out on the kitchen garden. These upper ones have a view on each side, but through windows that can be closed—especially in these walls that do not face the inner garden—to make the house safer" (77). In Edward Coke's formulation, quoted earlier in this chapter, an Englishman's home served not only "for repose" but also "for defense against injury and violence." Juan Luis Vives, writing on poor relief, had shown just why the homes of the rich needed barred and shuttered windows:

> In the commonwealth the weaker may not be neglected without peril to the more powerful; for the former, driven by necessity, sometimes steal. . . . The poor envy the rich and are incensed and indignant that they have abundance to lavish on jesters, dogs, harlots, asses, pack-horses, and elephants; that in truth they themselves have not the wherewithal to feed their little hungering children, while their fellow-citizens revel splendidly and insolently in the riches which have been wrung from them and others like them. (6)

What might Eusebius have answered to such a charge, other than to deny the harlots or the elephants?

Renaissance great houses were lockable; and they had courtyards within courtyards and private spaces deep within the house, to which the family withdrew. In English house architecture, the first mentions of "the *interloquitorium,* or parlour (both meaning 'place of conversation')" (John Schofield 90) occur in the late fourteenth century; by the sixteenth century, "in larger houses, . . . a parlour would be found adjacent to the hall with a communicating door, but it was never entered directly from a courtyard. . . . The parlour was the innermost room of the household, a private space for the family, often looking out over the garden. This contrasts with the [eigh-teenth-century] status of the parlour . . . [as] the room . . . for entertaining *other* families, [when it was] moved nearer the street" (John Schofield 160). The sixteenth-century occulted parlor spoke to a perceived need for safety, which was found deep in the bowels of one's house. The interior of Sir Edward Darcy's house, rebuilt from a medieval original, was reached in 1598 through two gatehouses and a screens passage; tucked away inside this compound were two large gardens (John Schofield 160–61). This recalls the refreshing interior gardens of *Convivium Religiosum,* with their fountains, one garden within a courtyard shut up at night, another enclosed by the walls of the house (and overlooked by three galleries where Eusebius strolls with friends), and a third garden deeper within the walls, containing an herb garden, a meadow, and an orchard of exotic imported trees. Schofield documents the transformation of the Charterhouse—that brave dissident monastery—into "a great house with courtyards. . . . An outer and inner courtyard . . . was now fashionable" (142). Susan Frye writes of Queen Elizabeth's withdrawing, in later years, more and more into sequestered inner apartments, the innermost rooms reached through several other rooms that opened sequentially onto each other (124–26)—a significant withdrawal for a highly mobile, progress-making monarch.

Shakespeare's *Measure for Measure* features a doubly or trebly lockable garden house: Angelo has

> a garden circummured with brick,
> Whose western side is with a vineyard backed;
> And to that vineyard is a planchèd gate,
> That makes his opening with this bigger key.
> This other doth command a little door
> Which from the vineyard to the garden leads. (4.1.28–33)

Within that is a "garden house," sequestered through being reached via a locked vineyard and garden (5.1.236). "Circummured" ("walled around"), apparently a Shakespearean coinage, is an apt invention for an age when the rich encased themselves in layers of protective walls. Another Shakespearean brick-walled garden, the one in *2 Henry VI* where Iden, like Eusebius, enjoys his "quiet walks" (4.10.17) and takes pride in being charitable to the poor at his gates, is invaded: Jack Cade climbs the brick wall and encounters the shocked homeowner in the garden. Reflecting the ambivalence of the well-off during this period, Iden is torn between his usual charitable instincts—he calls Cade "a poor famished man" (4.10.43)—and his horror that a poor man would dare to "break into my garden / and like a thief . . . come to rob my grounds, / Climbing my walls" (4.10.32–34). His queasiness about killing the invader is assuaged by the news that Cade is a political insurrectionist, a "monstrous traitor" (4.10.65)—a fear that the spectacle of the poor outside the gates often inspired in those days.

Houses of the Renaissance well-to-do were circummured because the world beyond them was seen as dangerous, full of criminals and poor folk. Those who fancied the countryside could have a walled garden. In one of Harman's tales, a parson lives in an impressively garrisoned house, but the vagrants get him anyway. Two rogues contemplate this house, which seems vulnerable because isolated, with no other house near "by almost a quarter of a mile" (75); but to their chagrin it is "stone-walled about, and . . . we cannot well break in. . . . The windows be thick of mullions, that there is no creeping in between" (76). "Mullions"—vertical bars—were an architectural feature of Elizabethan origin. The rogues return at midnight, and one makes "a rueful and pitiful noise, requiring for Christ sake some relief, that was both hungry and thirsty, and was like to lie without the doors all night and starve for cold, unless he were relieved by him with some small piece of money" (76). When the parson reaches between the bars to bestow alms, the vagrants seize his arm and threaten to smite it off, until he gives them three pounds. So dangerous is the world that an honest soul is not safe even putting an arm out a window.

Renaissance works on homelessness are often set in comfortable homes. (And I am writing this work, I admit, in a comfortable home.) Writing of the hordes begging at his gate, Harman sketches details of his mansion, noting its copper cauldrons and pewter, servants and fine horses. Starkey sets his dialogue on poverty in Pole's ancestral mansion at Bisham, reassuringly surrounded by portraits of forbears "of great nobility" (21). Of Erasmus's many "convivia," the only one set in a fine home with sturdy walls and interior gardens is the one that takes up beggary as a social issue, *Convivium Religiosum*. *Utopia*'s conversation about English beggary takes place in More's Antwerp residence, where men converse in a garden awaiting lunch. Clearly the place to discuss homelessness and hunger was in the safety of home, while dining. Why did Renaissance writers adapt the medieval *hortus conclusus* to the discourse of vagrancy? What does this trope reveal?

I think the cozy domestic settings of Renaissance discussions of vagrancy function like chimney-corner settings of ghost stories and armchair mise-en-scènes of murder mysteries. Anthony Vidler writes that "a domesticated version of absolute terror, to be experienced in the comfort of the home and relegated to the minor genre of the *Märchen* or fairy tale, the uncanny found its first home in the ghost stories of E. T. A. Hoffmann and Edgar Allan Poe.

Its favorite motif was precisely the contrast between a secure and homely interior and the fearful invasion of an alien presence" (3). Vidler dismisses as "a minor genre" a world of oral tales that was a major Renaissance locus of terror. *The Winter's Tale* takes its title from the telling of ghost stories on a winter's night, as Mamillius proposes: "A sad tale's best for winter. I have one / Of sprites and goblins. . . . / . . . / . . . / There was a man . . . / Dwelt by a churchyard" (2.1.25–30). Shakespeare often links tales with a winter's fireside. Puck describes old women telling stories while eating roasted crab apples (*MND* 2.1.47–57). Lady Macbeth, inhabiting a tale of terror, mentions a "story at a winter's fire" (3.4.65). The contrast between winter outside (linked with the terror in the tale) and the fire's warmth inside creates a special effect, the coziness heightening the tale's terror, the terror making more precious the warm domestic safety. In Renaissance references to storytelling, the fireside-in-winter pattern recurs insistently. The tale-teller in George Peele's *Old Wives Tale* (first acted in 1590) offers "a crab in the fire" (l. 48) and "a merry winter's tale" (l. 83). The tale collection *The Cobbler of Canterbury* addresses farmers "turning (in a winter's evening) the crab in the fire" (sig. A3–A3ᵛ). Richard of Gloucester links storytelling with winter: "Let Aesop fable in a winter's night" (*3H6* 5.5. 25–26]). Terror's cozy domestic settings suggest that horror and domesticity are defining opposites. Vidler describes analogous settings from the nineteenth century:

> a cheerful household, generally following dinner, the men smoking pipes before the blazing fire, the women sewing, the children allowed to stay up late. This was the nostalgic evocation of the *veillee*, a 'cottage' vision of house and home especially relished in the age of rural displacement and urban emigration. In such a secure setting, stories of terror might be tasted with delight; many writers insisted on the need for a storm outside, to reinforce by contrast the snugness within. Thus the setting of Hoffmann's "Uncanny Guest" . . . , where "the four ingredients, autumn, a storm, wind, a good fire, and a jorum of punch," engendered a strange sense of the awesome, provoked a fear of the supernatural, that was then deliciously prolonged. (36)

Vidler finds this a nineteenth-century topos, but the early modern texts quoted in this chapter show its essential elements—tale of terror, fireside, bad weather—in place in the sixteenth century, also an "age of rural displacement and urban emigration."

Some murder mysteries draw on similar conventions. Ernst Bloch notes the "cozy" setting in which mysteries are enjoyed: "In a comfortable chair, under the nocturnal floor lamp with tea, rum, and tobacco, personally secure and peacefully immersed in dangerous things" (245). This genre's association with domesticity helps explain its association with female authors, "queens of crime" (Christie, Marsh, Sayers) who set tales in opulent country houses. The hard-boiled mystery whose tough-guy detective sleeps in his office seems deliberately antidomestic; but male authors also set macabre tales of murder in a cozy home—consider Holmes and Watson's digs or the domestic bliss of Nero Wolfe's gourmet dinners. Homely safety is central to the classic mystery; "curling up with a good mystery" suggests the fetal position.

I think the trope of cozy domesticity versus winter, crime, and terror took shape in early Tudor times, when homemaking was idealized and beggars outside the walls of the home, demonized as predatory criminals, had become terrifying. John Taylor's nurse frightened him into behaving by threatening him with abduction by "the beggar" (97). (Could the "bogeyman" of nursery imaginings—whose etymology is unknown—be a variant of "beggarman"?) In the Renaissance imagination vagrants inhabited a land of terror because they were called criminal and because, in their squalor and their frequent deaths from hunger, cold, disease, and hanging, they must have seemed like the walking dead.[14]

The trope of setting the cozy parlor against the dangerous outdoors also appears, as Garrett A. Sullivan Jr. notes, in depictions of map-reading, where curling up with a map in the safety of a warm study allows vicarious journeys, a safe substitute for the perils of travel. Sir Thomas Elyot recommends it: "What pleasure is it, in one hour, to behold those realms, cities, seas, rivers, and mountains; . . . incredible delight is taken in beholding the diversities of people, beasts, fouls, fishes, trees, fruits, and herbs; to know the sundry manners and conditions of people, . . . in a warm study or parlour, without peril of the sea, or danger of long and painful journeys" (1:77–78). Samuel Lewkenor helpfully published *A Discourse . . . for Such as Are Desirous to Know the Situation and Customs of Foreign Cities without Travelling to See Them.* Ironically, the great age of exploration, mapmaking, Richard Hakluyt's *Principal Navigations,* and England's first North American colonies was also an age when the well-off were growing nervous about leaving the house. Among many impetuses to mapmaking during this great cartographic age was a wish to provide gentlemen with a safe (because imaginary) way of going abroad in the world.

Thomas Harman's *Caveat* invokes this trope:[15] he invites us to imagine him in his cozy home, into which intrude the alien presences of vagrants. At one point he has been burgled; thieves have made off with a valued cauldron, which by his cleverness Harman is eventually able to retrieve. His text offers a comforting spectacle of control: a strong, resolute man with authority suffers—even (courageously) courts—intrusion of his domestic space by terrifying Others, whom he then controls through punishment and torture, and thus defangs for the anxious reader, through the reassuring publication of information that will arm his readers against similar invasions. Harman is an early, poor man's Prospero, exercising his power to control the forces threatening to invade what in Prospero's case is an island, in Harman's, a comfortable manor house.

The house-threatening vagrant as a bogeyman was successor to the home-invading friar. Itinerant friars, preaching from town to town, had long been caricatured as seducers of housewives—this most mobile of clerics proved the most menacing. The threat of house invasion is conjured at the end of *Piers Plowman:* as the forces of Antichrist gather, at the church door appears a figure named Sir Penetrans Domos ("penetrator of the house"). As Penn R. Szittya points out, the name comes from the Latin version of 2 Timothy 3:1–6: "In the last days, dangerous times will come. Men will be lovers of self, covetous, haughty, proud. . . . Avoid these. For of such are they who make their way into houses [*qui penetrant domos*]" (Szittya 3). This fearsome house-penetrator is presented by *Piers Plowman* in the habit of a friar.

Contemporary with idealized domesticity, and with the domestic architecture emphasizing sequestration, was a newly privatized sexuality. Noting that the influential architect Alberti recommended separate bedrooms for husband and wife with a communicating door "to enable them to seek each other's company unnoticed," Mark Wigley argues that domestic architecture was "the agent of a new kind of modesty and . . . played an active part in the constitution of the private subject" (345). Where servants had shared bedchambers with masters, house architecture now allowed more private sexuality. If the palisaded sequestration of Tudor houses was partly a response to fear of vagrants outside the door, one can thank vagrancy in some degree for fostering the new privacies of the age. And it is against a newly private sexuality that one should view the charges of Harman and others that vagrants' sexuality was animal-like in its publicness.

Though some ascribed the miseries of the vagrant poor to the decay of traditional hospitality, Harman ascribes the decay of hospitality to a fear of rampaging vagrants. To abolish vagrancy would "encourage a great number of gentlemen and others, seeing this security, to set up houses and keep hospitality in the country, to the comfort of their neighbors, relief of the poor, and to the amendment of the commonwealth" (63). Fear of witchcraft, too, reflected a sense that one's little domestic paradise was beleaguered by needy people seeking to penetrate its sanctuary. In the commonest scenario for witchcraft charges, the accuser, having uncharitably turned away an old woman who had come to the door begging, assumed she bore him malice and accused her of sorcery when some affliction struck (Keith Thomas, *Decline* 560–69). As Alan Macfarlane notes, the reason for the alleged witch attack "was almost always an unneighbourly action on the part of her . . . victim" ("Tudor Anthropologist" 147)—the witchcraft scene crucially involved the repulsion of beggars from one's door. Not only were witches potential house invaders, begging at one's door, but the belief that they were accompanied by supernatural familiars points to their lives' being conceived as a grotesque parody of domesticity. Cats, the commonest familiars, traditionally symbolize hearth and home, and witches' supposed suckling of familiars parodies maternal domesticity. (On texts that show witches as "engaged in a demonic form of domesticity," see Dolan [181]; see also Comensoli.) The iconography of witches made contact with that of beggars; for example, witches were often represented as lame. In the woodcut on the title page of *The Wonderful Discovery of the Witchcrafts of Margaret and Phillip Flower,* three witches carry canes; one props herself up on two canes. One thing feared about witches that allies them again with beggars was their mobility—a supernatural mobility, in this case, that allowed them to fly, go out of their bodies invisibly, and travel anywhere, another crime against the ideology of homekeeping.

* * *

We keep accumulating, then, crucial building blocks of English Renaissance culture—the Reformation, the new humanism, the political patriarchalism and centralizing tendencies of English government, the new sense of English nationhood, the valorization of domesticity—which *all* involved disclaiming and penalizing vagrancy. The period's preoccupation with vagrancy was overdetermined in the extreme; as I argued in the introduction, the vagrant poor became such figures of terror not because they were *big* bogeymen so much as because they were *everybody's* bogeymen. I turn now to the last two pieces of this complex cultural puzzle—issues of hygiene and of civility.

Notes

1. As Roger B. Manning notes, "The main rationale for all vagrancy and poor laws remained the preservation of public order. Hence, there was always a greater emphasis upon punishment of idleness than upon poor relief" (165).

2. Tudor centralization did not occur ex nihilo, of course; Palliser notes the existence "already by the early Tudor period [of] a relatively centralised state with a long, stable and unified tradition, in marked contrast to France, Spain, Italy, and the Empire" (9). Ironically, even the fifteenth-century civil wars had paved the way for a more firmly centralized system, since the focus of strife had not been increased local autonomy but control of the throne. The anthropologist Max Gluckman shows how civil wars can actually

enhance centralized authority if "contenders for power against established authority [seek] only to acquire the same positions of authority for themselves" (127).

3. The martial law of the provost-marshal, pioneered upon vagrants, ultimately proved influential in the colonies: "The first well-documented example of the use of provost-marshals against civilians who were not rebels was in Ireland in 1556, when martial law was employed to sweep up and punish vagrants. . . . Nowhere were provost-marshals given more extensive powers than in Elizabethan Ireland. Since Ireland was where the pattern of English colonial government was first developed and refined before being transplanted across the Atlantic, it should cause no surprise that a provost-marshal was regarded as an officer necessary for the government of early seventeenth-century Virginia, and that the royal governors of Barbados and Jamaica relied upon them to maintain order" (Manning 180).

4. For important modifications to Elton's view, showing greater continuity with the late fifteenth century than he allowed, see Coleman and Starkey's edited collection *Revolution Reassessed: Revisions in the History of Tudor Government and Administration,* which also shows that some innovations that Elton dated to the 1530s did not really appear until a decade or more later. Though the Coleman and Starkey volume rejects, in Starkey's words, Elton's "creationist" view in favor of an "evolutionary" view of Henrician events (200), contributors do not deny the importance of Henrician developments to the emerging English state.

5. A "subsidy man" is "a person liable to pay subsidy; hence, a man of means or substance" (*OED*); those rich enough to be contributing heavily to the underwriting of poor relief were given a substantial say in its disposition—he who pays the piper calls the tune.

6. That Elton exaggerated the newness of "a genuinely national administration" in the 1530s is argued by several authors in Coleman and Starkey's *Revolution Reassessed.*

7. Patrick Collinson provides a nuanced discussion of the contribution of Protestant thinking to emergent English nationalism in "The Protestant Nation" (*Birthpangs,* chap. 1), which considers the recurring Protestant claim that "God is English."

8. On England's disowned, barbaric medieval self, see Mikalachki's *Legacy of Boadicea: Gender and Nation in Early Modern England.*

9. Samuel Johnson's well-known remark on *Lycidas*—"its form is that of a pastoral, easy, vulgar, and therefore disgusting" (94)—is typical of a centuries-long English critical vendetta against the pastoral.

10. A fine example of a displaced country person turning handily into an urban trickster is the Country Wench in Middleton's *Chaste Maid in Cheapside:* in blackmailing various men into providing support for babies she claims they have fathered, and abandoning a baby by wittily palming it off on some corrupt citizens, the Country Wench seems to have migrated into city comedy from some cony-catching pamphlet, carrying with her all the usual vagrants' baggage of sexual profligacy, negligence toward her offspring, and trickiness. That the play invites audiences to enjoy her witty initiative rather than frown on her corrupt morals is part of the *enjoyment* of a tricksy underworld that is characteristic of the basically comic tenor of rogue literature; and it may also signal comment on "respectable" society, which is as morally corrupt as the Country Wench—an erasure of the line between rogues and civil society that is also found in texts such as Walker's *Man-*

ifest Detection of the Most Vile and Detestable Use of Dice-Play and Aleman's *Rogue; or, The Life of Guzman de Alfarache.*

11. On the analogy between the Commonwealth and the household, see Susan Dwyer Amussen, Christopher Hill (*Society and Puritanism in Pre-Revolutionary England,* chap. 13), Mary Beth Rose (chap. 3), and Deborah Kuller Shuger (chap. 6).

12. As R. W. Chambers writes, "It is significant that *the religious houses are the one European institution which the Utopians are said to approve.* . . . In Utopia, . . . the monastic idea is at work. . . . The Utopian, like the monk or friar, may possess nothing. Everyone in Utopia must wear the common habit. . . . Their hours of work, of recreation, the very games they may play, are all regulated. . . . The Utopians eat in refectories" (136).

13. For several contrasting opinions on what was new in sixteenth-century marriage, see Kathleen M. Davies, Margo Todd, Alan Macfarlane (*Marriage and Love*), Barbara A. Hanawalt (218–19), and Patrick Collinson (*Birthpangs,* chap. 3).

14. The idealization of domesticity also gives special force to the lurid depictions of domestic crime that were a prominent feature of the literary landscape, which "express fears that the home was unsafe and could not be protected against those who would rise against it from within" (Dolan 29)—a version, I suggest, of the horror of house invasion. Similar to the faithless servants who deserted their masters to hit the road as vagrants were those who stayed home and murdered their masters in "texts that focus on the ambitious, frustrated servant" (Dolan 41; see also Comensoli).

15. I am grateful to Lena Orlin for helping me make this connection.

5. Hygiene, Civility, and Homelessness

Of Undesirables and Disease

Beggars did wear rags; but the iconography of beggars' ragged clothing also expressed a fear of disease—beggars wore clothing full of holes in an era when tightly woven cloth was said to protect against plague (Vigarello 10). The chronically poor were confined in hospitals with the chronically ill, conflating poverty and disease—a logical extension of equating the deserving poor with the disabled poor. A 1580 royal proclamation provides a glimpse of the human rabbit warren in which destitute Londoners lived:

> The Queen's majesty, perceiving the state of the city of London (being anciently termed her chamber) and the suburbs and confines thereof to increase daily by excess of people, [and acknowledging that] where there are such great multitudes of people brought to inhabit in small rooms (whereof a great part are seen very poor, yea, such as must live of begging or by worse means, and they heaped up together, and in a sort smothered with many families of children and servants in one house or small tenement) it must needs follow if any plague or popular sickness should by God's permission enter amongst those multitudes that the same would not only spread itself and invade the whole city and confines (as great mortality should ensue to the same where her majesty's personal presence is many times required) . . . but would be also disperse through all other parts of the realm to the manifest danger of the whole body, . . . [doth] command all manner of persons . . . to desist and forbear from any new buildings of any house or tenement within three miles from any of the gates of the said city of London. (Hughes and Larkin 2:466–67)

London is here troped as the queen's private chamber ("anciently termed her chamber") within her home, England; its "excess of people" appear as house

invaders who, having penetrated the queen's chamber, are nightmarishly pro-
liferating there. Nation was identified with home, and the queen is here a
housewife, concerned with promoting the "preservation of her people in
health," just as wives consulted domestic handbooks for cures for illness. The
implied metaphor shifts from England as a house whose innermost chamber
is in danger of invasion by hordes of poor to England as a body in danger of
invasion by disease. The identification of poor people with disease is crucial
to understanding Renaissance attitudes toward beggary and vagrancy.[1]

Tudor centralized bureaucracy administered not only Poor Laws but also
regulations dealing with plague, which acquired a mental link with Poor Laws.
Cardinal Wolsey, that "inventor of Tudor paternalism,"

> began in 1517, not only with his famous enclosure commission, but also with a
> more general attack on social problems in London. The occasion was partly the
> disorders evident in the riots of Evil May Day 1517, and partly epidemics of the
> sweating sickness and plague which threatened the health of the Court in the
> same year. In January 1518 the Council interrogated the mayor and aldermen
> about the state of the city, and told them to act against rogues and beggars. Sim-
> ilar campaigns [were launched] against the wandering and mendicant poor in
> Coventry, Lincoln, Leicester and Shrewsbury between 1517 and 1521. . . . In-
> fluenced by humanist physicians such as Linacre, and by their aspiration to apply
> medical knowledge to the health of the commonweal in general, Wolsey founded
> the College of Physicians in 1518. In the same year he and More were responsi-
> ble for the first efforts by an English government to prevent the spread of plague.
> Infected houses in London and Oxford were to be identified and marked so that
> people might avoid them. Copied from foreign models, this early step towards
> the practice of quarantine was gradually developed in London and in provin-
> cial cities until the isolation of infected households became a standard public-
> health procedure. (Slack, *Poverty and Policy* 117; see also Barroll, chap. 3)

Quarantine was apt for an age prizing domesticity and fearing mobility—
one cured plague by keeping the sick home, as the deserving poor were envisioned as sickly and housebound. And Wolsey's antiplague campaign, as
Slack notes, also included rounding up vagrants.

The typically late-Tudor policy of supporting the poor through compulsory taxes rather than solely by voluntary charity seems in several cases to have
grown out of emergency taxes dealing with plague. York experimented with a
tax for plague victims in 1538, and eventually "assessments for the poor which
were begun . . . in the middle of another crisis caused by dearth and disease
proved permanent" (Slack, *English Poor Law* 123). The link was not arbitrary:
famine helped ensure "the predominance of the indigent among victims of the
disease" (Mollat 193). Outbreaks of disease were most common in crowded,
unhygienic slums, and the poor were seen as a kind of disease in themselves.

[The new, or] newly virulent, infectious diseases of the early sixteenth century, syphilis and the sweating sickness, . . . help to explain the horror at the "in-
curable diseases and filthiness of body" and the "maladies tedious, loathsome
or abhorrible to be looked upon" . . . associated with the poor. . . . There was
an increasing use of the paradigm of the body politic, not to bind together a
varied social whole, but to show the damage which untreated disease, disorder
or decay in any one member might do to the rest: the diseased members should
be cut off. (Slack, *Poverty and Policy* 24)

In *A Caveat for Common Cursetors, Vulgarly called Vagabonds,* Thomas Harman emphasizes beggars' lice. From nauseating accounts of the infestation
of the poor by insects and worms, Piero Camporesi concludes that preindustrial people lived "in a verminous universe unimaginable today" (152). To
many, beggars themselves seemed like lice, parasitic on the body politic:
Thomas Dekker calls them "the Egyptian lice of a kingdom" (*Bellman* 82),
alluding to that biblical nightmare, the dust turned into lice to plague Egypt
(Exodus 8:16–17). As Camporesi shows, propertied classes conflated "fear of
the multiplication of the poor" with fear of "a tide of human insects that
would rise until finally submerging them"; a world-wide insect attack "was
darkly feared as a possible universal catastrophe for all humanity" (158). Vagrants "were feared as voracious insects that devastated the countryside"
(163).

In his poor relief treatise *Concerning the Relief of the Poor,* Juan Luis Vives
evinces horror at the disease and filth of the poverty-stricken: beggars' ulcers give off a stench (8), their filth is polluting (13), they should be segregat-
ed lest they infect the community (19). Despite advocating relief, Vives cannot hide his distaste at running a gauntlet of beggars on his way to church:
"A common peril besets the citizens from contact with disease. . . . In every
church, especially at the established high festivals, one is obliged to enter the
sanctuary between two lines of sick, cancerous, ulcerous, and persons afflicted
with other diseases" (7). The Venetian Sanudo found that watching people
starve took the shine off Christmas, and the poor have the same effect on
Vives at "high festivals." They seem contagious, and he blames the peril on
their shamelessness: ulcers are "forced upon the eyes" and "assail the nostrils, the mouth, and are almost communicated to the hands and the body
of those passing by, . . . so shameless is the begging" (8). Vives advises a
roundup of vagrants, since even the healthy are so filthy as to be polluting:
"In regard to the beggars who wander about with no fixed dwelling places:
let those who are in health declare their name and the reason for their mendicancy in the presence of the Senate [i.e., authorities enforcing poor laws]
in some open place or vacant lot, that their filth may not pollute the Senate

chamber; let those who are sick do likewise, . . . that the eyes of the Senate may be spared" (13). Andreas Hyperius, too, is aghast at diseases assaulting the eyes of the decent: "Those monstrous bodies or deformed with sundry diseases, blood, matter, wounds, and loathesome filthiness, shall not be set in sight to terrify and dismay women great with child, or any other, which are soon troubled with the sight of such ghastly and sudden shows" (sig. D3).

Thomas Starkey advocates education to cure the "great dropsy" of unemployment: "Good education of youth . . . is the ground of the remedying all other diseases in this our politic body," just as with "bodily diseases the correction of corrupt and indigest humours is the chief point in the cure of them all, as the thing without the which all other medicines little shall avail" (143–44). "Corrupt and indigest humours" and dropsy, with its buildup of excess fluid, necessitated a purge; the medical metaphor commits Starkey to thinking in terms of bodily excess and voidance. Purging, though, is quite different from educating.

As Renaissance medicine often worked via bleeding or violent purges like hellebore, so the idea of dropsy puts into Starkey's mind a cure by expulsion: he who has "no craft at all, but, delight[s] in idleness, . . should be banished and driven out of the city, as a person unprofitable to all good civility" (142). The age saw purging, banishment, and exorcism as kinds of "cure," alternate modes of expelling evil (Woodbridge, *Scythe* 104–7). Banishment purged a nation of an enemy; Shakespeare's political banishments often sound like medical purges. Henry VI speaks of contagious disease when exiling Suffolk, fearing he will "breathe [out] infection in this air" (*2H6* 3.1.287); Duke Frederick calls banishment a "purgation" (*AYL* 1.3.51). On the civic level, expelling beggars from towns had the same quasimagical effect. Purging the body politic of a social evil as one purged the body of disease helped link the poor with disease in people's minds.

The theme of feigned illness looks different through this lens. If vagrants themselves had told stories about faking illness (as Erasmus has one do in "Beggar Talk"), one might read it as wish fulfillment: as folklore's Loathly Lady tales seem an old storyteller's fantasy of turning young, so feigned disability anecdotes could reflect disabled vagrants' pathetic wish to turn into robust lubbers by night. But these tales, told not by but against vagrants, seem a complacent evasion: onlookers revolted by beggars' open sores could reassure themselves that salves and cunning bandages accounted for everything. If these beggars were not really ill, there was no need to provide them with hospitals or alms. Many in the discourse of vagrancy regard all beggars' ailments as faked; but the revulsion of others reveals that they believe the illnesses to be quite real.

Anxiety about contagious diseases invading the body was persistently connected with fear of dangerous rogues outside the house. Thomas Nashe's *Unfortunate Traveller,* whose picaresque form owes something to rogue literature (*picaro* means "rogue") and whose early episodes read like a jest book (Nashe's trickster hero, like Howlglas, plays malicious practical jokes on alehouse-keepers and braggarts), incorporates a description of a wealthy home that could have come from Erasmus. This "summer banqueting house" rejoices in paintings, exotic plants, orchards, mechanical birds (327–30). But in a horrific episode immediately following the description of the idyllic house, rogues carry out what Nashe describes as a common practice in plague-ridden Italy: they break into the home of a wealthy man recently dead of the plague, rape his wife, and plunder the house (331). Juxtaposing ravaging house invaders with the plague, which also has invaded the house, structurally identifies outlaw house-violators with invasive disease. Mark Wigley shows that in Renaissance architectural treatises, "the dominant figure for the body [was] the house. But with the plague, the very walls of that house are seen as porous" (359).

In "Ben Jonson and the Centered Self," Thomas M. Greene interprets in terms of Jonson's personal psychology the many house invasions in his plays (*The Case Is Altered, Epicoene, The Alchemist*), as well as the poet's identification of selfhood with retreat into a safe home: "the act of dwelling at home with dignity, style, and integrity, . . . involves a kind of inner homing, a capacity to come to rest within" (330). Jonson's characters wish variously to "live at home, / With my own thoughts" (*Sejanus* [4.296–97]) or to "devise a room, with double walls, and treble ceilings; the windows close shut, and caulk'd" (*Epicoene* 1.1.184–85). "Inviting a Friend to Supper" and "To Penshurst" identify selfhood with a home. Once, in Jonson's own absence from home, plague invaded the house and killed his only son. But the motif of a self ensconced in a home, set against plague or frightening crowds outside, is not unique to Jonson: here speak crucial anxieties of the age. Camporesi discusses the horrific psychological impact of the plague and the way that this increased fear of the poor: "The universe of fear seemed to extend indefinitely" (89). Writing of the period's "terrifying dreams," he notes that "those on the margins of society, always and everywhere watched with suspicion and fear, became the potential vehicle of contagion and carrier of epidemics" (89).

Of Beggary, Filth, and Pollution Beliefs

As well as disease, an "aura of dirt, pollution and peril . . . was firmly attached to the Tudor poor" (Slack, *Poverty and Policy* 24). Robert Copland's *High-*

way to the Spital-house calls them "crooked, lame and blind, / Scabby and scurvy, pock-eaten flesh and rind, / Lousy and scald," also deriding them as "breechless, barefooted, all stinking with dirt" (3). Those faking illness also feign filth: Thomas Harman's fraudulent epileptics "wear filthy cloths on their heads" (85); and as one of their brotherhood, Nicholas Jennings is careful to get the costume right: he wears "a filthy foul cloth" on his head, his jerkin is "all berayed with dirt and mire, and his hat and hosen also" (86). Hospitals saw themselves as licensed to cure the city of poverty, disease, and filth. St. Bartholomew's claimed that in a five-year period it had "cured 800 poor 'of the pox, fistules, filthy blanes and sores . . . which else might have . . . stunk in the eyes and noses of the city'; and its beadles were enjoined to throw vagrants in gaol and bring in any sick loitering in the streets 'to the noyance and infection of the passers-by.' Christ's Hospital housed foundling children whose 'corrupt nature' arose from the 'dunghills' from which they were taken" (Slack, *Poverty and Policy* 119). Poor Laws occupied the same conceptual space as street-cleaning: "Municipal by-laws against beggars and vagabonds were often issued at the same time as orders for cleaning the streets. Town councils wished to purify their communities from every kind of dirt and disorder" (115). In a sermon, John Donne advocates transporting vagrants to the colonies, which will cleanse English cities: "It shall sweep your streets, and wash your doors, from idle persons" (4:272). Street-cleaning was a humiliating punishment for Bridewell prisoners, who

> must purge the street
> Of noisome garbage, carry dirt and dung,
> The beadles following with a mighty throng.
> . . . Drive, till ye sweat again in dirt and dust,
> Barefac'd in public view throughout the city;
> While all men laugh, and few or none will pity. (R.M., *Micrologia*, sig. D6ᵛ)

Given Thomas Harman's stance as a vagrant-eradicating cleanser of the countryside, it is interesting to contemplate A. L. Beier's recent finding (discussed in chap. 1) that Harman was a commissioner of sewers.

Dirt included excrement. Widow Edith's ordeal in the coalhouse is condign punishment: she has pretended to gentility despite her yeoman roots and her current vagrancy, and she is forcibly reminded of her social inferiority by being purged with a violent laxative. That anxieties over ambiguous social class should call forth excrement as a signifier resonates with the pollution theories of anthropologist Mary Douglas. She argues, citing an Indian untouchable caste charged with disposing of excrement, that different classes of society are associated with different parts of the body, namely, ruling classes with the head and upper body and lower classes with what Mikhail Bakhtin (who argues similarly) calls the "lower bodily stratum." Since body and society are linked images, societies respond to threatened erosion of social boundaries, or to fear of foreign invasion, by guarding bodily orifices with pollution taboos and by rigidly demarcating various category boundaries.

I have elsewhere argued that, like the beleaguered societies Douglas discusses, England was deep-dyed in pollution beliefs, reflecting an anxiety about the safety of its borders—the preoccupation of many writers with stories about sieges reflects England's self-image as a besieged island (*Scythe,* chap. 1). Anxiety over border-violation also appears in Tudor fears concerning unstable social rank. According to Douglas, avoidance of creatures that stray out of class boundaries is symptomatic of that boundary obsession that generates pollution beliefs—in a society that feels endangered, clear boundaries divide Jew from Gentile, gentleman from tradesman. Fear of class invasion by the upwardly mobile and of national invasion by foreigners (the Spanish Armada, foreign workers in London) are two faces of the same fear. If Douglas is right, it is unsurprising that a society as committed as Tudor England to border patrolling was also fearful of pollution.

As one example, book 1 of Edmund Spenser's *Faerie Queene,* on holiness, treats sin largely as pollution. The words "filth," "filthy," and "dirty" loom large. Sunk in sin, the Redcross Knight lies in a dungeon reeking with a "filthie banefull smell" (1.8.39) and requires cleansing, "the filthy blots of sinne to wash away" (1.10.27.7). Error's body is "full of filthie sin" (1.1.24.7). The personifications Lechery and Gluttony are "filthy" (1.4.24.4, 1.4.21.2). As her name suggests, Una the heroine of holiness possesses a unitary nature, but the forces of sin, as Duessa's name hints, are double and hybrid. Archimago can become bird, fish, or fox (1.1.10). Error is half woman, half snake. When the beautiful Duessa is stripped, her filth is connected with hybridity: her "secret filth" includes "filthy scald" on her head, sour breath that smells abominable, scabby skin, and a dung-encrusted rump, and she is part fox, part eagle, part bear (1.8.46–48). Boundary confusion is here closely connected with pollution: as Victor Turner sums up Mary Douglas's principle, the unclear is unclean.

Fear of pollution seems connected, in Tudor thinking, with anxiety about boundary erosion—including fluidity of social rank and threats to national boundaries. Early in the sixteenth century, Henry VIII felt embattled by the papacy; later, Elizabeth was under siege from Spain and Catholic Europe. All through the Tudor century, England felt menaced at its boundaries, and the concomitant fear of pollution contributed, I believe, to the period's pervasive interest in beggars and vagrants, considered filthy and linked with dirt and dung. The closeness to animals of vagrants who slept in barns suggested filth *and* boundary crossing—of the line between human and beast. England's emerging sense of nationhood had as a driving engine a fear of invasion, not only by the Armada, but also by the filth of beggars.

As a logical corollary to Douglas's theory associating lower orders with the lower body, one might postulate that the lowborn are more despised in cultures that denigrate the body. A Christian humanist like Sir Thomas More inherited a double dose of body-denigrating philosophy: from Christianity, which valued soul over body, and from neoplatonic humanism, which defined human dignity in terms of *intellectual* capacities. Pico della Mirandola had celebrated humanity for its freedom of choice (humans had the option, unique in the universe, to be either beasts or angels), but responsible humans were to aim at the angelic: one "delivered over to the senses" is "a brute, not a man," declared Pico (6). For humanists no middle ground was possible: whoever was not a near-angel would sink into beastliness. Not to ascend was to descend. Little wonder that humanists felt revulsion toward the hungry, whose minds often seemed to rise no higher than the alimentary. During a time of famine, "the fall of man into bestiality constitutes a recurrent *topos* in the great dramatic frescos" (Camporesi 33).

Excrementalizing the Other: Filthy Language as Weapon

One body denigrator, Sir Thomas More, wore a hair shirt and flagellated to subdue his flesh. He passionately hated Martin Luther, largely on grounds of Luther's having violated his oath of celibacy, and attacked him using a language of bodily filth as a weapon. More wrote a violently scatological, 350-page polemic, *Responsio ad Lutherum* (Response to Luther), bursting with invective linking Luther with excrement, sewers, and vomiting: More snarls about the "obscenities, dirt, filth, muck, shit" and "sewage" Luther "vomited up through that foul mouth into that railers' book of his, like devoured dung" (61); Luther "bespatter[s] and besmirch[es] [Henry VIII's] royal crown with shit," and "the beshitted tongue of this practitioner of posterioristics [is] most fit to lick with his anterior the very posterior of a pissing she-mule" (181); Luther's "shitty mouth [is] truly the shit-pool of all shit, all the muck and shit which [his] damnable rottenness has vomited up" (311); More will "empty out all the sewers and privies" onto Luther's head (311). As Louis A. Schuster writes, the "*Responsio*'s Rabelaisian grossness . . . engulfs the figure of its anti-hero and sprays him steadily with its scattershot of four-letter words in their Latin equivalents" (1147). One dealt with an adversary by pushing his head into a sewer, associating him with bodily hindparts.

Luther himself would have recognized in More's rhetorical excesses the accepted idiom of theological dispute. Heiko Oberman, in a section of his book on Luther entitled "God's Word in Filthy Language," considers a typical moment in Luther's prose: "'If that is not enough for you, you Devil, I have also shit and pissed; wipe your mouth on that and take a hearty bite'" (107). Some, Oberman notes, have ascribed Luther's scatological rhetoric to his being anally arrested; some link his scatology with his chronic bowel complaints; some see it as a throwback to his peasant roots. "Or is it," Oberman engagingly ponders, "perhaps just the drastically literal expression of the proverbial call: Devil, get thee behind me?" (107). Oberman's own explanation of Luther's linguistic filth, eschewing psychoanalysis, situates the language in its historical and cultural context: scatology aimed at Satan or human malefactors was typical of monastic preaching (107–8). He notes that "the filthy vocabulary of Reformation propaganda was aimed at inciting the common man. A figure of respect, be he Devil or pope, is effectively unmasked if he can be shown with his pants down" (109). R. W. Scribner discusses scatology in the woodcuts of German Reformation polemics: in one, a soldier defecates into the papal tiara; in another, the pope carries steaming excrement on his palm; in a third, the devil defecates into the mouth of Luther's opponent Johann Cochleus, a jester in cap and bells holding a mirror up to Cochleus's open mouth as the excrement falls in (81–85).

English monasticism had similar rhetorical traditions: Protestant controversialist and playwright John Bale was a friar before the Reformation, and his Protestant writings reveal the heritage of monastic preaching: "His controversial writings touch depths of scurrility and obscenity remarkable even for that age" (Knowles 58). Bale was one who assailed monastic sexual depravity. The evocation of the lower bodily stratum in invective against ideological opponents is the rhetorical equivalent of official charges of sexual misconduct against monastics. More, who spent four years in a monastery and maintained lifelong affinities with the monastic life, was no doubt familiar with rhetorical scatology: it would have come naturally to an attack on that archscatological polemicist and former monastic, Luther.

During Edward VI's reign, the dissolution of chantries and royal asset-stripping from parish churches were accompanied, as Eamon Duffy shows, by "a flood of polemical Protestant literature, much of it scurrilous, rejoicing in the destruction of image and chantry, but above all attacking the Mass, the Pope's whore who infects all her lovers":

Good mistress missa
Shall ye go from us thissa?
Well yet I must ye kissa
Alack from pain I pissa. (460)

A Protestant polemic by Henri Estienne[2] attacked friars' scatological preaching, excoriating what one might call jest saints' legends, like those of Brother Juniper (a Franciscan friar), and friars' or monks' scatological combat with demons—in one such tale, a monk threatens to defecate into the devil's mouth. (Satan runs away.) Estienne keeps apologizing for relating such vulgarities— "It is hard to find modest words to express immodest things" (262)—but it is clear that in tarring friars with this scatological brush, he is literally demonizing them—turning excrement against them as they did against the devil. Jest books were not the only locus of merriment and excrement. The rhetorical uses of laughter and scatology should alert us to the serious cultural work performed by texts represented as jest. Cleansing a city of filthy vagrants or writing against ideological foes meant pushing others—whether the lowborn or one's philosophical enemies—outside of respectable society, either literally (through roundups and expulsions) or verbally (through jests or excremental invective). "Social boundaries were being redrawn and proper, respectable society being newly and more tightly defined" (Slack, *Poverty and Policy* 24). One's own refinement demanded others' defilement; and defilement provoked expulsion.

Enemies, then, were rhetorically associated with filth and excrement, and vagrants became public enemies insofar as they were naturally dirty or endowed with filth by the imaginings of the respectable. The most desperate poor sometimes slept on dunghills because recently piled dung was warm. In a pollution-wary society, this caused alarm.

The Articulation of Civility

As Norbert Elias has shown, this was exactly the era when the idea of civility fully emerged, posited in texts such as Erasmus's influential *De Civilitate Morum Puerilium* (On good manners for boys) (1530), which advises on manners befitting the gentle classes. Elias documents the gradual progress of refinement, the "advance of the threshold of embarrassment and shame" (101); polite folk gradually stopped not only farting uninhibitedly in public but talking about farts in public.[3]

To some extent, one can track increasing refinement even among humanist jest books. In the mid-fifteenth century, the humanist Poggio Bracciolini had purveyed the following misogynistic jest, concerning the "obstinacy of women," who are "sometimes so unbending" that

they would rather die than give in once they have made their point. Then someone said, "A woman from my country was always fighting with her husband, contradicting everything he said, making fun of him, and insisting on the last word to show that she was superior. One day during a grave battle with her husband, she called him 'lousy.' In order to make her retract her words the man beat her furiously, but the more he punished her, the more she called him lousy. Finally, . . . he put a rope around her and lowered her into a cesspool, threatening to drown her if she did not change her tune. But she persisted in her verbal barrage, even when she was immersed up to the chin. Then, in order to shut her up once and for all, the man plunged her completely under the excrementious muck, hoping that imminence of death would make her improve her language. She, however, suffocating and speechless, said with her fingers what she could not with her mouth. Raising her hands above her head, she pressed her thumbnails together, thus by gesture still calling her husband lousy. For women kill lice with just these fingernails." (66–67)

Poggio, who apparently borrowed this jest from a medieval sermon exemplum, proved true to his usual form in adding the excrement—in Jacques de Vitry's sermon the husband merely "threw her into the water" (Vitry 222–23). Poggio's nauseating jest proved a shade too scatological for the refined court of Urbino; a courtier, Castiglione writes, should never be "filthy and uncleanly": he should speak with "sweetness to refresh the hearers' minds, and with merry conceits and jests to provoke them to solace and laughter," but never in a "loathsome" manner (133). And so Castiglione retold Poggio's cesspool jest in a version so free of excrement as to be unintelligible: "Where obstinacy is bent, no doubt . . . ye shall find some women that will never change purpose, as she that could no longer call her husband pricklouse, with her hands made him a sign" (206). Similarly, Castiglione modifies the harshness of Cicero's comic theory, de-emphasizing its use of facetiae as weapons in vicious ad hominem arguments, and moderates the "personal hostility" of jokes he borrows from Cicero (Lipking 305), smoothing them into gentility. Compared to Poggio's full-blooded vulgarities, Castiglione's jests are "notably sedate" (Lipking 307). The sixteenth-century rhetorician Thomas Wilson places the new, polite code of jesting among gentility, repudiating that venue of vagrants, the alehouse: he warns against "gross boording, and alehouse jesting, . . . foolish talk, and ruffian manners" (138).

Where did all this refinement come from? Elias argues that the engine driving increased civility was upward mobility:

> At this period customs, behavior, and fashions from the court are continuously penetrating the upper middle classes, where they are imitated and . . . altered in accordance with the different social situation. They thereby lose . . . their character as means of distinguishing the upper class. They are somewhat devalued. This compels those above to further refinement and development of

behavior. And from this mechanism—the development of courtly customs, their dissemination downward, their slight social deformation, their devaluation as marks of distinction—the constant movement in behavior patterns through the upper class receives part of its motivation. (100–101)[4]

Elias does not inquire into why the aristocracy differentiated itself by increasing *refinement*—why not maintain distinctness through unsurpassed vulgarity, the strategy of the British monarchy in more recent times? I suggest that the nature of the change—favoring conduct that avoided bodily contact, shunned spitting, avoided touching food others had touched—reflected the desire Mary Douglas speaks of for a self-contained, sealed-off body, a desire that expresses fear of boundary violation. In her terms, the contemporaneous flowering of the ethic of civility and the rhetoric of Tudor nationalism is to be expected: bodily integrity goes along with the integrity of national borders and with social integrity segregating the elite from those below.

Civility involved Othering: good manners were taught by stigmatizing lower-class manners. "It is boorish to wipe one's nose on one's cap or clothing," decrees Erasmus: "to do so on one's sleeve or forearm is for fishmongers" (*De Civilitate* 274). Mocking the behavior of the lower orders buttressed one's own social identity, one's place in society. Invoking the king/beggar antithesis, Leontes in *The Winter's Tale* sees as "barbarism" any effacement of the "distinguishment" between "the prince and beggar," and the difference lies in manners: it is a "*mannerly* distinguishment" (2.1.85–88).

Erasmus's *De Civilitate* helped civility replace a waning medieval concept, courtesy, which had meant behavior appropriate at court, although Elias notes bourgeois appropriations of courtesy in the late Middle Ages (102).[5] But civility differed significantly. Throughout the sixteenth century, its two meanings modified each other: the first was "good breeding, culture, refinement"; the second comprised a cluster of meanings centering on "good polity, orderly state (of a country), social order, as distinct from anarchy and disorder, good citizenship" (*OED*). This dual concept was deeply embedded in the Henrician situation: it embodied the new sense of nationhood, a more civic-than court-centered idea of the polity (reflecting London's growth and importance), a sense that value resides in the *civic* (both city and polis, London and England), a belief in the citizen's duty to promote public order (and a strong fear of disorder), an emphasis on refined manners, and a granting of refinement to the *citizen*. Starkey's dialogue between Pole and Lupset, written shortly after the English translation of *De Civilitate* appeared, invokes the concept of civility throughout: "Our law . . . in the punishment of theft is over-strait [i.e., over-strict], and faileth much from good civility" (114); the idleness of bishops and abbots is "contrary to the institution of the law and all good civility" (125); the idle who refuse to learn a craft "should be banished and driven out of the city, as person[s] unprofitable to all good civility" (142); noblemen's living in the countryside shows "a lack of all civil order and humanity" (161). The same concept represented public order, good government, and good citizenship, on the one hand, and refined behavior, on the other. To denigrate Luther, or vagrants, by sneering at their unseemly bodiliness, and thus their impoliteness, was virtually an accusation of incivility in the sense of sedition, disorder, and promotion of anarchy. (More linked Luther with German peasant uprisings as well as with excrement and sewers.) To indict lower orders for impoliteness was, by way of a remarkably sliding signifier, *civility,* to indict them for bad citizenship. Jests about the filth, sexual immorality, and bodiliness of the poor did serious cultural work in implying that the poor could not be good citizens.

Jest books, repositories of the uncivil, associated their plenteous flatulence and excrement with the lower orders or with comic clergy. The eponymous fart bequeather of *Jill of Brentford's Testament* keeps an alehouse, a hospice of the vagrant poor; the author of this vulgar comic poem, Robert Copland, also wrote a poem on idleness leading to the poorhouse, *The Highway to the Spital-house.* Tudor jest dealt not in thin, suggestive indecency but in robust vulgarity: after dictating her flatulent will, Jill

> groan[s] as panged with pain
> Gripping her belly with her hands twain
> And lift[s] up her buttock somewhat awry
> And like a handgun, she let[s] a fart fly. (sig. Bii)

But how can one explain that during this century of increasing refinement, vulgar jest books were enjoyed by readers at many levels of society, including such members of the educated elite as More at the beginning of the century and Spenser at the end? When William Hazlitt, in the age of Victorian refinement, collected and published early modern jest books, he sprinkled Walter Smith's *Twelve Merry Jests of the Widow Edith* with asterisked excisions and felt obliged to comment, "For the gross coarseness which more than occasionally occurs in *Scoggin's Jests,* it may be pleaded as an apology, that they were collected for publication upward of 300 years ago, at a period of our literature and history, when neither the employment of indelicate expressions, nor the performance of indelicate acts, was thought to be inconsistent, even in the highest circles, with morality and virtue" (*Shakespeare Jest-Books* xviii), that is, in the time of Henry VIII. And how much had refinement advanced during the sixteenth century? Hazlitt observed primly that "the state of English manners in the time of Elizabeth was not altered so much for the better as might be expected" (ix). But it was altered enough for jest books to be read as stigmatizing the nongenteel for vulgar manners. In a humanist milieu grown perhaps oppressively fastidious, indulgence in occasional bawdy and bodily humor is unsurprising, but civility had created inhibitions to be overcome. The next best thing to abjuring vulgar tales was to relish such stories as evidence of the vulgarity of the masses. Like Victorian pornography, the jest books provided a *Ventilsitten*. Hazlitt, in an era similarly vexed with anxieties about the body, class consciousness, and the specter of vagrancy and poverty, prudishly disapproved of the jest books' coarseness and indelicacy at the very moment that he was reprinting them.

Castiglione, as I have shown, cleaned up the jests he borrowed—this suave Italian was no purveyor of fart jokes. The same cleansing occurred in other jest collections: for example, *Tales and Quick Answers, Very Merry, and Pleasant to Read* cleans up its borrowings from Poggio (Lipking 326–27). Castiglione worried about inappropriate jests. According laughter high status as a distinguishing feature of humankind, he describes it attractively in its innocent hurtlessness: man is "a living creature that can laugh: because this laughing is perceived only in a man, and . . . always is a token of a certain jocundness and merry mood that he feeleth inwardly in his mind, which by nature is drawn to pleasantness, and coveteth quietness and refreshing" (137). Laughter should relieve pain, not cause it: "Whatsoever . . . causeth laughter, the same maketh the mind jocund and giveth pleasure, nor suffereth a man in that instant to mind the troublesome griefs that our life is full of" (138). But a courtier is not a jester, a fellow contemptible in his low social status, for jesters are "common": "To make men laugh always is not comely for the Courtier, nor yet in such wise as frantic, drunken, foolish and fond men and . . . common jesters do" (138).

To Castiglione, making social inferiors the butts of jokes is an unworthy activity for a courtier: "It provoketh no laughter to mock and scorn a silly soul in misery and calamity. . . . and men's minds are not bent to scoff them in misery" (139). But in the main, Castiglione discourages his courtier from telling crude jokes about the lowborn not because that will hurt their victims' feelings but because it will make the courtier resemble the objects of derision, "filthy and uncleanly in his living, with certain rude and boisterous behaviors that smell of the plough and cart a thousand mile off" (129). Of such a crudely jesting courtier, "it is not only not to be hoped that he will make a good Courtier, but he can be set to no better use than to keep sheep" (129). Note the urban bias—Castiglione sneers not at a shepherd of the literary pastoral but at a yokel farmhand. Civility implies the civic, specifically in the sense of the urban. Though Castiglione leaned heavily on Cicero for jest theory, his notion of jest was usually less combative than Cicero's. However, when it came to jest's potential for keeping the genteel distinctive in their refinement, Castiglione had learned well the lesson of the master: "Merriment," Cicero had observed, "shatters or obstructs or makes light of an opponent . . . ; and it shows the orator himself to be a man of finish, accomplishment and taste" (2:236).

This study has discussed Gabriel Harvey's scornful allusions to "Scogginists," whom he contrasts with the educated, with Ciceronians. By the time Harvey was writing in the 1590s, the elite might indulge in reading jest books, but they seldom confessed to *producing* them. In about 1516, More himself had published a slapstick verse jest; by the 1590s, few persons remotely approaching More's stature would have dreamed of attaching their names to such a thing. "Jesters" and "rhymers," Samuel Ward declared in a sermon in 1617, belonged to "the rabblement" (85). By the later sixteenth century, humanists had disowned their own creation, jest books, preserving elite literature as civil and decorous by demoting jest books to a lower cultural category that was now seen as emanating from the masses. The grossness of jests finally offended against civility.

Some of the plebeians who take ship in *Cock Lorel's Boat* (ca. 1518–19) smell so bad that they cause Cock and his men to spew (sig. Bi^v). But their bad manners, like their moral lapses, are handily wiped out: a pardoner issues a pardon allowing each to frequent brothels and alehouses and "on your own sleeve to wipe your nose / Without rebuke" (sig. [B4]^v), a clear equating of sinful behavior with mere unmannerliness. In the sixteenth century, "manners" meant both "etiquette" and "morals," as Touchstone wittily demonstrates to Corin: "If thou never wast at court, thou never sawst good manners; if thou never sawst good manners, then thy manners must be wicked; and wickedness is sin, and sin is damnation" (*As You Like It* 3.2.38–42). That "manners," like "civility," implied both small refinements of etiquette and large moral and civic virtues restricted morality and citizenship to those with refined etiquette. Only those who demonstrated by polite manners their full possession of civility could legitimately exercise power. In the Renaissance polis, only the polite had a right to be political.

The new emphasis on civility, then, helps account for disgust with the poor. However, rogue literature concerned itself not only with dirt-poor vagrants of the sort Thomas Harman writes about but also with the well-to-do, deceptive con artists of the sort Gilbert Walker and Robert Greene write about, and civility is pertinent here too. Fear that rogues might infiltrate law-abiding society, expressed in rogue pieces like Gilbert Walker's *Manifest Detection of . . . Dice-Play* and Smith's *Widow Edith,* seems a projection onto "rogues" of the everyday fear that polite society might be infiltrated by the upwardly mobile. To Elias, such fear provided the engine of ever-escalating civility. But as Frank Whigham shows, handbooks of civility were a double-edged sword: aimed at buttressing the elite by *describing* their polite behavior, civility books became how-to manuals for those wishing to insinuate themselves into higher society. Handbooks providing armor for gentlemen also provided weapons for would-be gentlemen. What was meant as a "gesture of exclusion" by the elite was "read, rewritten, and reemployed by mobile base readers" (5–6). Michael Holmes suggests that one should view rogue writings as "a fairly coherent body of anti-courtesy literature that carnivalizes and destabilizes the very nature of the gentleman, and, in turn, the ideology of civility" (n.p.). Noting that the courtesy book *The Institution of a Gentleman* (1555) borrows a chapter on gentlemanly dice-play from Walker's closely contemporary *Manifest Detection of . . . Dice-Play*, Holmes argues that "the fact that in 1609 Thomas Dekker—one of the principal writers of rogue literature—actually prepared a satiric courtesy text entitled *The Gull's Hornbook* . . . is a strong indication that rogue-text authors recognized the parodic relations between their own writings and normative instructional treatises" (n.p.).

The Female Vagrant as Jest Book Hero: *The Twelve Merry Jests of the Widow Edith*

A jest book about a vagrant woman, Walter Smith's *Twelve Merry Jests of the Widow Edith* (1525), richly articulates the preoccupations of its age. Edith—who despite the title is never a widow—is the daughter of an Exeter yeoman. She leaves her husband and, when abandoned while pregnant by another man, becomes vagrant, and the child dies. The text tracks her from Exeter to Andover, then to Wainsworth, Kew, "Hormynger," Brandonbery, Coulme (Calne?) in Oxfordshire, Stratford at the Bow, Barking, and London. She puts up at alehouses and commits petty crimes as she goes. When London gets too hot for her, she repairs to Windsor and then via Southwark to Sussex. She also visits Towton, Sevenoaks, St. Mary Cray, Rochester, Arundel, Croydon, and Eltham. She returns to London by Battersea and then goes to Chelsea. When last seen, she is moving from Westminster through Holborn to destinations unknown. Like most vagrants, she does some stints in jail, including imprisonment for a year for failing to repay thirteen shillings that she has borrowed (sig. B3).

Edith's wanderings create a map of England; the roll call of place names echoes the age's great topographical inventories or the Poor Laws' address list of village and parish locations to which orders could be posted. Jest books took pride in Englishness, supported by a particularity of geographic place names; for instance, *A Hundred Merry Tales* resituates in English locales a number of tales originally set in other parts of Europe. That Edith's confident geographical awareness was not typical of real vagrants is suggested by Patricia Fumerton's account of the examination of a vagrant woman who "went out of Warwick to Kenilworth and lay there that night. The next night she lay at a town two miles beyond Coventry the name she knoweth not. And so from town to town in and out. And one night she lay in Noneton but where she hath been ever sithens she knoweth not." Fumerton comments, "The inability of vagrant subjects to name many of the towns they passed through, as [appears] in cases of itinerant pedlars arrested for vagrancy, underscores [their] unplaceable 'nowhereness.'" But *Widow Edith* cheerily creates a title figure who is more the self-confident tourist than the bemused and unmoored wanderer.

Adhering to an antifeminist literary tradition in which young women learn deceit and abuse of men from their mothers (Woodbridge, *Women* 224–43), Edith's life of crime begins when her mother brings her up to avoid "good huswifery" and to "forge and lie" (preface). "Life of crime," however, is an overstatement: Edith sets her sights low and has only a couple of strings to her bow: she skips out of inns without paying her bill, borrows petty cash (and occasionally clothing) which she does not repay, and feigns wealth so that men will court her. Despite a brief bigamous marriage, she does not aim to snag a husband: her goal in courtships is a few days' lodging and free meals. Not very competent even at modest scams, she keeps getting caught and exposed, often literally: she is repeatedly stripped.

Edith's pitiful exploits are so repetitious as to make readers grateful to have only "twelve merry jests" and not another "hundred merry tales." But herein lies a clue to her literary pedigree—Edith is a specialist whose modus operandi repeats because she belongs to a certain category of vagrants, like the *Liber Vagatorum*'s category *Over-Söntzen-goers*, who claim to have "suffered by war, fire, or captivity," and thus "lost all they had," dressing "prettily and with neatness, as though they were noble, though it is not so" (115). Edith at first claims to be homeless because of a great, unspecified wrong (sig. [A3]–[A3]ᵛ). Perhaps because other vagrants have more specific disaster stories, Edith is disbelieved, and she later fleshes out her stories with a few more details—after traveling through Eltham, she claims at her next stop to be a wealthy woman with a home in Eltham. Often with the help of a borrowed dress, she purports to be a wealthy widow from another part of the country who is on the lookout for a husband—or sometimes for a husband for her daughter—which suggests that Edith is not young. Clearly she has been conceived by Smith as a vagrant who specializes in one small scam and evades getting caught too often by taking care to keep moving. Her literary brothers and sisters, specialists in petty crimes and deceits, pepper the discourse of vagrancy, from the *Liber Vagatorum* to the texts of John Awdeley and Thomas Harman in the 1560s to Greene's cony-catching pamphlets in the 1590s.

Ratifying stereotype, Edith is a vagrant by choice, not necessity. De-emphasizing her abandonment by a lover, Smith emphasizes her leaving her husband for no reason but her corrupt nature and bad upbringing. Like other vagrants, she is deceitful by nature, promiscuous, and given to petty crime. Though not among the period's more ingenious tricksters, she pulls off one complex trick: she attracts the attention of some Canterbury-bound pilgrims by a feint at drowning herself in the Thames in despair after being robbed, a variant of a trick found in Greene's *Second Part of Cony-Catching, Puss in Boots, The Winter's Tale,* and the *Liber Vagatorum.* The pilgrims take her to the home of a friend, a scrivener. She expresses a desire to renounce the world and become a nun; the scrivener's wife lends Edith her best gown to go to church. All Edith is after is decent clothes, but before she can get away with the dress, the scrivener and his wife find her out, confiscate the gown, and vow to send her forth "stark belly naked" (sig. C4^v). Edith goes to a draper, whom she talks out of a new gown by claiming to be rich, and for payment she sends the draper to the scrivener. When these two learn how they have been cheated, they vow to keep it quiet, or "we shall be laughed to scorn" (sig. Dii^v).[6]

As in rogue literature, Edith is tricky and merry; a jokey tone prevails. The work is situated as a jest book by its title (*The Twelve Merry Jests*) and by chapters headed with the jest book "how" formula: "How this lying widow Edith made a poor man to unthatch his house" (sig Aii). As so often, vagrancy is made funny: Edith is "merry" though in jail for a year (sig. B3), merry upon returning to London after criminal adventures ("over Thames was rowed full merry" [sig. Eiii^v]), and "glad and merry" when released from three weeks in jail, sitting with her legs in "massive chains day and night" (sig. Fiiii^v).[7] The fear of being "laughed to scorn," as in Harman's *Caveat,* keeps cropping up—a man with whom Edith flirts finds her out but delays telling others for fear of being laughed at (sig. Fi^v). The invitation to readers to enjoy tricksters' cleverness creates a merry atmosphere in which nobody's pain is real—neither the pain of the cheated draper nor the pain of a stripped and humiliated Edith. Readers are not asked to believe in their pain any more than modern audiences experience a catharsis of pity and fear through watching the Roadrunner blow up Wile E. Coyote.

At one point this immediately pre-Reformation text draws on the comic tradition that made butts of the Catholic clergy. Edith cheats a cleric by telling him in confession that she is rich and wants to forsake the world, just as Howlglas correctly assumes that priests misuse information gained in confession. Hoping for some financial fallout from Edith's piety, the cleric entertains her to the tune of five nobles, at which point she skips out. He then makes a speech conventionally lamenting the clergy's worldliness, confessing to the usual wife-chasing: "Why do we not let men's wives alone?" (sig. Ci).

In an age in which domestic ideology, fostered by the Crown, was trumpeted from pulpits, Edith is antidomestic. Her mother turned her against "good huswifery." Her restless wanderings are the opposite of settled domesticity. She tricks an innkeeper into unthatching his house, apparently for the fun of it—Edith is a literally a homewrecker. (Again, one catches an echo of Howlglas, who unthatches the roof of one employer in revenge for being fired [Fiii^v–Gi].) Chaining up Edith is condign punishment, just as the stocks were apt punishment for beggars, since she has declined settled domesticity.

Deceit is Edith's middle name: her mother educated her to "study to forge and lie." "Forge" means "invent an imaginary story" (*OED*), and Edith grows fairly accomplished at inventing or at least embellishing stories. Vagrants were stripped and whipped for feigning destitution or disabilities; the frequency with which Edith is stripped, given that she never performs disability, suggests that divestment is a symbolic disclosure of deceit. The scrivener and his wife try to send her forth "stark belly naked." Another man takes Edith's kirtle and gown in lieu of money that she has failed to repay, sending her to the next town in her petticoat (sig. B3^v). In another episode, Edith, claiming wealth, takes up with a serving man of Sir Thomas Neville. After staying with him for a few nights' free lodging, she slips away, but after trying the same trick twice more she gets caught and is "stripped . . . out of her array" (sig. Eiii). Since this time she has not cheated anyone of clothing, the stripping seems purely an exposure of a deceitful nature, and the exposers are spitefully vindictive: "Walk, whore, they all gan say" (sig. Eiii). After her exposure at More's house, Edith is stripped of her gown before being sent to prison.

The stripping of this deceitful woman, like that of Spenser's Duessa in *The Faerie Queene,* belongs to the same realm as the popular tale (recently refamiliarized in A. S. Byatt's *Possession*) of Melusine, a beautiful bride whose clothes conceal a snaky tail of spectacular length—in some versions the husband finally sees Melusine in the bath, her tail touching the ceiling. (One is not supposed to ask what was wrong with his sense of touch in the bedroom—this is a folktale after all.) Edith's nature is only metaphorically snaky—but the old tales often expressed, by naïve serpentine appendages, something metaphoric, something inward. The Melusine tale, like related monster bridegroom tales, expresses anxieties of the newly married, the fear of finding something monstrous in the beloved. Stripping expressed folk fear when accused witches were searched for devil's tokens, and I suspect similar terror was expressed in early modern stripping of beggars, which ostensibly verified disability: if the body were genuinely disabled, sympathy could officially be extended. But fear of beggars was not unrelated to fear of witches, and at some level of consciousness decent folk *wanted* to strip the bodies of the poor and find them monstrous—and were willing to whip them until they *were* monstrous—because to find the poor monstrous was to put some distance between them and one's own species.

In an age when women's dresses were long and concealing and modesty valued, being stripped even of outer garments—down to a petticoat—ought to have been painfully shaming. But through all her strippings, Edith never shows a hint of humiliation. She is always "merry," because she is beneath humiliation; she is shameless. At a time when (in Elias's formulation) thresholds of shame were rising and the polite were denying their bodiliness to retain distinction from social inferiors, the stripping of an Edith—or of beggars and vagrants—showcased the physicality of the poor, putting their naked bodies on display while the bodies of the polite were discreetly shielded from public gaze. Clothing was a sign of social standing, regulated by sumptuary laws, and one reason Edith is so often divested is that she lies about her social status, pretending to wealth. Ann Rosalind Jones has shown that the part of the Patient Griselde tale that most struck contemporaries was the episode wherein Griselde is stripped and sent home to her impoverished father (chap. 4); and this tale deals with a woman who marries above herself (see also Baskins, Jaster).[8] The poor could not afford shame. Even if they avoided public stripping, nakedness peeked through the holes in their clothes. In literature, people from good homes get to stay dressed and appear in tragedies; the poor are stripped and appear in jest books, where their nakedness is funny.

Though Edith repeatedly gets her comeuppance for pretending to be rich, she is also a vehicle to expose the social climbing of those who try to marry her for her supposed money. Three hangers-on of the rich and famous— followers of Sir Thomas More, William Roper, and Sir Thomas Neville— evoke a society whose social fluidity called forth threats of exposure, of being laughed to scorn. One of these young men in the slippery category "servant"—More's own man—wrote *Widow Edith*. In placing himself among those taken in by Edith, was Walter Smith making some gesture of self-effacement, some disclaimer of social ambition? In fact, Smith did pretty well:

the year More became Lord Chancellor, he obtained for Smith, his personal servant for nine years, an important office, Sword-Bearer to the Lord Mayor (A. W. Ward 154). Perhaps it was through his comic literary tastes that Smith found favor; he was to bequeath to More's son John his copies of *The Canterbury Tales* and of Boccaccio (A. W. Ward 154).[9]

As *Widow Edith* shows, almost as insidious as vagrants pretending to disability were vagrants who pretended not to be vagrants: those who feigned respectability. Gilbert Walker's *Manifest Detection of . . . Dice-Play,* one of the earliest English rogue texts, features only "respectable" rogues and explains their ability to pass as genteel—many of them *are* wellborn, having been recruited into the gambling underworld after losing their fortunes at dice, a kind of vampire syndrome. Here is a glimpse of the way economic changes that shifted wealth away from the landed were being displaced onto a supposed criminal underworld. John Awdeley's only three developed anecdotes (apparently added to the 1575 edition of his *Fraternity of Vagabonds*) concern "a courtesy man," a "cheater or fingerer," and a "ring faller" who pass as respectable citizens. The courtesy man, "cleanly appareled" and able to "behave himself mannerly" (as if he had been reading Erasmus's *De Civilitate*), claims to be one of many fortune-fallen men who "have been wealthily brought up" and are now "ashamed to declare [their] misery" (sig. [A3]^v). These phony shamefaced poor, trusted in hostelries because they "have the port of right good gentlemen" (sig. [A4]^v), often check out early, stealing the sheets. The cheaters or fingerers are almost undetectable as "idle vagabonds" since "they go gorgeously, sometime with waiting men" ([A4]^v). Unlike beggars shunned for their disgusting personal habits, courtesy men, cheaters and fingerers, and ring fallers cause anxiety by mimicking gentility, and this is the sort of vagrant Widow Edith is. Like courtesy men, she is "cleanly appareled" (in borrowed clothes), can "behave [her]self mannerly," and uses these class markers to work petty swindles. The criminal infiltrator of polite society became a character type in mainstream literature—the well-dressed, literate cutpurse Edgeworth in Jonson's *Bartholomew Fair* passes as a civil young gentleman.

Since accent was already becoming a class marker in England (see Mugglestone), feigning gentility must have meant replicating genteel speech— "courtesy man" suggests behavior that would pass muster even at court. Courtesy men, fingerers, ring fallers, and Widow Edith do not speak thieves' cant. The texts' very silence on the language of vagrants who pass as respectable citizens is eloquent: the energy devoted to warnings about cant, in the light of these "respectable" vagrants, looks like an evasion. Who, after all, would *need* a warning in print against those who declare their criminality so openly as to converse in thieves' cant? The ones you need to be warned about are those who sound civil. High indignation against beggars speaking an easily recognizable criminal dialect forms a mental refuge from what was *really* frightening about the new mobilities of the age—the prospect of polite society infiltrated by impersonators of respectability. The stripping of witches to look for devil's tokens expressed a fear that some who mingled with the respectable were merely *passing;* and stripping vagrants expressed the same fear—some who live in proper society are secretly unworthy of friendship or sympathy because they are not of high social rank.[10] In terms anticipating the 1950s' nightmare visions of communists infiltrating every neighborhood, Edward Hext, a Somerset justice, described the infiltration of decent society by well-dressed beggars. His paranoia recalls witch beliefs: "They have intelligence of all things intended against them, for there be of them that will be present at every assize, sessions, and assembly of justices, and will so clothe themselves for that time as any should deem him to be an honest husbandman; so nothing is spoken, done, or intended to be done but they know it" (Tawney and Power 2:345).[11]

Edith's strippings forcibly remind her of her low rank; but in one jest, that is not enough—when she feigns gentility in the very home of Thomas More, she is purged by a violent laxative. The age was fascinated by practical jokes. Castiglione, the first theorist of such jests, declared only non-cruel jokes proper to a courtier. Many Renaissance practical jokes, however, *are* hurtful, and their aim is often, as in *Widow Edith,* to expose pretense. Earlier, literary practical jokes were often played on the powerful by the less powerful—vagrant Howlglas performs many practical jokes on the prosperous; in fabliaux, including the Miller's Tale and the Reeve's Tale, the joke is on rich husbands cuckolded by poor students. Medieval practical jokes often operated within one social class—like the god-game perpetrated on Sir Gawain by Lord and Lady Bercilak and Morgan-le-Faye. But Renaissance practical jokes more typically work socially downward—the lord's joke on Christopher Sly; Prince Hal's on Francis and on Falstaff, Henry V's on Williams, Faustus's on the horse courser. Renaissance practical jokes also betray uneasiness about unstable social hierarchy, an instability that they sometimes enact while creating a virtual reality for their victims. In *The Taming of the Shrew*'s induction, a lord hires actors to create a god-game wherein the "beggar" (Ind.1.40) Christopher Sly is waited on like a "mighty lord" (64);[12] and in *A Midsummer Night's Dream,* Bottom the Weaver is attended by servants who treat him like royalty. As if to assuage fears that except for the attentions of servants there may actually *be* no difference between lords and beggars, both figures continue behaving like louts or beasts though treated royally: Sly goes on calling for small ale though advised that noblemen drink sack (Ind.2.1–2), construes the question "How fares my noble lord?"—an inquiry into his mental health—to mean "How well are you eating?" (Ind.2.98–100), invites the "lady" to hop into bed with him (Ind.2.114), and displays lower-class taste in entertainment (Ind.2.133–34). Bottom, royally attended, remains devoted to scratching and to eating oats and hay (*MND* 4.1.7–33).

Enlisting actors and attendants who are in on the joke to create a virtual reality, a god-game into which a victim steps, Renaissance practical jokes often expose their victims' bodiliness, uncouth manners, and pretensions, thus pitting pretense against pretense, a play staged to expose someone's role-playing. To explode a Falstaff's or a Parolles's pretense to valor, costumes create a pretend world of counter-robbers (*1 Henry IV*), fairies (*The Merry Wives of Windsor*), or soldiers (*All's Well That Ends Well*). To explode Edith's pretense to gentility, a dinner party is staged into which she walks as if a genteel guest, although everyone else is in on the joke that her food has been spiked. Other guests keep up the charade that they simply enjoy conversation when in fact they are keeping Edith talking to discomfit her by preventing her rushing to the closestool. Such practical jests have the same aim as Harman's description of vagrant trickery: exposure. Like witchcraft prosecutions, such jests bring hidden realities to light.

One of Howlglas's practical jokes, though late medieval in operating socially upward, heralds the Renaissance in exposing cowardice. Howlglas creates a nighttime tableau starring a stuffed wolf with two children's shoes in its mouth; a boastful innkeeper, thinking the wolf alive, betrays craven terror, at which Howlglas "laughed at this hardy man, that would have slain ten wolves, and he was much afraid of one dead wolf" (sig. [I4]). The host "was ashamed, and he wist not what to say. And then he left his boasting, and jesting" (sig. [I4]ᵛ–Ki). The tale anticipates the exposure of cowardice in a Falstaff or a Parolles, and as in those later jests confederates aid in the scheme: three merchants are in on the joke, and the whole town hears about it. In many Renaissance practical jokes, several people gang up on a victim, who becomes isolated in exposure and humiliation. Henri Bergson's generalization that "in laughter we always find an unavowed intention to humiliate, and consequently to correct our neighbour" (477) holds true at least in regard to Renaissance practical jokes. Oberon's making Titania fall in love with an ass is a move in a power struggle, as were many Renaissance jests. Henry V predicts the serious consequences of the tennis ball jest, a calculated insult enmeshed in international power maneuvering: "This jest shall savour but of shallow wit, / When thousands weep, more than did laugh at it" (1.2.295–96). Jests are often about more than merriment; but in the Renaissance they were bound up in class tensions and, in their exposures and humiliations, grew nastier than ever.

The practical joke with the laxative is more than just an exposure. Gail

Paster has shown that women were considered leaky vessels, at both ends: they were sexually loose, they menstruated, they suffered bladder incontinence, and their incontinent mouths were always talking and could not keep a secret. But Edith *can* keep a secret, and that fact proves equally repugnant: because she holds her tongue, concealing a deceitful life, she is violently opened up, *caused* to be leaky and incontinent. The poor were considered filthy, and the letting loose of a flood of diarrhea in a host's coalhouse is a fairly filthy act. Yet this filth is imposed on Edith by supposedly refined, upper-crust hosts, just as the vagrant poor had filth imposed on them by circumstance and by the gross imaginations of polite people who held their noses when vagrants passed, just as dirty jests written by humanists were later ascribed to the lower orders.

More's house resembles Eusebius's home, imagined by More's friend Erasmus in his colloquy *Convivium Religiosum* (The godly feast) at about the time More moved to Chelsea. The well educated withdrew to such homes to discuss, often over a good meal, social problems like homelessness. But hospitality within one's home—unlike alms dispensed at the gate—was for social equals: when an actual member of the homeless set has the effrontery to *join* the meal, the response is an act of antihospitality: they spike her food. Given the developing polarity between the safety of the parlor and the terrors of the road, between settled householder and mobile vagrant, the most shocking thing a vagrant could do was invade a house, just as the most terrifying ghost stories—which are told around a fireside, emblem of domestic safety—are about haunted houses. When an exterior threat moves indoors, blurring the boundary between inside and out, terror reigns. Edith really gets threatening and needs a humiliating punishment when she invades the home of a humanist. Just as her bowels are forcibly evacuated, so she is expelled from the house, as the language expelling beggars from towns resembled that of the medical purge. Keeping an Edith outside the house, or expelling her if she manages to get in, replicates the way vagrants were fed at the gate. Vagrants were to be kept at bay emotionally, too, by ideologies that made pity a sucker's emotion: they were not allowed past the doorposts of erected severity into the human heart.

During Edith's stay in the More home, she meets Margaret Giggs, a historical figure[13] whom Nicholas Harpsfield called one of the household's most prominent and interesting members, "furnished with much virtue and wisdom, and with the knowledge of the Latin and Greek tongues, yea, and physic too, above many that seem good and cunning physicians" (103). In 1537, twelve years after the publication of *Widow Edith,* Giggs performed one of the age's heroic acts. When Henry VIII's henchmen arrived at the Charterhouse monastery, where More had lived for four years, the recent execution of several abbots of other monasteries did not dampen the courage of the determined Charterhouse men. Faced with the demand to swear an oath of allegiance to Henry as supreme head of the English church, "ten remained, 'unmoved, unshaken, unseduced, unterrified,' who would not swear" (235):

> They were immediately lodged in a filthy ward of Newgate. . . . Chained without possibility of movement in a foul atmosphere, and systematically starved, they were thus left, . . . to "be dispatched by the hand of God." Abandoned by all, and dying slowly of hunger and fever, they received a moiety of succour and a more precious instance of love from a devoted woman. Margaret Giggs, the adopted daughter of Sir Thomas More, had learnt from him to practise charity and knew well of her father's admiration for the Carthusians. She now bribed her way to their prison and, acting the part of a milkmaid, carried in a bucket on her head food, which she placed with her own hands between their lips. . . . She brought also clean linen which she put on them, and cleansed them as they stood unable to move hand or foot. The effects of her ministration betrayed her; the authorities, finding the prisoners still alive, reprimanded the gaoler and [she] was denied entrance. Undeterred, she obtained access to the roof and endeavoured, by removing some tiles, to let food down in a basket. She failed in her design, and the Carthusians died one by one through the summer months. (Knowles 235–36)

Giggs is the antitype of a trickster hero. Though like Howlglas and Edith she deconstructs a roof, her action serves a merciful deed, as does her pretense to be of a lower social rank (a milkmaid), reversing Edith's pretense to a higher. Edith and Howlglas cheat people out of food; Giggs gives food. Where in jest books young women sneak into monastic chambers for immoral purposes, Giggs sneaks into the chambers of monastic men for benevolent purposes. She undresses them for humane purposes, reversing the immoral motives of the same action in a jest book. This woman had guts; she stood up for those despised by others. Because she had learned "to practice charity," she could overcome the repugnance of a woman of good family to filthy surroundings and visit a hellhole prison; she could overcome womanly modesty toward male bodiliness to the extent of stripping and washing the prisoners. Though refined etiquette demanded keeping one's hands away from others' food, she put food between the prisoners' lips with her own hands.

But this saintly antitrickster *does* appear in a jest book. In *Widow Edith,* Giggs makes a cameo appearance, reveling and gossiping at More's house (sig. Fiᵛ). Smith does not tell us if Giggs was there when Edith was slipped the laxative, or when she was stripped and taken to prison, bound and unable to move, not unlike the heroic Carthusians in her punishment, if not her principles. Smith does not tell us—because he is not interested, one feels—

whether Giggs's charity extended to vagrants. But monastics and vagrants were similar in being pariahs, and Giggs seems not the sort of woman to let public contempt override her plain human sympathy for imprisoned people who had no other friends. Would Margaret have visited Edith in prison? Would she have changed that petticoat, filthy from three weeks in leg irons, for clean linens, with her own hands? The Walter Smith who created and/or embellished "Widow Edith" did not ask that kind of question.

It is hard, though, when reading the jokey accounts of the poor and homeless in this period, not to long for a few maverick sympathetic voices. Were there not *any* jest book readers who slammed the smirking book shut and declared, "This story isn't very funny"? Where were you, Margaret Giggs, when Widow Edith needed you?

Notes

1. Considering the association of disease with the poor, and the fear of disease on the part of those in power, Carroll interestingly posits disease as "the inverse energy of power: Power operates *down* the social hierarchy, while social and political 'infection' operate *up* the chain, threatening those of 'better disposition'" (*Fat King* 128).

2. The work, published in France in 1566, was translated into English as *A World of Wonders* at a later period of virulent anti-Catholic feeling, 1607 (in the wake of the Gunpowder Plot).

3. The ultimate result, after four centuries' further refinement, was that my computer's spellchecker recognizes "flatulence" but not "farts" as a word: it suggests that I might mean "facts" or "warts."

4. The stylish Latinate diction by which the educated distinguished themselves from those below, which I discussed in Harman's case (see chap. 1), belonged to this drive toward increased civility. As Richard Halpern observes, it is no accident that "Erasmus, who reorganized the teaching of Latin around the concept of style, also wrote the first modern book of manners. . . . Social manners and literary style . . . cooperated to produce a subject 'well fashioned in soul, in body, in gesture, and in apparel'" (32).

5. John Hale notes the spread across Europe during the sixteenth century of the phrase "civil conversation," in the sense of "discussion amongst civilized people of civilized subjects" (366). Stefano Guazzo's *Civil Conversation* (1574), was translated into French, English, German, Spanish, and Latin; the Dutchman Johann Althusen published *Two Books of Civil Conversation* (1611). Edmund Spenser wrote that "in Princes hall / That vertue should be plentifull found, / Which of all goodly manners is the ground / And roote of civil conversation" (qtd. in Hale 366). The spread was contemporary with the rise of nation-states across Europe.

6. There are few later allusions to Widow Edith, but Dekker seems to have her in mind in his cony-catching piece *Lantern and Candlelight*, published nearly a century after *Widow Edith*. Here a "harlot" manages to infiltrate polite society because she is "civilly attired": "And where must her lodging be taken up but in the house of some citizen whose known reputation she borrows, or rather steals, putting it on as a cloak to cover her deformities.

... For example, she will lie in some Scrivener's house. ... The first man that she meets of her acquaintance shall, without much pulling, get her into a tavern. Out of him she kisses a breakfast and then leaves him. The next she meets does, upon as easy pulleys, draw her to a tavern again. Out of him she cogs a dinner, and then leaves him" (247). The borrowed clothing, sexual trickery earning no more than a good meal, lodging in a respectable house, and even the conning of a scrivener bespeak the Edith story.

7. In the public jollity attending the spectacle of vagrants' being imprisoned and/or whipped, one recalls that visits to Bedlam were a popular public entertainment. Carroll notes that "for many the spectacle of the lunatic poor was essentially comic" (107); he cites the visit to "Bethlem Monastery" in Dekker's *The Honest Whore, Part I*, where the confined mad folk enact "such antic and such pretty lunacies, / That spite of sorrow they will make you smile" (5.2.160–61).

8. In Queen Elizabeth's celebrated remark "I thank God I am endued with such qualities that if I were turned out of the realm in my petticoat I were able to live in any place in Christendom," Jones see an "extraordinary and unexpected casting of herself as Griselda" (chap. 4). But the allusion may be wider, and it may involve an extraordinary and unexpected identification with the realm's beggars, witches, Widow Ediths, and all others subject to humiliating strip searches.

9. As I point out in appendix B, *Widow Edith* can be placed in a tradition of jest biographies; these have many points of contact, as I have shown, with rogue biographies such as that of Ned Brown in Robert Greene's *The Black Book's Messenger*. That *Widow Edith* was written by a member of More's household perhaps reflects the More circle's interest in biography—More's biography of Richard III and the biographies of More himself by Roper and Harpsfield. One might well read *Widow Edith* as parodic of this tradition, a carnivalization of straight biography.

10. Michael Holmes argues that "of central importance to cony-catching literature is the debasement of gentlemanliness by the cunning misappropriation and misuse of civility's material and performative signifiers; . . . sartorial and behavioral masquerade is a staple topic of the genre" (n.p.).

11. Of beggars' supposed histrionic ability to feign poverty and disability on the one hand or gentility on the other, Carroll writes, "There seems little, in these accounts, that such beggars cannot do: they can forge official documents, feign disease and mutilation, . . . even 'play' the role of middle-class citizen. . . . Rarely has any culture fashioned so wily and powerful an enemy out of such degraded and pathetic materials" (*Fat King* 47).

12. Sly is situated in the discourse of vagrancy by being called "a tinker and a beggar" in the dramatis personae (one recalls that tinkers were regularly included in rogue rosters by writers like Awdeley and Harman), by his frequenting of alehouses, and by an alehouse hostess's threatening him with "a pair of stocks, you rogue!" (Ind.1.2). Carroll places Sly in the discourse of poverty (*Fat King* 158–67).

13. There may be a number of historical figures in *Widow Edith*, prefiguring Harman's naming of actual beggars like Nicholas Jennings. Giving these tales the trappings of verisimilitude seems a hallmark of Tudor scam artist pieces. A. W. Ward reports, "Of the characters actually named in *Widow Edith*, I have traced all but the widow's father John Hawkins, her husband Thomas Ellys, Master Guy and his sister of Stratford, John Frank and his wife of Fulham, Goodman Rosse of Sevenoaks, the two servants of Roper and Lington, and John Coates of Holborn" (155).

6. Lear, the Homeless King

> Adequate and permanent shelter is a basic need, and its absence has a
> deleterious effect upon physical and mental health, personal
> development, and the ability to exercise individual rights and
> obligations.
> —"Resolution on Homelessness," American Psychological Association

THE LAST CHAPTER CLOSED with a wish for what *King Lear,* I think, can offer: a few maverick sympathetic voices. The play takes a hard look at homelessness. Sometimes, as happens in the discourse of vagrancy, the play looks through the eyes of a jester, this time an actual court jester. The polarity between home and homeless had been sharpening during the sixteenth century, and in this early seventeenth-century tragedy the exploration of the centered sense of home and the nomadic diaspora of the homeless is at its most intense.[1] The play's shattering questions about humanity and mortality may invite universalist readings; but I will foreground a more specific context: the plunge into homelessness of so many characters is imagined precisely in terms of the discourse of vagrancy, and the play's language of violence and anger draws on a familiar lexicon from vagrancy texts. Unlike many new historicist and cultural materialist critics, however, I will not read the play as a text of despair or conclude that it finally collapses into the politically conservative or reactionary. Read against many texts I have explored in this book—and I think they represent the mainstream of English Renaissance thought—*King Lear* is, I will argue, politically and socially radical.

Others have questioned the play's degree of social awareness: Lear's eyes are opened to the inequities of his reign only when he lacks agency to change the system. As Jonathan Dollimore says, "Insofar as Lear identifies with suffering it is at the point when he is powerless to do anything about it. . . . His compassion emerges from grief only to be obliterated by grief" (192–93). Walter Cohen notes that Lear's "social experience . . . precludes a return to the throne; although he simply transcends interest in worldly power with a sublime indifference, the final scene of the play brutally reveals the hopeless inadequacy of this attitude" (334). But this is too narrow, too king-centered a view of the play's wide-ranging social and economic critique—Lear was not responsible for all the realm's social ills, and he alone could not have cured them. The cure the play points toward is more radical than royalty-centered readings have imagined.

For years, in my teaching and writing, I have combated the idea that Shakespeare stood head and shoulders above his culture or was centuries ahead of his time. I have argued that Shakespeare was *not* a feminist ahead of his time, did *not* consistently demystify the magical thinking to which his age was prone, and did *not* always resist the temptation to scapegoat marginal groups or individuals. I have argued that while we complain of those who turn Shakespeare into a cultural icon transcending time, we literary scholars do it ourselves when we "exempt him from the rigorous historicizing to which we subject his contemporaries: how many times have we read that Shakespeare demystified, exposed, treated with ironic detachment, parodied, inverted, played gracefully with the conventions and beliefs which his benighted contemporaries adopted blindly?" (Woodbridge, *Scythe* 19). It is, then, with some chagrin that I now argue that on the issue of poverty and homelessness Shakespeare, in *King Lear* at least, stood head and shoulders above his culture and was centuries ahead of his time—and perhaps ahead of ours.

Broken Homes

The domestic interiors of *King Lear* cannot be called homey. There is a chair to which Gloucester is bound when he is blinded; and mad Lear takes a joint stool for Goneril. Lear in his madness may be fantasizing the curtains in the hovel (3.6.83), but it does have cushions (3.6.34), a degree of comfort absent from the play's castles, where no furniture or amenities are mentioned. What style of interior decoration would suit the taste of Goneril or Regan? Tapestries with violent and erotic mythological scenes? Lockable cabinets, in a Jacobean style, for poison storage? Readers are free to imagine, since nothing is specified: the absence of details conjuring domestic coziness fits perfectly a play where "home" is a myth to be exploded.

In many Renaissance texts, home represents personal centeredness, the focus of one's universe, a safe haven—one thinks of Ben Jonson's "Inviting a Friend to Supper" or the country house poems. *King Lear* is not one of those texts. Its many outdoor scenes decenter the individual: on the heath, winds blow indiscriminately on Lear, not caring whether he is beggar or king. The monarch so accustomed to command that he has come to believe that the elements will obey him—a true centered self—now shrinks miserably. The thunder will not peace at his bidding (4.6.101–2). But indoor scenes too are antihavens, arenas of division where kingdoms and bodies are mutilated.

In a brutal corollary of Tudor and Stuart domestic ideology, which declared the family a little commonwealth with the father as king, this play collates divided family with divided kingdom.[2] What Thomas M. Greene notes as a central structural principle in Jonson's works—an analogy between governor, householder, "inner self," and "identity," radiating from circles within circles (326)—was an underpinning ideology of the period; and if home was a series of concentric circles—body, family, state—one sees in *King Lear* mutilation within every circle.

"Home" means "the body" in Edmund's false report of Edgar: "With his preparèd sword he charges home / My unprovided body" (2.1.50–51). From the mid-sixteenth century, "home" was used adverbially to suggest the penetration of a human body by a thrusted weapon, as in "to strike home" (*OED*). Edmund's conflation of body and household is even stronger in that "provided" was used of preparations for hospitality—for example, in the context of Timon's excessive hospitality (*Timon of Athens* 1.2.192–93) or the sinister double entendre of Lady Macbeth's preparations for the arrival of King Duncan: "He that's coming / Must be provided for" (*Macbeth* 1.5.66–67). Regan refuses hospitality to Lear with the words "I looked not for you yet, nor am provided / For your fit welcome" (2.4.234–35). Home in *King Lear* becomes a locus of revenge and punishment. Two speakers allude to home as a punished human body just after being shut out of a house: "These injuries the King now bears will be revenged home" (3.3.11–12), vows Gloucester, after crying, "they took from me the use of mine own house" (3.3.3–4); and "I will punish home," snarls Lear, incredulously marveling, "in such a night / To shut me out?" (3.4.16–18).

Households are mutilated in the breakup of families (Lear's and Gloucester's), of marriages (the Albany and Cornwall families are threatened by adultery), and in the breakdown of master-servant relations in the Cornwall household. Hospitality violations abound. The Cornwalls are both poor guests and poor hosts: Cornwall blinds Gloucester while a guest in his home, and of Lear and his knights, Regan keeps her vow "if they come to sojourn at my house / I'll not be there" (2.1.103–4). When the Cornwalls decamp to avoid offering him hospitality, Lear is at first merely puzzled: "'Tis strange that they should so depart from home / And not send back my messenger" (2.4.1–2). And well he might be: one recalls Jonson's praise of Penshurst's providedness to receive the king and his entourage even in its owners' absence ("To Penshurst" 76–88). Gloucester, to whose home Regan repairs uninvited, gets a cryptic explanation of the Cornwalls' abrupt departure from home and their abrogation of hospitality: they have received letters from her father and sister, "which I least thought it fit / To answer from our home" (2.1.125–26); Regan will not favor Lear with, as it were, even a Cornwall postmark. As the action moves from Lear's castle to Albany's palace to Gloucester's house to a hovel, not even the audience is invited inside the Cornwall home—if warmth of hospitality were measured by thermometer, this establishment would approach absolute zero. Edmund also strategically abandons home: asked whether Edmund knew about his father's blinding, a messenger replies, "'Twas he informed against him, / And quit the house on purpose that their punishment / Might have the freer course" (4.2.93–95). Households in this play are not places of refuge for either victims or villains; people flee *from* more often than *to* home.

Though other texts envision England as a nation-home analogous to a household, *King Lear* drains all sense of home out of England. This decentralized, feudal scene predates Tudor centralizing policies. Kent's ignorance of the details of Gloucester's life—his need to be told how many sons Gloucester has and that one is illegitimate—suggests that these earls seldom come to court (1.1). England will soon fly apart; but from the outset it has a weakly centralized government.[3]

The word "England" does not appear in *King Lear,* and "English" appears once, but only in the Folio, not in the Quarto (4.6.253). Audiences are not invited to feel very threatened by an event that in another context (say, anywhere in the English history plays) would be horrific—France's invading England. That it is *France* invading (rather than merely vague forces allied with Cordelia) is softened by the substitution of a fuzzy "our land" for "England" at the few points where Frenchness is mentioned: "It touches us as France invades our land" (5.1.26); "France spreads his banners in our noiseless land" (4.2.57). Perhaps de-emphasizing "England" is a strategy to mute audience anxiety at the prospect of French invasion. Or perhaps "English" and "England" are effaced because England does not exist anymore, since the kingdom was divided. The two new kingdoms are never given names. Rumors of war between Cornwall and Albany, representing the new kingdoms, mooted from the start, raise expectations that they will fight it out until one wins and reunifies England, Lear's division having simply produced a Lancaster-York scenario. But this does not happen.

Who can blame audiences for being confused when, on a battlefield located in an unknown setting, Albany arrests Edmund for capital treason? (5.3.84–85). Audiences are not certain of Albany's jurisdiction over Edmund as Duke of Gloucester: which new kingdom is Gloucestershire in, Albany's or Cornwall's? Since fourteen of the play's twenty-six scenes take place near Gloucester's seat, for much of the play audiences do not know what kingdom the characters are in. When Lear bemusedly asks, "Am I in France?" what is the force of Kent's answer, "In your own kingdom, sir" (4.7.80)? Whose kingdom *is* this at the moment? In a nation-building age, when England was the center of the universe, the action in *King Lear* is often radically placeless, recalling the wanderings of vagrants unable to "name many of the towns they passed through" in an England that was for them a land of "unplaceable 'nowhereness.'"

In the limbo of authority at play's end, the Cornwall kingdom is up for grabs because both Cornwalls are dead, and Lear lives for only eleven lines after Albany reassigns to him his half of the kingdom. Albany then offers sovereignty of "this realm" (the Albany kingdom only, or the Albany and Cornwall kingdoms reunited?) to the Earls of Kent and Gloucester; one declines and the other does not answer. There is little sense of England as a nation-home.

Recent criticism pressing an analogy between King Lear and King James I is problematic, among other reasons, in that James's publicity campaign stressed his role as the unifier of England, Scotland, and Wales, while *King Lear* radically disarticulates England. In his first speech to Parliament in 1604, James proudly declared that Britain "united, [in] the right and title of . . . my person, . . . is now become like a little world within itself" (272). Works closely contemporary with *King Lear* stress James's reversal of the mythic Brutus's frightening, Lear-like division of the kingdom: Anthony Munday's *Triumphs of Re-united Britania* (1605) notes that "England, Wales, & Scotland, by the first *Brute* severed and divided, is in our second *Brute* reunited" (7); Thomas Heywood's *Troia Britanica: or, Great Britain's Troy* (1609) rejoiced that in James "three kingdoms, first by Brute divided, / United are" (437). In the context of contemporary royal self-congratulation on the unification of Britain, *King Lear*'s vivisecting England must if anything have been *more* disturbing.

The play, then, unsettles key Renaissance signifiers of stability: making home dispersible, penetrable, unsafe, it strikes at domestic ideology; allowing England to be dissected, the play unravels the new centralized nationalism the Tudors and King James had so triumphantly constructed. An important dual signifier of home as nation and as household, the 100 knights represent both Lear's political power and his patriarchal authority as the head of a household. Are such feudal retainers soldiers or servants? Goneril categorizes them with household servants, suggesting that Lear be attended by her own or Regan's servants (2.4.245–46); she speaks of their inhabiting "one house" with her servants, and Regan's reference to the possibility of their happening to "slack" Lear recalls Goneril's direction for household servants deliberately to "come slack of former services" (1.3.10–13). That she means servants rather than military retainers is underlined by her directions to Oswald, who is her steward—the official in charge of a household's domestic affairs. But Lear, when they are gone, laments "I lack soldiers" (4.6.117). Their dismissal marks both household dissolution and lost political power, for they bear on both sides of the patriarchalist view of householding and kingship.

Tudor history had been punctuated by royal sanctions against armed retainers of powerful nobles; getting rid of these and centralizing—in the monarchy—a monopoly of violence worked to replace the decentralized feudal system with a national state. Reversing the Tudor scenario, *King Lear* locates the band of dangerous armed retainers with the monarch (or former monarch). Stripping the central governing authority of its military power to create dispersed loci of power in two smaller fiefdoms is a step back from Tudor-style centralizing into feudalism. Deconsolidating central power, *King Lear* foreshadows the English civil war and picks up on fears of a disaffected nobility and a seditious underclass that had haunted the Tudors.

Goneril, Regan, and Cornwall situate the knights in the context of such fears. Both dismissed servants and demobilized soldiers became vagrants; the "ruffler" (former soldier) heads Thomas Harman's list of rogues in *A Caveat for Common Cursetors, Vulgarly Called Vagabonds*. The knights, the first of many in the play to become homeless, are construed as a rabble by Goneril and Regan and are used to fan fears of disorder, as Tudor authorities used vagrants as a pretext for buttressing their powers. Goneril calls Lear's indulging of his men-at-arms a "crime" (1.3.5). Declaring their behavior "riotous" (1.3.7), a term for both alehouse revelry and seditious uprisings,[4] she directs Oswald deliberately to provoke them (1.3.24–27). She identifies them with "disorder" (another term suggesting both drunken debauch and political insubordination) and with the tavern world, associated with vagrancy:

> Men so disordered, so debauched and bold
> That this our court, infected with their manners,
> Shows like a riotous inn, . . .
> . . . more like a tavern or a brothel
> Than a graced palace. (1.4.239–43)

Her term for them recalls the description of the plebeians in the closely contemporary *Coriolanus:* they are a "disordered rabble" (1.4.253). Lear vigorously denies "riotous" behavior by his knights: to him, these gentlemanly thanes scrupulously observe royal decorum:

> Thou liest!
> My train are men of choice and rarest parts,
> That all particulars of duty know
> And in the most exact regard support
> The worships of their name. (1.4.261–65)

Goneril expects outright thuggery from them: "He may enguard his dotage with their powers / And hold our lives in mercy"; but her husband finds this unreasonable: "You may fear too far" (1.4.325–27). Regan exploits others' difficulties to scapegoat her chosen enemies—her father and his knights. Accepting the story of Edgar's treachery, she besmirches Lear by gratuitously calling Edgar "my father's godson, . . . / He whom my father named" (2.1.91–92) and then demanding, "Was he not companion with the riotous knights / That tended upon my father?" (2.1.94–95), an association that no evidence supports and that Gloucester doubts, though Edmund loyally agrees, "He was of that consort" (2.1.97). Regan then blames Edgar's alleged parricide attempt on the knights: "'Tis they have put him on the old man's death, / To have th' expense and spoil of his revenues" (2.1.99–100), presumably by moving in with Edgar as the new Duke of Gloucester after being dismissed from Lear's service. The word "riotous" (2.1.94) begins to stick to the knights, defining them as a loose, dangerous, seditious rabble, the usual suspects in any assassination attempt on peers of the realm. Soon Regan speaks again to her father of "the riots of your followers" (2.4.142) and complains of the "danger" of keeping them (2.4.241). Cornwall puts Kent in the stocks because his disorderly fight with Oswald resembles the knights' behavior; he is "a fellow of the selfsame color" (2.2.141). Regan scapegoats the knights when locking Lear out: "He is attended with a desperate train" (2.4.306); she fears "what they may incense him to" (2.4.308).

The language of infection and contagion in Goneril's claim that the knights "infected" the court (1.4.240) reminds one of "better" neighborhoods sealing themselves off from contact with poorer from fear of diseases raging in slums. And what allegedly places the knights in such a contaminated milieu is their "manners," that double-edged word meaning both "polite etiquette" and "good morals" (*OED*). At one end of the social scale, words like "rogue" and "rascal" connoted both low social class and poor moral character; at the other, good "manners" suggested behavior both appropriate to the polite classes and morally good. Since uncouth manners spelled moral evil, it is an easy step for Goneril to move from stigmatizing the knights' tavern etiquette to maintaining their aptness for political sedition.

The text gives no warrant for the knights' riotousness or danger to the state and in fact treats them sympathetically. Audiences do not know what becomes of the fifty knights dismissed in act 1, but of the other fifty, thirty-five or thirty-six brave the storm as "hot questrists," searching for Lear (3.7.17). Since Lear is not especially hard to locate—Gloucester keeps stepping out to talk to him on the heath—this reported action seems pointless except as a bid for audience sympathy for these retainers faithful to a fallen master. The casting of the knights by Goneril, Regan, and Cornwall as a dangerous, seditious rabble behaving more like vagrants than men-at-arms replicates the way vagrants were scapegoated: the supposed need to control them justified repressive laws buttressing royal authority. An imaginary political threat has been manufactured by the authorities as a pretext for consolidating power—in Stephen Greenblatt's terms, a subversion manufactured to give scope for containment. As Machiavelli advised, "a shrewd prince will . . . subtly encourage some enmity to himself" to increase his power "by overcoming it" (61).

Fear of sedition from ranks lower than knights is voiced in the play, too. Albany reports defections among those "whom the rigor of our state / Forced to cry out" (5.1.22–23); the injustice of his own cause means that Albany's heart is not in the battle: "Where I could not be honest, / I never yet was valiant" (5.1.24–25). Similarly, Edmund fears revolt from the "impressed lances" of his troops (5.3.52). Such passages show the rebellion of common people as only to be expected under harsh, unjust regimes. Especially considering the dangerous political climate in which the play was produced—a year after *King Lear* was first acted, the Midlands Rising engulfed ten counties—this sympathetic view of disaffected common people is surprising, paving the way for other politically radical moments in the play.

Naked Wretches and the Question of "Distribution"

If the play's interestingly sympathetic references to sedition flicker briefly, its visions of a poverty-stricken underclass are pervasive. "Fortune, that arrant whore, / Ne'er turns the key to the poor" (2.4.51–52). Beggars are but a step above beasts:

> Our basest beggars
> Are in the poorest thing superfluous.
> Allow not nature more than nature needs,
> Man's life is cheap as beasts. (2.4.266–69)

Talk of famine recurs: "he that keeps nor crust nor crumb" (1.4.195). The Fool, like Harman, links homelessness with lice:

> He that has a house to put 's head in has a good headpiece.
> The codpiece that will house
> Before the head has any,
> The head and he shall louse;
> So beggars marry many. (3.2.25–30)

Lear's night in the hovel makes Cordelia think of homeless people sleeping in freezing barns, as in Harman's *Caveat,* and she uses Harman's term "rogues": "poor Father, / To hovel thee with swine and rogues forlorn / In short and musty straw" (4.7.39–41).

Lear thinks often of wretches, those punished by whipping: "Tremble, thou wretch, / That hast within thee undivulgèd crimes / Unwhipped of justice" (3.2.51–53); "poor naked wretches, wheresoe'er you are" (3.4.28). Enshrining ambivalence toward poverty, the word "wretch" meant one "sunk in deep distress, sorrow, misfortune, or poverty," thus meriting pity and relief, but it also meant "one of opprobrious or reprehensible character" (*OED*), a cony-catching rogue worthy of whipping. (Similarly ambiguous, the word "forlorn" in Cordelia's "rogues forlorn" meant either "abandoned, forsaken, desolate," and thus worthy of pity, or "morally lost, depraved," and thus— in many Renaissance eyes—ineligible for pity [*OED*].) In the space of two scenes, on the heath, Lear's social attitudes progress from seeing wretches as evil rogues (guilty of "undivulgèd crimes") to seeing wretches as pitiable and worthy of relief.[5] Given the Renaissance suspicion of mobility, it is of interest that "wretch" derives ultimately from the Anglo-Saxon *wraecca,* exile or wanderer[6]—one recalls "The Wanderer" as a poignant Anglo-Saxon text of lonely alienation. Lear's most famous speech of social consciousness directs compassion specifically at *homeless* wretches:

> You *houseless* poverty—
> . . . .
> Poor naked wretches, wheresoe'er you are,
> That bide the pelting of this pitiless storm,
> How shall your *houseless* heads and unfed sides,
> Your looped and windowed raggedness, defend you
> From seasons such as these? O, I have ta'en
> Too little care of this! Take physic, pomp;
> Expose thyself to feel what wretches feel,
> That thou mayst shake the superflux to them
> And show the heavens more just. (3.4.26–36; emphasis added)

Lear's new social consciousness goes farther than anybody else's. Edgar's account of how Poor Tom became poor blames profligacy and riotous living rather than crop failure or enclosures: "Wine loved I deeply, dice dearly, and in woman out-paramoured the Turk. Keep thy foot out of brothels, thy hand out of plackets, thy pen from lenders' books" (3.4.89–96). This is in the tradition of Erasmus's "Beggar Talk" or Sir Thomas Elyot's *Book Named the Governor,* or of Robert Copland's *Highway to the Spital-house,* wherein a procession of social types (rufflers, masterless men, crooked innkeepers) dissolves into the seven deadly sins—indigency, the result of sin, invites no sympathy. Speaking as Poor Tom, Edgar adopts the orthodox early Tudor line on the causes of poverty. Raman Selden sees a double consciousness in Edgar, who shows "a precise awareness of the degraded condition of the displaced vagabond but retain[s] the point of view of the disguised aristocrat who sees beggary as the due punishment for bad servants and not as the result of neglect by bad masters" (157). Lear, however, strikingly does not inquire into poverty's causes; he is simply devastated by seeing its effects, and far from scapegoating the homeless for their misery, he bravely accepts responsibility himself: as king, he could have ensured a more equitable or at least more generous distribution of food and shelter.[7] Many readers find "shake the superflux to them" an inadequate approach to poverty, smacking of the "crumb theory" of economics—indeed, the image suggests shaking the crumbs out of a tablecloth.[8] But if Lear does not go far enough, he deserves credit for how far he goes. Audiences accustomed to hearing vagrants reviled for "beastly life" in works like Harman's and seeing the homeless disqualified from relief under the Poor Laws must have been signally unprepared for Lear's stunning proclamation of royal responsibility for the homeless, his resounding cry of compassion for those who *for whatever cause* have no house to cover their heads.

Lear suddenly sees that legal inequities reproduce economic disparities: the law favors the rich and oppresses the poor. He declares, "See how yond justice rails upon yond simple thief. Hark in thine ear: change places and, handy-dandy, which is the justice, which is the thief?" (4.6.151–54). Gaining intensity as he thinks about it, Lear shifts from hard-hitting prose into memorable blank verse:

> Through tattered clothes small vices do appear;
> Robes and furred gowns hide all. Plate sin with gold,
> And the strong lance of justice hurtless breaks;
> Arm it in rags, a pygmy's straw does pierce it. (4.6.164–67)

Iconographically across Europe (for good practical reasons) "tattered clothes" spelled beggary. Lear's new perception reveals economic conditions to be conspiring with legal inequalities to keep the homeless down.

How radical is Lear's perception "through tattered clothes small vices do appear; / Robes and furred gowns hide all"? Compare it with a similar statement in a handbook for Poor Law administrators, *An Ease for Overseers of the Poor* (1601): "The very ornament of wealth doth add a kind of grace and majesty to a man, although he be destitute of the chief habit of a man, whereas poverty makes a man despisable, which by his properties is commendable" (9). Lear is discovering something desperately wrong in this double standard; *An Ease for Overseers* accepts it as the way of the world—this is why the wealthy, not the poor, should be chosen as overseers. The handbook's attitude is typical, while Lear's perception is atypical to the point of being revolutionary. Other writers had said that clothes make the man and exposed the hypocrisy of the well-dressed; but in juxtaposing "tattered clothes" with "robes and furred gowns," Shakespeare localizes the critique within the discourse of poverty. To place this in turn within a discussion of inequality before the law was to challenge the very system that made laws against wandering and prosecuted the ragged as criminal.

Gloucester's attitudes follow a similar trajectory to Lear's. At first beggars are repulsive, and he is shocked to find Lear with Poor Tom: "What, hath Your Grace no better company?" (3.4.140). He then tries to get Lear into the house and relegate Tom to the hovel (3.4.173). When Lear refuses to be parted from Tom, Gloucester humors him. That the sight of a beggar makes a great impression on Gloucester suggests a sheltered life; how often did dukes see beggars? After being blinded Gloucester recalls Tom: "Is it a beggar-man? /... / ... / I' the last night's storm I such a fellow saw, / Which made me think a man a worm" (4.1.29–33); "Is that the naked fellow?" (4.1.40). Now himself "wretched," turned out of his home and approaching the condition of the homeless, Gloucester, like Lear, accepts some responsibility for their plight. "Bring some covering for this naked soul" (4.1.44), he asks.

> Here, take this purse, thou whom the heavens' plagues
> Have humbled to all strokes. That I am wretched
> Makes thee the happier. Heavens, deal so still!
> Let the superfluous and lust-dieted man,
> That slaves your ordinance, that will not see
> Because he does not feel, feel your pow'r quickly!
> So distribution should undo excess
> And each man have enough. (4.1.63–70)

Both Lear and Gloucester speak of superfluity, excess wealth arrogated by the haves to the deprivation of the have-nots. Their epiphany is not a warm, fuzzy sense of human brotherhood but a specific recognition of economic inequality in this realm. But is "distribution should undo excess" a plea for radical reorganization of the social and economic system, on communist lines? In 1951 John Danby identified Gloucester's words with the Christian communism of radical Anabaptism; Walter Cohen associates them with radicalism of the Digger type; while Jonathan Dollimore finds Gloucester's words potentially revolutionary. But arguing against taking "distribution" in the Marxist sense of redistribution of wealth, Judy Kronenfeld adduces Renaissance texts on charity to show that "'distribution' is the actual word for private and personal almsgiving, as well as for government-regulated charity" (760) and that even very conservative preachers regularly enjoined parishioners to curb their excess and give their "superfluity" to the poor (762). Kronenfeld is right in seeing "superfluous" as often having referred to almsgiving. For example, in *A Sermon Exhorting to Pity the Poor,* Henry Bedel wrote: "If the rich would once become liberal, there is *superfluous* enough to keep the poor and needy" (sig. [C3]ᵛ); "Ye . . . that live in this *excess* with *superfluity,* have some remorse to the poor in their misery" (sig. E1). Similarly, John Downame wrote that "the godly man spareth from his *superfluities,* and sometimes necessaries, that he may have the more to spend in bounty and beneficence" (14; emphasis added).

But radical views of almsgiving were voiced: for example, the anonymous *A Supplication to Our Most Sovereign Lord, King Henry the Eighth* (1544) argues that a "godly *distribution*" should be made of seized church lands, because the "gorgeous and sumptuous . . . houses, manors, and castles" of worldly churchmen were built with money that rightfully belonged to the poor (48–49). For churchmen to give alms out of their superfluity is an act not of virtue but of restitution: "my Lord Bishop should give the superfluity of his goods to the poor (*whose goods justly they be*)" (49; emphasis added). Although early in the English Reformation, writers of inflammatory pieces advocating seizure of church lands did not foresee that these seizures would mainly make some courtiers rich, they did view monastic wealth as a blatant inequality—the clergy were the rich, and their lands should be seized and given to the poor. *A Supplication to Our Most Sovereign Lord* also advocates that "all such lands and possessions, whereupon so many idle hypocrites and deceivers be great burden and charge to your realm, which hitherto have lived ungodly and unprofitably, may, from henceforth, be partly converted to the supportation and maintenance of common schools," a "godly *distribution* (most prudent Sovereign) of the lands and possessions, ordained and appointed for the comfort, succour, and help of your poor . . . subjects" (44;

emphasis added). More's *Supplication of Souls* rightly suspects that such hopes are naïve, but that does not obscure the fact that some religious reformers had in mind a radical redistribution of wealth when they used words like "distribution" and "superfluity."

By no means limited to almsgiving, "distribution" often referred more generally to a radical redistribution of wealth, as it does in More's *Utopia:* "Unless private property is entirely done away with, there can be no fair or just distribution of goods, nor can mankind be happily governed" (28). "Fair or just distribution of goods" translates *"res aequabili ac iusta aliqua ratione distribui"* in More's Latin original, and Robinson's 1551 English translation also uses the word "distribution": "equal and just distribution of things" (sig. Ei^v). Again, More writes that in Utopia, "nothing is *distributed* after a niggish sort, neither there is any poor man or beggar" (Robinson, Sig. [R7]–[R7]^v; Latin *distributio*). Elyot front-loads the issue of communism at the beginning of his *Book Named the Governor.* Far from being a marginal political discourse limited only to Anabaptists, the call for redistribution of wealth is central enough to political thinking that it helps define, by contrast, Elyot's whole conception of the state, and it affects the choice of his central term, "public weal," which he prefers to "commonweal" because the latter suggests communism. Kronenfeld is not persuasive when she implies that notions of radical redistribution of wealth were limited to the lunatic fringe or that no one would have taken Anabaptists seriously because they were persecuted and made bogeymen and subject to official denunciations by bishops and homilists—the very need for such action against Anabaptist sentiments suggests that people *did* take them seriously, as Charles Hobday argues (77). And texts firmly in the humanist mainstream—*Utopia, The Governor*—make highly visible the idea of radical redistribution of wealth. Whether praising or condemning it, they give it prominence and a serious hearing.[9] When notions of "distribution" and "superfluity" were voiced in *King Lear,* a range of meanings, some more radical than others (and some very radical indeed), were available to Shakespeare's audience. It is true that wealth is not redistributed in *King Lear;* as Margreta de Grazia notes, despite all the play's upheavals, both "superfluous" property and titles remain within the ruling classes, descending to heirs. But that the play entertains the idea of redistributing wealth as a compassionate and even just social outcome is radical in itself.

Neither Gloucester nor Lear invokes heaven in order to abdicate responsibility or leave social action to Providence: Lear's "show the heavens more just" and Gloucester's "heavens, deal so still!" recognize that to help the poor, heaven must open the eyes of those in power to the need for action. Glouces-

ter sees because he feels: he relieves a beggar's distress because he has become a vagrant himself, just as Lear saw "houseless poverty" once he became
homeless.

The Plunge into Homelessness

King Lear makes the privileged experience homelessness. Like the "shamefaced
poor"—"members of the middle or even upper classes who have lost their
social status and been reduced to poverty" (Geremek 40)—Cordelia, Lear,
Edgar, Gloucester, Kent, and a hundred knights become homeless. Most are
forced out, though Lear turns himself out, resolving to visit his daughters in
monthly cycles, a permanent houseguest (1.1.132–35). When Regan and Goneril abrogate their part of the deal, Lear becomes homeless, and Lear's vanishing castle is more than a textual crux: that he never considers, when his
daughters close up their houses, simply going back to the castle where the
opening scenes took place suggests the text's commitment to homelessness
as a theme. ("I abjure all roofs," he cries [2.4.209].)[10] Edmund seems to have
no settled home—he has been "out" for nine years and is soon to go abroad
again (1.1.32–33); but like other uncompassionate people in the play, he never
confronts absolute houselessness or learns fellow feeling from that experience.

For the others, the fall into houselessness is precipitous and terrifying.
Edgar's and Gloucester's plummet into outdoor living reveals what flimsy
circumstances may tip a person onto the skids. Characters in this period often
imagine such abrupt reversals of fortune. In *Richard II,* a banished Bolingbroke—who, as is later shown, retains plenty of allies and resources after his
banishment—demands, "Will you permit that I shall stand condemned / A
wandering vagabond, my rights and royalties / Plucked from my arms per-
force?" (2.3.119–21). Advised to flee his home, Orlando in *As You Like It* (with
better reason than Bolingbroke) jumps to the conclusion that the only alternatives to life at home are beggary and highway robbery: "What, wouldst thou
have me go and beg my food? / Or with a base and boist'rous sword enforce
/ A thievish living on the common road?" (2.3.31–33). Such extreme reactions
may reflect the pervasive stylistic habit of antithesis; Lear's fall from the
heights of monarchy to the depths of beggary draws on the traditional mon-
arch/beggar antithesis. But the terms in which the extreme reactions are
couched point toward the discourse of vagrancy, which posits "the common
road" as the opposite of "home." The trope of a plunge into vagrancy suggests a widespread cultural anxiety, prompted by the high visibility of poverty, that provoked fear of beggary as a response to any serious setback. In

real life, fortune-fallen aristocrats do not necessarily slip to the bottom of the social ladder: they have relatives, old patrons, friends, loans, borrowed lodgings, various shifts to avoid absolute penury; but in *King Lear,* the fallen are forced not into shabby gentility but onto the heath and into the hovel, where they confront the lowest levels of the economic hierarchy and experience what society's poorest members endure daily.

This is a radical move: Shakespeare by no means had to go this far to dramatize the unpleasantness of poverty. The vagrant poor were the great bogeymen of the age. Lear or Gloucester could have been taken in by respectable cottagers; Renaissance ideology would have sanctioned their learning from the hardworking, householding poor. The social depths to which the mighty here plunge are of an altogether different order, and pity for the true homeless, the bogeymen vagrants themselves, is a note sounded very rarely by Renaissance writers.

Cordelia is disinherited, Kent banished from England; recalling the homology between the domestic and national senses of "home," she becomes domestically homeless, while he becomes nationally homeless. A chiasmus then occurs: Cordelia gains a domestic home in marrying and leaves her national home, while Kent dodges banishment but elects domestic homelessness to follow Lear. The link between domestic and national homelessness is built into Lear's thinking, a product of Tudor ideology identifying nation with home. Disinheriting his daughter, Lear turns her into a foreigner. He has "stripped her from his benediction, turned her / To foreign casualties" (4.3.44–45). Conjuring the legendarily barbaric Scythian, he orientalizes her:

> The barbarous Scythian,
> Or he that makes his generation messes
> To gorge his appetite, shall to my bosom
> Be as well neighbored, pitied, and relieved
> As thou my sometime daughter. (1.1.116–20)

This, of course, means that she will not be "well neighbored" at all: Lear's Britain hardly provides foreign aid to Scythians or cannibals. The word "neighbored" suggests an idealized world where neighbors spontaneously help the poor, a world before wandering beggars were exempted from pity. "Relieved" could suggest private charity, but a primary meaning of "relief" was "assistance . . . given to the indigent from funds administered under the Poor Law or from parish doles" (*OED*). To Lear, Cordelia is ineligible even for poor relief; she is among the undeserving poor. "Stranger," which he twice calls her (1.1.115, 1.1.207), often meant "foreigner," and it was also the term parish registers used for a person not of the parish and hence ineligible for poor relief—vagrants were strangers. Kent emphasizes her shelterlessness: "the gods to their dear shelter take thee, maid" (1.1.185). Even after the King of France takes Cordelia up, her precarious position in a world of changing fortunes and reliance on almsgiving is emphasized by Goneril: "your Lord . . . hath received you / At Fortune's alms" (1.1.281–82). Lear has turned his daughter into a vagrant. Later, when the shoe is on the other foot and Lear needs charity, the word "relieve" recurs: Gloucester resolves to "relieve him" (3.3.14), declaring, "The King my old master must be relieved" (3.3.19).

Gloucester's mention of "unstating" himself (1.2.101) is unwittingly prophetic: "unstate" meant "deprive of state, rank, or estate" (*OED*). He begins to learn what the poor experience when he is "pinion[ed] like a thief" (3.7.24). Blinded and expelled from home with the brutal injunction to "smell / His way to Dover" (3.7.96–97), he becomes a vagrant on the road and receives private relief from one of his old tenants. Like rags, blindness belonged to the iconography of beggary. With his two purses, Gloucester is better off than most blind beggars; but he experiences something of their wretched life.

Locking Kent in the stocks is a punishment fit for the dregs of society, who live by small thieving, like Harman's vagrants: this

> low correction
> Is such as basest and contemned'st wretches
> For pilferings and most common trespasses
> Are punished with. (2.2.145–48)

The stocks were associated with fraudulent poverty: "The pillory . . . had been employed against fraudulent beggars since the late Middle Ages" (Jütte 165). Again the word "wretches" appears: Kent too has exposed himself to feel what wretches feel. The word "correction" for disciplinary punishment would have suggested houses of correction, to which thieving vagrants were sent ever since a 1575–76 Elizabethan act had specified, "Within every county . . . one, two or more abiding houses . . . shall be provided, and called the house or houses of correction for setting on work and punishing . . . of such as shall be taken as rogues" (*An Act for the Setting of the Poor on Work . . .* sig. Bi–Bi^v). Kent ironically calls the stocks a "lodging." However philosophical he is trying to be, as an earl he must steel himself against the overwhelming shame of being treated like a common thief: "Take vantage, heavy eyes, not to behold / This shameful lodging" (2.2.174–75). He identifies with people who pilfer clothing because their own is worn out, and their stockings are threadbare: "A good man's fortune may grow out at heels" (2.2.160). When Lear first banished Kent, he envisioned hasty preparations to take enough supplies to prevent destitution: "Five days we do allot thee for provision / To shield thee from disasters of the world" (1.1.176–77); without that five days, utter dispossession and beggary would loom (in the Quarto, Kent is given only *four* days). Kent does not avail himself of the five days but sets off in disguise, not "provisioned" but unprovided, like the unprovided body Edmund says Edgar assaulted, like the unprovided household Regan claims. Given the world's dangers, his very unprovidedness is a measure of his courage and loyalty. In the end, virtually none of the characters in *King Lear* is able to shield himself from disasters of the world. Where anyone might at any moment plunge into depths of poverty, five days' provisioning would never be enough.

As the disguised Kent's punishment in the stocks invokes the fraudulent poverty rampant in rogue literature, Edgar's disguise comes right out of the literature of roguery and vagrancy:

> Whiles I may scape
> I will preserve myself, and am bethought
> To take the basest and most poorest shape
> That ever penury, in contempt of man,
> Brought near to beast. My face I'll grime with filth,
> Blanket my loins, elf all my hairs in knots,
> And with presented nakedness outface
> The winds and persecutions of the sky.
> The country gives me proof and precedent
> Of Bedlam beggars who with roaring voices
> Strike in their numbed and mortifièd arms
> Pins, wooden pricks, nails, sprigs of rosemary;
> And with this horrible object, from low farms,
> Poor pelting villages, sheepcotes, and mills,
> Sometimes with lunatic bans, sometimes with prayers,
> Enforce their charity. (2.3.5–20)

Tom o' Bedlam, first alluded to by Edmund (1.2.139) and then adopted as a persona by Edgar, was a signature figure of rogue literature (Carroll, "'The Base Shall Top the Legitimate'"). This figure who feigned madness and created sores on his body was not unique in being considered a charlatan: rogue texts treat nearly all beggars and vagrants as charlatans, performing disability though able-bodied, pretending poverty though they have money stashed away. Edgar sees his disguise not as unique to one specialized type of counterfeit disabled person but merely as an extreme form of generic poverty: "the basest and most poorest shape / That ever penury . . . / Brought near to beast." His plan to "march to wakes, and fairs and market-towns" (3.6.73–74) names haunts common to vagrants (Beier, *Masterless Men* 72–80). He knows how beggars were kept moving from parish to parish by humiliating punishments: "whipped from tithing to tithing and stock-punished and imprisoned"(3.4.133–34).

The counterfeit madman was the first of the "cozeners and shifters" discussed in John Awdeley's *Fraternity of Vagabonds:* "An abram-man is he that walketh bare-armed, and bare-legged, and feigneth himself mad, and carryeth a pack of wool, or a stick with bacon on it, or suchlike toy, and nameth himself Poor Tom" (53). Chapter 9 of Harman's *Caveat* is devoted to "abram-men," who

> feign themselves to have been mad, and have been kept either in Bethlem or in some other prison a good time, and not one amongst twenty that ever came in prison for any such cause. Yet will they say how piteously and most extremely they have been beaten and dealt withal. . . . Either when they come at farmers' houses, they will demand bacon, either cheese, or wool, or anything that is worth money. And if they espy small company within, they will with fierce countenance demand somewhat. Where for fear the maids will give them largely, to be rid of them. (83)

The details of the counterfeit bedlamite repeat from text to text: in the two passages above, for example, *A Caveat,* published several years after *The Fraternity,* transmutes two signs by which to know an abram-man—his pack of wool or his stick with bacon on it—into commodities the abram-man begs for: "they will demand bacon . . . or wool." The one passage in rogue literature that comes closest to the language of *King Lear* is Thomas Dekker's description in *The Bellman of London* (1608) of the false madman who "swears that he hath been in Bedlam, and will talk frantically of purpose; you see pins stuck in sundry places of his naked flesh, especially in his arms, which pain he gladly puts himself to . . . only to make you believe he is out of his wits; he calls himself by the name of Poor Tom, and coming near any body cries out, Poor Tom is a cold" (101). In fact, *The Bellman of London,* published some two years after the first acting of *King Lear,* was probably itself influenced by *King Lear:* authors, while denouncing abram-men as what Carroll calls "a theatrical fiction" ("'The Base Shall Top the Legitimate'" 434), were not above flagrantly plundering other theatrical fictions (such as *King Lear*) for material for their allegedly firsthand portraits of Elizabethan beggars.

From earlier accounts of Poor Toms, Shakespeare keeps the nakedness, feigned madness, and the preying on others—particularly on country people, who respond with fear (this last trope is repeated by Dekker in *O Per Se O* [1612]). What Shakespeare stresses about the figure differs significantly, though, from the rogue literature: Awdeley and Harman simply issue warnings against this phony, cheating beggar, who lacks the decency to be honestly insane and takes advantage of gullible folk whom Harman merely calls "farmers." Shakespeare adds details to the costume (such as the griming with filth), emphasizes the beggar's vulnerable naked body exposed to the elements, and in place of Harman's farmers introduces *very* poor people, living in "low farms, / Poor pelting villages, sheepcotes." ("Pelting" means contemptible, worthless [*OED*].) Tom's forcing charity by his fearsome appearance and "roaring voice" (recalling Harman's "fierce countenance") is "horrible" (2.3.17), I suggest, not only in involving extortion—"enforc[ing] their charity" through fear—but also in that this beggar worms money out of people almost as poor as he is, a cut above him only in having a place to live, however low and pelting. Even the housed poor could be very hungry. Tom's revolting regimen of frogs and newts is usually regarded as part of the semiotics of madness, but given what the poor were sometimes reduced to eating, it could just as well belong to the semiotics of hunger. "In some regions," wrote the Bolognese Giovan Battista Segni, "salted locusts are the food of the poor" (qtd. in Camporesi 139).

The prominent presence of a Tom o'Bedlam evokes rogue literature, a provocative move: rogue texts maintain that in a vagrant's world, all disability is feigned. And Edgar is doubly feigning: an aristocrat pretending to be a lowborn abram-man, who was an able-bodied beggar pretending disability. Shakespeare had introduced the counterfeit disabled person early in his career: in *2 Henry VI*, Simpcox, faking blindness and lameness, is whipped by a beadle (the typical punishment for vagrants) until he runs away, revealing his lameness as false, to the merriment of nearby courtly figures (2.1.145–58). The episode clearly belongs to the same anecdotal genre as Harman's account of torturing the counterfeit dumb man until he bursts into speech. Consistent with the Poor Laws, Simpcox and his wife are whipped and returned to their home parish: "Let them be whipped through every market-town, till they come to Berwick, from whence they came" (2.1.161–63). As in rogue literature, the trickery and harsh punishment of vagrants are treated as funny. When a similar episode is recounted in Sir Thomas More's *Dialogue Concerning Heresies*, with several other faked-disability anecdotes, a marginal gloss identifies these as "merry tales," allying them with jest books (83–87). Even this early episode, though, as Thomas Cartelli notes, allows Simpcox's wife to defend herself by "testimony that she and her husband pursued their fraud 'for pure need'" (58), and between this early comic account and his tragic use of similar material in *King Lear*, Shakespeare's social awareness seems to have increased.[11] Readers are invited to *sympathize* with Edgar as faking madman, to see his fraud as legitimated by homelessness and persecution. In a sense, Edgar's disguise is no disguise at all—he really has lost everything, and he really is homeless. Does the play suggest that other Poor Toms are put to such desperate shifts by necessity? Edgar's other disguises include that familiar figure, the lame beggar,[12] "a most poor man, made lame by [Folio: "tame to"] fortune's blows, / Who, by the art of known and feeling sorrow, / Am pregnant to good pity. Give me your hand" (4.6.224–26). Compassion has been fostered by the fall into beggary.

Here, then, is the pattern: the princess Cordelia, expelled from home and dying a criminal's death, hanging; the Duke of Gloucester, reduced to an icon of blind beggary and vagrancy; his elder son, turned into a homeless bedlam beggar; the Earl of Kent, clapped in the stocks like a thieving vagrant; the king himself, sleeping in straw like the vagrants who sheltered in barns, hustled from county to county, just ahead of hostile authority. This play, which rewrites in a tragic key so many conventions of comedy—disguise, a subplot, a daughter's dowry threatened by her *senex iratus* father, an old father outwitted by a clever son—also offers a striking instance of the *tragic* carnivalesque: royalty and aristocracy fall out of their place and plummet to the bottom of society, where they reproduce the sad repertoire of beggars, phony madmen, and vagrants familiar in rogue literature. Naomi Liebler notes that *King Lear* offers "no view of the large population of Jacobean poor. The actual wretches Lear sees before him were, are, and remain members of the court" (200). Audiences might wish that Shakespeare *had* incorporated "real" poor folk; but Kent is treated as real beggars were treated, and Lear's hovel evidences how real poor people lived. It may be a pity that Shakespeare did not go farther down this road; but that he traversed it with sympathy at all—and in a tragic rather than comic context—is unusual for his time. In comedies such as John Fletcher and Philip Massinger's *Beggar's Bush,* which idealize vagrancy, beggars turn out to be disguised aristocrats in keeping with rogue literature's dogma that beggars are secretly wealthy. (Indeed, in that text, the beneficent deployment of beggars' considerable wealth saves the day.) But *King Lear* trades in no such dogmas: the well-off must experience what it is like to be *truly* destitute. *King Lear* is one of the only texts of the English Renaissance to give beggary tragic rather than comic or farcical treatment.

"Change places and, handy-dandy, which is the justice, which is the thief?" Viewing *King Lear* through the lens of homelessness rather than of universal human suffering casts suffering in terms of class: people of the highest rank experience pain through falling to the lowest social stratum, and they express the need for the highborn to develop sympathy for the low through enduring what they endure. Lear's stripping off his clothes, often read as a search for the essentially human under culture's artificial vestments, is also specific to the discourse of vagrancy—the near-nakedness of a beggar's rags or of beggars stripped as a prelude to whipping. Cordelia's loss of Lear's favor aptly evokes the language of punished vagrancy: Lear has "*stripped* her from his benediction" (4.3.44). The word "stripped," rare in Shakespeare, was elsewhere often paired with "whipped," as in George Wyther's *Abuses Stripped and Whipped*. The image recalls Widow Edith and the punishment of beggars.

If mobility was feared and settled domesticity valued, it is notable how much traveling goes on in *King Lear* and how many households simply fly apart. When the court breaks up, Cordelia goes to France; Gloucester, Edgar, and Edmund go to Gloucester's house; Albany, Goneril, Lear, Kent, the Fool, and 100 knights go to the palace of Albany and Goneril; Cornwall and Regan go to their own house. After a violent family quarrel at the Albany-Goneril palace, that household disintegrates. Lear sets forth to the home of Cornwall and Regan, sending Kent ahead; for confusingly explained reasons, Kent ends up at Gloucester's house instead (he may or may not have called at the Cornwall house on the way [see 2.4.26–38, which may or may not be a true account]); and for unexplained reasons, Lear ends up at Gloucester's house too. Cornwall and Regan arrive at Gloucester's house first, having gone there to avoid receiving Lear at their house. All characters from the opening scene in Lear's castle (except for Cordelia, France, and Burgundy) are now gathered at Gloucester's house. This household also blows apart: Edgar, Lear, Kent, the Fool, and some fifty (now dismissed) knights go to the open country. Edgar hides in a hovel; Gloucester oscillates between his house and wherever Lear is—in the open and in the hovel; thirty-five or thirty-six of the knights dash around the countryside looking for Lear. Cornwall takes over Gloucester's house, denying Gloucester the use of his own home (3.3.3–4). Edmund leaves Gloucester's house, going off with Goneril to avoid being part of his father's blinding, but he turns back before reaching the Albany-Goneril house. Albany and Goneril arrive separately at their palace. Even the hovel eventually breaks up in haste: Lear, Kent, and Edgar head for Dover, and Gloucester goes separately there. After Cornwall dies and everyone else decamps, Regan and Oswald remain for some time at Gloucester's house. Nobody ever stays home for long, and the play ends with everyone outdoors. The play's numerous letters emphasize how physically separated people are. Many messengers travel about, including Oswald (whose movements I have left out here, but who is always traveling). Travel is physically stressful: Kent, Cornwall, and Regan claim to be tired out from journeying all night (2.2.158, 2.4.86–87). The extremes of travel and home-leaving, and the outdoor setting of the conclusion, resemble homelessness and vagrancy. These highborn characters learn something of what vagrants' lives are like—all because of Lear's fatal decision to break up his household and travel from daughter to daughter on a *monthly* cycle, which suggests regularity but is also allied with the phases of the moon—emblem of instability—and perhaps even with the monthly cycles thought to ally women with lunar changefulness. The play mimics the alleged aimlessness of vagrant wandering.

Identity, bound up in social roles (Lear starts questioning who he is after losing the roles of king and father), is also a function of place. Some of the play's many uses of "place" situate the individual according to his or her rank in society, and some situate individuals geographically—or at least they try to. Lear early on explains his extreme obstinacy as a result of his temperament and social rank:

> Thou hast sought to make us break our vows,
> Which we durst never yet, and with strained pride
> To come betwixt our sentence and our power,
> Which nor our nature nor our *place* can bear. (1.1.171–74; emphasis added)

Here "place" indicates a locus in society so fixed and unchangeable that it warrants an apogee of inflexible behavior. This firmly centered fixity is soon exploded, however: Lear learns that the psyche can quite easily be moved from what seemed a fixed "place":

> O most small fault,
> How ugly didst thou in Cordelia show!
> Which, like an engine, wrenched my frame of nature
> From the fixed *place*. (1.4.265–68; emphasis added)

Edgar is deplaced by persecution: "No port is free, no *place* / That guard and most unusual vigilance / Does not attend my taking" (2.3.3–5; emphasis added). That there is no safe *place* for Edgar is a phenomenon that he experiences as a radical assault on his identity, and he responds by annihilating identity: "Edgar I nothing am" (2.3.21). When Kent becomes a displaced person through a punishment unbefitting his rank, Lear puns on "place": "What's he that hath so much thy *place* mistook / To set thee here?" (2.4.11–12; emphasis added). That shocking "place," the stocks, is a startling misplacement for someone of Kent's place (or station) in society—even as the king's messenger, let alone in his true identity as an earl. In *King Lear*'s England audience members lose their geographic bearings—for much of the play they do not know what kingdom the characters are in—and this radical decentering, coming after the opening in a recognizable center, the court, reproduces the loss of *social* place of those who become homeless. In the poignant scene where an awakening Lear sees Cordelia, his uncertainty about identity ("methinks I should know you, and know this man, / Yet I am doubtful" [4.7.65–66]) and about his own sanity ("I fear I am not in my perfect mind" [4.7.64]) expresses itself as confusion about geographical location ("I am mainly ignorant / What *place* this is") and about the whereabouts of home ("nor I know not / Where I did lodge last night" [4.7.68–69]). An individual's identity is bound up in where home is. Those who become homeless are strangers to themselves.

The psychologists Lisa Goodman, Leonard Saxe, and Mary Harvey, complicating the view of psychologists who have discussed mental health problems as a cause of homelessness, argue that "homelessness is itself a risk factor for emotional disorder" (1219). Noting that 53 percent of a random sample of homeless people exhibit full-blown cases of post-traumatic stress disorder, suffering from collapse of affiliative bonds with others, desperate feelings of helplessness, symptoms such as depression, irritability, angry outbursts, sleep disturbance, and the general sense that they "have experienced a malevolent world," Goodman, Saxe, and Harvey posit mental illness as an *effect,* not solely a cause, of homelessness (1220). The trauma symptoms they discuss are present in King Lear's increasingly disordered personality. But then, is a homeless person's sense of having "experienced a malevolent world" mental illness or an accurate perception of reality?

King Lear's doubleness of "place"—as geographic location and social rank—again links Renaissance anxiety about vagrants, whose geographic place is fluid, with social fluidity. Exploring what it would mean to "change places" with the poor, *King Lear,* more than any other monument of high culture, enacts what it meant to be placeless in the Renaissance.

A Stigmatizing Lexicon

In this angry play, rage adopts a language of invective and insult from the discourse of vagrancy. Drawing on Erving Goffman's *Stigma: Notes on the Management of Spoiled Identity,* Robert Jütte describes a "labelling process . . . based on moral judgments concerning beggars. The belief that the undeserving poor have no morality (i.e., steal, cheat, are loose sexually), are lazy, work-shy and do not want to be educated and improve themselves, emerged in the late Middle Ages and persists in one form or another to this very day" (158–59); the poor, Jütte continues, have been stigmatized as gamblers, squanderers, fornicators, and defamed with "terms like beggar or rogue" (162). Paul Slack thinks that the labeling process actually created the vagrant class: "the image of the vagrant rogue produced laws which manufactured a vagrant class out of an amorphous group of poor migrants. The system made paupers and delinquents by labelling them" (*Poverty and Policy* 107).[13] Name-calling, like judicial labeling, was a serious matter: in seventeenth-century England, a man was arraigned for calling a neighbor "a burn cast rogue, drunken bad fellow, rascal, rogue publicly in the street" (Addy 115). In London in 1584, a riot involving up to a thousand people was precipitated by a gentleman saying publicly that apprentices were "little better than rogues" and were "but the scum of the world" (Archer, *Pursuit of Stability* 4). People call each other worse than this in *King Lear,* and its language of insult is in line with the way vagrants and the poor were stigmatized.

Kent calls Oswald a "rogue" six times in act 2, scene 2; the seriousness of this insult to a steward no doubt contributes to the harshness of his punishment. This word, new in the mid-sixteenth century, came directly from thieves' cant in rogue literature. Beginning as a technical term for one kind of suspicious vagrant, "rogue" by the 1570s became generalized as a term of moral and social disapprobation. It meant "a dishonest, unprincipled person, a rascal" (*OED*), retaining connotations of low rank—such generalizing shows how vagrants became models of moral turpitude. But the word is used sympathetically later in *King Lear,* after highborn characters become homeless. A servant who takes a risk to aid the blinded, homeless Gloucester recognizes the affinity between an abram-man and a rogue, describing Poor Tom's "roguish madness" (3.7.107). Cordelia's use of the word brims with sympathy for the "forlorn" homeless who sleep in barns and for her father, who has shared their condition: "poor Father, / To hovel thee with swine and rogues forlorn" (4.7.39–40).

One of Kent's insults, "lubber" (1.4.89), connoted both low social status (a servant who did the meanest drudgery) and—contradictorily—extreme idleness (the Land of Cockaigne where no one worked was called Lubberland). Harman applies the term to vagrants sturdy enough to sneak out at night to pitch the bar and cast the sledge but too idle to work; they beg by day "with clouts bound about their legs, and halting with their staff in their hands" (81–82). Goneril trains on Lear's domestic tyrannies terms not of overbearing monarchy, as one might expect, but of criminal idleness: "Every hour / He flashes into one gross *crime* or other" (1.3.5–6), ultimately declaring him an "*Idle* old man" (1.3.17; emphasis added).

When Goneril and Regan cast the knights as a seditious mob, tarring them with criminal, underworld terms, one term especially—"disordered rabble" (1.4.253)—bears the stigma of the vagrant poor. "Rabble," a sixteenth-century coinage, meant both the lowest orders and dangerous mobs. "Dunghill" (which Oswald calls Edgar, thinking him a peasant [4.6.246]), became a mid-sixteenth-century term of contempt for "a person of evil life, or of base station" (*OED*) and was applied to vagrants. For example, a marginal comment on Acts 17:5 in the Geneva Bible excoriates "vagabonds . . . which do nothing but walk the streets, wicked men, to be hired for every man's money to do any mischief, such as we commonly call the rascals and very sink and dunghill knaves of all towns and cities."

Kent calls Oswald "beggarly" (2.2.15) and "beggar" (2.2.21), associating him with lowbrow sports ("base football player" [1.4.85], a term utterly incomprehensible as an insult at my university). He calls him "one-trunk-inheriting slave" (2.2.18–19); analyzing early modern inventories of poor people's possessions, Jütte found that the wooden chest

> was the quintessential mobile piece of furniture in every man's home. Its use
> was not only dictated by the lack of means for buying more expensive furni-
> ture. It also suited the mobility and instability which characterized the life-style
> of the poor. One of its many advantages was that the few wretched belongings
> in a poor man's home could be quickly grabbed and stuffed into those chests
> without fear of breakage or great expense in moving [which was often neces-
> sary, to dodge creditors]. Household and bed linen, in which the poor invest-
> ed a considerable portion of their meagre savings, were kept in them most of
> the time. (71)

The "one trunk" must have been a common icon of poverty, though of less extreme poverty than that of Harman's vagrants, some of whom possess not even a sheet, much less a trunk to keep it in. Kent calls Oswald "eater of broken meats" (2.2.14), meaning scraps distributed to the poor. Other insults that Kent hurls at Oswald include "knave" (2.2.14), "base" (2.2.15), "slave" (2.2.19), and "villain" (2.2.67), all terms applied to society's poorest people. Even a good man like Kent chooses as insults words denoting the poor.

Some of these words were new ("rogue," "rabble"), and others evoke medieval values only to reinscribe them in a drastically changed Renaissance context. Lexical shifts reflect the desanctification of poverty and its acquisition during the Renaissance of an aura of moral turpitude. *King Lear*'s language repeatedly jars audiences out of a feudal world where lower station was given by God and poverty was honorable. In *King Lear*'s world, to be put in the same category as the poor is a serious insult. The insult "miscreant" (1.1.164), meaning "infidel," oozes chivalry, romance, and jousting, but in such a feudal atmosphere it seems odd that Lear uses "vassal" to insult Kent (1.1.164), who precisely *is* a vassal, "one holding lands from a superior on conditions of homage and allegiance" (*OED*). In the Middle Ages this would not have been a term of opprobrium. Loyal Kent, in fact, behaves like a model vassal. Not until 1589, when socially lower had begun to mean morally lower, does the *Oxford English Dictionary* list "vassal" as a term of abuse. "Knave," used as an insult eleven times in *King Lear*,[14] denoted in the feudal system a male servant or one of low condition, often contrasted with "knight"; but late in the Middle Ages, it came also to mean a crafty rogue, often contrasted with "fool"—again, low social rank coming to mean disgraceful moral condition. Another degenerated feudal term used as an insult (or literally, as a synonym for "criminal") is "villain," occurring seventeen times.[15] A feudal "villein" was simply a serf; in act 3, scene 7, which uses "villain" as an insult four times, the word is also used to mean feudal retainer (3.7.81). "Varlet," used twice as an insult (2.2.28, 2.4.188), in the feudal system meant an attendant on a knight or other military officer; only in the mid-sixteenth century did "varlet" come to signify "a person of a low, mean, or knavish disposition; a knave, rogue, rascal"—a term of abuse (*OED*). In a favorite insult, Lear calls Oswald "rascal" before striking him (1.4.83); Kent calls Oswald "rascal" four times in act 2, scene 2. Of late medieval origin, the word referred to one of the lowest social status, sometimes an army hanger-on. Like "rogue," "rascal" was generalized in about the 1580s to mean "unprincipled or dishonest fellow" (*OED*), another designation of low social standing that became synonymous with poor moral character. In a fine moment, socially awakened Lear turns this insult upon an authority figure dispensing the punishment so many vagrant women received: "thou *rascal* beadle, hold thy bloody hand! / Why dost thou lash that whore?" (4.6.160–61). "Slave" occurs twelve times as an insult and term of contempt.[16] To live in outright slavery or in menial servitude lacking in rights was regarded as pitiable in the Middle Ages; in the mid-sixteenth century, "slave" blossomed as a term of contempt for the low-born. To hold in contempt persons in *involuntary* servitude, not responsible for their condition, is to blame the victim; but as Lear on the heath "changes places" with the poor, he comes to see himself as a "slave" (3.2.19). Again, while one certainly would not idealize medieval concepts of poverty, which had their own deleterious effects on the poor, it is important to emphasize the definite move toward moral blame of the poor that appears in Renaissance lexical shifts, so plainly visible in the fact that the insults permeating this passionate, violent play draw heavily on the discourse of vagrancy and poverty.

Since low rank had waxed contemptible, one insulted the highborn by pushing them down, verbally, among the low. But uncannily, action here replicates language: the highborn *are* pushed down among the low, like Rosalie Colie's "unmetaphoring" (*Living Art* 145), wherein, for example, a love tragedy makes literal the Petrarchan oxymoron "dear enemy" and the Petrarchan hyperbole "dying for love." High-caste characters who smear members of their own social group with the stigma of poverty are forced to experience poverty's degradations, to contemplate their own contempt from the perspective of the contemptible.

All the major meanings of "poor"—"impoverished," "unfortunate," and "inadequate"—occur in the play. The most negative meaning, "inadequate" or "incompetent," is used only by Goneril, who mendaciously claims to feel "a love that makes breath *poor*" (1.1.60) and accuses her father of "*poor* judgment" (1.1.294–95). "Poor" often refers to poverty, to poor people as a class, to beggars (1.1.254, 2.3.7, 2.3.18, 2.4.52, 2.4.267, 3.2.88, 4.1.1, 4.6.240, 5.1.40). During the play, "poor" increasingly means "unfortunate." Act 1's only use in this sense is Cordelia's momentary self-pity, "poor Cordelia!" (1.1.76). Act 2's only use of the word is Lear's self-pitying "you see me here, you gods, a poor old man" (2.4.274). One can track the dawning of compassion, of concern for *others'* misery, in the great increase, in acts 3 and 4, of "poor" as "unfortunate": in act 3 Lear uses the word that way four times, Gloucester does so three times, and Edgar does so twice; in act 4 Cordelia uses it that way twice, while Gloucester, the Old Man, Kent, a Gentleman, and Albany all use "poor" that way once each. Those called "poor" out of sympathy and compassion include Lear, the blinded Gloucester, the Fool, the "poor naked wretches," and "a poor unfortunate beggar."[17] Act 5 offers two important further instances: Lear imagines that "poor rogues" will be his fellow prisoners (5.3.13) and cries out at Cordelia's death, "my poor fool is hanged" (5.3.311). Alternating between "poor" as "impoverished" and "poor" as unfortunate or pitiable, *King Lear* tropes suffering in terms of the misery of poverty. The unhappy attract the economically oriented term "poor," recapitulating the fall into beggary of the play's highborn characters. In that central human embodiment of poverty and misery, Poor Tom, does "poor" mean "impoverished" or "deserving of compassion"? The play invites audiences not to decide, instead asking them to obliterate the line between these two meanings. Impoverishment should by definition merit compassion.

"Expose Thyself to Feel What Wretches Feel"

Taking a cue from the play's sense of a society in crisis, where old rules no longer apply (see, for example, 1.2.106–20; 4.1.10–11, 46, 5.3.31–32), many critics situate the play in the historical transition from feudalism to capitalism or parliamentary democracy.[18] Much is wrong with this view.[19] But if the play does not engage explicitly with feudalism as a political or economic system, what about feudal values? With the values of the "new" society being embodied in ruthless figures—Goneril, Regan, Edmund, Oswald—does *King Lear* endorse feudal values of faithful vassalage? If so, was this reactionary? Was Shakespeare a confirmed conservative? Raymond Williams argues that to valorize "a pre-capitalist and therefore irrecoverable world" (36) is to avoid confronting present ills; and although *King Lear* does confront the contemporary evil of homelessness, Annabel Patterson feels that, disappointingly, "Lear *recovers* from his wisdom-as-madness, and takes nothing from it into his reconciliation with Cordelia" (*Shakespeare and the Popular Voice* 116). But just as "distribution" does not necessarily imply medieval almsgiving, so compassion for the poor, while a value of the Middle Ages, is not exclusively medieval. Renaissance voices *were* raised against the denigration of almsgiving and the criminalization of poverty—not many voices, but important voices—and their protests (like those of Macbeth's opponents) were "not loud, but deep." It is possible to read in Marlowe's *Doctor Faustus* a sophisticated critique of humanists, reveling in worldly sensuality while insisting their goals were intellectual; but such antihumanism is routinely construed instead as a relapse into simplistic Christian orthodoxy. Criticism of one's own age need not imply nostalgia for another. Why must critics read *King Lear*'s critique of the heartlessness of its age as feudal nostalgia?

And even an appeal to feudalism is not necessarily reactionary. As Richard Halpern shows, both King James I and his parliamentary opponents called on a feudal discourse to justify as ancient prerogative the new political powers each wanted to claim (220–21). Just as in the history plays Shakespeare defines political modernity against a vanishing feudal world (e.g., Bolingbroke versus Richard II or Hal versus Hotspur), so a new discourse of feudalism was forged in Jacobean times to define modern politics (Halpern 220–21). Though the feudal tenure and vassalage they idealized had largely disappeared by the fourteenth century, even radical thinkers among Renaissance working people harked back to an idealized past when struggling for a better future. As James C. Scott argues, "it is the revolutionary character of capitalism that casts them in a defensive role. If they defend a version of the older hegemony, it is because those arrangements look good by comparison with the current prospects. . . . The defense and elaboration of a social contract that has been abrogated by capitalist development is perhaps the most constant ideological theme of the peasant and early capitalist worker" (346–47).

If harking back to feudal values is nostalgia, then, it is nostalgia in the service of political and economic critique and protest. And is not nostalgia a kind of temporal homesickness, a feeling that one's society has gone astray and needs calling home again? A longing for feudal values functions on the national level as Lear's desire to return to childhood, to Cordelia's "kind nurs-ery" (1.1.124), functions on the domestic level, a homology suiting a society that theorized the political and the domestic in similar patriarchal terms. The lost world of Lear's childhood forms a psychic parallel to the nation's lost feudal childhood: as nation and family disintegrate, an intense feeling of homelessness results. But this is not politically reactionary: the experience of homelessness is what creates, among the highborn, compassion for the low. The king who cries "O, I have ta'en / Too little care of this!" will not neces-sarily take more care in the future; but he is better equipped to do so, to make real economic changes, than the king who has never accepted responsibility for the poor.

Though their political orientation is congenial to me, I think historicist readings of *King Lear* fail to respond to the play's tutelage of homelessness, to heed the implications of its decentering forces. Lear learns he is not the center of the universe; but historicist and cultural materialist critics have kept him at the center, along with his supposed analogue, King James I. It is vital-ly important, given the autocratic power he has wielded, that Lear come to recognize that he has "ta'en / Too little care." It is vitally important, but it is not everything. The poor are poor in *King Lear* because of widespread eco-nomic conditions for which a king is not solely responsible, and because the common assumption that the poor are responsible for their poverty impedes action that might change the economic system. Lear is not alone in neglect-ing the poor; to neglect and despise them is endemic in the play as it was in Renaissance society. Characters habitually use words signifying poverty and vagrancy as terms of insult and abuse; even Kent does this. Not only Lear but also Gloucester, Edgar, Kent, Cordelia, and the knights must experience pov-erty firsthand, because the problem of poverty is of such magnitude that opening the king's eyes is nowhere near enough: society's eyes must be opened. From Kent's demand, "See better, Lear!" (1.1.159) to Gloucester's recognition that before being physically blinded he was morally blind—"I stumbled when I saw" (4.1.19)—*King Lear* is about seeing, about understand-ing what is before one's eyes. The play makes *everyone* "see better"—not only the king, but all the characters and the audience too. Contemptuous, piti-less attitudes toward the poor typify not only the monarchy. The power un-dergirding this unjust, uncompassionate system resides in every well-off member of the nation.

The overwhelming size of the poverty problem, the need to change the hearts of thousands, not just the king, is daunting. But it has its bright side: that Lear sadly "recovers from his reason-in-madness," as Patterson says, that he loses interest in the poor just before he dies and is by then incapable of

helping them anyway, is no sign that Shakespeare has collapsed into reactionary views or dwindled into despair, or that modern audiences should either.
Dollimore argues, despairingly, that "in a world where pity is the prerequi-
site for compassionate action, where a king has to share the suffering of his
subjects in order to 'care,' the majority will remain poor, naked and wretched. . . . Princes only see the hovels of wretches during progresses . . . , in flight
or in fairy tale" (191). But the king did not cause the whole problem; he alone
could not have solved it. If the problem is atomized among all the play's
characters and members of the audience, so is the solution: their changed
hearts may now begin to address in small daily ways the creation of a society less contemptuous of the poor.

King Lear *did* resemble King James[20]—both went hunting to escape state
duties, both admired absolutist power, both regarded kingship as property
ownership, both had sons or sons-in-law who were dukes of Albany and of
Cornwall, both were subject to budget-trimming (by daughters in one case,
by Parliament in the other). But to reduce the play to a message to James
would again focus the nation's economic problems solely on the king. To
ascribe all power in Renaissance England to the king and court or to Parliament is an act of scapegoating, blaming all ills on the government and ab-
solving individual citizens. Poverty was created and/or increased by faceless
market forces and by the amoral pursuit of financial gain regardless of social cost; and the power that created and sustained this system and then treated its victims with contempt—this power lay, and now lies, with every comfortably well-off member of society. The households that fly apart, the
kingdom that disintegrates, the aristocrats who restlessly and homelessly
wander the countryside in *King Lear* attest to a centrifugal force. The play
reminded Jacobean audiences, for all the centralizing tendencies of their
government, and reminds modern readers, for all the king-and-court centered nature of recent historicist criticism, that the early modern English
nation consisted not only of king and court but of all its people. A nation's
injustices, its creation of an underclass and its contempt for the dispossessed,
concern not only kings and governments but every citizen. To help create a
more equitable society, to treat the homeless with both respect for their rights
and compassion for their misery, is as much in the power of ordinary citizens as is the ability to insult them, fear them, and hold them in contempt.
We forget the tutelage of the hovel if we disclaim this power.

Notes

1. In Lear's "unaccommodated man is no more but . . . a poor, bare, forked animal"
(3.4.105–7), "unaccommodated" may mean "homeless": "accommodation" could mean
"lodgings" (e.g., *Othello* 1.3.241).

2. It was commonplace to link national disorder with household disorder, as in Francis Dillingham's "a great cause of disorders, both in church and Commonwealth, is a disordered family" (sig. H3–H4). It is no accident that Milton, as a supporter of revolution, would also support a loosening of divorce laws; that a wide interest in divorce laws attended the English Civil War was a logical consequence of the persistent equation between monarch and patriarch—to depose and kill a monarch was to open the door to the dissolution of families as well.

3. I cannot agree with Walter Cohen that "the opening abdication scene makes sense only if Lear is not a traditional feudal king but a neofeudal absolute monarch. . . . The alarm caused by his decision to divide the country necessarily rests on the prior establishment of the relatively modern category of nationhood" (329). In fact, alarm over division of the country is notable for its absence. In act 1, scene 1, Gloucester and Kent discuss the division only in speculating over whose portion will be largest and what this says about the king's affections. Goneril and Regan find evidence of their father's instability in his exiling Cordelia and banishing Kent, but if they find anything alarming in his dividing the kingdom, they do not mention it. Gloucester's list of omens of disaster (1.2.106–20) does not mention the division of the kingdom. The dissection of England might well have proved alarming to the play's Jacobean audience, but within the play itself it is represented more in familial than in national terms.

4. "Riot" as "violence, strife, disorder, tumult, especially on the part of the populace" (i.e., the lower classes), dates to the late fourteenth century; riot as "wanton, loose, or wasteful living; debauchery, dissipation, extravagance" dates to the thirteenth century (*OED*). The more general word "crime" modulated during the sixteenth century from a more strictly legal medieval meaning ("an act punishable by law") to an early Renaissance meaning including "offense or sin," morally or theologically conceived (*OED*)—another instance of the mentality of crime and criminal law beginning to permeate everyday life, as they did when words like "rogue" began to be used as all-purpose insults.

5. The locale where Lear undergoes this education is one explicitly associated with the vagrant poor: "The heath was the . . . home of escapees from village order, paupers denied a parish settlement, vagrants escaping the oppression of wage labour, masterless men without land or trade of their own, madmen like Tom O'Bedlam, fugitives from justice and old people abandoned or thrown out of their families" (Ignatieff 40; on the heath, see also Christopher Hill's *Century of Revolution, 1603–1714* and *Society and Puritanism in Pre-Revolutionary England*, R. H. Tawney's *Religion and the Rise of Capitalism* and *The Agrarian Problem in the Sixteenth Century*).

6. I am indebted to Naomi Liebler for pointing this out.

7. He also at one point asks Tom, "Didst thou give all to thy daughters, and art thou come to this?" (3.4.48–49), reflecting the idée fixe of madness. That Lear's progress in social awareness is not linear, that he relapses into solipsism and madness, is not a sign of incomplete commitment to social awareness on Shakespeare's part but of the tragic hero's complex subjectivity in Shakespeare's mature period.

8. Halpern, for example, thinks "'shake the superflux' has a decidedly aristocratic cachet of largesse" (261). Earlier, however, Lear has defined even beggars' rags as "superfluous" ("our basest beggars / Are in the poorest thing superfluous" [2.4.266–67]); here, a wide variety of goods are only allegedly "superfluous": both beggars and kings need them. Patterson interprets the passage as radically redistributive of wealth: "'shake the superflux,'

that is, the superfluous wealth that he knows the economy produces, to the 'wretches' whose condition he now experiences" (*Shakespeare and the Popular Voice* 113). On the word "superfluity" as part of the discourse of both almsgiving and economic redistribution, see pages 212–18.

9. Beggars were sometimes said to have goods in common. Gilbert Walker's imagined rogue community has a treasurer, "a trusty secret friend," to whom they convey their ill-gotten gains, and "of every purse that is cleanly conveyed, a rateable portion is duly delivered into the treasurer's hands, to the use that whensoever by some misadventure any of them happen to be taken and laid in prison, this common stock may serve to satisfy the party grieved, and to make friends to save them from hanging" (83). If this system resembles union dues more than full-blown rogue communism, a more thoroughgoing sharing of goods appears in John Fletcher and Philip Massinger's comedy *The Beggar's Bush.*

10. As Heather Dubrow points out, "Surely it would not have been difficult for him to divest himself of most property but with the 'reservation' (1.1.133) of both one hundred knights and a castle or two in which to house them" (107). Naomi Liebler discusses the way in which, by holding court in the domestic space of the hovel, Lear desperately tries to recreate a sense of home (202–4).

11. A similar shift in attitude is visible in Rembrandt's beggars. In the 1630s, his beggars were cruelly comic caricatures in the vein of Jacques Callot or Pieter Quast, but "between the representations of beggars of c. 1630 and the *Beggars Receiving Alms at the Door of a House,* dated 1648, there is a change in Rembrandt's attitude toward beggars. . . . The faces of the adults are individualized, unlike the distorted, shadowy visages of the beggars in the etchings of the 1630s. . . . The gentleman who offers the coin at the open doorway wears a gentle and kindly expression that immediately gives notice that these beggars are not objects of ridicule" (Stratton 80).

12. Lameness was prominent in the iconography of beggary, and in this play, like so many other items in the semiotics of poverty, it can either provoke pity or prompt curses: Lear curses Goneril not only with sterility but with lameness (2.4.163).

13. Tracing the insidious expansion of the term "vagabond" in successive pieces of Tudor legislation, C. S. L. Davies notes the crucial contribution to this process of simple name-calling: "By 1572 the definition of a vagabond as one refusing to work for reasonable wages had become normal. Thus there has been a shift from treating the man refusing work as if he were a vagabond, to the concept that he *was* a vagabond. The earlier practice was part of the Tudor technique of expressing extreme disapprobation of a crime by calling it a bad name; as in the famous act declaring that poisoners should be treated as traitors. Vagrancy was a useful emotive concept of this sort" (535).

14. "Knave" is used as an insult in *King Lear* at 1.2.125, 2.2.14, 2.2.16, 2.2.20, 2.2.70, 2.2.89, 2.2.90, 2.2.128, 2.2.140, 2.4.74, 2.4.82–83.

15. "Villain" is used as an insult in *King Lear* at 1.2.80, 1.2.118, 1.2.124, 1.2.168, 2.1.37, 2.1.40, 2.1.76, 2.1.80, 2.2.67, 3.7.3, 3.7.35, 3.7.87, 3.7.90, 4.2.55, 4.6.249, 4.6.255, 5.3.101.

16. "Slave" is used as an insult and a term of contempt in *King Lear* at 1.1.80, 1.4.51, 2.2.19, 2.2.41, 2.2.72, 2.4.186, 2.4.217, 3.7.99, 4.6.239, 4.6.249, 5.3.225, 5.3.279.

17. "Poor" is used in the sense of "unfortunate" in *King Lear* at 3.2.20; 3.3.72, 3.4.28, 3.4.98, 3.4.169, 3.6.50, 3.7.57, 3.7.62, 4.1.28, 4.2.80, 4.3.40, 4.3.49, 4.6.68, 4.7.35, 4.7.38.

18. See, for example, works by John Danby, Paul Delany, Paul Siegel, Franco Moretti, Walter Cohen, John Turner, Rosalie Colie ("Reason and Need"), Richard Halpern, and Julian Markels.

19. For example, the supposed "new men" they identify have much that is feudal about them: Oswald, whose "status as the 'new man' of the court secures Kent's status as the 'old man' of feudalism" (Halpern 243) is in his way a perfectly faithful feudal retainer to Goneril. As Halpern notes, there is much of the feudal about Edmund, whose "opening lines ('Thou, Nature, art my goddess; to thy law / My services are bound') strongly allude to the language of knightly enfeoffment and courtly love, [while] his illegitimate affair with Goneril . . . puts him squarely in the position of the feudal courtly lover. . . . He turns out . . . to be no mean soldier and even attains in his last moments to something like a knightly sense of honor" (242). Theorists such as Julian Markels find a new spirit of bourgeois capitalism in Goneril, Regan, and Edmund, an argument that is based on no firmer grounds than their competitiveness and acquisitiveness, as if feudalism was a stranger to competition and acquisitiveness. Feudalism's signature competitiveness, the sibling rivalry built into primogeniture, is all over the play; Goneril and Regan object to Lear's abrogating this system by dividing land rather than passing it intact to the eldest—does this align the sisters with feudal values? To Halpern, a weakness of many historicist readings is to "equate the collapse of the play's social order with the collapse of feudalism, whereas in fact the play collapses *back into* feudalism" (242). And Halpern finds nowhere in *King Lear* "anything like a pro-parliamentary ideology" (224).

20. For critics who draw specific parallels between King Lear and King James, see, for example, Patterson (*Shakespeare and the Popular Voice* 106–16) and Halpern (222–33).

Conclusion: New Place or No Place?

Give me your tired, your poor,
Your huddled masses yearning to breathe free,
The wretched refuse of your teeming shore.
Send these, the homeless, tempest-tost to me,
I lift my lamp beside the golden door.

—Emma Lazarus

SOME OF THE FINEST MOMENTS in rogue literature efface the line between rogue life and respectable life, exposing the Othering process that projected the sins of the respectable onto the poor. In *A Manifest Detection of the Most Vile and Detestable Use of Dice-Play,* Gilbert Walker hints broadly that cheating at dice and cards parodies life in the legal profession: "cheating" stems from the legal term "escheat," and it is no accident that various kinds of card-sharping are known colloquially as "laws." A speaker in this dialogue argues that the landed aristocracy and most professional men are sharpers, no less than the dicing sharks:

> Think you that noble men could do as they do if in this hard world they should maintain so great a port only upon their rent? Think you the lawyers could be such purchasers if their pleas were short and all their judgments, justice, and conscience? Suppose ye the offices would be so dearly bought and the buyers so soon enriched if they counted not pillage an honest point of purchase? Could merchants, without lies, false making their wares and selling them by a crooked light to deceive the chapman in the thread or color, grow so soon rich, and to a baron's possessions, and make all their posterity gentlemen? (74).

Laying bare the process by which "rogues" were scapegoated for crimes committed at all levels of society, such remarks reveal how anxiety over social mobility—here, the upward movement of merchants—was displaced onto "rogues" who insinuated themselves into a higher social caste. These texts suggest that the apparent downward mobility of aristocrats whose position was being eroded by the jetting middle classes was also displaced onto the world of roguery: dicing-house masters, not a changing socioeconomic system, take the blame for "spoiling gentlemen of their inheritance" (71).

The Italian Francesco Vettori penned an encomium to rogues that implicated much of "respectable" society: "The world becomes beautiful, the brain of one person is made more acute in the search for new ways of defrauding, and that of another becomes sharper in order to guard himself against it. And in effect, all the world is imposture; and it begins with the men of religion, and continues with the lawyers, the doctors, the astrologers, the worldly princes, those who participate at any time in all arts and trades; and day by day everything gets sharper and more refined" (qtd. in Camporesi 59). And the Spanish novelist Matheo Aleman's character Guzman de Alfarache comments dryly, "As for your great rich thieves, such as ride on their foot-cloths of velvet, that hang their houses with hangings of tissue and costly arras, and cover the floors of their chambers with gold and silk, and curious Turkey carpets, and often hang such poor snakes as we are, . . . we are far inferior unto them, and are those little fishes, which these great ones do devour. . . . They call me Rogue, . . . [but no man should] make himself such a saint, as to take offence when he hears the name of a thief, . . . till he ask this question of himself, whether . . . he hath not in his lifetime played the thief himself" (3:338–42).

At another extreme from such wonderful demystifying moments is one of the largest mystifications in the discourse of vagrancy: the very writers who generally demonized or at best patronized vagrants, at other times downright idealized them. While one side of the Renaissance psyche felt anxiety about vagrants' mobility, another side yearned for it.

In literature, the "merry beggar" trope abounds. Whole plays dramatize beggars' jovial lives—usually, as in Brome's *Jovial Crew* and Fletcher and Massinger's *Beggar's Bush,* their lives are the merrier in that they are actually disguised aristocrats who can cast off the beggar's life at will. A Dekker character says, "although [beggars'] bodies beg, their souls are kings" (Dekker and Middleton, *Honest Whore* 5.2.504–5); in Nashe's *Summer's Last Will and Testament,* Ver defends the beggar's happy, free life; a vagrant in Dekker's *Bellman of London,* making "an oration in praise of beggary," rejoices that "the whole kingdom is [a beggar's] walk, a whole city is but his parish" (82). William Carroll places Autolycus in Shakespeare's *Winter's Tale* in the merry beggar tradition (*Fat King* 168–69; see also Mowat; Timpane, chap. 5).[1] The title figure of "The Cunning Northern Beggar," traveling with his "doxy," claims to be a disabled soldier or shipwrecked sailor, feigns disease, blindness, epilepsy, and body sores; the ballad foregrounds, however, his delightful freedom from care:

I scorn to work,
But by the highway lurk,
And beg to get my living;
. . . Yet, though I'm bare,
I'm free from care,—
A fig for high preferments!" (137)

What is so good about a beggar's life, according to such fantasies, is freedom: geographic freedom to wander, mental freedom from the worries and responsibilities of the settled and the powerful. Just as anxiety about vagrants' geographic wandering was displaced onto more nebulous social mobilities, so envy of vagrants' geographic license was extended to encompass envy of their mental liberty. Geographic freedom is emphasized in Alexander Barclay's *Ship of Fools*, offering two motives for people taking up a beggar's life: idleness and a wish to "wander at their will" (cxxviii). Mental freedom appears in Erasmus's "Beggar Talk," in which Irides calls begging "the next best thing to possessing a kingdom," because beggars are free from obligations that afflict the powerful (*Colloquies* 253). Carroll writes, "The beggar ironically turns back into a kind of monarch in his supposed freedom" (*Fat King* 17), and in reversing the king/beggar antithesis, the merry beggar trope indeed carnivalizes monarchy and beggary. Paul Slack discusses this carnivalesque side of depictions of poverty:

> The use of the poor as a yardstick, against which approved social norms could be measured out, may be seen most clearly in the representation of vagrants and idle paupers as the complete obverse of all that was acceptable. . . . They belonged in fact to the World Turned Upside Down. . . . [Beggars' inversions] were ambivalent. They were conservative in that they reinforced by contrast contemporary notions of right order. Yet they were also a relatively harmless outlet for criticism of that order and for the open presentation of alternatives. Much of the rogue literature as it developed in the later sixteenth century served a similar purpose. Combining fact and fiction, writers from Thomas Harman onwards dramatized the dangerous rogue, exaggerated his eccentricity, and even romanticized him. They portrayed vagabonds as men enjoying a unique freedom, no less attractive for the fact that it was condemned as licence. (*Poverty and Policy* 25)

The criticism of "contemporary notions of right order" and the "open presentation of alternatives" suggests that beggars offered a mute criticism of the life of power and of settled respectability. Did the trope praising the beggar's "unique freedom" call into question the value of "right order," from the monarchical down to the domestic? Had the sacrifice of freedom to attain either power or security come to seem too great a cost? Did the happy beggar topos suggest that the life of power and respectability might not be worth it?

The merry beggar is part of a complex trope involving also the miserable king. A well-developed example in Aleman's novel *The Rogue; or, The Life of Guzman de Alfarache* (1599/1623) idealizes the beggar's life for its liberty and merriment but concludes that "the office of a king, that is no good place; there is no sport in it, no mirth, no jollity" (2:39):[2]

> For a king neither sleepeth so soundly, nor resteth so quietly as the poor por-
> ter doth; neither doth he eat his meat with that merry heart, and free from all
> care, as doth the tradesman. . . . Nor any grand so great, but that the troubles
> and griefs which attend a king are far greater. He must keep watch and ward,
> when others securely sleep. . . . He sighs and groans when others sport and play;
> yet few are they that take pity of him, or are sensible of his sorrows. . . . Whereas
> indeed, . . . he ought of all to be both loved, feared, and respected. (2:39–40)

In a similar vein, a sleepless Henry IV comes close to saying "power is not worth it":

> Why, rather, sleep, liest thou in smoky cribs,
> Upon uneasy pallets stretching thee,
> · · · · · · · · · · · · · · · · · ·
> Than in the perfum'd chambers of the great,
> Under the canopies of costly state? (*2H4* 3.1.9–13)

New historicists typically dismiss passages like this one (and like Henry V's pre-battle insomniac lament) as hypocritical—as rhetorical ploys to justify privileged position. Stephen Greenblatt writes,

> Perhaps in a society in which the overwhelming majority of men and women
> had next to nothing, the few who were rich and powerful did lie awake at
> night. . . . The sufferings of the great are one of the familiar themes in the lit-
> erature of the governing classes in the sixteenth century. . . . We are invited to
> take measure of his suffering, to understand . . . the costs of power. And we are
> invited to understand these costs in order to ratify the power, to accept the gro-
> tesque and cruelly unequal distribution of possessions: everything to the few,
> nothing to the many. The rulers earn . . . their exalted position through suffer-
> ing. . . . At such moments *2 Henry IV* seems to be testing and confirming an
> extremely dark and disturbing hypothesis about the nature of monarchical
> power in England: that its moral authority rests upon a hypocrisy so deep that
> the hypocrites themselves believe it. (*Shakespearean Negotiations* 40–41)

William C. Carroll's reading of the merry beggar trope complements Green-blatt's reading of the miserable king trope: "The life of the beggar is claimed to be actually superior to that of the rest of us. This delusion of course flies in the face of the reality of social conditions, . . . a perfect illustration of how those comfortably placed within the social hierarchy rationalize the continued exclusion of the marginal. Beggars are thus usually either demonized by the prevailing discourse or their suffering suppressed through idealization" (*Fat King* 181).[3] I think this is true; but I also believe that it is not the whole truth. Professions of the miseries of power, like warped idealizations of poverty, are not necessarily hypocritical. A life of power *does* have costs, and they are precisely sacrifices of freedom. Granted, the powerful were looking for freedom from care in a pretty unpromising place—the beggar's life—but it is of real interest that they felt the lack of freedom keenly enough to indulge in such fantasies.

This lack was experienced in homes as well as palaces. Texts like Brome's *Jovial Crew,* which expressed envy of beggars' freedom, did rationalize neglect of the vagrant poor; but they also responded to the wistful fantasies of a too-settled, too-respectable people. In *A Jovial Crew,* Springlove, responsible steward to an old aristocratic family, experiences a "gadding humor" (1.1.175) every summer and goes "wand'ring like a vagabond" (1.1.188) to escape the stultifying routine of a life devoted to his employer and to duty, and to indulge his "inborn strong desire of liberty" (1.1.249), since "among beggars, each man is his own" (1.1.259). Springlove finds a beggars' song quite ravishing:

> From hunger and cold, who lives more free,
> Or who more richly clad than we?
> Our bellies are full; our flesh is warm;
> And, against pride, our rags are a charm.
> Enough is our feast, and for tomorrow
> Let rich men care; we feel no sorrow. (1.1.339–44)

Most people's workplaces were their homes—they did not even travel to work. They were constantly preached at to stay home and be domestic. The slightest irregularity of behavior was talked about by neighbors or punished with a ritualized laughing-to-scorn. During the Reformation, neighbors turned in old women for praying with rosaries. On top of all this enforced homekeeping and conformity, fear of vagrants made the respectable anxious about going out. Thomas Harman claims that vagrants commonly break into houses "when the owners be either at the market, church, or other ways occupied about their business" (71)—it is dangerous for a householder to go out at all. Rogue texts fostered the notion that to answer the door can be frightening. As Harman avers, "If [vagrants] ask at a stout yeoman's or farmer's house his charity, they will go strong as three or four in a company; where, for fear more than good will, they often have relief" (70). And so, ironically, those who were mullioned indoors projected onto vagrants a fantasy of liberty. In *A Jovial Crew,* two young women run off to join a troupe of beggars, whom they suppose "happier than we, . . . that are pent up and tied by the nose to the continual steam of hot hospitality here in our father's house, when they have the air at pleasure" (2.1.13); one sister, though suspecting that "we have merrier spirits than they," still agrees that "to live thus confin'd, stifles us" (2.2.13–14).

In his long poem "The Praise, Antiquity, and Commodity of Beggary, Beggars, and Begging," John Taylor ("The Water Poet") celebrates an unhoused life as an alternative to a more conventional home:

> Thus all degrees and states, whate'er they are,
> With beggar's happiness cannot compare:
> Heav'n is the roof that canopies his head,
> The clouds his curtains, and the earth his bed,
> The sun his fire, the stars his candlelight,
> The moon his lamp that guides him in the night. (95)

Citing the contemporary prosecution of a runaway apprentice, Richard Fletcher, who was resolute in his desire for freedom from his master, Patricia Fumerton emphasizes that there was a genuinely liberatory side to the vagrant's freedom from coercive authority and oppressively settled life: "such a free-ranging 'no where' subject was simultaneously alienated and free." Christopher Hill views woodland and pasture squatters and urban vagrants as seekers after freedom from prying authority (*World Turned Upside Down* 32–40).

The dullness of bourgeois respectability added glitter to the underworld's supposed freedom, and rogues' criminality, like beggars' freedom, was glamorized. In Ben Jonson's *Bartholomew Fair,* a bawd wooing a housewife into a life of prostitution scoffs at the honest woman's "scurvy dull life" (4.5.30), offering to make her "a free woman" (4.5.34). Such glamorization of an urban underworld complemented pastorals' idealization of rural poverty: though wildly unrepresentative of actual poverty, both obliquely expressed dissatisfaction with the settled respectability so relentlessly trumpeted as the norm.

Idealizing beggary has a gender dimension: as home was gradually gendered as a female space, a macho man was bound to feel uneasy, if not emasculated, in a cozily appointed, tapestried home.[4] Formal misogynistic writings sometimes staged an antidomestic revolt by the manly. Joseph Swetnam's

Robert Bly-like allegation that men relish roughing it in the outdoors, preferably on the battlefield, earned him the scorn of the pseudonymous Constantia Munda. To Swetnam's claim that men love "to lie on the cold grass, but a woman must be wrapped in warm mantles" (qtd. in Munda 32), Munda replies, "I never heard of any that had rather lie in the cold grass than in a feather-bed, if he might have his choice; yet you make it a proper attribute to all your sex" (32). Othello glorifies the freedom of a soldier's unhoused condition, and it augurs ill for his marriage that from the outset he conceives of married domesticity, that converse of a soldier's free life, as stultifying confinement:

> But that I love the gentle Desdemona,
> I would not my unhousèd free condition
> Put into circumscription and confine
> For the sea's worth. (*Othello* 1.2.25–28)[5]

Here domestic ideology confronts the ideology of martial masculinity. Male yearning for an undomestic existence helps make sense of the romanticizing of vagabonds.

Civility, too, had its downside for the masculine man: as John Hale points out, "From the mid-sixteenth century the effeminating effect of civility was fairly widely deplored" (369). Such anxiety helps account, Hale thinks, for the continuing fascination with the "Wild Folk," "naked denizens of forests and remote valleys, . . . liable to spring from among the trees with a lifted club to batter travellers" (369). This medieval/Renaissance sasquatch bears an obvious resemblance to the vagrant highwayman of Renaissance imaginings, especially rogues like the Upright Man, and it is telling that this figure's manliness was admired even as his lawlessness was feared, revealing a nagging suspicion that civility was for sissies.

Rogue literature's odd double tone—sober moralizing about wicked vagrants joined to mirthful relish of rogue trickery—nicely captures the ambivalence with which vagrants, genuinely feared and loathed, also enjoyed a certain amount of sneaking admiration. Robert Greene routinely wants it both ways: he revels in the posture of a streetwise tough guy who has dared to penetrate the underworld and is au fait with its tricks: "Gentlemen, I have seen the world and rounded it, though not with travel, yet with experience" (*Notable Discovery* 119). In this voice, he luxuriates in the superiority his shady experience confers: he is ever so much shrewder than the wide-eyed country folk continually taken in by urban cardsharks; and in learning everything there is to know about cheating at cards and other rogues' tricks (mostly from earlier rogue literature rather than experience, as he claims), he basks in knowledge superior even to that of any single member of the underworld. This polymath of roguery also lords it over the "gentlemen" he addresses in his dedication: however socially exalted their position, they are but babes in the woods compared with Greene's sophisticated persona, who patronizingly enlightens them on everything a poor, sequestered gent might never have had the excitement to learn. But Greene's other voice, the moralist ensconced upon high ground, sententiously denounces cony-catchers' "licentious abuses," donning the mantle of moral counselor to the nation: "I would wish the Justices appointed as severe censors of such fatal mischiefs" (*Notable Discovery* 121). Greene preserves his double persona by claiming he has not dirtied his hands by slumming—he has (like Prince Hal) been in this world without being of it. Impressive possibilities for self-congratulation inhere in possessing both the worldly sophistication of the chief of sinners and the moral authority of a conscience to the nation. Greene's persona is both master rogue and justice of the peace. If Mikhail Gorbachev failed because he could not decide whether to be Luther or the pope, Greene succeeds by being both the upright man and Harman.

Underworld envy soars to an apex in Jonson's *Bartholomew Fair*. Here some well-to-do Londoners visit a famous fair, whose carnies, drawn mainly from rogue literature, are under scrutiny by the authorities. The official gaze and the citizens' gaze reproduce the censorious but fascinated scrutiny the respectable often trained upon the underworld. One of the carnies belittles these slumming bourgeoisie as "sippers o' the city; they look as they would not drink off two penn'orth of bottle-ale amongst 'hem" (3.2.111–13). They get a thrill out of the underworld's violence and colorful language. Just as modern suburban teenagers, in revolt against dull respectability, sometimes ape the style of urban gangs, the bourgeois Quarlous and Wasp wax as violent and quarrelsome as the underworld denizens. The fair is a noisy world, pulsating with the raucous cries of vendors selling toys, gingerbread, ballads. The phenomenon of "roarers"—gentlemen turned bluff bullyboys— hints that increasing civility involved changing thresholds of noise: lower orders probably had louder voices. Unlike *King Lear*'s Cordelia, whose "voice was ever soft, / Gentle, and low" (5.3.277–78), the figure of Poor Tom was fearsome partly because he was roaring and noisy. But always speaking in a well-modulated, decorous voice may have palled, with mettlesome young gentleman: Quarlous and Wasp are young bloods cutting loose in a relieving flood of pure noise after too long a muffling by civility.

Bartholomew Fair is infiltrated by an authority in disguise: Justice Overdo adopts the persona of a mad orator to spy out abuses: "I, Adam Overdo, am resolved . . . to spare spy-money hereafter, and make mine own discoveries" (2.1.39–41). Like Greene's persona, who claims to have been a spy in the underworld so as to gain insight into the "knaveries" of the rogues who comprise a "dangerous enormity" (*Notable Discovery* 119, 121), Overdo calls the abuses "enormities" (4.4.182, 4.4.196). Since Overdo is a justice of the peace, one inevitably thinks of Thomas Harman, going to London and spying into the abuses of phony epileptics. That Jonson actually modeled Overdo on Harman is suggested by one character's mentioning, while discussing Overdo, a work called *A Caveat against Cutpurses* (3.1.34–35), thus evoking Harman's *Caveat for Common Cursetors*. Overdo's madman disguise allies him to fools; he is called "a justice in the habit of a fool" (2.1.7–9). As I have shown, the Renaissance fool weirdly combined the numskull with the clever trickster, and whether Overdo is more trickster than numskull is a question. His disguise consists of a species of feigned disability—he is "mad Arthur of Bradley, that makes the orations" (2.2.124–25), a kind of Poor Tom; and the disguise calls forth a preaching voice not far from the one Edgar at times uses for Poor Tom. Overdo wants to be a "middling thing, between a fool and a madman" (2.2.144–45).

Though he adopts Greene's worldly-wise pose, declaring Jordan Knockem "a cutpurse of the sword, the boot, and the feather! those are his marks" (2.3.11–12), Overdo is easy to fool. He quickly takes the word of another underworld character, Mooncalf, that Knockem is really an honest horse-courser: "Here I might have been deceived now, and have put a fool's blot upon myself, if I had not played an after game of discretion" (2.3.40–42). When he meets a real cutpurse, Edgeworth, Overdo mistakes him for a "civil young gentleman" (2.4.24). Overdo is a "serious ass," one who "takes pains to be one, and plays the fool, with the greatest diligence that can be" (3.5.265–67); his foolishness makes him putty in the hands of the clever underworldlings, and here again appears the perniciousness of such glamorized cleverness: from a real-life vagrant's point of view, justices of the peace were not nearly so harmless, so downright lovable. The play presents Overdo's pontifications as ultimately mere harmless rant: his wife (who does not see through his disguise) declares, "He hath something of Master Overdo, methinks" (2.6.272–73), and Cokes agrees, locating the resemblance in Overdo's voice (2.6.74–75). Overdo's pose as a mad orator, it appears, is largely indistinguishable from his usual moralizing voice as justice of the peace. Both are merely sideshows, no real threat to the rogue community, which is displayed as self-sufficient to the point of invulnerability.

A dramatized fraternity of vagabonds, Jonson's carnival rogues are organized into a smoothly running society: Edgeworth cooperates with a ballad singer in filching and conveying purses, and Ursula acts as a fence. Wasp alludes to John Awdeley's and Thomas Harman's descriptions of the personnel of rogues' fraternities, calling the disguised Overdo "the Patrico, . . . the patriarch of the cutpurses" (2.6.150–51) and purveys the all-things-in-common stereotype: "You share, sir, they say" (2.6.151–52).

Bartholomew Fair's cony-catching underworld wins the reader's sympathy as it wins the respectable characters' fascination, by its shrewdness and vitality. Making respectability dull and roguery glamorous caters to certain yearnings in the staunchly respectable Renaissance middle classes. Overdo is made the butt of jest, just as the underworld often makes fools of the respectable in rogue literature; but this supposed underworld self-sufficiency undercuts its claim on public sympathy. None of the play's underworld characters is shown suffering any deprivation. The obesity of Ursula the Pig Woman, a kind of female Falstaff, replaces the lean hunger common among real-life rogues. Homelessness is not an issue: the carnies have a rather settled life, however temporary to the fair—Ursula's booth is called a "mansion" (2.5.40). This play illustrates what happened to real poor people when roguery was glamorized: admiration for rogues' witty trickery, and the notion that they had a "fraternity" to take care of them, granted them an agency and self-sufficiency that disabled pity and seemed to render unnecessary public assistance for the poor or policies to change the economic system so as to ameliorate poverty.

If there is one thing I hope my literary study of vagrancy has accomplished, it is to show that the genres in which "rogues" appear have everything to do with cultural perceptions about them. Historians discuss a dismal array of imprisoning devices designed to arrest the mobility of vagrants: the parish boundary, the stocks, poor hospitals, Bridewell, and that final immobilizer, the gallows. And literature offers additional shackles: vagrants were imprisoned in hostile literary genres (Protestant polemics against mendicancy, humanist treatises on order and decency, sermons against idleness); in genres whose comic tenor trivialized vagrancy (rogue literature, comic celebrations of life on the road); in genres whose lowliness in the literary hierarchy made impossible a stature of heroism (or even dignity) for a rogue protagonist or a claim on the reader's sympathy for a victimized vagrant (cony-catching pamphlets, jest books). Even from Bridewell, it was possible to escape. But how does one get out of a jest book?

The Ambiguous Valuation of Mobility

Texts glamorizing vagrants' freedom reveal a fissure in Renaissance attitudes—should mobility be feared or envied? In a founding Renaissance text, *Oration on the Dignity of Man,* Pico della Mirandola had unsettled the fixity of the Great Chain of Being by making mobility the distinguishing human feature: God informs mankind that "a limited nature in other creatures is confined within the laws written down by Us. In conformity with thy free judgment, in whose hands I have placed thee, thou art confined by no bounds; and thou wilt fix limits of nature for thyself" (4). Man can degenerate to "the lower levels which are the brutes" or, by the use of reason, recreate himself at level of the divine (5). Yet an anxiety about such mobility appears in the way Pico constrains it: man's dignity may be based on his freedom to wander about in the Great Chain of Being, a cosmic vagrant, but if he wanders in the wrong direction—toward a life of beasts or plants rather than of angels—he forfeits his human identity altogether: one "delivered over to the senses" is "a brute, not a man" (6).

In this age of discovery, of globe-encompassing odysseys to the New World, around the Cape of Good Hope, to foreign places strange and spicy, poets sang of voyages. Christopher Marlowe's imagination was fired by "huge argosies," and the wealth that Spain garnered in America reminded him of Jason's golden fleece (*Faustus* 1.1.131–32). Shakespeare endowed supernatural agents with powers of globe-trotting travel: "I'll put a girdle round the earth / In forty minutes," cries Puck (*MND* 2.1.175–76), while Titania jets between her Athenian wood and India; in *The Tempest,* Ariel runs errands to the still-vexed Bermudas (1.2.230). Richard Hakluyt's voyages thrilled English readers. But as "The Water Poet" John Taylor put it, "a beggar is a right perpetual motion" (99), and the Renaissance was edgy about mobility.

Alongside mouthwatering mantras about exotic lands, a body of antitravel literature sprang up. Travel corrupted the young; it could turn a manly English Protestant into a downright Italian. Roger Ascham had known many who, "parting out of England fervent in the love of Christ's doctrine, and well furnished with the fear of God, returned out of Italy worse transformed, than ever was any in Circe's court" (226). Toward the end of Thomas Nashe's *Unfortunate Traveller,* an involuntary tourist (a banished English earl) patriotically lectures a voluntary traveler (the book's protagonist) on the evils of the journey: "Countryman, tell me, what is the occasion of thy straying so far out of England? . . . The first traveller was Cain, and he was called a vagabond runagate. . . . God had no greater curse to lay upon the Israelites, than by leading them out of their own country" (341). As Sara Warneke shows, "One of the strongest images of the traveller in early modern England was that of the dissolute Englishman corrupted by the pleasures and temptations freely available on the Continent" (191).

Sir Francis Bacon's essay "Of Travaile" distills conflicting attitudes: travel is valuable as "a part of education" but needs strict controlling (56). Young men are to venture abroad only "under some tutor, or grave servant"(56), and

Bacon specifies the sights that should be seen—princely courts, churches, fortifications, harbors, gardens, armories, respectable comedies. As distinct from mere tourism, educational travel aims at "profit" (57), and Bacon's metaphors are acquisitive—the traveler should *acquire*, gather things in. He should not "change his country manners, for those of foreign parts; but only prick in some flowers, of that he hath learned abroad, into the customs of his own country" (58). To avoid danger, this gathering should be accomplished as quickly as possible, and Bacon recommends ways to shorten and condense travel: a young man who seeks out ambassadors' secretaries "shall suck the experience of many" and thus "abridge his travel with much profit" (57). But are not such short cuts educationally suspect, a sign of laziness? Bacon's diction suggests uncertainty about whether travel is an industrious or an idle activity. The period spelling of "travel," "travail," paints it as industrious hard work; but Bacon's economizing, ambassadorial schmoozing looks more like idleness, and his phrase "suck the experience of many" recalls the common representation of the idle unemployed as bloodsuckers on those who work. The goal of travel—"if you will have a young man to put his travel into a little room, and in short time to gather much" (57)—is to acquire education like mercantile goods and then to condense the gatherings "into a little room." The goal of purposeful travel is retirement to the sequestration of a small, safe room, to hoard up what one has pillaged from abroad. As if to lock up this treasure house, Bacon recommends fixing experience by keeping a diary.

Among many reasons for the popular suspicion of friars—the most demonized of all religious orders—was their mobility: they were itinerant preachers. This, along with their ministering to the poor, allied them with vagrants in many eyes. But even cloistered monks were denounced for mobility: one of the first moves of Thomas Cromwell's emissaries early in the Reformation was to forbid monks to travel out of their monasteries. Another antimobility move of Cromwell's was an assault on pilgrimages, which had been central to medieval religion (see Jusserand, Sumption). In 1536 and 1538, he issued injunctions attacking "wandering to pilgrimages" (Duffy 398–409). A ballad by William Gray, a member of Cromwell's household, celebrating the reformers' stripping of shrines also attacked pilgrimages, linking them to the disability of beggars:

> To Walsingham a gadding,
> To Canterbury a madding,
> As men distraight of mind;
> With few clothes on our backs,
> But an image of wax,
> For the lame and for the blind. (qtd. in Duffy 408–9)

Harman exhibits some genteel anxieties about print, whose promiscuous availability to readers at many social levels made it seem corrosive of social hierarchy. I suspect that Renaissance squeamishness about print also had to do with its mobility. Medieval manuscripts stayed in one place, in a monastery or the library of a great house; and one sat in one place to read them, poring over, glossing, and reglossing a few texts. But like beggars on the move, printed texts multiplied alarmingly and swept across the land. A medieval manuscript was not only read by monks, it was *like* a monk; but printed texts behaved like vagrants. Pedlars, routinely stigmatized as vagrants, purveyed (among other goods) printed ballads and books. As Elizabeth Eisenstein writes, print enabled a new kind of analytical thinking: instead of endlessly reannotating a few books, readers now cut rapidly across dozens of books, picking out similar topics in each book. Printing promoted a movement of the mind, both exciting and fearsome, like other kinds of mobility. In some ways print represented authority, legitimacy, and containment of vagrancy, as seen in Harman; but print also enabled a vagrancy of texts, promoting agile hoppings of the mind as unsettling as they were invigorating. Printing was one of many cultural innovations sparking anxieties about change, and it was projected onto the visibly mobile—vagrants.

Tales of rogues' infiltration of genteel society look in retrospect like a displacement of anxieties about social mobility more generally—and they were comforting, insofar as a rogue can be exposed and driven away while less easily identifiable interlopers cannot. Walter Smith deflects any household unease about his own social climbing onto an easily exposable social pretender, the vagrant Widow Edith. The very genre of rogue warnings may have rendered social confusion simple and manageable: social upstarts, recognizable by their lingo, brands, and whipping scars, can be placed on a grid of categories. The readily identifiable was readily controllable, and language was a social marker. Barry Taylor argues that "the disguising of the vagrant"— with deceptive clothing and language—"tip[ped] the world towards illegibility" (3). But I think the world already bordered on illegibility, and vagrants were scapegoated for this. To learn to read a rogue was more appealing than trying to make sense of social fluctuations generally, because rogue-reading was, or seemed, easier.

Contemporaries made some efforts to stabilize slippery ideas about mobility. One way was to pit good mobility against bad. For example, tension between domestic homekeeping ideology and new practices of international trade was defused by distinguishing between good merchants and bad, the former including wealthy international traders and settled city and town shopkeepers and the latter including itinerant salesmen (pedlars, chapmen) and peripatetic tradesmen (tinkers, cobblers), who were consigned to the category of vagabond—a particularly clear example of the privileged projecting onto vagrants qualities they felt uneasy about in themselves. Another strategy was for each social group or gender to value mobility for itself but proscribe mobility in the group just below. Well-to-do international traders valued their own freedom of travel but sought to immobilize "illegitimate" merchants like pedlars or chapmen by supporting legislation defining them as vagrants. The male sex cherished its own right to move freely about London but agreed with preachers who sought to relegate women strictly to the home. Men were consumers of satires criticizing women for "gadding" about the streets.

Distinguishing between (as it were) deserving and undeserving mobility, Renaissance thinkers approved of controlled, organized movement, of planned forays from a center to a periphery and back again. The national figure for this was Queen Elizabeth, who made progresses into the countryside and back to the court; a domestic version of this national journey was the trip to the marketplace and back to the house. In "Inviting a Friend to Supper," Ben Jonson plans a foray to the Mermaid Tavern for canary wine and to the market for foodstuffs; then he ensconces himself in his home to perform duties of hospitality. Jonson thinks of that paradigmatic home-seeker Aeneas when anticipating a traveler's return:

> May all thy ends,
> As thy beginnings here, prove purely sweet,
> And perfect in a circle always meet.
> So, when we, blest with thy return, shall see
> Thy self, with thy first thoughts, brought home by thee,
> We each to other may this voice enspire;
> This is that good Aeneas, past through fire,
> Through seas, storms, tempests: and imbark'd for hell,
> Came back untouch'd. This man hath travail'd well. ("To William Roe" 80–81)

In "A Valediction: Forbidding Mourning," John Donne's speaker journeys abroad but is kept circling in an orbit around his woman, who remains at home; they are like the feet of a drawing compass—immobile female foot, mobile male foot. Harman travels to London to confer with his printer, then returns to his manor house. What was disapproved was not purposive movement but aimless wandering. The regular beats of many vagrants, following the harvest or other seasonal work, were not enough. A center was needed, a home to which to return: legislation specified that vagrants be sent back to their *home* parishes. Purposive movement presupposed return to a center after a visit to the periphery. As William Carroll notes, "Vagrancy is objectionable per se, since there is no clear destination to wandering" (*Fat King* 5).

Moralists responded to ambivalence about mobility by calling on women to be homekeepers while men ranged abroad, as in Katharina's lecture to fellow housewives in Shakespeare's *Taming of the Shrew:*

> Thy husband is . . .
> . . . one that cares for thee,
> And for thy maintenance commits his body
> To painful labor both by sea and land,
> To watch the night in storms, the day in cold,
> Whilst thou liest warm at home, secure and safe. (5.2.150–55)

But here is an irony built into the mobility/immobility question that sheds light on the topsy-turvy idealization of vagrancy: the long tradition in Western thought linking mobility with the male and immobility with the female. Males were to range about and act; females were to stay home. Commending immobility and criticizing mobility—the deserving poor stay home, often immobilized by disability, while the undeserving poor wander abroad—the discourse of vagrancy reveals an unstable configuration of ideas, feminizing the deserving poor in contrast to the more stereotypically masculine position of the undeserving. Historians have shown that early modern women were more likely to receive public assistance at home in their parishes and be considered deserving poor, while the majority of "undeserving" vagrants on the road were men. But given the preferential attitudes that nearly always favored male over female, it is not surprising to find the homekeeping poor, while called deserving, regarded with contempt—the frequent ascription to these feminized folk of the term "impotent" is telling. Nor is it surprising that vagrants, whose mobility encoded them masculine, while called undeserving were sometimes admired.

Vagrants' wandering became, in the Renaissance imagination, much more than geographic travel. The passionate wish for planned itinerary and purposeful mobility, the need to impose destination if none is specified, is the compulsion of a culture bound on a journey to an undiscovered country. Where was English culture going, anyway? Where was religion going, when the old Christendom was shattered, when monasteries were burned and old parish churches blown up, saints decanonized, saints' days canceled, ancestors no longer prayed for? Under Queen Mary, the nation had tried to go back, to find its way home; but it could not. Where was intellectual life going? The Latin language had united Europe as Catholicism had united Christendom; but now the vernacular was gaining ground everywhere, a Tower of Babel rupturing the European family. New ideas like the dignity of man clashed with old ideas like original sin. The printing press was disseminating tidal waves of new knowledge, new ideas. Skeptical rationalism was assailing comfortable old habits of magical, superstitious thought. Where was political life going? The feudal system had broken up, all its little local centers supplanted by control from what was (for many parts of the country) an unseen, nearly hypothetical center of power in London. A new bureaucracy was thrusting into corners of life once belonging to church rather than state: where did a Christian's and a subject's allegiance lie? Where was economic life going? What used to be common land was being enclosed, bought, and sold. So much was changing. People could not see where their culture was going.

In this climate, good mobility became travel with a fixed destination and an itinerary; and bad mobility was aimless wandering. With good mobility, travelers knew where they were going, because it was where they had come from; they just went out and came back again. Their destination was home. It was ultimately because many felt that their culture had lost its way that they became committed to travel ending at home and persecuted travelers who had no home. Writers and thinkers were so passionate about vagrancy, finally, because homelessness was the dark side of the Renaissance.

Language and the Discourse of Vagrancy

This conflicted, change-wracked culture must remain to some degree a foreign country, forever beyond the modern world's understanding. Even to those within it, the culture often verged on incomprehensibility. While the passing of four centuries has clarified some things, it has darkened others. But if anything can open doors into a culture, it is language. First I will pull together from various chapters some of this study's observations on some words operating in the discourse of vagrancy.

Some words serve as signposts to various discourses. The use in tale titles or subtitles of words like "merry," "merry jest," "merry tales" and of the "how" formula links some rogue literature to jest books. Harman's reference to "duty," when the vagrant woman makes up the bed in the barn, suggests the "particular duties" in marriage sermons, and his provocative use of "till death us depart," a borrowing from the marriage service, also conjures a world of domesticity, in the antidomestic context of vagrant life on the road. Harman's apparently sarcastic use of domestic terms boomerangs on him by unsettling the boundary between homeless and domestic.

Protestant semantics affected the poor. The preacher Henry Bedel tried to redefine faith so that it included almsgiving; but for every word twisted to help the poor, many more were defined to their detriment. Translating the New Testament, William Tyndale mostly used "love" to render *caritas*, whereas John Wycliffe had used "charity." In the Middle Ages love had manifested itself as charity—generous almsgiving—but the Reformation stripped almsgiving out of the imperative for the Christian to love. Such changes in language *reflect* changing reality, new attitudes toward private charity; but they *affected* reality too: when the same word, "charity," meant both general love of neighbors and a material act—giving money to those neighbors—the mental link between feeling warm benevolence and reaching into the purse must have been more automatic than when the Bible said "love" *instead* of "charity."

Shifting attitudes are signaled, too, in what one might call sinking words—neutral or even positive medieval terms that acquired negative connotations in the Renaissance discourse of poverty: "beggar," "knave," "rascal," "villein," "vassal," and "varlet." Words that had neutrally indicated lower social rank were applied to vagrants and directed at enemies as insults.

Like the two-faced god, what I will call "Janus words" look in two directions, fusing together two widely differing denotations or even yoking together by violence two discourses, simply by applying one word to both. "Wretch" and "forlorn" encompass, as has been demonstrated, the age's fear of mobility and its indecisiveness about whether to pity or despise the poor; and "lubber" yokes a sense of degrading labor to the unwillingness to work at all. Unpacking "idleness" reveals a similar confusion about whether the jobless are lazy or energetic: as William Carroll shows, sixteenth-century writers often speak of the idle rushing dangerously about, and idleness "leads not to inactivity, but to the wrong kind of activity, and ultimately to rebellion" (*Fat King* 5). Such slippery attitudes toward idleness and activity, joblessness and wicked work, recall the "work"/"works" slippage in Protestant theology: melding good works and hard work made the employed seem godly, the unemployed ungodly. The two-edged term "vocation," as calling by God and as gainful occupation, reflects the same conflation of godly good works with paid occupation. Encoded in the use of "rabble" (for both low social status and dangerous mobs) is the assumption that low social status breeds sedition. Other Janus words include "servant" (as soldier and household servant) and "riot," "riotous," and "disorder" (connoting both alehouse revelry and seditious uprisings). Since words like "riot" and "disorder" linked alehouses with both drinking and sedition, vagrants, who stayed in alehouses because they were cheap, were suspected as traitors merely because of where they stayed.

The use of "beggar" and "mendicant" both for monks and friars and for secular beggars helped conflate lay beggary with clerical mendicancy, and rogue literature transferred "fraternity" from fraternal monastic orders to vagrants. Another Janus word, "fool," meant either clever trickster or stupid buffoon, either witty court jester or retarded person. "Clown," which entered English about the same time as "rogue"—the 1560s—meant both "country-man, rustic, or peasant" and "fool or jester," encapsulating the age's comic treatment of the rural poor. What was rustic was laughable, and "clown" as a stage role reminds us of the placement of lower-class characters in comic subplots.

The two meanings of the Janus word "civility" worked together to dis-franchise lower orders: on the one hand, it meant good breeding, culture, refinement; on the other, it denoted good polity, an orderly nation, good cit-izenship. And "manners" as both "good etiquette" and "upright morals" indicted anyone without refined manners for poor moral character. Simi-larly polysemous was "filth," which meant both bodily dirt and sin: those who owned only one suit of clothes and could not afford baths became morally evil. "Hospital" meant a place for the sick, the poor, and the crim-inal. The chronically poor were confined in hospitals alongside the ill, con-founding poverty with disease—a logical extension of equating "deserving poor" with "disabled poor." Such hospitals were called prisons and were places of punishment as well as healing. Another Janus word, "ill," meant both "sick" and "evil."

Key economic terms looked in two directions. "Relief" meant both pri-vate almsgiving and monies administered under the Poor Laws, reflecting a system in transition from private alms to public social programs. "Distribu-tion" meant both alms and radical communism: as traditional almsgiving became rarer, alms itself became a radical solution, continuous with rather than opposed to radical communism.

The overlapping discourses of domesticity, nationalism, and personal cen-teredness spawned several Janus words. "Unprovided" referred to an unpro-tected human body, a house unready for hospitality, or a nation unprepared to defend itself (for the last, see *3 Henry VI* 5.4.62–63). "Stranger," as both a foreigner to England and a person not on parish roles, encodes a homology between nation and parish. The conjuring up of one's house, one's parish, one's England, one's body by the single word "home" vividly illustrates the marriage of domestic and nationalistic ideology. Domesticity, parish author-ity, and nationalism seemed as natural as biology, especially when the word "home" meant one's body too. Because "home" meant all these things, home-lessness meant lacking all these things. Vagrants lacked not only a domicile but a parish to give them poor relief; they were also without a country that regarded them as citizens. Foreigners in their own land, they were said to speak cant rather than English. Vagrants even lacked a body to call their own: the vagrant body was others' to banish, to whip, to brand, to hang. As Witold Rybczynski writes, "The wonderful word, 'home,' which connotes a physical 'place' but also has the more abstract sense of a 'state of being,' has no equivalent in the Latin or Slavic European languages. German, Danish, Swedish, Icelandic, Dutch, and English all have similar sounding words for 'home,' all derived from the Old Norse 'heima'" (62). The very richness of "home" magnified the bleakness of homelessness.

Wider-ranging than double-meaning puns, Janus words often link two discourses, as when connotations subliminally link vagrants with Catholic clergy, uncouth manners with sedition, being employed with being called by God, or being dirty with being evil. "Sturdy beggar" acted as a pivot between Protestant polemic and the discourse of vagrancy, "civility" and "manners" as pivots between etiquette handbooks and political treatises; "vocation" linked works on Protestantism with texts on employment and the economy; "filth" conflated the world of hygiene with that of moral standards. Most important of all, the use of "place" to situate the individual in a geographical location and in a social rank subliminally encouraged fears identifying vagrants with the frightening social mobilities of the age. As Heather Dubrow argues, fear of overt crime may project more nebulous fears: one may deflect onto literal robbers metaphoric versions of the same crime: fear of robbers gains force from resentment of "the welfare mother, who metaphorically robs the taxpayer" (197). Words combining discourses—like "place" joining the geographical and the social—show language enabling such projections.

Cultural elements that were later divorced from each other—like theology and jest books—were, in the Renaissance, still married. Later, meanings became dissociated: one now refers separately to "manners" and "morals." But linguists have shown that those who apply one word to two different things may be incapable of distinguishing between those things. The linguists Brent Berlin and Paul Kay, for example, have shown that those speaking languages with one word to cover both "red" and "yellow" do not distinguish between red and yellow when shown a series of color chips (26–27). Language directly affects perception, and those who use "manners" to mean both "good etiquette" and "upright moral behavior" will not readily distinguish between crude-mannered peasants and dangerous rogues. Unhappily—and probably not fortuitously—such double-discourse words more often worked against than in favor of the disadvantaged. The two-facedness of many Janus words that I have discussed—"wretch," "lubber," "vocation," "rabble," "beggar," "mendicant," "riot," "disorder," "fool," "civility," "manners," "filth," "hospital," "stranger," "home," "place"—worked against the vagrant poor.

The modern era has its own Janus words. Since "comic" means both "funny"—especially in the lighthearted sense—and "having to do with comedy as a genre or with the comic spirit," one has trouble distinguishing happy, harmless funniness from serious comedic promotions of marital harmony on the one hand or from caustic satiric attacks on the other. Romantic comedy had serious functions: in promoting marriage against the medieval cult of celibacy, it helped valorize domesticity; and the satiric side of the comic mode helped demonize public enemies, whether the Catholic clergy or vagrants. But these serious effects are muted by the trivializing, overgeneralized term "comic." Or take the term "serious literature," which in the present day can mean either "excellent literature, worthy of attention by the discerning" or "literature which is not comic." Identifying excellent with noncomic literature has been prejudicial to comedy—few find it as "excellent" as tragedy. (This is why the poor are so often relegated to comedy.) And ascribing harmless triviality to comic works has blinded modern readers to one of the most potent weapons in the arsenal arrayed against the poor: laughter.

Finally, on the language issue as it relates to the discourse of vagrancy, I propose that the imagining of thieves' cant expresses in complex ways the linguistic anxieties of the age. Erasmus's *De Copia* (Concerning plenitude) presents copious language as a richly furnished house, perhaps like Eusebius's house in Erasmus's *Convivium Religiosum* (The godly feast) (see chap. 4). The enriched language of the educated classes was part of the engine of social distinction that Norbert Elias sees as driving the increased refinement and civility of the age. In blaming vagrants for speaking an exclusive and incomprehensible lingo, the educated were disowning one of their own cultural practices: the humanist equivalent of thieves' cant was inkhorn terms. Language demarcated social boundaries that might otherwise seem dangerously permeable: the cultured man says "excogitate" and "divulgate"; the rogue says, "Hast thou any lour in thy bung to bouse?" And never the twain shall meet.

The educated projected onto vagrants one of their own cultural practices, the importation of words into English, partly because, like all importations, this one courted resentment of the foreign. But that Latin had become a foreign import rather than an international language was itself a new and disturbing development: from one angle, the assertion of national vernaculars against Latin was a source of pride for each country; from another angle, it echoed the breakup of Christendom during the Reformation, the rupture of a European family, the creation of a broken home. Noting Renaissance fascination with the Tower of Babel story, Claire McEachern muses that Babel "very much resembles the event of the Reformation at large in sixteenth-century Europe, as the Latin Vulgate was translated into the vernaculars of many countries, and national churches broke with papal control" (114). The dethroning of Latin was threatening to humanists as well. John Hale shows that as ambassadorial Latin waned, "Babel stood revealed" (157). Hale maintains that the interpreter between vernaculars "now had more to offer than the humanistically educated secretary or tutor. . . . Travellers had begun to include glossaries of useful foreign words as appendixes to their narratives. Polyglot vocabularies were published with increasing frequency" (157).

In rogue literature, vocabularies of thieves' cant appended to narratives of travels in the land of the rogues seem a parody of such useful vernacular glossaries, hinting at the way the resentment of thieves' cant served a scapegoating function in drawing off hostility toward other jetting vernaculars. Dekker opens a rogue pamphlet, *Lantern and Candlelight,* with an account of Babel. After a sanguine celebration of foreign loanwords as a fruitful enrichment of the national language ("turning those borrowings into good husbandry" in an English that would otherwise have "dealt in nothing but monosyllables" [214]), Dekker relates the Babel story as a *fall* into vernaculars and nationhood, effected by that "strange linguist," Confusion (215). And ultimately, Confusion's masterpiece was thieves' cant, which Dekker describes in long passages fulsomely plagiarized from Harman and others. Dekker's argument itself seems to have suffered a brush with Confusion: does he experience pride or anxiety at the emergence of national vernaculars? Such confusion was endemic in the period. The move Dekker makes, to snatch a cause for pride out of what he has described as a kind of linguistic original sin, is illuminating: he distinguishes between, as it were, deserving and undeserving vernaculars—the *good* new language is a separate but enriched English; the *bad* new language is thieves' cant. The publicity surrounding cant expressed anxieties about changes in the English language—its newly hegemonic status after the dethroning of Latin and its adulteration with "foreign" terms. If the triumph of English seemed tainted with foreignness (loanwords), sedition (patriarchal language unseated by upstart vernacular), and homewrecking (the breakup of Latin Christendom), such unsavory traits could be disowned by projecting them onto another "language," thieves' cant.

Similar language anxieties appear in reactions to Puritans, who "amongst themselves . . . employed a private and heavenly language which Jacobean dramatists loved to parody" (Collinson, *English Puritanism* 20)—and thus which was not so different from the way Jacobean dramatists staged thieves' cant in plays like Middleton and Dekker's *Roaring Girl.* Indeed, Jonson calls

Puritans "the second part of the Society of *Canters*" (*Bartholomew Fair* 5.2.42). Puritans in turn reacted strongly against that in-group language of sinners, swearing: "what the author of *England's Summons* called 'this infernal dialect and language of the Devil,' [swearing] was considered the most dangerous sin of all because, like some sinister cloud of nuclear fall-out, it threatened the whole nation which tolerated it in its streets" (Collinson, *Birthpangs* 19). In an age of linguistic upheaval, anxiety about specialized vocabularies, whether Puritan godly terms, swearers' ungodly terms, or thieves' cant, expressed worry both about antisocial behavior of groups whose language set them apart and about language itself.

Placeless in the Renaissance

For an age that glorified home and exalted homekeeping, the Renaissance could be remarkably ambivalent about hospitality. The Middle Ages had located private hospitality within larger communal obligations, a network of duties toward neighbor, kin, and God. Hospitality had included almsgiving. The whole idea was modulating during the Renaissance toward a more recognizably modern, merely recreational notion of hospitality, but vestiges of sacredness lingered here and there—for example, in plays with medieval settings. Of Macbeth's four reasons for not killing King Duncan—he is his king, kinsman, guest, and a virtuous man—the third strikes modern ears as not in a league with the others; to modern audiences, killing a houseguest is only marginally more heinous than killing the same man elsewhere; but here hospitality retains something of its sacred aura. When, like Judas, Macbeth has left the chamber unable to sup with the man he will betray, his soliloquy recalls the Last Supper: "If it were done when 'tis done, then 'twere well / It were done quickly" (1.7.1–2). Macbeth later commissions the murder of another dinner guest, Banquo, with the same result: Macbeth cannot sit down to the feast. Mealtime murder is a common Elizabethan motif: in Robert Yarington's *Two Lamentable Tragedies*, Merry murders Beech at suppertime: "Let others sup, I'll make a bloodier feast" (1.3). Arden of Feversham is murdered just before dinner guests arrive. In Shakespeare the murder of Henry VI is called a "bloody supper" (*3H6* 5.5.85). For all the early modern insistence on the safety of one's home, many literary homes do not have a safe feel to them.

Even Shakespearean comedy, with its semiotics of hospitality, often raises the specter of rude inhospitality. In *The Merchant of Venice* Bassanio keeps an open house, with feasts and masques, and Portia entertains suitors of all nations, welcomes her friends' friends, opens her home to Jessica and Lorenzo; but Shylock's house is locked up, and he starves his servant. Lancelot's description of being "famish'd in [Shylock's] service" (2.2.101–2) is juxtaposed with Bassanio's giving his servant orders for a feast (2.2.108–9). Hospitality offered to Shylock elicits a sneer about pork odors, suggesting why he is not a popular dinner guest (1.3.29–33), and his eventual acceptance is hardly gracious: "I'll go in hate, to feed upon / The prodigal Christian" (2.5.15–16); such violence to the spirit of hospitality damages our sympathy for him. And even the hospitable become suspect: Portia mutters "gentle riddance" when one guest leaves (2.7.78); and Bassanio's behavior raises that shadow common in humanist writings—self-impoverishment through a generosity that may really be profligacy. *As You Like It* also valorizes hospitality: though homeless themselves, the duke's band set out a picnic and invite Orlando; the banished men have preserved, in harsh conditions, civilized hospitality, recalling when they have "sat at good men's feasts" (2.7.120). But in this world, inhospitality is the norm; a shepherd with disgracefully low wages reports that his "master is of churlish disposition, / And little recks to find the way to heaven / By doing deeds of hospitality" (2.7.76–78).

Even comedy, then, reveals anxieties about hospitality, and other literature abounds in scenes of yet deeper anxiety, the sort one might expect in a culture that valued home so highly and was confronted daily by the spectacle of the hungry homeless, people whom most householders did not feel they could provide with old-fashioned hospitality. Macbeth is not alone in abusing guests: Timon dashes water in guests' faces (3.6.93 s.d.) and later snarls at one guest, "Mend my company, take away thyself" (*Timon* 4.3.286–87). Titus Andronicus serves his guest her sons baked in a pie. In *Antony and Cleopatra,* Menas urges Pompey to murder his guests. Lady Macbeth suffers that nadir of a hostess's career, the need to dismiss guests unceremoniously: "Stand not upon the order of your going, / But go at once" (3.4.120–21). Reflecting a nation as a house divided against itself by civil war, the English history plays offer few hospitality scenes; and even in a rare example like Glendower's entertaining the Hotspurs and Mortimers, sociability is spoiled by the party's political agenda and mutual distrust of host and guest. In *1 Henry VI* the Countess of Auvergne invites Talbot to her home only to kidnap him. Audiences first meet Falstaff in Prince Hal's apartment, where Hal does not even offer his eternally thirsty friend a drink. Most scenes of conviviality in history plays occur in public taverns; shallow pub friendships and hospitality that must be paid for befit a world of civil war. The Gloucestershire dinner party in *2 Henry IV* is a remarkable anomaly—there is country hospitality in a home and talk of children's education. This reminder of homes, families, and hospitality signals the end of civil war, the return of stable government. But from this new domestic tranquillity, Falstaff is excluded. Does Falstaff *have* a home?

Did Shakespeare have a home? Of course, unlike so many of his homeless contemporaries, Shakespeare did not live on the streets or sleep in barns. Yet as Marchette Chute writes,

> Unlike the other actors in his company he had no wife and family in London and for nearly twenty years he lived there in hired lodgings. An actor's wife in Elizabethan times could be a great help to her husband in his profession. Although there was no actors' guild, the actors used the same system as other business and professional men in London and each of them took a boy into his home to be trained. . . . It was an important part of the apprentice system that the boy should be treated as an actual member of the family, and there is still a loving tribute to Mrs. Henry Condell and Mrs. Cuthbert Burbage from a boy who had worked with the company. Nearly all the actors in Shakespeare's company were settled householders, with competent wives and a large number of children, and the only exceptions were two or three men who never married, and William Shakespeare. (54–55)

Is it important that the man who gave us *King Lear* was never, in his London years, a settled householder? Seeing homeless people around on the London streets day after day might well have made a person nervous, especially if he lived alone in lodgings. Actors had as much reason as anyone to fear plummeting into indigence. The ease with which actors switched roles onstage might have brought home to them the precariousness of social place in real life: it made Donald Lupton think of that old king/beggar dichotomy: "A player often changes, now he acts a monarch, tomorrow a beggar" (81). Like beggars, actors were classified as vagabonds in the Poor Laws.[6] Is it no more than an innocent trope (allied to the humility topos) that speakers of epilogues, who address audiences on behalf of actors and playwrights, often position themselves as *beggars* for applause? (The actor-as-beggar conceit comes naturally to "beggar plays": the closing words of *The Beggar's Bush* situate the actors as beggars and the audience as almsgivers; and in *A Jovial Crew,* "a begging Epilogue yet would not be, / Methinks, improper to this comedy" [5.1.501–2]. Even self-confident Rosalind, speaking the epilogue of *As You Like It,* states, "I am not furnished like a beggar, therefore to beg will not become me" [9–10].) As a dweller in rented lodgings most of his adult life, Shakespeare knew what it was like not to have a settled home; as an actor, he could imagine what it was like to be a beggar.

When Shakespeare got rich, he bought houses. Before he bought the big house in Stratford in 1597, he and his family had never owned a home; Samuel Schoenbaum thinks that Anne and the children lived with Shakespeare's parents in Henley Street while he was in London (76). In 1601 Shakespeare inherited the Henley Street house from his father. His mother lived there until her death in 1608, with Shakespeare's sister and her family; Shakespeare kept the house, and he still owned it at his death. In 1613 he bought another house, this time in Blackfriars, perhaps as an investment (Schoenbaum 181, 222–23). At his death, then, this long-term renter owned three houses, two in Stratford and one in London. One of the upwardly mobile, Shakespeare had achieved a new rank, a new *place* in society. And when he finally purchased, improved, and inhabited a home of his own, it was called New Place.

> The house that he bought was the second largest in Stratford. It had a frontage of over sixty feet in Chapel Street, a depth (along Chapel Lane) of at least seventy feet in some parts, and a height of over twenty-eight feet at the northern end. . . . No fewer than ten fireplaces warmed New Place in winter, and there were probably more rooms than fireplaces. . . . [An eighteenth-century drawing of the house] depicts a handsome big house of three storeys and five gables, with ornamental beams. . . . [Another drawing] shows the gate and entrance at the corner of Chapel Lane, the courtyard before New Place, and, on either side of the court, buildings, one being the servants' quarters. . . . [An eyewitness describes] a brick wall, "with a kind of porch," at the end next to the chapel, and [neighbors] would cross "a small kind of green court before they entered the house which was . . . fronted with brick." . . . Shakespeare's house stood in ample grounds, . . . with two barns and two gardens, . . . [with] two orchards. . . . The garden must have been fairly small at first, but Shakespeare added to it land to the east, in Chapel Lane. This had formerly belonged to the dissolved priory of Pinley. (Schoenbaum 173–78)

New Place, in short, looked like the home of Eusebius in Erasmus's *Convivium Religiosum,* with enclosed gardens and graceful architecture; or perhaps it resembled More's house in Chelsea, with its gallery, orchard, and garden house. Like Angelo's house in *Measure for Measure,* with its "garden circummured with brick" (4.1.28) and its enclosed vineyards, New Place had a green court surrounded by brick walls, and it was "famous for its vines" (Schoenbaum 178). Like many a Renaissance house sequestered within gates and courtyards, New Place had a gate and a courtyard, and—a modest version of Charterhouse, which had been remodeled into a private residence with outer and inner courtyards—New Place absorbed some confiscated monastery lands. It was the quintessential Tudor/Jacobean home: comfortable, private, and withdrawn behind a screen of brick walls, gardens, courtyards, and gates. It was, in short, a lockable house.

Was New Place a mental refuge for a man who had once confronted the specter of those who had no place?

>   You houseless poverty
>   . . . .
>   Poor naked wretches, wheresoe'er you are,
>   That bide the pelting of this pitiless storm,
>   How shall your houseless heads and unfed sides,
>   Your looped and windowed raggedness, defend you
>   From seasons such as these? (*King Lear* 3.4.26–32)

Faced with a terrible vision of the hungry and the homeless, Shakespeare, like his contemporaries, had a choice of responses. He could turn away and lock them out, withdrawing into New Place. He could revile and demonize them, as does his character Iden in *2 Henry IV*, who murders a starving man who has ventured into his garden. Or, with King Lear, he could look for the cause of vagrants' misery in his own behavior: "O, I have ta'en / Too little care of this! . . . / Expose thyself to feel what wretches feel" (3.432–34). What choices Shakespeare made may matter less now than what choices we will make.

Four hundred years on, those who live in modern New Places are still haunted by those who live in no place. While those who can afford it retire into gated communities, in North American cities that have not expelled them, the homeless panhandle on sidewalks and sleep on grates. Since America has emptied mental hospitals and returned the insane to "their rightful place in the community," many of these have no need to play abram-men, merely feigning madness. The U.S. federal government recently took a step toward disclaiming responsibility for welfare, bestowing it on the states, just as in Renaissance England, the Crown legislated parish responsibility for the poor, contributing no central funds to help. Modern Americans have taken to speaking of "welfare reform" when they mean to abolish social programs, just as early modern Protestants and humanists used a progressive-sounding vocabulary of "reform" to discourage almsgiving, which helped to found the first national poor relief system with real benefits to the settled poor but also helped to demonize the vagrant poor at their expense. Modern pronouncements on the unemployed sound remarkably like early modern pronouncements: the jobless do not want to work, they are lazy; one should not be suckered by professional beggars—they make more money every week than an honest teacher in a month; the poor breed like rabbits, sucking out the lifeblood of hardworking citizens. In the tradition of rogue literature, modern tabloids feature "a sub-genre of stories depicting people who have faked their destitute conditions. . . . Tabloids frequently report on homeless people who are secret millionaires. . . . Between August and October 1993, the *Weekly World News* ran several stories implying that beggars were, in reality, rich people or otherwise not deserving of charity—'Man Makes $275,000 as Street Beggar'" (Hogshire 40–41).

Maybe the similar pronouncements should not surprise the modern reader: recent attitudes toward the poor and vagrant are the distant historical echo of attitudes that crystallized in the sixteenth century. But considering that modern society has surpassed the sixteenth century in science, technology, medicine, travel, communications systems, and a host of other human activities, the fact that present-day attitudes toward the vagrant poor have changed so little in four hundred years is cause for discouragement. Amid the crop failures and famines, the poverty and misery and homelessness of the sixteenth century, the New World stood as one shining beacon of hope, a land of plenty, a Eutopia, a new place. But already in those days the New World became a dumping ground, for vagrants were sent here; and many are vagrants now. Four centuries are gone, and the huddled masses yearning to breathe free have passed through the golden door, and many are still huddled, still yearning.

We have ta'en too little care of this.

Notes

1. For further discussions of the romanticization of beggary, see Carroll (63–69), Koch ("The Economy of Beggary" chap. 3), Timpane (chaps. 7 and 8), and Gaby.

2. The trope could apply to the well-off and socially powerful in general, as well as to kings: Oldrents in *A Jovial Crew*, beholding "how merry" are a band of beggars singing of "bowsing" and "harman-becks" in cant purloined from Harman's *Caveat*, rhapsodizes: "What is an estate / Of wealth and power, balanc'd with their freedom, / But a mere load of outward compliment, / When they enjoy the fruits of rich content? / Our dross but weighs us down into despair, / While their sublimed spirits dance i' th' air" (2.2.185–90).

3. A few Renaissance texts debunk the happy beggar trope; for example, in *A Jovial Crew*, two young gentlemen who have joined up with a company of beggars quickly find the blithe life and sound sleep ascribed to beggars a delusion—miserable in his rags and groggy after a sleepless night, one cries, "Is this the life that we admir'd in others, with envy at their happiness?" (3.1.1–2). Two gentlewomen who have joined up with the beggars find themselves "sorely surbated with hoofing, . . . crupper-cramp'd with our hard lodging, . . . numb'd i' the bum and shoulders" (3.1.73–76); one has "found the difference between a hard floor with a little straw, and a down bed with a quilt upon't" (3.1.77–79).

4. Patricia Fumerton discusses ballads that suggest that men took to alehouses to escape domestic spaces that were increasingly gendered female—the "threateningly constricting female space of the home."

5. Even committed matrimonial apologists, including such architects of companionate marriage as Erasmus and Spenser, tended to speak of marriage as a cage: in his colloquy *Courtship,* Erasmus compares a married person to a caged bird: "Ask him if he desires to be free. He'll say no, I think. Why? He's willingly confined" (*Colloquies* 86–87);

Spenser maintains, "Sweet be the bands, the which true love doth tye, / without constraynt or dread of any ill: / the gentle birde feeles no captivity / within her cage, but sings and feeds her fill" (*Shorter Poems* 65).

6. For suggestive ideas on actors and vagrants, including the fact that two prominent authors of rogue literature, Dekker and Greene, were also playwrights, see Jeffrey Knapp's "Rogue Nationalism."

Appendix A: Historical Contexts for the Study of Vagrancy and Poverty

The Vagrancy Problem

As A. L. Beier shows, "between the mid-fourteenth and the mid-seventeenth centuries England experienced major shifts in migration patterns: from mainly local to more long-distance moves, the latter rising significantly between 1580 and 1640, including a frightening increase in the numbers of transient poor" (*Masterless Men* 31). Crop failures, famine, and enclosures boosted London's phenomenal growth. Lena Orlin provides an account of the cheek-by-jowl existence of many Londoners in densely subdivided dwellings ("Boundary Disputes").

On the question of how many vagrants travelled England during various decades of the early modern period, Beier provides a nuanced discussion in his section "The Numbers Issue" (*Masterless Men* 14–16). There is evidence that "London vagrancy did rise dramatically in the period" (14), but the precise dimensions of the vagrancy problem are nearly impossible to reconstruct. Beier dismisses contemporary estimates as likely no more than wild guesses based on little or no evidence. William Harrison estimated the national total at 10,000 in 1577, a Cornish magistrate at 200,000 in the 1590s, King James at 80,000, and later Stuarts at figures ranging from 30,000 to 100,000. Beier proposes that the most nearly accurate estimate—because it *is* based on hard figures—may be one extrapolated from the figures of Edward Hext for Somerset in 1596, which projected to the national level "would mean 16,000 to 20,000 vagabonds" (15) in England and Wales. But because Hext's Somerset experience might have been untypical, "even his statistics are suspect" (15), Beier notes. I would add that Hext's political agenda, which is close to Thomas Harman's, also does not inspire confidence in his statistics: he is one of those who fulminate against soft-on-crime judges and a bleeding-heart public, and he believes that polite society has been infiltrated by rogues in fiendishly clever disguises (see chap. 4). On the national level, then, modern scholars are left with wild (and wildly disparate) guesses. Steve Rappaport, dealing with London only, estimates that vagrants may have represented about 2 percent of the city's population in 1600–1601 (5), and he thinks that Beier has exaggerated the problem; Beier cautions that "it would be simplistic to think that people are only considered threats to the social order if their numbers are great" (*Masterless Men* 15). Ian Archer, too, faults Rappaport for underestimating the extent to which the elite grew alarmed and experienced "a sense of crisis," whether such a sense was warranted or not (*Pursuit* 8). Indeed, the lack of fit between reality and perception when it comes to vagrancy is what intrigues me.

Of unemployment and vagrancy of demobilized soldiers, Beier writes that "no occupational groups increased as much as sailors and soldiers among vagrants from 1560 to 1640" (*Masterless Men* 93), noting that "troops were always likely to become vagrants, because they were chiefly recruited from the poor and criminal classes" (94) and that "because of their background, military men had greater potential for violence than most other vagrants" (94).

On early modern vagrancy, Paul Slack summarizes, "Interpretations of vagrancy have ranged between two poles. On the one hand, vagrants have been seen as innocent hapless victims, culpable only because the law made mobility and unemployment criminal. On the other hand, they have been branded as a segment of society readily indulging in crimes of other kinds, especially petty theft" (*Poverty and Policy* 91). (Is there necessarily a contradiction here? Many who committed petty theft did so because they *were* victims of an economic situation over which they had no control. As Sir Thomas More has Hythlodaye demand, "What . . . can these men do, but rob or beg? And a man of courage is more likely to steal than to cringe" [13]. Compared with begging, "petty theft" is at least self-help.) Slack includes Beier and himself as proponents of the "softer" view, and as paradigmatic of the harsher view he cites J. S. Cockburn's "The Nature and Incidence of Crime in England, 1559–1625." (Cockburn, as mentioned in the introduction, uses Thomas Harman's *Caveat for Common Cursetors* alongside records of court assizes as valid sources of historical information on "vagrant criminals and their methods" [62]). In 1976 Beier debated the issue with John F. Pound in *Past and Present.*

Poverty: Its Causes and Its Extent

Contrary to the belief of writers like Thomas Harman—who thought that people hit the road out of laziness, shiftlessness, or moral perversity—modern historians attribute vagrancy mainly to poverty, and poverty had many causes: a succession of poor harvests throughout the sixteenth century, especially harsh from 1520 to 1535 and in the 1590s; impoverishment through illness, warfare, booming population, rising grain prices, falling or stagnant wages, the breakdown of families by death or desertion of a breadwinner (children and the aged were disproportionately represented in poor rolls), low wages for women, rural depopulation owing to enclosures and agricultural depressions; too great a pressure by migrants on London's housing resources and the inability of building trades and capital to keep up with demand for housing, even of the most squalid sort; a metropolitan economy simply unable to provide enough jobs. A series of depressions in the textile industry, the backbone of the English economy, also shook other European economies; poverty among textile workers was a major social problem.[1] In times of famine, hunger left the poor open to waves of epidemics; sweating sickness, for example, hit London in 1528 (Marc'hadour lxxiii).

On how serious the poverty was, historians' opinions differ. Beier speaks of "profound social dislocations—a huge and growing poverty problem, disastrous economic and demographic shifts" (*Masterless Men* 3). Robert Jütte concludes that "grain prices rose, and not just occasionally as a result of bad harvests, but quite generally and extending over many generations. This . . . was a new phenomenon, since earlier centuries, particularly the first hundred years after the Black Death, had seen a consistent fall in agricultural prices" (29). Natalie Zemon Davis's study of Lyon shows that relief rolls included butchers, millers, bakers, cobblers, masons, carpenters, glassmakers, weavers, printers, and schoolteachers: "We expect it in the men who have no skills; . . . but poverty was also the plight of the skilled journeymen . . . and could sometimes grip their masters as well" (21–22).

Although studies by Rappaport, Donald Woodward, and others indicate that in London, price rises and wage stagnation were not as drastic or as widespread as previously believed, Archer notes that "although this research suggests that things were not quite as bad as was previously thought, it does not mean that they were rosy. The poor presented the City's rulers with an increasingly acute problem" (12). Revisionist historians who downplay social problems in favor of a thesis of stability and relative prosperity often emphasize the successes of the Poor Laws, ignoring those ineligible for poor relief. Rappaport and Valerie Pearl, for example, are taken to task by Archer for being "biased towards the success stories. Their attention is focused on upwardly mobile Londoners and the recipients of poor relief" to the neglect of "the social topography of poverty, and important dimensions of the city's social problems, in particular vagrancy" (*Pursuit* 15). Revisionists, Beier maintains, too often accept sixteenth-century definitions of poverty, and their relative optimism is "based upon assumptions about who required or deserved relief, which often meant whoever was deemed worthy by local officials" ("Poverty and Progress" 209). Such revisionism, in other words, addresses itself to the deserving poor. Concerning revisionist claims that historians have overestimated the seriousness of sixteenth-century poverty, overpopulation in relation to resources, falling real wages, and harvest failures, Beier asks, "If this optimistic view were correct, would it have been necessary to establish a system of state poor relief? None of the historians who take the optimistic view have provided an answer to this question" ("Poverty and Progress" 202). Beier concludes that "Hoskins may have exaggerated the numbers of the early Tudor poor, but recent downward revisions of his figures should be treated with caution" ("Poverty and Progress" 237). Theodora A. Jankowski cites objections by Ronald Berger, Keith Lindley, and Ian Archer to what she calls Rappaport's "reactionary opinion that the poor were not 'really' poor and that, despite drops in both real wages and purchasing power, they were able to get by quite well" (333). As Archer observes, "The perspective from which we view the statistical evidence for hardship affects our interpretation of it. . . . The data derived from the parish registers can only give the crudest indication of the extent of suffering because there are many degrees of human suffering short of death by starvation" (*Pursuit* 13).

As Bronislaw Geremek dryly observes, "vagrant" was "the official term for the unemployed" (154); he notes "how often those who are reproached with idleness or vagrancy are simply unemployed" (155). Only occasional writers recognized that some were jobless because work was unavailable. In the sixteenth century, Henry Arthington admitted that some "are willing to take pains, and cannot get work" (sig. B2ᵛ); but this briefly entertained notion is soon swamped by diatribes on the fecklessness of rogues who "would not work" (sig. A3). *An Ease for Overseers of the Poor* also regards unavailability of work as accounting for only a tiny portion of unemployment. First, *An Ease for Overseers* lumps those who cannot find work in with the disabled as "willing to work, but by reason either of the penury of their estates, or deficiency of credit, or scarcity of work, or disability in doing work, they are constrained to live idly against their wills" (18). And this "willing to work" category is only one of four; the others are the "willful" (idle by nature and/or addicted to begging and thieving rather than working), the "negligent" (workers so incompetent that no one will hire them), and the "fraudulent" (those rejected as employees because of their record of embezzlement and stealing from employers). Here again the tiny phrase "scarcity of work" is swamped by other explanations, most blaming the jobless for their condition, branding them lazy, incompetent, dishonest. The assumption that vagrants did not want to work was built into the definition of vagrancy, in the 1563 Statute of Artificers: "by statutory definition, a vagrant was a person able to labour who possessed neither land nor master, who worked at no recognized trade, and who refused to accept such employment as might be offered to him" (Manning 159). As David M. Palliser notes, "The Poor Law statutes until 1572 recognised only the impotent poor and the vagabonds, blandly assuming that all able-bodied persons could find work if they tried, and it was only in the last thirty years of the period that the state came to recognise, and try to alleviate, the problems of involuntary unemployment" (120).

Solutions to problems of poverty, vagrancy, and unemployment were hampered by the early modern habit of resolving all questions into moral questions. Joblessness was a moral failing. The binary of deserving/undeserving poor blocked comprehension of intermediate states (such as being willing but unable to find work or of working hard at a job yet not making enough to support a family). Some parish surveys began including, after the impotent, widows, and the disabled, "lists of 'poor able labouring folk,' or 'labouring persons not able to live off their labour'"; but it was too seldom recognized that wages might not sustain life (Slack, *Poverty and Policy* 28). Local censuses reveal an economic system unable to sustain the population under prevailing conditions. In Essex in 1598–99,

> a survey of three parishes showed that while just under 4 per cent of the population were among the impotent, 20 per cent "do work for their living" but "being not able to maintain themselves and their charge by their labour." . . . The threat of an escalating number of paupers was thus sharply perceived in the countryside by 1600, and it did not come from a gang of idle wastrels but from the respectable labouring classes. Most parishes might manage for most of the time by supporting the two, three or four per cent of the population who were impotent, as they had always done. But they could not ignore the ten or twenty per cent of the population who hovered around the poverty line and who might fall below it when the harvest failed, when sickness hit the chief breadwinner, when employment opportunities for wives and children in rural industries contracted, or simply when there was a particularly bad winter. (Slack, *Poverty and Policy* 65–66)[2]

Because of the moral framework in which the problem was understood, writers who possessed the information necessary to an *economic* analysis of the problem often retreated into moralizings about idleness. Writing from Wakefield in 1597, a serious famine year, the preacher Henry Arthington recognizes perfectly well that people are hungry because of bad harvests, but believing conventionally that God sends bad weather to punish sins, he finds no contradiction between blaming the weather and blaming the poor. Idle and wasteful in better times, they did not save for thin times, and this also caused the thin times: God visits bad weather upon the idle and wasteful.

It was an essentialist age, deeply committed to the view that *nature*, not culture, makes men strong and forceful, women weak and timid, and the poor idle and shiftless. As *An Ease for Overseers* assures its readers, "The poor are by nature much inclined to ease and idleness" (27); overseers must "hold the poor to work, for most are so by nature given to ease, that it is as hard to bring their bodies to labour, as the ox that hath not been used to the yoke to draw" (20).

And while cities such as Lyon sometimes employed vagrants in public works projects like ditchdigging for fortification systems (Davis 45), vagrants were often physically unfit for such heavy labor. In this period there is no recognition that vagrants' indolent demeanor might reflect malnutrition rather than morally culpable idleness. The economist Partha Dasgupta, defining undernourishment as "a state in which the physical functioning of a person is impaired to the point where she cannot maintain an adequate level of performance at physical work" (412), concludes from a large number of empirical studies that

> people enjoying superior nutritional status enjoy a greater capacity for physical work. They are also able to endure longer hours. . . . (412)

> At manual work they can perform a greater range of tasks (e.g., lift heavier loads) and accomplish them in less time. In short, they are capable of getting more done over a day. A person of low nutritional status suffers from the handicap that he has to work long hours if he is to earn his day's keep through manual work alone. His endurance being less than that of one enjoying superior nutritional status, he has to work at a slower pace, or take more frequent breaks, or both. (465)

The poor often subsisted on nothing but bread (Palliser 114), and it was often moldy, contaminated bread (see Camporesi); their lackluster performance of physical tasks might easily have struck employers as laziness. Summarizing findings on nutrition and labor power, Dasgupta writes, "It is often said that even when a person owns no physical assets she owns one asset that is inalienable, namely *labour power*. The last two chapters have revealed the important truth that this is false. What an assetless person owns is *potential* labour power. . . . Conversion of potential into actual labour power can be realized if the person finds the means of making the conversion, not otherwise. Nutrition and health-care are the necessary means to this" (474). The poorly nourished Renaissance masses lacked these necessary means.

On impoverishment through illness, Jütte's *Poverty and Deviance in Early Modern Europe* shows that although in the Middle Ages labor shortages caused by the Black Plague had resulted in increased wages, the long-term effect in Renaissance Europe of plague and other epidemics was to increase poverty: "Epidemic diseases incapacitated at least as many people as they killed, thus reducing income and assets as well as leaving orphans and widows in their wake. . . . Epidemics were not only a 'symptom of poverty' . . . in early modern Europe but were also one of the major causes of indigence" (22–23). Slack writes of disease as an indicator of where the poor lived and congregated: "As with crises of subsistence, [epidemics'] incidence tells us something about the location of the worst deprivation. Plague was most fatal in overcrowded unhygienic tenements in the suburbs of towns. . . . Plague epidemics were a symptom of poverty. But they were also one of its prime causes since they totally disrupted employment and marketing" (*Poverty and Policy* 51).

Poverty was also exacerbated by population growth, which was especially notable in London. Jütte notes that "contemporaries already surmised a link between a rising population and the scarcity of foodstuffs due to limited agricultural resources" (27).[3]

The Poor Laws

The major legislative initiatives resulting in what have come to be known as the Poor Laws, developed over the course of the sixteenth and early seventeenth centuries and lasting through the nineteenth century, began with laws punishing rogues and vagabonds and then, from 1547 onwards, also made provisions for the relief of poverty. The next two sections of this appendix deal respectively with the punishment and relief provisions of the Poor Laws.

The Punishment of Vagrancy

Vagrants were materially affected by changes in the criminal justice system—the punitive sections of the Poor Laws, royal proclamations, and local ordinances; and new institutions such as Bridewell came into being, which blurred the line between hospital, hospice, workhouse, and prison.

Penalties prescribed for vagrancy could be extremely harsh: the Vagrancy Act of 1536 prescribed for all vagrants mutilation for a second offense and hanging for the third; this law apparently lapsed in 1542 (C. S. L. Davies 535). A 1547 Vagrancy Act provided enslavement for two years for a first vagrancy offense and enslavement for life for escaped slaves. The 1572 Vagrancy Act had a "three strikes and you're out" provision, in which the third offense was punishable by death. Shortly after this act came into effect, two men and a woman in Middlesex were hanged on grounds of their "being over 18 years old and fit for labour, but masterless and without any lawful means of livelihood" (Leonard 70–71). Palliser reports vagrants hanged under this statute but notes that "in 1593 these savage penalties were again repealed" (124). The 1598 statute, however, reinstituted slavery for vagrancy (Palliser 72); periods of harshness and relative leniency alternated.

Vagrancy itself was a serious crime, punishable by death. And vagrants' poverty tempted them into crimes against property, which were felonies and thus capital offenses: though it included offenses as serious as murder, "felony consisted overwhelmingly of property offences: larceny, burglary, housebreaking, highway robbery, robbery and pickpocketing" (Sharpe, *Crime* 79). Though acknowledging the difficulty of arriving at reliable statistics at an almost five-hundred-year historical remove, J. A. Sharpe still finds the English Renaissance remarkable for its hangings: "All surviving evidence suggests that levels of execution were much higher in the Elizabethan and Jacobean periods than they were in the first half of the eighteenth century. . . . A person accused of felony at the assizes in Elizabeth's reign stood a one in four or five chance of being executed; for his or her counterpart under Queen Anne, the chances were more like one in ten" (*Crime* 92–93). Though justices of the peace were supposed to leave capital offenses to higher courts, "there is nevertheless sufficient evidence that the lay magistrates were also hanging felons at a considerable rate" (Barker 240).

England was among the earliest of European countries to formulate plans for prison workhouses as places of enforced labor: "national plans in England for the forcible employment of vagrants date back to the 1530s" (Spierenburg, *Prison Experience* 23), and Bridewell, envisioned mainly as a repository of beggars, was the first true prison founded in Europe. Palliser notes that the number of vagrants sent to Bridewell was 69 in 1560–61, 209 in 1578–79, and 555 in 1600–1601 (123). Slack writes that "in the early 1560s, . . . only 16 per cent of all offenders were vagrants. After that, however, the proportion grew rapidly, reaching 62 per cent of the total in 1600–1601 and then levelling off: it was 50 per cent in 1624–25" (*Poverty and Policy* 93).

The period's theory of condign punishment—that the punishment should fit the crime—sheds light on ways vagrants were conceptualized. (For a classic statement of the idea that a culture's punishments comprise an echo of its concepts of productiveness, see Rusche and Kirchheimer.) The policy of enforced labor, initiated in the period's new houses of correction, reflects hatred of idleness and the Protestant valorization of work. The immobilization of vagrants in the stocks and prisons (and that ultimate immobilizer, hanging) stresses that their overriding offense was mobility.

Why was whipping considered a punishment appropriate to vagrants? Since vagrants were stereotyped as sexually promiscuous, it is relevant that whipping is often connected with sexual misdemeanors in texts of the period; its appropriateness as a punishment seems related to the sexual kinkiness connected with spankings and whippings. (For a contemporary account of a "whipping Jew" who gets sexual thrills from whipping naked women, see Thomas Nashe's *Unfortunate Traveller* [353, 359].) That whipping also involved stripping underlines its sexual connections—the prurience of the whipper appears in *King Lear*'s oft-quoted

> thou rascal beadle, hold thy bloody hand!
> Why dost thou lash that whore? Strip thine own back;
> That hotly lusts to use her in that kind
> For which thou whipp'st her. (4.6.160–63)

Laura Knoppers discusses the fact that public whipping of (especially female) offenders while naked became "excessive, voyeuristic, pleasurable for the spectator, publicizing and eliciting the very sexual transgression it aim[ed] to suppress" (459). The nakedness of the whipped may also allude to beggars' ragged seminakedness. The title page woodcut of Harman's *Caveat* features two beggars drawn behind a cart, followed by an officer upraising a huge, triple-thonged whip to strike them; they are naked except for loose loincloths, a costume closely approximating that of Nicholas Jennings in the same work, when he is first seen in his role as a begging, pretended epileptic: "He was naked from the waist upward, saving he had an old jerkin of leather patched, and that was loose about him, that all his body lay out bare" (85). Whipping was also a kind of writing on the body: "whipping, which was standard after 1531, and boring through the ear and branding, which were inflicted on some offenders, made social labels plainly visible" (Slack, *Poverty and Policy* 100). Such punishments were the physiological equivalent of stigmatizing terms like "rogue" and "vagabond." The badges that beggars were sometimes required to wear had the same stigmatizing effect (John Howes wrote in 1587 that "the shame of this badge will make some . . . not to go abroad" [qtd. in Tawney and Power 3:426]); but whipping, which could leave scars, was less removable than a badge.

The Relief of Poverty: Early Modern Secularization of Poor Relief

The most important single fact about poor relief, for the study of vagrancy, is that it excluded vagrants altogether. While considerable good will went into the creation of municipal and national poor relief schemes—historians such as Slack on England and Davis on France have depicted the new welfare schemes as a real achievement that relieved much distress—the vagrant poor were almost everywhere left out of such schemes, which typically operated via house-to-house censuses of the poor, thus presuming the possession of a dwelling. This was true all over Europe, owing partly to moral strictures against the nonrespectable poor and partly to the sheer magnitude of the poverty problem—not everyone could be relieved. For example, the great lay confraternities of Venice, the Scuole Grandi, "existed to serve the established, resident respectable poor. . . . They did not cater primarily to vagrants or displaced persons. . . . They provided for the pious, respectable poor, not for criminals and prostitutes. . . . They admitted many artisans, but did not plumb the lower depths of society" (Pullan, *Rich and Poor* 186–87).

Of equal importance to the exclusion of vagrants from government-sponsored relief schemes was the way they were increasingly cut off from private relief (alms to beggars) by the insistence that charity was to be exercised within government-sponsored schemes rather than by individuals on an ad hoc, one-on-one basis. A discourse of counterfeit disability—fostered by literary genres like rogue literature—underpinned doctrines disqualifying laymen from deciding whether a beggar deserved alms: ideally, no one was to beg, and alms were to be replaced by government relief given to those living in houses and staying within their parishes. In addition to having been, from the start, the primary target of the Poor Laws' provisions for punishment, vagrants alone were thus excluded from the "relief" provisions of the Poor Laws, and they suffered the brunt of the campaign against private almsgiving. I will now sketch in the processes by which vagrants became ineligible for most kinds of poor relief.

During the sixteenth century, responsibility for poor relief shifted from the church to secular authorities. Care of the poor had been central to the mission of the medieval church, which regularly allocated a quarter to a third of its resources to poor relief: "In English historiography the dissolution of the monasteries in 1535 and 1539 is traditionally seen as being central to the growth of poverty and the deterioration of living conditions among the poor in England, and indeed alms distributions fell sharply at that time" (Geremek 165). Secularizing poor relief across Europe left a fatal time lag—while the church was losing control over poor relief and municipalities were creating new bureaucratic structures, many poor people fell through the cracks of existing social programs and, hence, many became vagrant. In England, dissolving the monasteries not only abolished administrative structures for poor relief, it added monks and friars to the ranks of the homeless, a situation that quickly found its way into imaginative literature: Robert Copland's *Highway to the Spital-house,* exactly contemporary with the first monastery dissolutions, includes turned-out clergy amongst its roll call of vagrants.

Just as important as the secularization of poor relief was the passing of responsibility for the poor from individuals to the state. The 1552 English translation of a treatise on "almose" (alms), written by the Strassburg theologian turned Oxford professor Martin

Bucer, reveals the logic underlying this shift. Teaching people to distrust their own judgment about who was deserving opened the door to decision by experts; in Bucer this begins as early as the translator's dedication, which raises the specter of counterfeit disability: "In these days, many lusty and sturdy persons be suffered to beg, men counterfeiting horrible diseases and infirmities, sit by the common ways craving almost," and "good men's charities be abused" (sig. A2). Such fakery confounds the distinction between deserving and undeserving: alms are "given oftener to the unworthy than to the worthy (for every man cannot know and try such poor people as he meeteth suddenly)" (sig. A4ᵛ). Bucer proposes what became a very common solution: money should not be given directly to beggars but should instead be put into the church charity box. Responsible deacons would distribute the money to poor people whose worthiness they had confirmed. However, deacons cannot "provide for the poor unless they have wherewith to distribute to the poor, and therefore it belongeth to magistrates to see that churches have sufficient to relieve the poor" (13). The magistrate, though here cooperating with deacons, was a secular officer; Bucer recognizes that responsibility for the poor is passing to secular authorities. Recalling the large role the Catholic Church had played in poor relief, Bucer in good Protestant fashion blames the shriveling of this role on the greed of mendicant orders: "In time long past, the fourth part of all revenues that belonged to the spirituality, by their possessions, or . . . by good men's gifts and oblations" (14) were given to the poor; but since wicked monastics ate and drank up all the proceeds, the task has passed to magistrates, who will use the money properly. Also in the wind is a shift away from alms altogether: "It is convenient that some taxes be set . . . for the relief of the poor" (16).

As can be seen in this text, fear of counterfeit disability was a pivotal element in the shift away from individual charity to beggars and toward a state-sponsored relief system. And it was precisely the fear of counterfeit disability that was so vigorously fostered—often by insidiously comic means—by rogue literature such as Harman's or John Awdeley's. Rogue literature thus did crucial cultural work, teaching readers to distrust their own judgment about who really needed alms, to fear being taken in by counterfeiting, made a fool of, and laughed to scorn.

An Elizabethan statute created the secular office of overseer of the poor, with powers and duties like those of churchwardens—to keep tallies of parish poor, set them to useful work where possible, raise money through taxation, and administer relief. The administrative manual *An Ease for Overseers,* which sets forth overseers' duties, insists that relief had to be legislated because religious charitableness had failed: "In this obdurate age of ours, neither godly persuasions of the pastors or pitiful exclamations of the poor can move to any mercy, unless there were a law made to compel them; . . . most give to the poor rather by compulsion than of compassion" (22). Overseers were to set up job-training programs that taught only the simplest tasks; otherwise "the loss will be greater in learning than the gain will be in working" (19). Overseers were authorized to pry, with demeaning thoroughness, into poor people's lives.

Many urged private philanthropy to take up the slack as religious charity waned, and private charity became an important component in society's total package of support mechanisms for the poor, though whether such charity increased during the sixteenth century is a matter of dispute among historians. But again, vagrants were excluded. Significantly, the ideology of poverty during the period favored "organized" charity—such as

the founding of carefully administered homes for a certain number of indigent aged people—against opening one's pocketbook to beggars on the streets. Good will was not lacking: Archer points out that in inauguration speeches, London mayors pledged the city to
charity and hospitality, that wealthy testators bequeathed much money (though rarely
more than 2 percent of their estates) to found poor houses and so forth, and that wealthy
merchants competed in acts of charity ("London Scene"). Still, secular charity fell far short
of the needs of the kingdom's mushrooming population of poor folk: "there were very
many more individuals in need of regular support by pensions than the relief system was
able to provide for" (Archer, *Pursuit* 182–83). And those who got left out, when funds ran
short, were largely those with no fixed abode. As even private philanthropy grew more
institutionalized, more oriented toward providing for poorhouses than toward acts of
charity to individual wandering beggars, the sort of act that was seen as redemptive in
the Middle Ages was strongly discouraged in the Renaissance. When it came to vagrants
rather than impoverished householders, this shift renders moot the historians' dispute
about whether private philanthropy succeeded in picking up the slack from deficiencies
in public relief: *both* private philanthropy and public relief were designed to exclude individual beggars and favor the housed poor.

Changing Concepts of Poverty

That this period drew such firm distinctions between poor folk to be given relief and
indigent people to be punished resulted from changing concepts of poverty. Over some
four hundred years between the twelfth and sixteenth centuries, the concept of almsgiving as redemptive—and indiscriminate charity as a spiritual good—modulated into a
concept of charity as a duty to be carried out circumspectly, distinguishing carefully between deserving and undeserving poor. Beier argues that in England, "the Tudor and early
Stuart concept of vagrancy arose from a general re-definition of poverty," a shift in thinking from the Franciscan concept of poverty as holy and worthy of charity to a later view
of begging as a moral and social threat (*Masterless Men* 3–4).

In the Middle Ages, almsgiving had been considered redemptive for the rich, and poverty was seen as spiritually ennobling for the poor. The gospels and patristic literature
exalted poverty "as a spiritual value. . . . *Pauperitas* is clearly assimilated to *humilitas*"
(Geremek 19). Medieval society had valorized begging in the great mendicant orders. But
in medieval satirists' eyes, the voluntary poverty of clerics came to resemble the voluntary beggary of the idle; and there was a strong sense already in the Middle Ages that, for
both paupers and mendicant friars, poverty was degrading rather than ennobling. "The
degrading aspects of poverty were frequently stressed in ideological attacks on movements
of voluntary poverty and mendicant orders. Innocent III made explicit his opposition to
mendicancy as a shameful and undignified condition which ill befits the clergy and de-
grades all who practise it" (Geremek 28). The shift from indiscriminate charity to the
reservation of alms only for the deserving was under way as early as the twelfth century,
in Gratian's Decree and writings of twelfth-century decretists, who reinterpreted church
fathers to divide beggars into the "honest" and the "dishonest." The dishonest, though
able to work, "choose rather to beg or steal" (Tierney 59). Gratian "at one point urg[ed]
openhanded generosity to all, and at another point insist[ed] on the need for cautious
discrimination in the bestowal of alms," but finally developed "a whole theory of the
'deserving poor' and the 'undeserving poor'" (Tierney 54–55). Many late medieval wills

demanded that executors distinguish between deserving and undeserving poor when distributing doles (Thomson 182–83). Dissent against the sanctifying of poverty, emergent in the Middle Ages, became dominant in the Reformation. (This was treated at length in chapter 2 of this study.)

Modern writings on the early modern "new poor" may overstate the uniqueness of Renaissance poverty and the magnitude of the shift in attitude toward poverty and beggary between medieval and Renaissance times. Such changes in weltanschauung took place over some four centuries rather than being instantaneous, and they involved theology, economic and political factors, demographic shifts, and even changes in the weather. Individual ingredients of this brew of attitudes were not new in the Renaissance. Some in the Middle Ages had recognized, for example, that beggars might be idle, that they might fake disability: "Infirmity as a professional strategy appears frequently in medieval literature in the form of parables about cripples miraculously healed," in which beggars avoid being healed because that would mean having to work (Geremek 49). In a medieval preacher's humorous tale, "two lazy beggars, one blind the other lame, try to avoid the relics of St. Martin, borne about in procession, so that they may not be healed and lose their alms" (Vitry 182). The shift, however, while subtler than is often suggested, was discernible and did affect material conditions of life. What was distinctive in the Renaissance was that harsh attitudes toward the poor flourished in new soil: the decline of the medieval idea that almsgiving was redemptive coincided with the enfeeblement of the church as an institution of social policy and aid and with poverty that was more widespread and more desperate: "Poverty as a mass phenomenon . . . did not appear until the medieval world was already giving way to a new era" (Geremek 11); "in the early Middle Ages, . . . people intent on living off charity caused the agrarian civilization of Western Christendom no serious discomfort" (16–17). But now, "waves of poverty which swept Europe as a result of economic and food crises exceeded the scope of social policy; poverty on so vast a scale was met only with fear, threats and closed doors" (Geremek 99).

Political Unrest Stemming from Poverty

Geremek documents pan-European poor harvests and famines in the 1520s and 1530s that led to political unrest: "The final cycle of unfruitfulness, from 1526 to 1535, revealed the extent of the disparity between demographic growth and food supply; vagrancy assumed mass proportions and the wave of repressive legislation aimed at paupers intensified. . . . It marked a turning-point after which it became impossible to live or govern as before" (122). As Lis and Soly show,

> The period 1520 to 1535 was the turning-point. . . . From 1520, rebellious movements, often of dangerous proportions, pressed local and central authorities to act on social problems. Whole regions were set aflame: the *Communeros* in Spain in 1520–21, followed by the *Germanias* in 1525–26; the revolts of textile workers in south-east England in 1525–26 and 1528; the *Grande Rebeyne* at Lyon in 1529; the revolt of the *Straccioni* at Lucca in 1531–32, and the Pilgrimage of Grace in 1536–37, five revolts which gripped a great part of England. Also, in numerous Netherlandish regions (Land van Waas, Luxemburg, Limbur, Liège) and towns (The Hague, Hertogenbosch, La Roche, Utrecht, Brussels, Amsterdam, Leyden), serious disturbances took place in the period 1520 to 1535. (84–85)

Appendix A

Steve Rappaport, noting that continental uprisings were more widespread and more violent than those in England, maintains that later historians have exaggerated the extent of
unrest in England. Ian Archer has responded that "because Rappaport defines his position in terms of reaction against an extremist position never seriously held (that London
was characterised by a pattern of 'pervasive instability'), he is prone to underestimate the
tensions in civic society" (*Pursuit* 9). Again, the slippage between what Archer terms "a sense
of perceived crisis" and what Rappaport downplays as a noncrisis is precisely what interests me. If twentieth-century historians have exaggerated early modern instability, they have
taken their cue from early modern panic. And, crucially, the fomenters of the unrest were
misidentified: it was not wandering beggars who incited the textile workers' rebellions in
1525–26 and 1528 or the Pilgrimage of Grace in 1536–37; but whenever such unrest took place,
the authorities typically rounded up vagrants, a clear example of scapegoating.

Sources for Further Reading

On early modern English vagrancy, see A. L. Beier's *Masterless Men: The Vagrancy Problem in England* and "Vagrants and the Social Order in Elizabethan London"; A. L. Beier
and Roger Finlay's "Significance of the Metropolis"; and John F. Pound's *Poverty and
Vagrancy in Tudor England*. On early childhood homelessness caused by widespread abandonment of poor children, see John Boswell's *Kindness of Strangers: The Abandonment of
Children in Western Europe from Late Antiquity to the Renaissance* and Keith Thomas's
"Fateful Exposures."

On the late medieval origins of the vagrancy situation, the increase after the thirteenth
century in "the number of *extranei* or *vagrantes*, landless paupers trekking here and there
in search of work" (Lis and Soly 16) as the feudal system began to break up, see Catharina
na Lis and Hugo Soly's *Poverty and Capitalism in Pre-Industrial Europe* (3–16). On pro-
toindustrial growth from 1450 to 1630, which "led in the long run to rural depopulation,
deforestation, agrarian stagnation and consequently an absolute impoverishment of the
rural masses" see Robert Jütte's *Poverty and Deviance in Early Modern Europe* (34–40).

To get a sense of divergent views among historians on whether vagrants should be regarded as victims or as culpably criminal, see (on the "victim" side) Paul Slack's *Poverty
and Policy in Tudor and Stuart England* and A. L. Beier's *Masterless Men* and (on the "criminal" side) J. S. Cockburn's "Nature and Incidence of Crime in England, 1559–1625: A Preliminary Survey." See also "Vagrants and the Social Order in Elizabethan England," a debate between Beier and Pound in *Past and Present;* Peter Clark and David Souden, editors,
Migration and Society in Early Modern England; Peter Clark's "Migrant in Kentish Towns,
1580–1640"; Slack's "Vagrants and Vagrancy in England, 1598–1664"; and Pound's "Elizabethan Census of the Poor: The Treatment of Vagrancy in Norwich, 1570–80."

On the legal definition of actors as vagabonds, see Peter Roberts's "Elizabethan Players and Minstrels and the Legislation of 1572 against Retainers and Vagabonds."

On vagrancy of demobilized soldiers, see Beier's *Masterless Men* (93–94); Charles Greig
Cruickshank's *Elizabeth's Army;* and Henry J. Webb's "Elizabethan Soldiers: A Study in
the Ideal and the Real."

Older studies of vagrancy, still sometimes cited, are C. J. Ribton-Turner's *History of
Vagrants and Vagrancy and Beggars and Begging* and Frank Ayledotte's *Elizabethan Rogues
and Vagabonds*.

On the alehouse culture so often familiar to vagrants, see Peter Clark's classic study *The English Alehouse: A Social History, 1200–1830* and Alan Milner Everitt's "English Urban Inn, 1560–1760." Patricia Fumerton's work in progress on vagrancy includes a chapter on alehouses as alternate versions of home.

On early modern poverty in general, see Andrew B. Appleby's *Famine in Tudor and Stuart England;* A. L. Beier's *Problem of the Poor in Tudor and Early Stuart England* and "Poverty and Progress in Early Modern England"; Paul Slack's *Poverty and Policy in Tudor and Stuart England;* David M. Palliser's *Age of Elizabeth: England under the Later Tudors, 1547–1603;* Steve Rappaport's *Worlds within Worlds: Structures of Life in Sixteenth-Century London;* Keith Wrightson and David Levine's *Poverty and Piety in an English Village: Terling, 1525–1700;* Bronislaw Geremek's *Poverty: A History;* Elaine Clark's "Social Welfare and Mutual Aid in the Medieval Countryside"; John Walter and Keith Wrightson's "Dearth and the Social Order in Early Modern England"; Paul A. Fideler's "Poverty, Policy and Providence: The Tudors and the Poor"; and Brian Pullan's *Rich and Poor in Renaissance Venice: The Social Institutions of a Catholic State to 1620.* For a succinct introduction to "subsistence crises," see the first two chapters of R. B. Outhwaite's *Dearth, Public Policy, and Social Disturbance in England, 1550–1800.* For the most thorough early census of the poor—from Norwich, then England's "second city"—see John F. Pound, editor, *The Norwich Census of the Poor 1570.*

On harvest failures and famine, see Buchanan Sharp's *In Contempt of All Authority: Rural Artisans and Riot in the West of England, 1586–1660;* Barry Supple's *Commercial Crisis and Change in England, 1600–1642;* C. G. A. Clay's *Economic Expansion and Social Change: England, 1500–1700;* Palliser's *Age of Elizabeth* (182–84); Penry Williams's *Tudor Regime,* 185–95; Ian Archer's *Pursuit of Stability: Social Relations in Elizabethan London* (9–14); Piero Camporesi's *Bread of Dreams: Food and Fantasy in Early Modern Europe;* and Brian Pullan's "Famine in Venice and the New Poor Law, 1527–29." On inflation, Geremek writes: "The simplest explanation that has been proposed attributes this sudden rise to a massive influx of silver from the newly discovered American continent and the disturbances which this entailed in the value and circulation of money. This is how people explained it at the time, and most modern historians concur with this theory. However, the chronology of events alone makes this unlikely. . . . Prices were already on the upward trend by 1460–70, well before the influx of precious metals from America. . . . The relation between currency and precious metals is only one of a long list of factors contributing to inflation" (89–90). See also Appleby's "Grain Prices and Subsistence Crises in England and France, 1590–1740"; Peter Bowden's "Agricultural Prices, Farm Profits, and Rents"; C. J. Harrison's "Grain Price Analysis and Harvest Qualities, 1465–1634"; William George Hoskins's "Harvest Fluctuations and English Economic History, 1480–1619"; Palliser's chapter "The Great Inflation" in *The Age of Elizabeth* (130–60); chapter 5, "The Standard of Living" (123–61), and appendix 3, "Prices and Wages in London, 1490 to 1609" (401–7), in Rappaport's *Worlds within Worlds* (which argues that modern historians have overestimated the effects of inflation during the sixteenth century); and Outhwaite's "Dearth and Government Intervention in English Grain Markets, 1590–1700." On changes in the weather and possible long-term climatic changes during the period, see Palliser (3–4).

On stagnant or falling wages, Jütte writes, "Wages did not keep up with the rapid development of prices. At the beginning of the seventeenth century weavers and carpenters earned twice as much as at the beginning of the sixteenth century, while the price for food had almost tripled" (29; see also Christopher Hill, *Century* 24). The most frequently cited authority on falling wages, Steve Rappaport, estimates that earning power declined by 29 percent during the sixteenth century (150), while other historians claim up to 60 percent; either figure represents a serious loss of purchasing power. See also Donald Woodward's "Wage Rates and Living Standards in Pre-Industrial England"; Palliser's *Age of Elizabeth* (130–60, 385–87); Peter Ramsey's *Tudor Economic Problems* (113–21); and Clay's *Economic Expansion and Social Change,* (1:27, 1:197–213).

On enclosures, see Eric Kerridge's *Common Fields of England;* E. M. Leonard's *Early History of English Poor Relief* (73–74); R. H. Tawney's *Agrarian Problem in the Sixteenth Century* (147–73, 213–30); Pound's *Poverty and Vagrancy in Tudor England* (7–11); Clay's *Economic Expansion and Social Change* (1:67–101); Palliser's *Age of Elizabeth* (178–85); Joan Thirsk's "Tudor Enclosures"; Roger B. Manning's *Village Revolts: Social Protest and Popular Disturbances in England, 1509–1640* (23–131); Penry Williams's *Tudor Regime* (180–85); and William C. Carroll's *Fat King, Lean Beggar: Representations of Poverty in the Age of Shakespeare* (chap. 4). As Lis and Soly summarize:

> Although historians dispute the causes, extent, and results of the enclosure movement, it undeniably turned many small farmers into beggars. . . . In all areas where a systematic shift from arable to pasture took place the demand for labour dropped drastically. Underemployment and unemployment rose. The enclosure movement undoubtedly favoured economic growth in England by promoting changes in agrarian structure which brought along greater efficiency and specialization, but these technological improvements were to the cost of small farmers and rural labourers, who not only lost their rights to the commons . . . but simultaneously were confronted by fewer opportunities for work. (60)

Noting that Sir Thomas More's analysis of the effect of enclosures on the poor was later "quoted approvingly and taken over in all its essentials by Marx in *Capital*" (129), Carroll cites some progressive effects of enclosures and reviews the Renaissance debate on this issue (*Fat King* 129–33). For the debate on Marx's views, see J. D. Chambers's "Enclosure and the Labor Supply in the Industrial Revolution"; John Saville's "Primitive Accumulation and Early Industrialization in Britain"; William Lazonick's "Karl Marx and Enclosures in England"; J. R. Wordie's "Chronology of English Enclosure, 1500–1914"; and John E. Martin's *Feudalism to Capitalism: Peasant and Landlord in English Agrarian Development* (132–40).

On the impact of illness and famine on poverty, see Jütte's *Poverty and Deviance;* John Walter and Roger S. Schofield's *Famine, Disease and the Social Order in Early Modern Society;* Schofield's "Impact of Scarcity and Plenty on Population Change in England, 1541–1871"; Andrew B. Appleby's "Disease or Famine? Mortality in Cumberland and Westmorland, 1580–1640," "Nutrition and Disease: The Case of London, 1550–1750," and *Famine in Tudor and Stuart England;* Mary J. Dobson's *Chronology of Epidemic Disease and Mortality in Southeast England, 1601–1800;* John Hatcher's *Plague, Population, and the English Economy, 1348–1530;* Charles Mullett's *Bubonic Plague and England: An Essay in the History of Preventive Medicine;* Thomas R. Forbes's "By What Disease or Casualty: The Changing Face of Death in London"; Patrick R. Galloway's "Annual Variations in Death by Age,

Deaths by Cause, Prices, and Weather in London, 1670–1830" and "Basic Patterns in Annual Variations in Fertility, Nuptiality, Mortality, and Prices in Pre-Industrial Europe"; Leslie A. Clarkson's *Death, Disease, and Famine in Pre-Industrial England;* Outhwaite's "Food Crises in Early Modern England: Patterns of Public Response" and "Dearth, the English Crown and the 'Crisis of the 1590s'"; Slack's "Mortality Crises and Epidemic Disease in England, 1485–1610," *The Impact of Plague in Tudor and Stuart England,* and "Dearth and Social Policy in Early Modern England"; Walter and Wrightson's "Dearth and the Social Order in Early Modern England"; Margaret Pelling's "Healing the Sick Poor: Social Policy and Disability in Norwich, 1550–1640" and "Illness among the Poor in an Early Modern Town: The Norwich Census of 1570," which indicates how widespread was disability; Andrew Wear's "Caring for the Sick Poor in St. Bartholomew's Exchange, 1580–1676"; and Natalie Zemon Davis's *Society and Culture in Early Modern France* (23–24).

On the growth of London, see Peter Ramsey's *Tudor Economic Problems;* Palliser's *Age of Elizabeth;* Roger Finlay's *Population and Metropolis: The Demography of London, 1580–1650;* Roger Finlay and Beatrice Shearer's "Population Growth and Suburban Expansion"; Clay's *Economic Expansion and Social Change;* and Edward Anthony Wrigley and Roger S. Schofield's *Population History of England, 1541–1871.* On population growth in England more generally, Beier estimates in *Masterless Men* that the country's population nearly doubled from about 2.7 million in 1541 to 5.2 million in 1651 (19); Palliser writes that "by the end of Elizabeth's reign the population of England may have been as much as 35 per cent higher than it was at the start" (37). See also Palliser (30–59).

For a succinct discussion of the developing Poor Laws, see Slack's *Poverty and Policy* (113–37); for a fuller treatment, see Slack's *English Poor Law, 1531–1782.* See also Outhwaite's *Dearth, Public Policy, and Social Disturbance in England, 1550–1800* (35–44); Penry Williams's *Tudor Regime* (196–215); and Rosalind Mitchison's "Making of the Old Scottish Poor Law."

On justices of the peace and their duties, see W. Lambard, *Eirenarcha: or, Of the Office of Justices of the Peace* (1581), and M. Dalton, *Country Justice* (1618). For further contemporary comment on those charged with enforcing the poor laws, see the anonymous manual *An Ease for Overseers of the Poor* (1601).

For earlier accounts of Bridewell and Bethlehem Hospital, see Thomas Bowen's *Extracts from the Records and Court Books of Bridewell Hospital* and *An Historical Account of the Origin, Progress, and Present State of Bethlem Hospital.* See also Edward G. O'Donoghue's *Bridewell Hospital: Palace, Prison, Schools from the Death of Elizabeth to Modern Times;* Joanna Innes's "Prisons for the Poor: English Bridewells, 1555–1800"; E. D. Pendry's *Elizabethan Prisons and Prison Scenes;* Alfred J. Copeland's *Bridewell Royal Hospital: Past and Present;* Carroll's *Fat King, Lean Beggar: Representations of Poverty in the Age of Shakespeare* (97–126); Patricia Allderidge's "Bedlam: Fact or Fantasy?"; Pieter Spierenburg's *Prison Experience: Disciplinary Institutions and Their Inmates in Early Modern Europe* (esp. 69–86); Anthony Masters's *Bedlam;* and Beier's "Foucault *Redux?* Creating Bridewell, 1500–1560."

Material on vagrancy is to be found in sources dealing with crime—indeed, the whole topic of vagrancy is sometimes (prejudicially, I believe) subsumed under the heading of crime. On crime in general, see Timothy Curtis and James A. Sharpe's "Crime in Tudor and Stuart England"; Timothy Curtis and F. M. Hale's "English Thinking about Crime,

1530–1620"; Sharpe's *Crime in Early Modern England, 1550–1750* and "The History of Crime in Late Medieval and Early Modern England: A Review of the Field"; Peter Lawson's "Property Crime and Hard Times in England, 1559–1624"; Jennifer Kermode and Garthine Walker, editors, *Women, Crime, and the Courts in Early Modern England;* John H. Langbein's *Prosecuting Crime in the Renaissance;* John G. Bellamy's *Criminal Law and Society in Late Medieval and Tudor England;* and Gary V. Dubin and Richard H. Robinson's "Vagrancy Concept Reconsidered: Problems and Abuses of Status Criminality." On the question of whether vagrants were organized into criminal societies, see Beier's *Masterless Men* (123–45) and his "Vagrants and the Social Order in Elizabethan London"; and Ian Archer's *Pursuit of Stability* (204–56). John L. McMullan offers a compromise position in "Criminal Organization in Sixteenth- and Seventeenth-Century London" and *The Canting Crew: London's Criminal Underworld, 1550–1700.* On thieves' cant, see McMullan's *Canting Crew;* Beier's "Anti-language or Jargon? Canting in the English Underworld in the Sixteenth and Seventeenth Centuries"; D. B. Thomas's "Preface" to *The Book of Vagabonds and Beggars with a Vocabulary of Their Language and a Preface by Martin Luther;* and Jodi Mikalachki's "Women's Networks and the Female Vagrant: A Hard Case" and "Gender, Cant, and Cross-Talking in *The Roaring Girl.*"

The other side of the coin from the punishment of vagrants, poor relief, is of interest within my topic, even though vagrants were specifically exempted from such relief, because research on poor relief often turns up attitudes toward vagrants as "undeserving poor" and also documents the extent and causes of the poverty that often threw people into vagrancy. As I argue in the introduction, the very condemnation of vagrants enabled relief of the "deserving" poor. On local poor relief, see Marjorie K. McIntosh's "Local Responses to the Poor in Late Medieval and Tudor England"; Frederick George Emmison's "Poor-Relief Accounts of Two Rural Parishes in Bedfordshire, 1563–98" and "The Care of the Poor in Elizabethan Essex"; Ethel Mary Hampson's *Treatment of Poverty in Cambridgeshire, 1597–1834;* John Webb, editor, *Poor Relief in Elizabethan Ipswich;* and S. J. Wright's *Parish, Church, and People: Local Studies in Lay Religion, 1350–1750.* For a nuanced discussion of varying attitudes among Protestant denominations over where responsibility for poor relief ought to reside, see Elsie Anne McKee's *John Calvin on the Diaconate and Liturgical Almsgiving* (115–37). Other studies on poor relief include Leonard's *Early History of English Poor Relief;* Geoffrey W. Oxley's *Poor Relief in England and Wales, 1601–1834;* Pound's *Poverty and Vagrancy in Tudor England;* Sidney and Beatrice Webb's *English Poor Law History,* Part 1: *The Old Poor Law;* Brian Tierney's *Medieval Poor Law: A Sketch of Canonical Theory and Its Application in England;* and G. R. Elton's "Early Tudor Poor Law."

On the poor-relief system of monastic charity that the Poor Laws replaced, see Barbara F. Harvey's *Living and Dying in England, 1100–1540: The Monastic Experience* (146–78). On changing attitudes toward charity and hospitality, see Felicity Heal's *Hospitality in Early Modern England;* Daryl W. Palmer's *Hospitable Performances: Dramatic Genre and Cultural Practices in Early Modern England;* and J. A. F. Thomson's "Piety and Charity in Late Medieval London." On the development of secular philanthropy to replace medieval almsgiving, W. K. Jordan's *Philanthropy in England, 1480–1660: A Study of the Changing Pattern of English Social Aspirations* and *The Charities of London, 1480–1660: The Aspirations and the Achievements of the Urban Society* can still prove useful, although they are seriously flawed by his not allowing for inflation. See J. F. Hadwin's critique of Jordan, "Deflating Philanthropy," which concludes that private endowments did not make up for the loss of monastic charity at the Dissolution until the 1580s (and, if rising population is also taken into account, not until the 1650s). See also Slack's *Poverty and Policy* (163); William G. Bittle and R. Todd Lane's "Inflation and Philanthropy in England: A Reassessment of W. K. Jordan's Data," which presents evidence of an almost continuous decline in charitable giving from 1510 to 1600, followed by a partial recovery in the early seventeenth century; and Susan Brigden's "Religion and Social Obligation in Early Sixteenth-Century London." On the interaction of public assistance and private charity, see Archer's *Pursuit of Stability* (163–82). When using all these sources, one must keep in mind the crucial fact, discussed above, that after the decline of medieval almsgiving, both private philanthropy and public poor relief discriminated against the unhoused vagrant.

On the dissolution of the monasteries and chantries, which abolished the principal medieval mechanism of poor relief, necessitating a shift to secular poor relief and adding former monastics to the vagrant population, see Eamon Duffy's *Stripping of the Altars: Traditional Religion in England, 1400–1580;* David Knowles's *Religious Orders in England;* A. G. Dickens's *English Reformation;* Christopher Haigh's *Reformation and Resistance in Tudor Lancashire;* Christopher Haigh, editor, *The English Reformation Revised;* Alan Krieder's *English Chantries: The Road to Dissolution;* and J. Thomas Kelly's *Thorns on the Tudor Rose: Monks, Rogues, Vagabonds, and Sturdy Beggars.* As Palliser summarizes, "the dissolution of the monasteries (1536–40) produced what was unquestionably the greatest transfer of land since the Norman Conquest" (89).

On experiments in setting up trade schools to stem unemployment, see Joan Thirsk's "England's Provinces: Did They Serve or Drive Material London?" On make-work trade "projects," see Thirsk's *Economic Policy and Projects: The Development of a Consumer Society in Early Modern England.*

On early modern unrest and disorder and the governmental measures taken to contain perceived threats of disorder, see Anthony Fletcher and John Stevenson, editors, *Order and Disorder in Early Modern England;* Alan Macfarlane and Sarah Harris's *Justice and the Mare's Ale: Law and Disorder in Seventeenth-Century England;* Buchanan Sharp's *In Contempt of All Authority;* David Underdown's *Revel, Riot, and Rebellion: Popular Politics and Culture in England, 1603–1660;* Rappaport's *Worlds within Worlds;* Manning's *Village Revolts;* Outhwaite's *Dearth, Public Policy, and Social Disturbance in England* (45–56); Andrew Charlesworth's *Atlas of Rural Protest in Britain, 1548–1900;* Peter Clark's "Popular Protest and Disturbance in Kent, 1558–1640"; Penry Williams's *Tudor Regime* (217–52, 313–50); and John Walter's "'Rising of the People'?: The Oxfordshire Rising of 1596." Though these historians differ among themselves on how widespread and how serious political disorder was in this period, they agree in producing a portrait of disorderly elements as comprising mainly settled local people—clothworkers, apprentices, laborers—rather than vagrants, a striking contradiction of early modern fulminations against "seditious" vagabonds.

Notes

1. Writing of depressions in the European textile industry, Lis and Soly note that "the Brugge rhetorican Cornelis Everaert in the 1520s and 1530s showed a deep understanding of the socio-economic relationships dominant in the textile industry. In his plays, repeat-

edly banned by the authorities, he unambiguously portrayed the underpayment of the textile workers and the scandalous practices of their employers, who paid in debased coinage or in produce" (70).

2. Europe offered similar evidence against the idea that the poor simply did not want to work: as Geremek shows, the response to a suggestion by a Parisian official that the poor be employed in public works projects was a fear of oversubscription: "if only six or seven hundred people are put to work in this way, after two days there will be more than two thousand; they will revolt and sack the city" (129). As Geremek notes, this gives the lie to the "common assumption . . . that the unemployed were simply idle": "The fact that the prospect of work, however badly paid, was so attractive indicates clearly that a shortage of jobs was the cause of the increased number of beggars on the streets of Paris" (129). The conviction that vagrants are idle freeloaders averse to work has persisted, a legacy (at least in its remote origins) of the Renaissance. In 1983, presidential adviser Edwin Meese called soup kitchens a "free lunch" for people not really in need (Engel and Sargent A1); President Reagan said the homeless lived on the streets "by their own choice" (Green and MacColl 162; see also Steven V. Roberts). For more on recent American homelessness and public attitudes toward it—so reminiscent of Renaissance attitudes—see Foscarinis, Ely, Donovan, and Hopper; Hopper and Hamberg; Oreskes; Reyes and Waxman; Rossi; E. Smith; Toro, Trickett, Wall, and Salem; Barak; Baumohl; Talmadge Wright; Blau; White; Demko and Jackson; Van Whitlock, Lubin, and Sailors; Roleff; and the U.S. Congress report *Homelessness in America*.

3. Although it is often assumed that population growth per se influenced fundamental changes in methods of poor relief and legislation concerning the poor, Pieter Spierenburg argues that "the reform of poor relief in the sixteenth century antedated the most conspicuous wave of population growth" (*Prison Experience* 34). Many conditions—from poor harvests to sweeping religious renovations—combined to produce such changes, as I show throughout this study.

Appendix B: English Renaissance Jest Books

The charts that begin on page 286 give the chronological distribution of early modern English jest books, the printing history of which falls into three distinct phases: 1510–34, 1555–ca. 1585, and 1590–1609. The first jest collection in English was perhaps the small clutch of Poggio's jests that Caxton appended to his *Aesop's Fables* (see Robert H. Wilson). But a truly English movement, the founding phase of Henrician jest books (1510–34), saw nine single jests in verse, six collections in prose, and one collection in verse (Walter Smith's *Twelve Merry Jests of the Widow Edith*). In 1533 and 1535, the printers Rastell and de Worde died; they had printed a number of jests, and their deaths coincide with the end of this first phase. The repetition among jest book printers suggests that they played an important role in fostering this genre as well as rogue literature: of the nine single verse jests, de Worde printed four, Julian Notary printed two, P. Treveris printed one (possibly two), and an unknown printer printed one. (Treveris was also associated with Rastell, who printed one of the prose collections and the one verse collection.)[1] This first phase of jest books is contemporary with a crisis in poverty, a cycle of poor harvests, newly articulated Poor Laws, the English Reformation, the dissolution of the monasteries, the first great generation of humanists, and a revolution in education. The pseudonymous Till Eulenspiegel's *Merry Jest of a Man That Was Called Howlglas* and Smith's *Widow Edith* are jest books that track the careers of vagrants; and this period also produced antibeggary texts such as Robert Copland's *Highway to the Spital-house*.

Up until the mid-1520s, this genre comprised single-story jests in verse, called "merry jests":[2] *A Merry Jest of the Friar and the Boy;* Sir Thomas More's *Merry Jest How a Sergeant Would Learn to Be a Friar; A Merry Jest of the Milner of Abington; A Merry Jest of Dane Hew, Monk of Leicester, and How He Was Four Times Slain and Once Hanged; A Merry Jest and a True How Johan Splinter Made His Testament; A Merry Jest of a Shrewd and Curst Wife Lapped in Morel's Skin; A Merry Jest of an Old Fool with a Young Wife.* After the 1520s, "merry jest" was supplanted by "merry tales" or simply "jests." At the transition point stands *Widow Edith* (1525): its title uses "merry jest," and it is in verse; but it collects tales rather than being a single jest, and it was followed by prose collections, including *A*

The First Phase of English Jest Books, 1510–34

Single Jests in Verse	Tale Collections in Prose	Tale Collection in Verse
ca. 1510 *Plowman . . . Paternoster*	early 16th c.[?] *Scoggin's Jests*[a]	1525 *Widow Edith*
ca. 1510–13 *Friar & Boy*	early 16th c.[?] *Mad Men of Gotham*[b]	
ca. 1516 *Sergeant . . . Friar*	ca. 1519 *Howlglas*	
1520[?] *Johan Splinter*	1526, 1530 *100 Merry Tales*	
1520s[?] *Dane Hew*	pre-1529[?] *Skelton's Jests*[c]	
ca. 1525 *Morel's Skin*	1532 *Tales & Quick Answers*	
ca. 1530 *Old Fool . . . Young Wife*		
ca. 1532–34 *Milner of Abington*		
1534[?] *Christ Cross Me Speed*		

The Second Phase of English Jest Books, 1555–ca. 1585

New Jest Books	Reprints of Single Jests in Verse	Reprints of Prose Collections	Reprint of Verse Collection
ca. 1557 *Sackful of News*	1560 *Plowman . . . Paternoster*	1555, 1560 *Howlglas*	1573 *Widow Edith*
	1560[?] *Dane Hew*	1565 *Mad Men of Gotham*	
	1568–69 *Friar & Boy*	1565–66 *Scoggin's Jests*	
	1575 *Sergeant . . . Friar*	1567 *Tales & Quick Answers*	
	1575 *Milner of Abington*	1567 *Skelton's Tales*	
	ca. 1580 *Morel's Skin*	1576 *Tales & Quick Answers* entered	
	1584–89 *Friar & Boy*	1582 *Sackful of News* entered to Awdeley	

The Third Phase of English Jest Books, 1590–1609

New Jest Books

1590 *Cobbler of Canterbury*
pre-1592[?] *Tarlton's Jests*
1604 *Jack of Dover*
1605–7 *Jests of Peele*
1607 *Dobson's Dry Bobs*
1607 *Make You Merry*
1607 *Old Hobson*
1609 "*Conceits & Jests*"
1609 *Pasquil's Jests*

a. All extant editions date to the mid-sixteenth century or later, but Scoggin was a court jester in the reign of Edward IV (late fifteenth century) and those who allude to these jests often intimate that the collection emanates from the early sixteenth century.

b. The only extant editions date to 1565, though this was probably first published early in the sixteenth century.

c. Skelton died in 1529. His biographer William Nelson presents evidence suggesting that a work called *The Jests of Skelton*, listed as being in Thomas Cromwell's possession in 1530–32 but now lost, was an earlier edition of the extant *Merry Tales Newly Imprinted and Made by Master Skelton, Poet Laureate* (1567) (Nelson 109).

Key to Abbreviated Titles (for full bibliographic information, consult the works cited list at the end of the book):

Christ Cross Me Speed   *A Little Proper Jest Called Christ Cross Me Speed. ABC. How That Good Gossips Made a Royal Feast*
Cobler of Canterbury   *The Cobbler of Canterbury; or, An Invective Against Tarlton's News Out of Purgatory*
"*Conceits & Jests*"   "Certain Conceits and Jests," in *The Philosopher's Banquet, Furnished with Few Dishes for Health, but Large Discourse for Pleasure* (see under Scott, Michael)
Dane Hew   *A Merry Jest of Dane Hew, Monk of Leicester, and How He Was Four Times Slain and Once Hanged*
Dobson's Dry Bobs   *Dobson's Dry Bobs, Son and Heir to Scoggin*
Friar & Boy   *A Merry Jest of the Friar and the Boy*
Howlglas   *A Merry Jest of a Man That Was Called Howlglas* (see under Eulenspiegel, Till [pseud.])
Jack of Dover   *Jack of Dover, His Quest of Inquiry; or, His Privy Search for the Veriest Fool in England* (later called *The Merry Tales of Jack of Dover*)

Hundred Merry Tales; Tales and Quick Answers, Very Merry, and Pleasant to Read; and [Andrew Borde's] *Merry Tales of the Mad Men of Gotham.*

The second phase extends from around 1555 to approximately 1585, with a dense concentration during the 1560s. (Between the first two phases, the dormant period 1535–55 saw little activity except for new editions of *The Friar and the Boy* [1545] and *A Hundred Merry Tales* [1548?]). During this second phase of jest book printing, one apparently new prose collection was entered in the Stationer's Register (*A Sackful of News* [ca. 1557]), and seven of the nine single verse jests were reprinted. Seven reprints of prose collections appeared, and two more were entered in the Stationers' Register. This second phase coincides with the publication of rogue literature—John Awdeley's *Fraternity of Vagabonds* and Thomas Harman's *Caveat for Common Cursetors, Vulgarly Called Vagabonds.*

For about a quarter of a century, from the reprinting of *The Friar and the Boy* (1584–89) to *The Jests of Scoggin* (1613), none of the Henrician jest books was reprinted. But starting in the 1590s, the tradition reblossomed with nine new jest books, all prose collections. This third phase coincides with the publication of Robert Greene's cony-catching pamphlets, which share many verbal tags with jest books. And scattered allusions suggest that despite a paucity of reprints in the later Elizabethan and early Jacobean period, the elder jest tradition was not entirely dead—indeed, it may have flourished in late Elizabethan editions now lost. Though *The Jests of Scoggin* was not reprinted until 1613, a 1597 herbal by John Gerard refers to "Scoggin's heirs" (258). References to *The Jests of Scoggin* appear in a 1578 marginal note by Gabriel Harvey (Furnivall xlviii); in Harvey's *Three Proper and Witty Familiar Letters, Lately Passed between Two University Men* (1580), the two "university men" being Harvey and Edmund Spenser; in *A Whip for an Ape; or, Martin Displayed* (1589), one of the Martin Marprelate tracts; and in Harvey's *Pierce's Supererogation; or, A New Praise of the Old Ass* (1593). Though *Howlglas* had not been reprinted since 1560, Spenser loaned a copy to Harvey in 1578; Jonson mentions it in *The Poetaster* (1601); and in Jonson's *Alchemist* (acted 1610), Subtle pretends his servant is named Ulen Spiegel— the German name for "Howlglas" (2.3.32, 2.3.249). The old play *Wily Beguiled,* printed in 1606, refers to *The Jests of Scoggin* and *A Hundred Merry Tales.* The new jest book by George Dobson, *Dobson's Dry Bobs* (1607), was subtitled *Son and Heir to Scoggin;* in its address to the reader, the author says that he has outdone "Tiell" (i.e., Till Eulenspiegel) and "Skoggin." Jonson's *Masque of the Fortunate Isles* (1624) introduced Skelton and Scoggin as characters. Spenser loaned Harvey his copy of three early Tudor jest books—*Howlglas, The Jests of Scoggin,* and [John Skelton's] *Merry Tales Newly Imprinted and Made by Master Skelton, Poet Laureate.* William Hazlitt cites several early seventeenth-century works that mention the jests of Skelton and Scoggin in the same breath (*Shakespeare Jest-Books* 1:42). Though no sixteenth-century editions of *A Hundred Merry Tales* are extant after approximately 1548, Harvey refers to *A Hundred Merry Tales* in the second of his *Four Letters* (1592) and in his *Pierce's Supererogation* (1593); in addition, a young woman's preferring the tale of Robin Hood to Gabriel Harvey's pompous discourse on earthquakes seems an allusion to tale 52 in that jest book (Harvey, *Three Proper and Witty Familiar Letters* 13). References to *A Hundred Merry Tales* appear in William Bathe's *Brief Introduction to the True Art of Music* (1584) and in Dekker's *Wonderful Year* (1603). In Shakespeare's *Much Ado about Nothing* (1600), Beatrice claims to have got her wit out of *A Hundred Merry Tales* (2.1.124). Sir John Harington's *New Discourse on a Stale Subject, Called*

The Metamorphosis of Ajax (1596) refers to *A Hundred Merry Tales* but really means *Tales and Quick Answers*. Through whatever channels—fresh editions now lost, old editions still knocking around—early Tudor jest collections in prose remained very familiar during the period 1590–1609, when the nine new prose collections also came out. And even some of the new jest books look like revivals from the earlier period: *Dobson's Dry Bobs* is set during the aftermath of the dissolution of the monasteries; Richard Johnson's *Pleasant Conceits of Old Hobson the Merry Londoner* (1607) is set early in Elizabeth's reign, with one episode in Mary Tudor's reign.

Following Ernst Schulz, F. P. Wilson divided jest books into three classes: anthologies of detached jokes;[3] *Schwankbiographien*, or jest "biographies" relating the tricks of a single hero;[4] and collections of comic tales (or *novelle*). Wilson's taxonomy included only prose jests. Joanna Lipking used the same classification system but reinstated verse jests, some as a separate category, with *Widow Edith* under jest biography. I have tried not to be schematic or dogmatic about what counts as a jest book or how these books should be classified; but in trying to draw provisional boundaries around English jest books for the sake of this appendix, I have imposed a few ground rules. Unlike Schulz, Wilson, and Lipking, I have not included *novelle*, since the vague boundlessness of this category muddies thought. I *have* included verse jests, since for purposes of this book, I am more interested in representations of comic figures and their actions than in formal qualities of prosody; and from that standpoint, pate-buffeting, cuckolding, and farting look (and smell) pretty much the same, whether in prose or tetrameter. Unlike Schulz, Wilson, and Lipking, I have not made a hard-and-fast distinction between anthologies of detached jokes and jest biographies: instead, I have treated the biography as a specialized form of the anthology of detached jokes. I accept Lipking's observation that the biography stories "are read with a sense of comfortable expectation," while the anthologies "are designed for diversity and surprise" (174); but individuality is so effaced in the biographies' "heroes" that grouping tales around one figure seems merely a formal device, and the difference between these two types of jest collection remains relatively unimportant for my purposes, except insofar as the choice of a *vagrant* as hero (as in Widow Edith or Howlglas) sheds light on some of the cultural work these jests are performing.

I have shown how jest and laughter were common tools of Renaissance polemic, and contemporaries acknowledged debts to jest books. Reformer Henri Estienne, for example, attacks friars' preaching for its literariness and comic touches, for its narrative and dramatic techniques amplifying Bible stories: "They play with the holy Scripture as comedians are wont, or rather convert it to mere comical conceits" (246) to "enrich their tale" (251). The translator links such comic preaching specifically to *The Jests of Scoggin*: Scripture is disgraced by those who "turn it to jibes and jests, and merry conceits; especially the deep dissembling ducking friars, . . . [who play] the Scoggins with the Scriptures, . . . buffoons who abuse the Scripture in their sermons to move laughter" (253). Although these "jolly preachers" taught that "Christ never laughed in all his life, yet they followed not his example. . . . They took such pleasure in ridiculous and Scoggin-like speeches, as that they were not ashamed in preaching of the passion, to use sundry ridiculous jests, and diverse sorts of quips and girding taunts" (281). Significantly, though, the way to deal with friars is to laugh them to scorn—the tale of St. Francis preaching to the birds will give a man a "belly full of laughing cheer" (263). In the very chapters that rail at friars' use of jest, Estienne turns laughter against them. Similarly, as Lipking shows, "More compares Tyndale to 'an abbot of misrule' given to 'mad apish jesting' . . . and makes Tyndale's mocking, scoffing, jesting and railing a major theme" of his *Confutation of Tyndale's Answer* (363); but in this same theological diatribe, More incorporates jests from Poggio's *Facetiae* and *Tales and Quick Answers*.

English jest books, unlike continental jest books, seldom flaunt their humanist credentials or advertise elegant authorship. "Curiously indifferent to tradition, all are written in the vernacular; almost all are anonymous. None refers directly to learned models, and no contemporary observer makes for them the claims they neglect to make for themselves" (Lipking 168). The lack of specific humanist trappings has perhaps contributed to English jest books' having been classified as popular culture. The term "popular" was first applied to them, tellingly, in the late eighteenth and early nineteenth century, when Romantics were valorizing "folk" culture. Joseph Ritson's *Pieces of Ancient Popular Poetry* (1791) included *A Merry Jest of the Friar and the Boy* alongside such folksy items as "Clim o' the Clough" and "The King and the Barker," all of which he calls "favourites of the people" and locates within the oral tradition, to be sung "at marriages, wakes and other festive meetings, . . . [to] the tinkling of a harp" (506). Edward Vernon Utterson's *Select Pieces of Early Popular Poetry* (1817) includes the verse jest *A Merry Jest of a Shrewd and Curst Wife Lapped in Morel's Skin*, which a few years later William Hazlitt called a "valuable record and illustration of the manners of the *lower classes* in England" (*Remains* 4:179; emphasis in original). Hazlitt's collection, like Ritson's and Utterson's, promulgated the category "popular poetry," being titled *Remains of the Early Popular Poetry of England* (1864). The Merrie Olde England flavor of Hazlitt's four volumes, with their "folk" pieces like "The Nutbrown Maid" and "Tom Thumb," was spiced with gamier, often slapstick jests, and he also reprinted, in *Shakespeare Jest-Books* (1864), nearly all the prose jest collections plus *Widow Edith*, calling these pieces "light literature" (2:x). I have already shown, however, multiple links between the More circle and jest books such as *A Hundred Merry Tales, Tales and Quick Answers,* and *Widow Edith*. Intellectuals such as the Protestant preacher Hugh Latimer, the rhetorician Thomas Wilson, and the courtier Sir John Harington drew many illustrative tales from jest books. The English jests' refusal of filiation with continental humanist jest collections might express English nationalism. *A Hundred Merry Tales* has a very English feel, with its many English place names, but few of the tales are native; and here, as in many English jest books, continental place names have been changed to English ones. At any rate, English jest books are not folksy effusions of popular culture— they are embedded in the humanist movement like their continental cousins.

Of some interest are the multiple commitments of printers and the cultural linkages these might imply. John Awdeley, printer and perhaps author of *The Fraternity of Vagabonds,* owned the rights to *A Little Jest How the Plowman Learned His Paternoster,* which he entered in the Stationer's Register in 1560, to *A Sackful of News,* entered in 1582, and to *A Hundred Merry Tales* (see Hazlitt, *Shakespeare Jest-Books* 1:iv). And other evidence indicates that rogue literature occupied similar categories to jest books in printers' minds: Henry Bynneham, prosecuted in 1567 for pirating Harman's *Caveat,* entered in the Stationers' Register in 1576 an edition of the jest book *Tales and Quick Answers.* The world of jest had printing links with humanism, too: *Widow Edith* and *A Hundred Merry Tales* were printed by John Rastell, Sir Thomas More's brother-in-law, who had a number of more soberly humanist printing projects. Thomas Berthelet, who printed Sir Thomas Elyot's profoundly humanist *The Book Named the Governor* in 1531, the following year published the jest book *Tales and Quick Answers*. Suggesting links with the growing valorization of domesticity, Berthelet also printed Xenophon's marriage treatise, *Treatise of the Household* (1532). I am not arguing that printers deliberately shaped ideologies but that their (perhaps wholly commercial) response to the market is revealing—they knew books on humanism, domesticity, jests, and rogues would sell.

Joanna Lipking, in her richly detailed (and unfortunately never published) dissertation *Traditions of the "Facetiae" and Their Influence in Tudor England,* one of the best resources on European Renaissance jest books, makes the perceptive points that "the merry tale expresses and invites us to express something audacious, irregular, a little bit *bad*" (10) and that "the joke's real justification seems to lie . . . in a spontaneous, restless impulse to break off serious matters, to play the truant" (1). In many ways, the Renaissance passion for jests—especially salacious or scatalogical jokes—seems to have fulfilled a similar function to idealizations of beggary—both allowed an exhilarating if vicarious release from the stultifying pressures of refined civility, hard work, orderly citizenship, and respectable domesticity. This desire to "play the truant" often issued in jests that featured truant characters, including vagrants like Widow Edith or Howlglas. (The very pan-European circulation of jokes in the jest collections has a kind of vagrancy about it, too.) To jest about disreputable elements of society was to become "a little bit *bad*," like them; and jesting about vagrants simultaneously took a slap at their turpitude and paid homage to their freedom.

The greatest icon of achieved English nationhood, of royal power, of dedication and responsibility, and of civility was Queen Elizabeth I, and it is pleasing to conclude with a vision of the great queen ending her career with an act of consummate truancy: neglecting "discourses of government and state" (Lipking 447), she listened instead to readings from *A Hundred Merry Tales:* "In March of 1603, as the Queen lay dying, a Catholic at court wrote to an English Jesuit at Rome of the 'dumps at Court,' describing the Queen's ailments and disturbance of mind, 'besides notable decay in judgement, and memory insomuch as she cannot attend to any discourses of government and state, but delighteth to hear some of the 100 merry tales, and such like, and to such is very attentive'" (Lipking 448). Like the dying vagrant Howlglas, Queen Elizabeth on her deathbed played the truant and the jester.

Notes

1. On sources of the English jest books and their continuity with continental jest materials, see Ernst Schulz, Harold V. Routh, F.P. Wilson, Stanley J. Kahrl, Douglas Bush, Henry De Vocht, and Joanna Lipking.

2. The exception was the English translation of [Till Eulenspiegel's] *Howlglas* (ca. 1519), printed in Antwerp, the only *collection* earlier than the mid-1520s. The impulse in *A Hundred Merry Tales* (1526) to put together a collection of prose jests, rather than the single verse jests in vogue during the previous few years, does not seem to reflect the influence of *Howlglas,* a prose collection published abroad just seven years earlier; at least, *A Hundred Merry Tales* borrows no jests from *Howlglas.* The models seem to have been the collection of humanist facetiae (the twenty-fourth tale of *A Hundred Merry Tales* is repeat-

ed nearly verbatim from Poggio Bracciolini's *Facetiae*) and the framed tale collection (the second tale in *A Hundred Merry Tales* is borrowed from Boccaccio's *Decameron*). The "hundred" in the title suggests the titles of collections of novelle (see Lipking 189). For further discussion of jest books, see chapter 3.

3. Such anthologies include *A Hundred Merry Tales*, *Tales and Quick Answers*, *The Merry Tales of the Mad Men of Gotham*, and *Jack of Dover, His Quest of Inquiry; or, His Privy Search for the Veriest Fool in England* (also called *The Merry Tales of Jack of Dover*).

4. Archer Taylor provides useful background on the German antecedents of the six-teenth-century jest biography, going back to Der Stricker's *Pfaffe Amis* (ca. 1225), the jests about Neidhart (thirteenth century), and the internationally known *Salomon and Mar-colphus*, which came to Germany about 1482: "This form is marked by the concentration of a single type of narrative about a central figure. It comes to a climax in *Kalenberger* (ca. 1473), *Eulenspiegel* (1515), *Peter Leu* (1550), which calls itself a 'second Kalenberger,' *Finkenritter* (1560), and *Lalebuch* (1597) soon rebaptized as *Schiltbürger* (1598)" (102). Taylor's wonderful suggestion that critics might assimilate some of the Faust material to this tradition (103) helps make sense of the Howlglas-like tricks played by this jokiest and most elusive of tragic heroes. There were English versions of *Salomon and Marcolphus* and *The Parson of Kalenberger* (or *The Parson of Kalenborowe*); Lipking suggests that literary historians include among English jest biographies the jests of Skelton, Scoggin, George Peele, Tarlton, Smith's Widow Edith, and Long Meg of Westminster.

Works Cited

Note: The designation "STC" refers to *A Short Title Catalogue of Books Printed in England, Scotland and Ireland and of English Books Printed Abroad, 1475–1640*, ed. A. W. Pollard and G. R. Redgrave, 2d ed. (London: The Bibliographical Society, 1976). The designation "Wing STC" refers to *A Short Title Catalogue of Books Printed in England, Scotland, Ireland, Wales and British America and of English Books Printed in Other Countries, 1641–1700*, comp. Donald Wing (New York: Columbia University Press, 1945).

An Act Concerning Punishment of Beggars and Vagabonds. 1530–31. In *English Historical Documents.* Vol. 5: *1485–1548.* Ed. C. H. Williams. New York: Oxford University Press, 1967. 1026–29.
An Act for the Continuance of the Statute Made in the 39th Year of Our Late Queen Elizabeth, Entitled, An Act for the Punishment of Rogues, Vagabonds, and Sturdy Beggars. Chapter 7 of Anno Regis. Iacobi Primo. London: Robert Barker, 1604. STC 9500.
An Act for the Punishment of Vagabonds, and for the Relief of the Poor and Impotent. London: Richard Jugge, 1572. STC 9478.
An Act for the Relief of the Poor, and *An Act for the Punishment of Rogues, Vagabonds, and Sturdy Beggars.* 39 Elizabeth, 1597. London: Deputies of Christopher Barker, 1598. STC 9494.3.
An Act for the Setting of the Poor on Work, and for the Avoiding of Idleness. Chapter 3 of Anno 18 Regina. Elizabeth. London: Richard Jugge, 1575. STC 9481.
Addy, John. *Sin and Society in the Seventeenth Century.* London: Routledge, 1989.
Agnew, Jean-Christophe. *Worlds Apart: The Market and the Theater in Anglo-American Thought, 1550–1750.* Cambridge: Cambridge University Press, 1986.
Aleman, Matheo. *The Rogue; or, The Life of Guzman de Alfarache.* Ca. 1599/1623. Trans. James Mabbe. 4 vols. London: Constable, 1924.
Allderidge, Patricia. "Bedlam: Fact or Fantasy?" In *The Anatomy of Madness: Essays in the History of Psychiatry.* Ed. W. F. Bynum, Roy Porter, and Michael Shepherd. 2 vols. London: Tavistock, 1985. 2:17–33.

Allen, Robert. *A Treatise of Christian Beneficence*. London: John Harrison, 1600. STC 367.

American Psychological Association. "Resolution on Homelessness." *American Psychologist*, November 1991, 1108.

Amussen, Susan Dwyer. *An Ordered Society: Gender and Class in Early Modern England*. Oxford: Basil Blackwell, 1988.

Appleby, Andrew B. "Disease or Famine? Mortality in Cumberland and Westmorland, 1580–1640." *Economic History Review* 26 (1973): 403–31.

———. *Famine in Tudor and Stuart England*. Stanford, Calif.: Stanford University Press, 1978.

———. "Grain Prices and Subsistence Crises in England and France, 1590–1740." *Journal of Economic History* 39 (1979): 865–87.

———. "Nutrition and Disease: The Case of London, 1550–1750." *Journal of Interdisciplinary History* 6 (1975): 1–22.

Archer, Ian. *The Pursuit of Stability: Social Relations in Elizabethan London*. Cambridge: Cambridge University Press, 1991.

———. "Setting the London Scene." Plenary lecture read at the conference "Material London, ca. 1600." Folger Shakespeare Library, Washington, D.C., March 16, 1995.

Arlotto, Piovano. *Motti e facezie del Piovano Arlotto* (Sayings and jests of Piovano Arlotto). Ca. 1480. Ed. G. Folena. Milan: Ricciardi, 1953.

Arthington, Henry. *Provision for the Poor, Out of the Storehouse of God's Plenty*. London: Thomas Creed, 1597. STC 798.

Ascham, Roger. *The Schoolmaster*. 1570. Ed. Lawrence V. Ryan. Ithaca, N.Y.: Cornell University Press, 1967.

Attardo, Salvatore, and Jean-Charles Chabanne. "Jokes as a Text Type." *Humor* 5 (1992): 165–76.

Awdeley, John. *The Fraternity of Vagabonds*. Ca. 1561. In *Awdeley's "Fraternity of Vacabondes, Harman's Caveat, Haben's Sermon," &c*. Ed. Edward Viles and Frederick J. Furnivall. London: Early English Text Society, 1869. 1–16. (Version of 1561 presumed lost; version of 1565, title page only, STC 993; earliest extant full version is London, 1575, STC 994; shorter version entitled *The 24 Orders of Knaves* [London: John Awdeley, ca. 1561], STC 995.5.)

Ayledotte, Frank. *Elizabethan Rogues and Vagabonds*. Oxford: Clarendon Press, 1913.

Bacon, Sir Francis. "Of Travaile." In *The Essayes or Counsels, Civill and Morall*. 1625. Ed. Michael Kiernan. Cambridge, Mass.: Harvard University Press, 1985. 56–58.

Bakhtin, Mikhail. *The Dialogic Imagination.* Ed. Michael Holquist. Trans. Caryl Emerson and Michael Holquist. Austin: University of Texas Press, 1981.

———. *Rabelais and His World*. Trans. Helene Iswolsky. Cambridge, Mass: M.I.T. Press, 1968.

Bale, John. *Acts of English Votaries, Comprehending Their Unchaste Practices and Example by All Ages, from the World's Beginning to This Present Year*. London: Thomas Raynalde, 1548[?]. STC 1270.

Barak, Gregg. *Gimme Shelter: A Social History of Homelessness in Contemporary America*. New York: Praeger, 1992.

Barclay, Alexander. *Ship of Fools*. London: Richard Pynson, 1509. STC 3545.

Barker, Francis. "*Titus Andronicus* and Death by Hanging." In *The Production of English*

Renaissance Culture. Ed. David Lee Miller, Sharon O'Dair, and Harold Weber. Ithaca, N.Y.: Cornell University Press, 1994. 226–61.

Barlandus (von Baarland), Adrian. *Iocorum Veterum ac Recentium Duae Centuriae* (Two hundred old and new jokes). Louvain: Petrum Martinum Alonstenseum, 1524.

Barroll, Leeds. *Politics, Plague, and Shakespeare's Theater.* Ithaca, N.Y.: Cornell University Press, 1991.

Baskins, Cristelle L. "Griselda; or, The Bride Stripped Bare by Her Bachelor in Tuscan *Cassone* Painting." *Stanford Italian Review* 10 (1991): 153–75.

Bathe, William. *A Brief Introduction to the Skill of Song.* London: Thomas Este, 1596. STC 1589.

———. *A Brief Introduction to the True Art of Music.* 1584. London: Thomas Este, 1596[?]. STC 451.

Baumohl, Jim, ed. *Homelessness in America.* Phoenix: Oryx Press, 1996.

Bebel, Heinrich. *Heinrich Bebels Facetien: Drei Bücher* (Bebel's *facetiae:* Three books). Ed. Gustav Bebermeyer. Leipzig: Hiersemann, 1931.

Bedel, Henry. *A Sermon Exhorting to Pity the Poor.* London: John Awdeley, 1571. STC 1783.

Beccadelli, Antonio (Panormita). *De Dictis et Factis Alphonsi Regis Aragonum* (Concerning the words and deeds of Alphonsus, king of Aragon). 1538. Frankfurt: Minerva, 1967. (First compiled in 1455.)

Beier, A. L. "Anti-language or Jargon? Canting in the English Underworld in the Sixteenth and Seventeenth Centuries." In *The Social History of Language: Language and Jargon.* Ed. Peter Burke and Roy S. Porter. 3 vols. London: Polity Press, 1995. 3:64–101.

———. "Foucault *Redux*? Creating Bridewell, 1500–1560." Paper read at the Shakespeare Association of America Annual Meeting, Washington, D.C., April 1997.

———. *Masterless Men: The Vagrancy Problem in England.* London: Methuen, 1985.

———. "Poverty and Progress in Early Modern England." In *The First Modern Society: Essays in English History in Honour of Lawrence Stone.* Ed. A. L. Beier, David Cannadine, and James M. Rosenheim. Cambridge: Cambridge University Press, 1989. 201–39.

———. *The Problem of the Poor in Tudor and Early Stuart England.* London: Methuen, 1983.

———. "Vagrants and the Social Order in Elizabethan London." *Past and Present* 64 (1974): 3–29.

Beier, A. L., and John F. Pound. "Debate: Vagrants and the Social Order in Elizabethan England." *Past and Present* 71 (1976): 126–34.

Beier, A. L., and Roger Finlay. "The Significance of the Metropolis." In *London, 1500–1700: The Making of the Metropolis.* Ed. A. L. Beier and Roger Finlay. London: Longman, 1986. 1–33.

Bellamy, John G. *Criminal Law and Society in Late Medieval and Tudor England.* New York: St. Martin's Press, 1984.

Berger, Arthur Asa. "What's in a Joke? A Micro-Analysis." *Elements: Journal of Slavic Studies and Comparative Cultural Semiotics* 1 (1994): 321–30.

Bergson, Henri. *Laughter.* 1900. Trans. Fred Rothwell. In *Comedy: Meaning and Form.* Ed. Robert W. Corrigan. San Francisco: Chandler, 1965. 471–77.

Berlin, Brent, and Paul Kay. *Basic Color Terms.* Berkeley: University of California Press, 1969.

Bittle, William G., and R. Todd Lane. "Inflation and Philanthropy in England: A Reassessment of W. K. Jordan's Data." *Economic History Review,* 2d ser., 29 (1976): 203–10.

Blau, Joel. *The Visible Poor: Homelessness in the United States.* New York: Oxford University Press, 1992.

Bloch, Ernst. *The Utopian Function of Art and Literature: Selected Essays.* Trans. Jack Zipes and Frank Mecklenburg. Cambridge, Mass.: M.I.T. Press, 1988.

Boccaccio, Giovanni. *The Decameron.* Composed in 1350–52; first published in 1471. Trans. J. M. Rigg. London: Dent, 1978.

The Book of Vagabonds and Beggars with a Vocabulary of Their Language and a Preface by Martin Luther. Ca. 1509. Ed. D. B. Thomas. Trans. J. C. Hotten. London: Penguin, 1932. (Also called *Liber Vagatorum* [The book of vagabonds].)

[Borde, Andrew?]. *The Merry Tales of the Mad Men of Gotham.* London: T. Colwell, 1565. Wing STC 3749. (Possibly printed 1549 or earlier; reprinted in *Shakespeare Jest-Books,* ed. William Hazlitt, 3 vols. [London: Willis and Sotheran, 1864], 3:4–26.

Boswell, John. *The Kindness of Strangers: The Abandonment of Children in Western Europe from Late Antiquity to the Renaissance.* New York: Pantheon, 1988.

Bowden, Peter. "Agricultural Prices, Farm Profits, and Rents." In *The Agrarian History of England and Wales.* Vol. 4: *1500–1640.* Ed. Joan Thirsk. Cambridge: Cambridge University Press, 1967. 593–695.

Bowen, Barbara C. *One Hundred Renaissance Jokes: An Anthology.* Birmingham, Ala.: Summa Publications, 1988.

Bowen, Thomas. *Extracts from the Records and Court Books of Bridewell Hospital.* London: Bridewell Hospital, 1798.

———. *An Historical Account of the Origin, Progress, and Present State of Bethlem Hospital.* London: Bridewell Hospital, 1783.

Brant, Sebastian. *Liber Faceti* (The book of *facetiae*). N.p., 1496.

———. *Narrenschiff* (Ship of fools). 1509. Trans. Alexander Barclay. Ed. Phyllis C. Robinson. Seal Harbor, Maine: High Loft, 1983.

Breen, T. H., and Stephen Foster. "Moving to the New World." *William and Mary Quarterly,* 3d ser., 30 (1973): 189–222.

Brigden, Susan. "Religion and Social Obligation in Early Sixteenth-Century London." *Past and Present* 103 (1984): 67–112.

Bryskett, Lodowick. *Discourse of Civil Life.* In *Literary Works of Lodowick Bryskett.* Ed. J. H. P. Pafferd. Farnborough: Gregg, 1972. xxiii–279.

Brome, Richard. *A Jovial Crew.* First acted in 1641. Ed. Ann Haaker. Lincoln: University of Nebraska Press, 1968. (Sometimes subtitled *The Merry Beggars.*)

Brown, Pamela. "Laughing at the Cony: A Female Rogue and 'The Verdict of the Smock.'" *English Literary Renaissance* 29 (1999): 201–24.

Bucer, Martin. *A Treatise How by the Word of God, Christian Men's Almose Ought to Be Distributed.* London: N.p., 1557[?]. STC 3965.

Burke, Peter. "Urban History and Urban Anthropology of Early Modern Europe." In *The Pursuit of Urban History.* Ed. Derek Fraser and Anthony Sutcliffe. London: Edward Arnold, 1983. 69–82.

Bush, Douglas, "Some Sources for the *Mery Tales, Wittie Queries, and Quicke Answeres.*" *Modern Philology* 20 (1923): 275–80.

Camporesi, Piero. *Bread of Dreams: Food and Fantasy in Early Modern Europe.* 1980. Trans. David Gentilcore. Chicago: University of Chicago Press, 1989.

Carbone, Lodovico. *Cento Trenta Novelle o Facetie* (A hundred thirty novellas or *facetiae*). 1469–71[?] Ed. Abd-El-Kader Salza. Livorno: Giusti, 1900.

Carnes, Pack. "The Dynamics of the Joke as a Conversational Genre." In *Storytelling in Contemporary Societies.* Ed. Lutz Röhrich and Sabine Wienker-Piepho. Tübingen: Narr, 1990. 137–46.

Carroll, William C. "'The Base Shall Top the Legitimate': The Bedlam Beggar and the Role of Edgar in *King Lear.*" *Shakespeare Quarterly* 38 (1987): 426–41.

———. *Fat King, Lean Beggar: Representations of Poverty in the Age of Shakespeare.* Ithaca, N.Y.: Cornell University Press, 1996.

Cartelli, Thomas. "Jack Cade in the Garden: Class Consciousness and Class Conflict in *2 Henry IV.*" In *Enclosure Acts: Sexuality, Property, and Culture in Early Modern England.* Ed. Richard Burt and John Michael Archer. Ithaca, N.Y.: Cornell University Press, 1994. 48–67.

Castiglione, Baldassare. *The Courtier.* 1561 (Thomas Hoby translation). Ed. W. E. Henley. London: David Nutt, 1900.

Chambers, J. D. "Enclosure and the Labor Supply in the Industrial Revolution." *Economic History Review,* 2d ser., 5 (1953): 319–43.

Chambers, R. W. *Thomas More.* 1935. London: Jonathan Cape, 1958.

Chandler, Frank Wadleigh. *The Literature of Roguery.* Boston: Houghton Mifflin, 1907.

Charlesworth, Andrew. *An Atlas of Rural Protest in Britain, 1548–1900.* London: Croom Helm, 1983.

Chaucer, Geoffrey. *The Works of Geoffrey Chaucer.* Ed. F. N. Robinson. 2d ed. Boston: Houghton Mifflin, 1957.

Cheke, Sir John. *The Hurt of Sedition.* London: Day and Seres, 1549. STC 5109.5.

Chester, Allan G. "The Date and Authorship of *The Fraternitye of Vagabonds.*" *Modern Language Notes* 54 (1939): 347–51.

Chute, Marchette. *Shakespeare of London.* New York: Dutton, 1949.

Cicero. *De Oratore* (Concerning oratory). Trans. E. W. Sutton and H. Rackham. 2 vols. Cambridge, Mass.: Harvard University Press, 1977–79.

Clark, Elaine. "Social Welfare and Mutual Aid in the Medieval Countryside." *Journal of British Studies* 33 (1994): 381–406.

Clark, Peter. *The English Alehouse: A Social History, 1200–1830.* London: Longman, 1983.

———. "The Migrant in Kentish Towns, 1580–1640." In *Crisis and Order in English Towns, 1580–1700: Essays in Urban History.* Ed. Peter Clark and Paul Slack. London: Routledge and Kegan Paul, 1972. 117–63.

———. "Popular Protest and Disturbance in Kent, 1558–1640." *Economic History Review* 29 (1976): 365–82.

Clark, Peter, and David Souden, eds. *Migration and Society in Early Modern England.* London: Hutchinson, 1987.

Clarkson, Leslie A. *Death, Disease, and Famine in Pre-Industrial England.* Dublin: Gill and Macmillan, 1975.

Clay, C. G. A. *Economic Expansion and Social Change: England, 1500–1700.* 2 vols. Cambridge: Cambridge University Press, 1984.

Cleaver, Robert. *A Godly Form of Household Government: For the Ordering of Private Families, According to the Direction of God's Word.* London: F. Kingston, 1598. STC 5383.

Clemen, Otto. *Luther und die Volksfrömmigkeit seiner Zeit* (Luther and the "popular piety" of his time). Dresden: Ungelenk, 1938.

The Cobbler of Canterbury; or, An Invective against Tarlton's News Out of Purgatory. London: Robert Robinson, 1590. STC 4579.

Cockburn, J. S. "The Nature and Incidence of Crime in England, 1559–1625: A Preliminary Survey." In *Crime in England, 1550–1800.* Ed. J. S. Cockburn. London: Methuen, 1977. 62–63.

Cock Lorel's Boat. London: Wynkyn de Worde, ca. 1518–19. STC 5456.

Cohen, Walter. *Drama of a Nation: Public Theater in Renaissance England and Spain.* Ithaca, N.Y.: Cornell University Press, 1985.

Coleman, Christopher, and David Starkey, eds. *Revolution Reassessed: Revisions in the History of Tudor Government and Administration.* Oxford: Clarendon Press, 1986.

Colie, Rosalie L. "Reason and Need: *King Lear* and the 'Crisis' of the Aristocracy." In *Some Facets of "King Lear": Essays in Prismatic Criticism.* Ed. Rosalie L. Colie and F. T. Flahiff. Toronto: University of Toronto Press, 1974. 185–219.

———. *Shakespeare's Living Art.* Princeton, N.J.: Princeton University Press, 1974.

Collinson, Patrick. *The Birthpangs of Protestant England: Religion and Cultural Change in the Sixteenth and Seventeenth Centuries.* New York: St. Martin's Press, 1988.

———. *English Puritanism.* London: Historical Association, 1983.

Comensoli, Viviana. *Household Business: Domestic Plays of Early Modern England.* Toronto: University of Toronto Press, 1996.

Cony-Catcher, Cuthbert (pseud.). *The Defense of Cony-Catching.* London: Abel Jeffes, 1592. STC 5654.5.

Cook, G. H., ed. *Letters to Cromwell and Others on the Suppression of the Monasteries.* London: John Baker, 1965.

Copeland, Alfred J. *Bridewell Royal Hospital: Past and Present.* London: W. Gardner, Darton, and Co., 1888.

Copland, Robert. *The Highway to the Spital-house.* 1536[?]. In *The Elizabethan Underworld.* Ed. A. V. Judges. 2d ed. New York: Octagon, 1964. 1–25. (1536[?] Robert Copland edition, STC 5732.)

———. *Jill of Brentford's Testament.* 1563. In *Robert Copland: Poems.* Ed. Mary Carpenter Erler. Toronto: University of Toronto Press, 1993. 164–86. (Written ca. 1535–36; 1563 W. Copland edition, STC 5731.)

Corrigan, Robert W., ed. *Comedy: Meaning and Form.* San Francisco: Chandler, 1965.

Cortesi, Paolo. *De Cardinalatu* (Concerning cardinalship). [Rome]: Castro Cortesio, 1510.

Cotgrave, Randle. *A Dictionary of the French and English Tongues.* London: Adam Islip, 1611. STC 5830.

Crane, Thomas Frederick. "Analysis and Notes." In Jacques de Vitry, *The Exempla or Illustrative Stories from the Sermones Vulgares of Jacques de Vitry.* Ed. Thomas Frederick Crane. London: Folk-Lore Society, 1890. 135–269.

Cressy, David. *Literacy and the Social Order: Reading and Writing in Tudor and Stuart England.* Cambridge: Cambridge University Press, 1980.

Croft, Henry Herbert Stephen. "Life of Elyot." In Sir Thomas Elyot, *The Book Named the Governor.* 1883. 2 vols. New York: Bert Franklin, 1967. 1:xix–clxxxix.

Crowley, Robert. *An Information and Petition against the Oppressors of the Poor Commons of This Realm.* 1550. In *Select Works of Robert Crowley.* Extra Series #15. London: EETS, 1872. 151–56.

———. *One and Thirty Epigrams.* London: Robert Crowley, 1550. STC 6888.3.

———. *The Way to Wealth: By What Means Sedition May Be Put Away, and What Destruction Will Follow If It Be Not Put Away Speedily.* 1550. In *Select Works of Robert Crowley.* Extra Series #15. London: EETS, 1872. 130–50.

Cruickshank, Charles Greig. *Elizabeth's Army.* 2d ed. Oxford: Clarendon Press, 1966.

Cunningham, Richard. "The Attraction of the Truth: Navigating Experience in Early Modern Literature." Ph.D. dissertation, Pennsylvania State University, 1999.

"The Cunning Northern Beggar." 1869. In *The Roxburghe Ballads.* Ed. William Chappell. Vol. 1, pt. 1. Hertford: Stephen Austin, 1977. 137–41.

Curtis, Timothy, and F. M. Hale. "English Thinking about Crime, 1530–1620." In *Crime and Criminal Justice in Europe and Canada.* Ed. Louis A. Knafla. Waterloo, Ont.: Wilfrid Laurier University Press, 1981. 111–26.

Curtis, Timothy, and James A. Sharpe. "Crime in Tudor and Stuart England." *History Today* 38 (1988): 23–29.

Dahlberg, Charles. "Chaucer's Cock and Fox." *Journal of English and Germanic Philology* 53 (1954): 277–90.

Dalton, M. *The Country Justice.* London: Adam Islip, 1618. STC 6205.

Danby, John. *Shakespeare's Doctrine of Nature: A Study of "King Lear."* London: Faber and Faber, 1951.

Dasgupta, Partha. *An Inquiry into Well-Being and Destitution.* Oxford: Clarendon Press, 1993.

Davies, Christie. "Language, Identity, and Ethnic Jokes about Stupidity." *International Journal of the Sociology of Language* 65 (1987): 39–52.

Davies, C. S. L. "Slavery and Protector Somerset: The Vagrancy Act of 1547." *Economic History Review,* 2d ser., 19 (1966): 533–49.

Davies, Kathleen M. "Continuity and Change in Literary Advice on Marriage." In *Marriage and Society: Studies in the Social History of Marriage.* Ed. R. B. Outhwaite. New York: St. Martin's Press, 1981. 58–80.

Davis, Natalie Zemon. *Society and Culture in Early Modern France.* Stanford, Calif.: Stanford University Press, 1965.

De Grazia, Margreta. "The Ideology of Superfluous Things: *King Lear* as a Period Piece." In *Subject and Object in Renaissance Culture.* Ed. Margreta de Grazia, Maureen Quilligan, and Peter Stallybrass. Cambridge: Cambridge University Press, 1996. 17–42.

Dekker, Thomas. *The Bellman of London.* 1608. In *The Non-Dramatic Works of Thomas Dekker.* Ed. A. B. Grosart. 1885. 5 vols. Rpt., New York: Russell and Russell, 1963. 3:61–169. (1608 edition [London: Nicholas Okes], STC 6480.)

———. *Lantern and Candlelight.* 1608. In *Rogues, Vagabonds, and Sturdy Beggars: A New Gallery of Tudor and Early Stuart Rogue Literature.* Ed. Arthur F. Kinney. 2d ed. Amherst: University of Massachusetts Press, 1990. 213–60. (1608 edition [London: G. Eld], STC 6485.)

————. *O Per Se O.* London: T. Snodham, 1612. STC 6487.

————. *The Wonderful Year.* London: Thomas Creede, 1603. STC 6535.

Dekker, Thomas, and George Wilkins. *Jests to Make You Merry: With the Conjuring Up of Cock Watt.* London: Nicholas Okes, 1607. STC 6541.

Dekker, Thomas, and John Webster. *Westward Ho.* First acted in 1604. In *The Dramatic Works of Thomas Dekker.* Ed. Fredson Bowers. 4 vols. Cambridge: Cambridge University Press, 1953–1961. 2:313–403.

Dekker, Thomas, and Thomas Middleton. *The Honest Whore, Part 1.* First acted in 1604. In *The Dramatic Works of Thomas Dekker.* Ed. Fredson Bowers. 4 vols. Cambridge: Cambridge University Press, 1953–1961. 2:1–131.

Delany, Paul. "*King Lear* and the Decline of Feudalism." *PMLA* 92 (1977): 429–40.

Demko, George J., and Michael C. Jackson. *Populations at Risk in America: Vulnerable Groups at the End of the Twentieth Century.* Boulder, Colo.: Westview Press, 1995.

De Vocht, Henry. "'Merry Tales, Wittie Queries, and Quicke Answeres' and Their Sources." *Anglia* 33 (1910): 120–32.

The Dialogue; or, Communing between the Wise King Salomon and Marcolphus. Ed. E. Gordon Duff. London: Lawrence and Bullen, 1892. (1492 edition [Antwerp: Geraaert Leeu], STC 22905.)

Dickens, A. G. *The English Reformation.* 2d ed. University Park: Pennsylvania State University Press, 1991.

Dillingham, Francis. *Christian Oeconomy or Household Government.* London: J. Tapp, 1609. STC 6880.

Dobson, George. *Dobson's Dry Bobs, Son and Heir to Scoggin.* London: Valentine Simmes, 1607. STC 6930.

Dobson, Mary J. *A Chronology of Epidemic Disease and Mortality in Southeast England, 1601–1800.* Historical Geography Research Series No. 19. London, 1987.

Dolan, Frances E. *Dangerous Familiars: Representations of Domestic Crime in England, 1550–1700.* Ithaca, N.Y.: Cornell University Press, 1994.

Dollimore, Jonathan. *Radical Tragedy: Religion, Ideology, and Power in the Drama of Shakespeare and His Contemporaries.* 2d ed. Brighton: Harvester Wheatsheaf, 1989.

Domenichi, Ludovico. *Facetie et Motti Arguti di Alcuni Eccellentissimi Ingegni, et Nobilissimi Signori.* (*Facetiae* and witty sayings of some most excellent wits, and most noble gentlemen). Florence: Lorenzo Torrentino, 1548.

Donne, John. *The Sermons of John Donne.* Ed. Evelyn M. Simpson and George R. Potter. 10 vols. Berkeley: University of California Press, 1953.

Douglas, Mary. *Purity and Danger: An Analysis of the Concepts of Pollution and Taboo.* London: Routledge and Kegan Paul, 1966.

Downame, John. *The Plea of the Poor; or, A Treatise of Beneficence and Alms-Deeds.* London: E. Griffin, 1616. STC 7146.

Drayton, Michael. "To the Virginian Voyage." 1619. In *The Works of Michael Drayton.* Ed. J. William Hebel. 5 vols. Oxford: Blackwell, 1931–41. 2:363–64.

Dubin, Gary V., and Richard H. Robinson. "The Vagrancy Concept Reconsidered: Problems and Abuses of Status Criminality." *New York University Law Review* 37 (1962): 102–36.

Dubrow, Heather. *Shakespeare and Domestic Loss: Forms of Deprivation, Mourning, and Recuperation.* Cambridge: Cambridge University Press, 1999.

Duffy, Eamon. *The Stripping of the Altars: Traditional Religion in England, 1400–1580.* New Haven, Conn.: Yale University Press, 1992.

Durant, David N. *Bess of Hardwick: Portrait of an Elizabethan Dynast.* New York: Atheneum, 1978.

An Ease for Overseers of the Poor. London: John Leggatt, 1601. STC 7446.

Eichmann, Raymond, and John DuVal, eds. and trans. *The French Fabliau B.N. MS. 837.* 2 vols. New York: Garland, 1985.

Eisenstein, Elizabeth. *The Printing Revolution in Early Modern Europe.* Cambridge: Cambridge University Press, 1983.

Elias, Norbert. *The Civilizing Process.* 1939. Trans. Edmund Jephcott. New York: Urizen, 1978.

Elsky, Martin. *Authorizing Words: Speech, Writing, and Print in the English Renaissance.* Ithaca, N.Y.: Cornell University Press, 1989.

Elton, G. R. "An Early Tudor Poor Law." In *Studies in Tudor and Stuart Politics and Government.* Vol. 2: *Parliament/Political Thought.* Ed. G. R. Elton. Cambridge: Cambridge University Press, 1974. 137–54.

———. "The Real Thomas More?" In *Reformation Principle and Practice: Essays in Honour of A. G. Dickens.* Ed. Peter Newman Brooks. London: Scolar, 1980. 21–31.

———. *The Tudor Revolution in Government: Administrative Changes in the Reign of Henry VIII.* Cambridge: Cambridge University Press, 1953.

Ely, L., S. Donovan, and Kim Hopper. *Over the Edge: Homeless Families and the Welfare System.* Washington, D.C.: National Coalition for the Homeless, 1988.

Elyot, Sir Thomas. *The Book Named the Governor.* 1531. Ed. Henry Herbert Stephen Croft. 2 vols. 1883. Rpt., New York: Bert Franklin, 1967.

Emmison, Frederick George. "The Care of the Poor in Elizabethan Essex." *Essex Review* 62 (1953): 7–28.

———. "Poor-Relief Accounts of Two Rural Parishes in Bedfordshire, 1563–98." *Economic History Review* 3 (1931): 102–16.

Enck, John J., Elizabeth T. Forter, and Alvin Whitley, eds. *The Comic in Theory and Practice.* New York: Appleton-Century-Crofts, 1960.

Engel, M., and E. Sargent. "Meese's Hunger Remarks Stir More Outrage among Groups." *Washington Post,* December 11, 1983, A1.

Erasmus, Desiderius. *The Colloquies of Erasmus.* 1518–40. Trans. Craig R. Thompson. Chicago: University of Chicago Press, 1965.

———. *De Civilitate Morum Puerilium* (On good manners for boys). 1530 (Latin)/1532 (English). In *Collected Works of Erasmus,* vol. 25. Ed. J. K. Sowards. Trans. Brian McGregor. Toronto: University of Toronto Press, 1985. 269–89.

———. *De Copia* (Of plenitude). 1512. In *Collected Works of Erasmus,* vol. 24. Ed. Craig R. Thompson. Trans. Betty I. Knott. Toronto: University of Toronto Press, 1978. 279–659.

———. Letter 999 to Ulrich von Hutten. 1519. In *Collected Works of Erasmus,* vol. 7: *The Correspondence of Erasmus.* Ed. Peter G. Bietenholz et al. Trans. R. A. B. Mynors. Toronto: University of Toronto Press, 1987. 15–25.

———. *The Praise of Folly.* Ed. and trans. Clarence C. Miller. New Haven, Conn.: Yale University Press, 1979.

Erickson, Carolly. "The Fourteenth-Century Friars and Their Critics." *Franciscan Studies* 35 (1975): 107–35; 36 (1976): 108–47.

Estienne, Henri. *A World of Wonders.* 1566. Trans. Richard Carew. London: John Norton, 1607. STC 10553.

Eulenspiegel, Till (pseud.). Ca. 1519. *A Merry Jest of a Man That Was Called Howlglas.* London: W. Copland, 1560. STC 10563.5. (ca. 1519 edition [Antwerp], STC 10563; translation of a late fifteenth-century work.)

Everitt, Alan Milner. "The English Urban Inn, 1560–1760." In *Perspectives in English Urban History.* Ed. Alan M. Everitt. New York: Barnes and Noble, 1973. 91–137.

Fabricius, Johannes. *Syphilis in Shakespeare's England.* London: Jessica Kingsley, 1994.

Farnham, Willard. "The Medieval Comic Spirit in the English Renaissance." In *Joseph Quincy Adams Memorial Studies.* Ed. James G. McManaway, Giles E. Dawson, and Edwin E. Willoughby. Washington, D.C.: Folger Shakespeare Library, 1948. 429–39.

Feibleman, James K. *In Praise of Comedy: A Study in Its Theory and Practice.* 1939. New York: Russell and Russell, 1962.

Fideler, Paul A. "Poverty, Policy, and Providence: The Tudors and the Poor." In *Political Thought and the Tudor Commonwealth.* Ed. Paul A. Fideler and T. F. Mayer. London: Routledge, 1992. 194–222.

Finlay, Roger. *Population and Metropolis: The Demography of London, 1580–1650.* Cambridge: Cambridge University Press, 1981.

Finlay, Roger, and Beatrice Shearer. "Population Growth and Suburban Expansion." In *London, 1500–1700: The Making of the Metropolis.* Ed. A. L. Beier and Roger Finlay. London: Longman, 1986. 37–59.

Fish, Simon. *A Supplication for the Beggars.* Ca. 1529. Ed. Frederick J. Furnivall. London: Early English Text Society, 1871.

Fleisher, Mark S. *Beggars and Thieves: Lives of Urban Street Criminals.* Madison: University of Wisconsin Press, 1995.

Fleming, John. "The Antifraternalism of the Summoner's Tale." *Journal of English and Germanic Philology* 65 (1966): 688–700.

Fletcher, Anthony, and John Stevenson, eds. *Order and Disorder in Early Modern England.* Cambridge: Cambridge University Press, 1985.

Fletcher, John, and Philip Massinger. *The Beggar's Bush.* First acted in 1615. Ed. John H. Dorenkamp. The Hague: Mouton, 1967.

Flood, John L. "The Winchester Geese." (Review of Johannes Fabricius's *Syphilis in Shakespeare's England.*) *Times Literary Supplement,* January 13, 1995, 12.

Forbes, Thomas R. "By What Disease or Casualty: The Changing Face of Death in London." In *Health, Medicine, and Mortality in the Sixteenth Century.* Ed. C. Webster. Cambridge: Cambridge University Press, 1979. 117–39.

Foscarinis, Maria. *Beyond Homelessness: An Agenda for the 1990s.* Washington, D.C.: National Law Center on Homelessness and Poverty, 1990.

———. "The Politics of Homelessness: A Call to Action." *American Psychologist* 46 (1991): 1232–39.

———. *Social Security: Broken Promise to America's Homeless.* Washington, D.C.: National Law Center on Homelessness and Poverty, 1990.

Freud, Sigmund. *Jokes and Their Relation to the Unconscious.* 1905. Trans. James Strachey. New York: W. W. Norton, 1960.

Frischlin, Nicodemus. *Facetiae.* N.p.: pre-1560.

Frye, Susan. *Elizabeth I: The Competition for Representation.* New York: Oxford University Press, 1993.

Fuller, Ronald. *The Beggars' Brotherhood.* London: Allen and Unwin, 1936.

Fumerton, Patricia. "Spacious Voices/Vagrant Subjects in Early Modern England." Book-length ms., University of California at Santa Barbara, n.d.

Furnivall, Frederick J., ed. *Captain Cox, His Ballads and Books; or, Robert Laneham's Letter.* London: Ballad Society, 1871.

Gaby, Rosemary. "Of Vagabonds and Commonwealths: *Beggar's Bush, A Jovial Crew,* and *The Sisters.*" *Studies in English Literature* 34 (1994): 401–24.

Galenson, David W. *White Servitude in Colonial America.* Cambridge: Cambridge University Press, 1981.

Galloway, Patrick R. "Annual Variations in Death by Age, Deaths by Cause, Prices, and Weather in London, 1670–1830." *Population Studies* 39 (1985): 487–505.

———. "Basic Patterns in Annual Variations in Fertility, Nuptiality, Mortality, and Prices in Pre-Industrial Europe." *Population Studies* 42 (1988): 275–304.

Gascoigne, George. *The Steel Glass.* London: H. Bynneman, 1576. STC 11645.

Gast, Johann. *Convivialum Sermonum Liber* (The book of convivial sermons). Basel, Switzerland: Westhemerus, 1541.

Gerard, John. *The Herbal or General History of Plants.* London: E. Bollifant, 1597. STC 11750.

Geremek, Bronislaw. *Poverty: A History.* Trans. Agnieszka Kolakowska. Oxford: Blackwell, 1994.

Gilbert, William. *De Magnete.* (Concerning the magnet). 1600 (Latin)/1893 (English). Trans. P. Fleury Mottelay. New York: Dover, 1958.

Gluckman, Max. *Order and Rebellion in Tribal Africa.* London: Cohen and West, 1963.

Goffman, Erving. *Stigma: Notes on the Management of Spoiled Identity.* Englewood Cliffs, N.J.: Prentice-Hall, 1963.

Goodman, Lisa, Leonard Saxe, and Mary Harvey. "Homelessness as Psychological Trauma: Broadening Perspectives." *American Psychologist* 46 (1991): 1219–25.

Gosynhyll, Edward. *The Praise of All Women, Called Mulierum Paean.* London: William Middleton, ca. 1542. STC 12102.

Gouge, William. *Of Domestical Duties.* 1622. London: G. Miller, 1634. STC 12121.

Green, Mark J., and Gail MacColl. *Reagan's Reign of Error.* Rev. ed. New York: Pantheon, 1987.

Greenblatt, Stephen. *Shakespearean Negotiations: The Circulation of Social Energy in Renaissance England.* Berkeley: University of California Press, 1988. 21–65.

———. *Marvelous Possessions: The Wonder of the New World.* Chicago: University of Chicago Press, 1991.

———. *Renaissance Self-Fashioning: From More to Shakespeare.* Chicago: University of Chicago Press, 1980.

Greene, Robert. *The Black Book's Messenger, Cuthbert Conny-Catcher; The Defence of Conny-Catching.* 1592. Edinburgh: Edinburgh University Press, 1966.

———. *A Disputation between a He Cony-Catcher and a She Cony-Catcher.* 1592. In *The Elizabethan Underworld.* Ed. A. V. Judges. 2d ed. New York: Octagon, 1964. 206–47. (1592 edition [London: A. Jeffes]. STC 12234.)

———. *A Notable Discovery of Cozenage.* 1591. In *Rogues, Vagabonds, and Sturdy Beggars:*

A New Gallery of Tudor and Early Stuart Rogue Literature. Ed. Arthur F. Kinney. 2d ed. Amherst: University of Massachusetts Press, 1990. 163–86. (1591 edition [London: John Wolfe], STC 12279.)

———. *A Quip for an Upstart Courtier.* London: John Wolfe, 1592. STC 12300.5.

———. *The Second Part of Cony-Catching.* 1591. In *The Elizabethan Underworld.* Ed. A. V. Judges. 2d ed. New York: Octagon, 1964. 149–80. (1591 edition [London: John Wolfe], STC 12281.)

———. *The Third Part of Cony-Catching.* 1592. In *The Elizabethan Underworld.* Ed. A. V. Judges. 2d ed. New York: Octagon, 1964. 180–205. (1592 edition [London: T. Scarlet], STC 12283.)

Greene, Thomas M. "Ben Jonson and the Centered Self." *Studies in English Literature* 10 (1970): 325–48.

Greenhill, Pauline, Kjerstin Baldwin, Michelle Blais, Angela Brooks, and Kristen Rosbak. "25 Good Reasons Why Beer Is Better Than Women and Other Qualities of the Female: Gender and the Non-Seriousness of Jokes." *Canadian Folklore Canadien* 15 (1993): 51–67.

Groundwork of Cony-Catching. London: N.p., 1592. STC 12789. (The main body of this work is a reprint of Thomas Harman's *A Caveat for Common Cursetors, Vulgarly Called Vagabonds.*)

Hadwin, J. F. "Deflating Philanthropy." *Economic History Review,* 2d ser., 31 (1978): 105–17.

Haigh, Christopher. *English Reformations: Religion, Politics, and Society under the Tudors.* Oxford: Clarendon Press, 1993.

———. *Reformation and Resistance in Tudor Lancashire.* Cambridge: Cambridge University Press, 1975.

Haigh, Christopher, ed. *The English Reformation Revised.* Cambridge: Cambridge University Press, 1987.

Hale, John. *The Civilization of Europe in the Renaissance.* New York: Atheneum, 1994.

Hall, Kim F. *Things of Darkness: Economies of Race and Gender in Early Modern England.* Ithaca, N.Y.: Cornell University Press, 1995.

Halliday, M. A. K. *Language as a Social Semiotic: The Social Interpretation of Language and Meaning.* London: Arnold, 1978.

Halpern, Richard. *The Poetics of Primitive Accumulation: English Renaissance Culture and the Genealogy of Capital.* Ithaca, N.Y.: Cornell University Press, 1991.

Hampson, Ethel Mary. *The Treatment of Poverty in Cambridgeshire, 1597–1834.* Cambridge: Cambridge University Press, 1934.

Hanawalt, Barbara A. *The Ties That Bound: Peasant Families in Medieval England.* New York: Oxford University Press, 1986.

Harington, Sir John. *A New Discourse on a Stale Subject, Called The Metamorphosis of Ajax.* 1596. Ed. Elizabeth Story Donno. New York: Columbia University Press, 1962.

Harman, Thomas. *A Caveat for Common Cursetors, Vulgarly Called Vagabonds.* 1567. In *The Elizabethan Underworld.* Ed. A. V. Judges. 2d ed. [New York: Octagon, 1964], 61–118. (First printed in 1566; 1567 edition [London: W. Griffith], STC 12787; second edition [London: H. Middleton, 1573], STC 12788.)

Harpsfield, Nicholas. *The Life and Death of Sir Thomas More.* Ca. 1575/1932. In *Lives of Saint Thomas More.* Ed. E. E. Reynolds. London: Dent, 1963. 51–175.

Harriot, Thomas. *A Brief and True Report of the New Found Land of Virginia.* London, R. Robinson, 1588.

Harrison, C. J. "Grain Price Analysis and Harvest Qualities, 1465–1634." *Agricultural History Review* 19 (1971): 135–55.

Harrison, William. *The Description of England.* 1587. Ed. Georges Edelen. Ithaca, N.Y.: Cornell University Press, 1968.

Harvey, Barbara F. *Living and Dying in England, 1100–1540: The Monastic Experience.* Oxford: Oxford University Press, 1993.

Harvey, Gabriel. *Four Letters and Certain Sonnets.* London: John Wolfe, 1592. STC 12900.

———. *Gabriel Harvey's Marginalia.* Ed. G. C. Moore Smith. Stratford, England: Shakespeare Head Press, 1913.

———. *Pierce's Supererogation; or, A New Praise of the Old Ass.* London: J. Wolfe, 1593. STC 12903.

———. *Three Proper and Witty Familiar Letters, Lately Passed between Two University Men* [Gabriel Harvey and Edmund Spenser]. London: H. Bynneman, 1580. STC 23095.

Hatcher, John. *Plague, Population, and the English Economy, 1348–1530.* London: Macmillan, 1977.

Hazlitt, William, ed. *Remains of the Early Popular Poetry of England.* 4 vols. London: John Russell Smith, 1864.

Hazlitt, William, ed. *Shakespeare Jest-Books.* 3 vols. London: Willis and Sotheran, 1864.

Heal, Felicity. *Hospitality in Early Modern England.* Oxford: Clarendon Press, 1990.

Helgerson, Richard. *The Elizabethan Prodigals.* Berkeley: University of California Press, 1976.

———. *Forms of Nationhood: The Elizabethan Writing of England.* Chicago: University of Chicago Press, 1992.

Herman, Peter C., ed. *Rethinking the Henrician Era: Essays on Early Tudor Texts and Contexts.* Urbana: University of Illinois Press, 1994.

Herrup, Cynthia. *The Common Peace: Participation and the Criminal Law in Seventeenth-Century England.* Cambridge: Cambridge University Press, 1987.

Heywood, Thomas. *Troia Britanica; or, Great Britain's Troy.* 1609. Hildesheim, Germany: Georg Olms, 1972.

Hexter, J. H. "*Utopia* and Its Historical Milieu." In *The Complete Works of St. Thomas More.* 15 vols. Ed. Edward Surtz and J. H. Hexter. New Haven, Conn.: Yale University Press, 1963–84. 4:xxiii–cxxiv.

Hill, Carl. *The Soul of Wit: Joke Theory from Grimm to Freud.* Lincoln: University of Nebraska Press, 1993.

Hill, Christopher. *The Century of Revolution, 1603–1714.* Edinburgh: Nelson, 1961.

———. *Society and Puritanism in Pre-Revolutionary England.* London: Panther, 1979.

———. *The World Turned Upside Down: Radical Ideas during the English Revolution.* New York: Viking, 1972.

Hobday, Charles. "Clouted Shoon and Leather Aprons: Shakespeare and the Egalitarian Tradition." *Renaissance and Modern Studies* 23 (1979): 63–78.

Hogshire, Jim. *Grossed-out Surgeon Vomits inside Patient: An Insider's Look at Supermarket Tabloids.* Venice, Calif.: Feral House, 1997.

Holmes, Michael. "Gentleman Sirens: Friendship, Roguery, and Uncivil Seduction." Book-length ms., Brock University, n.d.

Hopper, Kim, and Jill Hamberg. *The Making of America's Homeless, from Skid Row to New Poor, 1945–84.* New York: Community Service Society of New York, 1984.

Hoskins, William George. "Harvest Fluctuations and English Economic History, 1480–1619." *Agricultural History Review* 12 (1964): 28–46.

Hughes, Paul L., and James F. Larkin, eds. *Tudor Royal Proclamations.* 3 vols. New Haven, Conn.: Yale University Press, 1964–69.

Hull, Suzanne W. *Chaste, Silent, and Obedient: English Books for Women, 1475–1640.* San Marino, Calif.: Huntington Library, 1982.

A Hundred Merry Tales. London: J. Rastell, 1526. STC 23664. (Reprinted in *Shakespeare Jest-Books,* ed. William Hazlitt, 3 vols. [London: Willis and Sotheran, 1864], 1:11–129.)

Hyperius, Andreas. *The Regiment of Poverty.* Trans. Henry Tripp. London: F. Coldock and H. Bynneman, 1572. STC 11759.

Ignatieff, Michael. *The Needs of Strangers.* London: Chatto and Windus, 1984.

Innes, Joanna. "Prisons for the Poor: English Bridewells, 1555–1800." In *Labour, Law, and Crime: An Historical Perspective.* Ed. Francis Snyder and Douglas Hay. London: Tavistock, 1987. 42–122.

The Institution of a Gentleman. London: T. Marshe, 1555. STC 14104.

Jack of Dover, His Quest of Inquiry; or, His Privy Search for the Veriest Fool in England. London: William White, 1604. STC 14291. (Later called *The Merry Tales of Jack of Dover.*)

James I, King. *The Political Works of James I, Reprinted from the Edition of 1616.* Ed. Charles Howard McIlwain. Cambridge, Mass.: Harvard University Press, 1918.

Jankowski, Theodora A. "Historicizing and Legitimating Capitalism: Thomas Heywood's *Edward IV* and *If You Know Not Me, You Know Nobody.*" In *Medieval and Renaissance Drama in England.* Vol. 7. Ed. Leeds Barroll. London: Associated University Presses, 1995. 305–37.

Jaster, Margaret Rose. "Painted Puppets: Dressing and Undressing Women in Early Modern England." Ms., Pennsylvania State University, n.d.

Johnson, Richard. *Pleasant Conceits of Old Hobson the Merry Londoner.* London: G. Eld, 1607. STC 14688. (Reprinted in *Shakespeare Jest-Books,* ed. William Hazlitt, 3 vols. [London: Willis and Sotheran, 1864], 3:1–52.)

Johnson, Robert C. "The Transportation of Vagrant Children from London to Virginia, 1618–1622." In *Early Stuart Studies: Essays in Honor of David Harris Willson.* Ed. Howard S. Reinmuth Jr. Minneapolis: University of Minnesota Press, 1970. 137–51.

Johnson, Samuel. "Milton." In *Johnson's Lives of the Poets.* Ed. J. P. Hardy. Oxford: Clarendon Press, 1971. 50–113.

Jones, Ann Rosalind. "(In)alienable Possessions: Griselda, Clothing and the Exchange of Women." In *Renaissance Clothing and the Materials of Memory,* by Ann Rosalind Jones and Peter Stallybrass. Cambridge: Cambridge University Press, forthcoming.

Jonson, Ben. *Ben Jonson.* Ed. C. H. Herford, Percy Simpson, and Evelyn Simpson. 11 vols. Oxford: Clarendon Press, 1925–52.

—*The Alchemist.* First acted in 1610. 5 (1937): 289–407.

—*Bartholomew Fair.* First acted in 1614. 6 (1938): 11–140.

—*The Case Is Altered.* First acted in 1597. 3 (1927): 93–190.

—*Epicoene.* First acted in 1609. 5 (1937): 161–272.

—"Inviting a Friend to Supper." ca. 1616. 4 (1932): 64–66.

—*The Masque of the Fortunate Isles.* First acted in 1624. 7 (1941): 701–29.

—*The Poetaster.* First acted in 1601. 4 (1932): 185–317.

—"To Penshurst." ca. 1616. 4 (1932): 93–96.

—*Sejanus.* First acted in 1603. 4 (1932): 327–485.

—"To William Roe." ca. 1616. 4 (1932): 80–81.

—*Volpone.* First acted in 1606. 5 (1937):15–136.

Jordan, W. K. *The Charities of London, 1480–1660: The Aspirations and the Achievements of the Urban Society.* New York: Russell Sage, 1960.

————. *Philanthropy in England, 1480–1660: A Study of the Changing Pattern of English Social Aspirations.* New York: Russell Sage, 1959.

Judges, A. V., ed. *The Elizabethan Underworld.* 2d ed. New York: Octagon, 1964.

Jusserand, Jean Adrien Antoine Jules. *The Wayfaring Life in the Middle Ages.* Trans. Lucy Toulmin Smith. 2d ed. London: T. F. Unwin, 1920.

Jütte, Robert. *Poverty and Deviance in Early Modern Europe.* Cambridge: Cambridge University Press, 1994.

Kahrl, Stanley J. "The Medieval Origins of the Sixteenth-Century English Jest-Books." *Studies in the Renaissance* 13 (1966): 166–85.

Kelly, J. Thomas. *Thorns on the Tudor Rose: Monks, Rogues, Vagabonds, and Sturdy Beggars.* Jackson: University Press of Mississippi, 1977.

Kelly [Kelly-Gadol], Joan. "Did Women Have a Renaissance?" In *Becoming Visible: Women in European History.* Ed. Renate Bridenthal and Claudia Koonz. Boston: Houghton Mifflin, 1977. 137–64.

Kempton, Murray. "The Shadow Saint." *New York Review of Books,* July 11, 1996, 4–5.

Kermode, Jennifer, and Garthine Walker, eds. *Women, Crime, and the Courts in Early Modern England.* Chapel Hill: University of North Carolina Press, 1994.

Kerridge, Eric. *The Common Fields of England.* Manchester: Manchester University Press, 1992.

Kinney, Arthur F., ed. *Rogues, Vagabonds, and Sturdy Beggars: A New Gallery of Tudor and Early Stuart Rogue Literature.* 2d ed. Amherst: University of Massachusetts Press, 1990.

Knapp, Jeffrey. "Rogue Nationalism." In *Centuries' Ends, Narrative Means.* Ed. Robert Newman. Stanford, Calif.: Stanford University Press, 1996. 138–50.

Knoppers, Laura Lunger. "(En)gendering Shame: *Measure for Measure* and the Spectacles of Power." *English Literary Renaissance* 23 (1993): 450–71.

Knowles, David. *The Religious Orders in England.* Vol. 3: *The Tudor Age.* Cambridge: Cambridge University Press, 1959.

Koch, Mark. "The Desanctification of the Beggar in Rogue Pamphlets of the English Renaissance." In *The Work of Dissimilitude: Essays from the Sixth Conference on Medieval and Renaissance Literature.* Ed. David G. Allen and Rovert A. White. Newark: University of Delaware Press; London: Associated University Presses, 1992. 91–104.

————. "The Economy of Beggary in English Literature from the Reformation to the Enlightenment." Ph.D. dissertation, State University of New York at Buffalo, 1987.

Krieder, Alan. *English Chantries: The Road to Dissolution.* Cambridge, Mass.: Harvard University Press, 1979.

Kronenfeld, Judy. "'So Distribution Should Undo Excess, and Each Man Have Enough':

Shakespeare's *King Lear*—Anabaptist Egalitarianism, Anglican Charity, Both, Neither?" *English Literary History* 59 (1992): 755–84.

Kuhn, Thomas. *The Structure of Scientific Revolutions.* 2d ed. Chicago: University of Chicago Press, 1970.

Kupperman, Karen. *Settling with the Indians: The Meeting of English and Indian Cultures in America, 1580–1640.* Totowa, N.J.: Rowman and Littlefield, 1980.

Lalebuch. 1597. New Haven: Connecticut Research Publications, 1970. (Microfilm.)

Lambard, W. *Eirenarcha; or, Of the Office of Justices of the Peace.* London: Ralph Newbery and Henry Bynneman, 1581. STC 15163.

Langbein, John H. *Prosecuting Crime in the Renaissance.* Cambridge, Mass.: Harvard University Press, 1974.

Laslett, Peter. *The World We Have Lost.* New York: Scribner, 1965.

Lauter, Paul, ed. *Theories of Comedy.* New York: Doubleday, 1964.

Lawson, Peter. "Property Crime and Hard Times in England, 1559–1624." *Law and History Review* 4 (1986): 95–127.

Lazonick, William. "Karl Marx and Enclosures in England." *Review of Radical Political Economics* 6 (1974): 1–59.

Leonard, E. M. *The Early History of English Poor Relief.* Cambridge: Cambridge University Press, 1900.

Lewis, C. S. *English Literature in the Sixteenth Century, Excluding Drama.* Oxford: Clarendon Press, 1954.

Lewis, Wyndham. "Studies in the Art of Laughter." *London Mercury* 30 (1934): 509–15.

Lewkenor, Samuel. *A Discourse . . . for Such as Are Desirous to Know the Situation and Customs of Foreign Cities without Travelling to See Them.* London: John Windet, 1600. STC 15566.

Liber Vagatorum (see *The Book of Vagabonds and Beggars*)

Liebler, Naomi. *Shakespeare's Festive Tragedy: The Ritual Foundations of Tragedy.* London: Routledge, 1995.

Life of Lazarillo de Tormes, The. 1553. Trans. Sir Clements Markham. London: A. and C. Black, 1908.

Life of Long Meg of Westminster, The. London: F. R. Bird, 1636. STC 17783.3.

Lipking, Joanna. "Traditions of the 'Facetiae' and Their Influence in Tudor England." Ph.D. dissertation, Columbia University, 1970.

Lis, Catharina, and Hugo Soly. *Poverty and Capitalism in Pre-Industrial Europe.* Trans. James Coonan. Atlantic Highlands, N.J.: Humanities Press, 1979.

A Little Jest How the Plowman Learned His Paternoster. Ca. 1510. In *Remains of the Early Popular Poetry of England.* Ed. William Hazlitt. 4 vols. London: John Russell Smith, 1864. 1:209–16. (Ca. 1510 edition [London: Wynkyn de Worde], STC 20034.)

A Little Proper Jest Called Christ Cross Me Speed. ABC. How That Good Gossips Made a Royal Feast. London: Wynkyn de Worde, 1534[?]. STC 14546.5.

Lloyd, Peter Cutt. *Slums of Hope? Shanty Towns of the Third World.* Manchester: Manchester University Press, 1979.

Lubarsky, Ruth Samson. "Telling a Book by Its Cover; or, How Harman Masquerades as Greene." *American Notes and Queries* 5 (1992): 100–102.

Lupton, Donald. *London and the Country Carbonadoed and Quartred into Several Characters.* London: Nicholas Okes, 1604. STC 16944.

Luscinius (*see* Nachtgall [or Nachtigall], Otmar)

Luther, Martin. "Exposition of Psalm 127." 1524. Trans. Charles M. Jacobs. Rev. ed. Walther I. Brandt. In *Works.* Ed. Jaroslav Pelikan and Helmut T. Lehmann. 55 vols. St. Louis: Concordia Press; Philadelphia: Fortress Press, 1955–86. 45:311–37.

———. "Ordinance of a Common Chest, Preface." 1523. Trans. Albert T. W. Steinhaeuser. Rev. ed. Walther I. Brandt. In *Works.* Ed. Jaroslav Pelikan and Helmut T. Lehmann. 55 vols. St. Louis: Concordia Press; Philadelphia: Fortress Press, 1955–86. 45:169–76.

———. "To the Christian Nobility of the German Nation Concerning the Reform of the Christian Estate." 1520. Trans. Charles M. Jacobs. Rev. ed. James Atkinson. In *Works.* Ed. Jaroslav Pelikan and Helmut T. Lehmann. 55 vols. St. Louis: Concordia Press; Philadelphia: Fortress Press, 1955–86. 44:123–217.

———. "Trade and Usury." 1524. Trans. Charles M. Jacobs. Rev. ed. Walther I. Brandt. In *Works.* Ed. Jaroslav Pelikan and Helmut T. Lehmann. 55 vols. St. Louis: Concordia Press; Philadelphia: Fortress Press, 1955–86. 45:245–310.

———. "Treatise on Good Works." 1520. Trans. W. A. Lambert. Rev. ed. James Atkinson. In *Works.* Ed. Jaroslav Pelikan and Helmut T. Lehmann. 55 vols. St. Louis: Concordia Press; Philadelphia: Fortress Press, 1955–86. 44:21–114.

Lüthi, Max. *The Fairytale as Art Form and Portrait of Man.* 1975. Trans. Jon Erickson. Bloomington: Indiana University Press, 1984.

Macfarlane, Alan. *Marriage and Love in England, 1300–1840.* Oxford: Basil Blackwell, 1986.

———. "A Tudor Anthropologist: George Gifford's *Discourse* and *Dialogue.*" In *The Damned Art: Essays in the Literature of Witchcraft.* Ed. Sydney Anglo. London: Henley; Boston: Routledge and Kegan Paul, 1977. 140–55.

Macfarlane, Alan, and Sarah Harris. *The Justice and the Mare's Ale: Law and Disorder in Seventeenth-Century England.* Oxford: Basil Blackwell, 1981.

Machiavelli, Niccolò. *The Prince.* 1513. Ed. and Trans. Robert M. Adams. New York: Norton, 1977.

Mann, Jill. *Chaucer and Medieval Estates Satire: The Literature of Social Classes and the General Prologue to "The Canterbury Tales."* Cambridge: Cambridge University Press, 1973.

Manning, Roger B. *Village Revolts: Social Protest and Popular Disturbances in England, 1509–1640.* Oxford: Oxford University Press, 1988.

Marc'hadour, Germain. "Introduction" to Sir Thomas More's *Supplication of Souls.* In *The Complete Works of Saint Thomas More,* vol. 7. Ed. Frank Manly, Germain Marc'hadour, Richard Marius, and Clarence H. Miller. New Haven, Conn.: Yale University Press, 1990. lxv–cxvii.

Markels, Julian. "Shakespeare's Materialism in *King Lear.*" *Rethinking Marxism* 4 (1991): 100–108.

Markham, Gervase. *The English Housewife.* 1615. Ed. Michael R. Best. Montreal: McGill-Queen's University Press, 1986.

Marlowe, Christopher. *Doctor Faustus.* First acted in 1592. In *The Complete Works of Christopher Marlow.* Ed. Fredson Bowers. Cambridge: Cambridge University Press, 1973. 121–272.

Marprelate, Martin (pseud. for John Lyly?). *A Whip for an Ape; or, Martin Displayed.* London, 1589. STC 17464.

Martin, John E. *Feudalism to Capitalism: Peasant and Landlord in English Agrarian Development.* Atlantic Highlands, N.J.: Humanities Press, 1983.

Marx, Karl. *Capital: A Critique of Political Economy.* Ed. Frederick Engles. Rev. ed. Ernest Untermann. Trans. Samuel Moore and Edward Aveling. New York: Modern Library, 1936.

Masters, Anthony. *Bedlam.* London: Michael Joseph, 1977.

Matza, David. "Poverty and Disrepute." In *Contemporary Social Problems.* Ed. R. K. Merton and R. A. Nisbet. 2d ed. New York: Harcourt, Brace, and World, 1966. 601–55.

Mauss, Marcel. 1925 (in French). *The Gift: The Form and Reason for Exchange in Archaic Societies.* Trans. W. D. Halls. London: Routledge, 1990.

McEachern, Claire. *The Poetics of English Nationhood, 1590–1612.* Cambridge: Cambridge University Press, 1996.

McFarlane, K. B. *England in the Fifteenth Century: Collected Essays.* London: Hambledon, 1981.

McKee, Elsie Anne. *John Calvin on the Diaconate and Liturgical Almsgiving.* Geneva: Librarie Droz, 1984.

McIntosh, Marjorie K. "Local Responses to the Poor in Late Medieval and Tudor England." *Continuity and Change* 3 (1988): 209–45.

McMullan, John L. *The Canting Crew: London's Criminal Underworld, 1550–1700.* New Brunswick, N.J.: Rutgers University Press, 1984.

———. "Criminal Organization in Sixteenth- and Seventeenth-Century London." *Social Problems* 29 (1982): 311–23.

Mensa Philosophica (The philosophical mind). Cologne: Johannes Guldenshaaf, 1475.

Merbury, Francis. *The Marriage between Wit and Wisdom.* First acted in 1579. Ed. Trevor N. S. Lennam. Oxford: Oxford University Press, 1971.

A Merry Jest of an Old Fool with a Young Wife. London: P. Treveris, ca. 1530. STC 14520.5.

A Merry Jest of a Shrewd and Curst Wife Lapped in Morel's Skin. Ca. 1525. London: H. Jackson, ca. 1580. STC 14521. (Ca. 1530 fragment, STC 14520.5.)

A Merry Jest of Dane Hew, Monk of Leicester, and How He Was Four Times Slain and Once Hanged. 1560[?]. In *Remains of the Early Popular Poetry of England.* Ed. William Hazlitt. 4 vols. London: John Russell Smith, 1864. 3:130–46. (Probably first printed in the 1520s; 1560[?] edition [London: Allde], STC 13257.)

A Merry Jest of the Friar and the Boy. Ca. 1510–13. In *Remains of the Early Popular Poetry of England.* Ed. William Hazlitt. 4 vols. London: John Russell Smith, 1864. 3:54–81. (Ca. 1510–13 edition [London: Wynkyn de Worde], STC 14522.)

A Merry Jest of the Milner of Abington. Ca. 1532–34. In *Remains of the Early Popular Poetry of England.* Ed. William Hazlitt. 4 vols. London: John Russell Smith, 1864. 3:98–118. (Ca. 1532–34 edition [London: Wynkyn de Worde], STC 78.)

Middleton, Thomas. *A Chaste Maid in Cheapside.* First acted in 1613. Ed. R. B. Parker. London: Methuen, 1969.

Middleton, Thomas, and Thomas Dekker. *The Roaring Girl.* First acted in 1608. Ed. Andor Gomme. London: Ernest Benn, 1976.

Mikalachki, Jodi. "Gender, Cant, and Cross-Talking in *The Roaring Girl.*" *Renaissance Drama* 25 (1994): 119–43.

———. *The Legacy of Boadicea: Gender and Nation in Early Modern England.* London: Routledge, 1998.

———. "Women's Networks and the Female Vagrant: A Hard Case." In *Maids and Mistresses, Cousins and Queens: Women's Alliances in Early Modern England.* Ed. Susan Frye and Karen Robertson. New York: Oxford University Press, 1999. 52–69.

Mirandola, Pico della. *Oration on the Dignity of Man.* 1487. Trans. Charles Glenn Wallis. Indianapolis: Bobbs-Merrill, 1965.

Mitchison, Rosalind. "The Making of the Old Scottish Poor Law." *Past and Present* 63 (1974): 58–93.

Mollat, Michel. *The Poor in the Middle Ages: An Essay in Social History.* 1978. Trans. Arthur Goldhammer. New Haven, Conn.: Yale University Press, 1986.

More, Sir Thomas. *Confutation of Tyndale's Answer.* In *Complete Works of Saint Thomas More,* vol. 8. Ed. Louis A. Schuster, Richard C. Marius, James P. Lusardi, and Richard J. Schoeck. New Haven, Conn.: Yale University Press, 1973. Parts 1–3.

———. *A Dialogue Concerning Heresies.* 1529. In *The Complete Works of Saint Thomas More,* vol. 6. Ed. Thomas M. C. Lawler, Germain Marc'hadour, and Richard C. Marius. New Haven, Conn.: Yale University Press, 1981. Part 1.

———. *A Dialogue of the Veneration and Worship of Images.* London: William Rastell, 1630. STL 18085.

———. *Latin Epigrams.* 1518. Trans. Leicester Bradner and Charles A. Lynch. Chicago: University of Chicago Press, 1953.

———. Letter to Peter Giles. In *Utopia.* 1516. Ed. and trans. Robert M. Adams. 2d ed. New York: Norton, 1992. 109–12.

———. *A Merry Jest How a Sergeant Would Learn to Be a Friar.* London: Julian Notary, ca. 1516. STC 18091.

———. *Responsio ad Lutherum* (Response to Luther). 1523. In *The Complete Works of Saint Thomas More,* vol. 5 (pt. 1). Ed. John M. Headley. Trans. Sr. Scholastica Mandeville. New Haven, Conn.: Yale University Press, 1969. 1–713.

———. *Supplication of Souls.* 1529. In *The Complete Works of Saint Thomas More,* vol. 7. Ed. Frank Manly, Germain Marc'hadour, Richard Marius, and Clarence H. Miller. New Haven, Conn.: Yale University Press, 1990. 107–228.

———. *Utopia.* 1516. Ed. and trans. Robert M. Adams. 2d ed. New York: Norton, 1992. (Occasional reference is made to the 1551 translation by Ralph Robinson [London: A. Vele], STC 18094.)

Moretti, Franco. "'A Huge Eclipse': Tragic Form and the Deconsecration of Sovereignty." Trans. D. A. Miller. In *The Power of Forms in the English Renaissance.* Ed. Stephen Greenblatt. Norman, Okla.: Pilgrim Books, 1982. 7–40.

[Morison, Richard] *A Remedy for Sedition.* London: Thomas Berthelet, 1536. STC 20877.

Moulton, Ian. *Before Pornography: Erotic Writing in Early Modern England.* New York: Oxford University Press, 2000.

Mowat, Barbara. "Rogues, Shepherds, and the Counterfeit Distressed: Texts and Infracontexts of *The Winter's Tale* 4.3." *Shakespeare Studies* 22 (1994): 58–76.

Mugglestone, Lynda. *"Talking Proper": The Rise of Accent as Social Symbol.* Oxford: Clarendon Press, 1995.

Mueller, Janel. "'The Whole Island Like a Single Family': Positioning Women in Utopian Patriarchy." In *Rethinking the Henrician Era: Essays on Early Tudor Texts and Contexts.* Ed. Peter C. Herman. Urbana: University of Illinois Press, 1994. 93–122.

Mullett, Charles. *The Bubonic Plague and England: An Essay in the History of Preventive Medicine.* Lexington: University Press of Kentucky, 1956.

Munda, Constantia (pseud.). *The Worming of a Mad Dog; or, A Sop for Cerberus the Jailor of Hell.* London: George Purslowe, 1617. STC 18257.

Munday, Anthony. *The Triumphs of Re-united Britania,* 1605. In *Pageants and Entertainments of Anthony Munday.* Ed. David Bergeron. New York: Garland, 1985. 1–23.

Nachtgall (or Nachtgall), Otmar (called Luscinius). *Ioci ac Sales Mire Festivi* (Wonderfully witty jokes and quips). 1524. Strasburg: N.p., 1529.

Nashe, Thomas. *Summer's Last Will and Testament.* 1600. In *The Unfortunate Traveller and Other Works.* Ed. J. B. Steane. London: Penguin, 1972. 146–207.

———. *The Unfortunate Traveller.* 1593. In *The Unfortunate Traveller and Other Works.* Ed. J. B. Steane. London: Penguin, 1972. 251–370.

Nelson, William. *John Skelton, Laureate.* New York: Columbia University Press, 1939.

Oberman, Heiko Augustinus. *Luther: Man between God and the Devil.* Trans. Eileen Walliser-Schwartzbart. New Haven, Conn.: Yale University Press, 1989.

O'Donoghue, Edward G. *Bridewell Hospital: Palace, Prison, Schools from the Death of Elizabeth to Modern Times.* London: Bodley Head, 1923.

Olson, Elder. "An Outline of Poetic Theory." 1949. In *Critics and Criticism: Ancient and Modern.* Ed. R. S. Crane. Chicago: University of Chicago Press, 1952. 546–66.

Oreskes, M. "Poverty Is Perceived as Increasing and State of the Poor Is Unimproved." *New York Times,* August 23, 1989, A11.

Orgel, Stephen. *Impersonations: The Performance of Gender in Shakespeare's England.* Cambridge: Cambridge University Press, 1996.

Oring, Elliott. *Jokes and Their Relations.* Lexington: University Press of Kentucky, 1992.

Orlin, Lena Cowen. "Boundary Disputes in Early Modern London." In *Material London, ca. 1600.* Ed. Lena Cowen Orlin. Philadelphia: University of Pennsylvania Press, 2000. 344–76.

———. "Chronicles of Private Life." In *Cambridge Companion to English Literature, 1500–1600.* Ed. Arthur F. Kinney. Cambridge: Cambridge University Press. 2000. 241–64.

———. *Elizabethan Households: An Anthology.* Washington, D.C.: Folger Shakespeare Library, 1995.

———. *Private Matters and Public Culture in Post-Reformation England.* Ithaca, N.Y.: Cornell University Press, 1994.

Ornstein, Robert. "Shakespearian and Jonsonian Comedy." *Shakespeare Survey* 22 (1969): 43–46.

Outhwaite, R. B. "Dearth and Government Intervention in English Grain Markets, 1590–1700." *Economic History Review* 34 (1981): 389–406.

———. *Dearth, Public Policy, and Social Disturbance in England, 1550–1800.* Cambridge: Cambridge University Press, 1991.

———. "Dearth, the English Crown, and the 'Crisis of the 1590s'." In *The European Cri-*

sis of the 1590s: Essays in Comparative History. Ed. Peter Clark. London: Allen and Unwin, 1985. 23–43.

———. "Food Crises in Early Modern England: Patterns of Public Response." In *Proceedings of the Seventh International Economic History Congress.* Ed. Michael W. Flinn. Edinburgh: Edinburgh University Press, 1978. 367–74.

Oxley, Geoffrey W. *Poor Relief in England and Wales, 1601–1834.* Newton Abbot, England: David and Charles, 1974.

Palliser, David M. *The Age of Elizabeth: England under the Later Tudors, 1547–1603.* London: Longman, 1983.

Palmenfelt, Ulf. "Stereotypical Characters in Erotic Jokes." In *Storytelling in Contemporary Societies.* Ed. Lutz Röhrich and Sabine Wienker-Piepho. Tübingen: Narr, 1990. 147–53.

Palmer, Daryl W. *Hospitable Performances: Dramatic Genre and Cultural Practices in Early Modern England.* Lafayette, Ind.: Purdue University Press, 1992.

Panormita (*see* Beccadelli, Antonio)

Parker, Patricia. *Shakespeare from the Margins: Language, Culture, Context.* Chicago: University of Chicago Press, 1996.

The Parson of Kalenborowe [or *Kalenberger*]. Antwerp: Jan van Doesborch, 1520. STC 14894.5.

Pasquil (W. Fennor?). *Pasquil's Jests: Mixed with Mother Bunch's Merriments.* London: John Windet, 1609. STC 19451.5.

Paster, Gail Kern. "Leaky Vessels: The Incontinent Women of City Comedy." *Renaissance Drama,* n.s., 18 (1987): 43–65.

Patterson, Annabel. *Reading Holinshed's Chronicles.* Chicago: University of Chicago Press, 1994.

———. *Shakespeare and the Popular Voice.* Oxford: Basil Blackwell, 1989.

Peacham, Henry. *The Complete Gentleman.* 1634. Ed. Virgil B. Heltzel. Ithaca, N.Y.: Cornell University Press, 1962.

Pearl, Valerie. "Change and Stability in Seventeenth-Century London." *London Journal* 5 (1979): 3–34.

Peele, George. *Merry Conceited Jests of George Peele.* London: Nicholas Okes, 1605. STC 19541.

———. *Old Wives Tale.* First acted in 1590. Ed. Patricia Binnie. Baltimore: Johns Hopkins University Press, 1980.

Pelling, Margaret. "Healing the Sick Poor: Social Policy and Disability in Norwich, 1550–1640." *Medical History* 29 (1985): 115–37.

———. "Illness among the Poor in an Early Modern Town: The Norwich Census of 1570." *Continuity and Change* 3 (1988): 273–90.

Pendry, E. D. *Elizabethan Prisons and Prison Scenes.* 2 vols. Salzburg: Institut für Englische Sprache und Literatur, 1974.

Petrarca, Francesco (Petrarch). *Rerum Memorandarum Libri* (The book of memorable things). Ca. 1343–45. Ed. Giuseppe Billanovich. Florence: Sanxoni, 1943.

Piccolomini (Aeneas Sylvius). *Antonii Panormitae de Dictis et Factis Alphonsi Regis Aragonum Libri Quattuor: Commentarium* (Antonio Panormita's *Concerning the words and deeds of Alphonsus, king of Aragon.* Book 4: *Commentary*). Basel, Switzerland: Ex Officina Herviagiana, 1938.

Poggio Bracciolini, Giovanni Francesco. *The Facetiae.* 1470. Trans. Bernhardt J. Hurwood. New York: Award Books, 1968.

Pontano, Giovanni. *De Sermone Libri Sex* (Six books concerning speech). 1518–19. Ed. S. Lupi and A. Risicato. Lugano, Switzerland: Thesaurus Mundi, 1954.

Pories, Kathleen. "The Intersection of Poor Laws and Literature in the Sixteenth Century: Fictional and Factual Categories." In *Framing Elizabethan Fictions: Contemporary Approaches to Early Modern Narrative Prose.* Ed. Constance C. Relihan. Kent, Ohio: Kent State University Press, 1996. 17–40.

Porter, Roy. "Preface." In Piero Camporesi, *Bread of Dreams: Food and Fantasy in Early Modern Europe.* Trans. David Gentilcore. Chicago: University of Chicago Press, 1989. 1–16.

Portman, Derek. "Vernacular Building in the Oxford Region in the Sixteenth and Seventeenth Centuries." In *Rural Change and Urban Growth, 1500–1800.* Ed. C. W. Chalklin and M. A. Havinden. London: Longman, 1974. 135–68.

Pound, John F. "An Elizabethan Census of the Poor: The Treatment of Vagrancy in Norwich, 1570–80." *University of Birmingham Historical Journal* 8 (1962): 135–61.

———. *Poverty and Vagrancy in Tudor England.* London: Longman, 1971.

Pound, John F., ed. *The Norwich Census of the Poor, 1570.* Norfolk, England: Norfolk Record Society, 1971.

Pratt, Alan R., ed. *Black Humor: Critical Essays.* New York: Garland, 1993.

Pullan, Brian. "The Famine in Venice and the New Poor Law, 1527–29." *Bollettino dell'Istituto di Storia della Società e dello Stato Veneziano* 5–6 (1963–64): 159–68.

———. *Rich and Poor in Renaissance Venice: The Social Institutions of a Catholic State to 1620.* Oxford: Basil Blackwell, 1971.

Puttenham, George. *The Art of English Poesie.* 1589. Ed. Gladys Doidge Willcock and Alice Walker. Folcroft, Pa.: Folcroft Press, 1936.

Quintilianus, Marcus Fabius. *Quintilian's Institutes of Oratory.* Trans. John Selby Watson. 2 vols. London: George Bell, 1891.

Ramsey, Peter. *Tudor Economic Problems.* London: Gollancz, 1963.

Rappaport, Steve. *Worlds within Worlds: Structures of Life in Sixteenth-Century London.* Cambridge: Cambridge University Press, 1989.

Rasmussen, Steen Eiler. *London: The Unique City.* 1934. Cambridge, Mass.: M.I.T. Press, 1982.

Rastell, John[?]. *The Nature of the Four Elements.* First acted in ca. 1517–18. In *A Select Collection of Old English Plays, Originally Published by Robert Dodsley in the Year 1744.* Ed. W. Carew Hazlitt. London: Benjamin Blom, 1874–76. 5–50.

Reinold, Lucinda Kate. "The Representation of the Beggar as Rogue in Dutch Seventeenth-Century Art." Ph.D. dissertation, University of California at Berkeley, 1981.

Reyes, Lilia M., and Laura DeKoven Waxman. *A Status Report on Hunger and Homelessness in America's Cities: 1989.* Washington, D.C.: United States Conference of Mayors, 1989.

Reynolds, E. E., ed. *Lives of Saint Thomas More.* London: Dent, 1963.

Ribton-Turner, C. J. *A History of Vagrants and Vagrancy and Beggars and Begging.* London: Chapman and Hall, 1887.

Rid, Samuel. *Martin Markall, Beadle of Bridewell.* 1610. In *The Elizabethan Underworld.*

Ed. A. V. Judges. 2d ed. New York: Octagon, 1964. 383–422. (1610 edition [London: All-de], STC 21028.5.)

Ritson, Joseph. *Pieces of Ancient Popular Poetry.* London: C. Clark, 1791.

R.M. *Micrologia: Characters, or Essays, of Persons, Trades, and Places, Offered to the City and Country.* London: T. Cotes, 1629. STC 17146.

Roberts, Peter. "Elizabethan Players and Minstrels and the Legislation of 1572 against Retainers and Vagabonds." In *Religion, Culture, and Society in Early Modern Britain: Essays in Honour of Patrick Collinson.* Ed. Anthony Fletcher and Peter Roberts. Cambridge: Cambridge University Press, 1994. 29–55.

Roberts, Steven V. "Reagan on Homelessness: Some Choose to Live in the Streets." *New York Times,* December 23, 1988, A1.

Röhrich, Lutz. *Folktales and Reality.* Trans. Peter Tokofsky. Bloomington: Indiana University Press, 1991.

Roleff, Tamara, ed. *The Homeless: Opposing Viewpoints.* San Diego: Greenhaven Press, 1996.

Roper, William. *The Life of Sir Thomas More, Knight.* 1626. In *Lives of Saint Thomas More.* Ed. E. E. Reynolds. London: Dent, 1963. 1–50. (Written before 1578.)

Rose, Mary Beth. *The Expense of Spirit: Love and Sexuality in English Renaissance Drama.* Chicago: University of Chicago Press, 1988.

Rossi, Peter Henry. *Down and Out in America: The Origins of Homelessness.* Chicago: University of Chicago Press, 1989.

Routh, Harold V. "The Progress of Social Literature in Tudor Times." In *Cambridge History of English Literature.* Ed. A. W. Ward and A. R. Waller. 15 vols. Cambridge: Cambridge University Press, 1909. 3:93–129.

Rusche, Georg, and Otto Kirchheimer. *Punishment and Social Structure.* 1939. New York: Russell and Russell, 1968.

Rybczynski, Witold. *Home: A Short History of an Idea.* New York: Viking, 1986.

A Sackful of News. London: Andrew Clark, 1673. Wing STC 223. (Earlier edition ca. 1557 has been lost.)

Sackville-West, Vita. *Knole and the Sackvilles.* London: Heinemann, 1922.

Sālgado, Gāmini, ed. *Cony-Catchers and Bawdy Baskets.* Harmondsworth, England: Penguin, 1972.

Salomon and Marcolphus. Ca. 1482 (see *The Dialogue*)

Saunders, J. W. "From Manuscript to Print: A Note on the Circulation of Poetic MSS. in the Sixteenth Century." *Proceedings of the Leeds Philosophical and Literary Society* 6 (1951): 507–28.

———. "The Stigma of Print: A Note on the Social Bases of Tudor Poetry." *Essays in Criticism* 1 (1951): 139–64.

Saville, John. "Primitive Accumulation and Early Industrialization in Britain." *Socialist Register* (1969): 247–71.

Schochet, Gordon J. *Patriarchalism in Political Thought: The Authoritarian Family and Political Speculation and Attitudes Especially in Seventeenth-Century England.* Oxford: Basil Blackwell, 1975.

Schoenbaum, Samuel. *William Shakespeare: A Documentary Life.* New York: Oxford University Press, 1975.

Schofield, John. *The Building of London from the Conquest to the Great Fire.* London: British Museum, 1984.

Schofield, Roger S. "The Impact of Scarcity and Plenty on Population Change in England, 1541–1871." In *Hunger and History.* Ed. Robert I. Rotberg and Theodore K. Rabb. Cambridge: Cambridge University Press, 1985. 67–93.

Schulz, Ernst. *Die englishchen Schwankbücher bis herab zu "Dobson's Drie Bobs"* (The English jestbooks down to "Dobson's dry bobs"). Palaestra, no. 117. Berlin: Mayer and Müller, 1912.

Schuster, Louis A. "Thomas More's Polemical Career, 1523–33." In *Complete Works of Saint Thomas More,* vol. 8 (pt. 3). Ed. Louis A. Schuster, Richard C. Marius, James P. Luscardi, and Richard J. Schoeck. New Haven, Conn.: Yale University Press, 1973. 1123–268.

Scoggin, John [sometimes attributed to Andrew Borde]. *The Jests of Scoggin.* 1565–66. In *Shakespeare Jest-Books.* Ed. William Hazlitt. 3 vols. London: Willis and Sotheran, 1864. 2:38–161. (First printed ca. 1547 or earlier; 1565–66 edition [London: T. Colwell], STC 21850.3.; 1613 edition [London: R. Blower], STC 21851.)

Scott, James C. *Weapons of the Weak: Everyday Forms of Peasant Resistance.* New Haven, Conn.: Yale University Press, 1985.

Scott, Michael. "Certain Conceits and Jests." 1609. In *Shakespeare Jest-Books.* Ed. William Hazlitt. 3 vols. London: Willis and Sotheran, 1864. 3:1–18. (1609 edition in *The Philosopher's Banquet, Furnished with Few Dishes for Health, but Large Discourse for Pleasure* [London: Nicholas Okes], STC 22061.5.)

Scribner, R. W. *For the Sake of Simple Folk: Popular Propaganda of the German Reformation.* Cambridge: Cambridge University Press, 1981.

Selden, Raman. "*King Lear* and True Need." *Shakespeare Studies* 19 (1987): 143–69.

Shakespeare, William. *Complete Works.* Ed. David Bevington. 4th ed. Glenview, Ill.: Scott, Foresman, 1992.

Sharp, Buchanan. *In Contempt of All Authority: Rural Artisans and Riot in the West of England, 1586–1660.* Berkeley: University of California Press, 1980.

Sharpe, J. A. *Crime in Early Modern England, 1550–1750.* 2d ed. London: Longman, 1999.

———. "The History of Crime in Late Medieval and Early Modern England: A Review of the Field." *Social History* 7 (1982): 187–203.

Sherry, Richard. *A Treatise on Schemes and Tropes.* London: John Day, 1550. STC 22428.

Shuger, Deborah Kuller. *Habits of Thought in the English Renaissance: Religion, Politics, and the Dominant Culture.* Berkeley: University of California Press, 1990.

Siegel, Paul. *Shakespearean Tragedy and the Elizabethan Compromise.* New York: New York University Press, 1957.

[Skelton, John]. *Merry Tales Newly Imprinted and Made by Master Skelton, Poet Laureate.* 1567. In *Shakespeare Jest-Books.* Ed. William Hazlitt. 3 vols. London: Willis and Sotheran, 1864. 2:2–36. (First printed before 1529[?]; 1567 edition [London: Thomas Colwell], STC 22618.)

Skipp, Victor. *Crisis and Development: An Ecological Case Study of the Forest of Arden, 1570–1674.* Cambridge: Cambridge University Press, 1978.

Slack, Paul. "Dearth and Social Policy in Early Modern England." *Social History of Medicine* 5 (1992): 1–17.

———. *The English Poor Law, 1531–1782.* Cambridge: Cambridge University Press, 1990.

———. *The Impact of Plague in Tudor and Stuart England*. London: Routledge and Kegan Paul, 1985.

———. "Mortality Crises and Epidemic Disease in England, 1485–1610." In *Health, Medicine, and Mortality in the Sixteenth Century*. Ed. C. Webster. Cambridge: Cambridge University Press, 1979. 9–59.

———. *Poverty and Policy in Tudor and Stuart England*. London: Longman, 1988.

———. "Vagrants and Vagrancy in England, 1598–1664." *Economic History Review*, 2d ser., 27 (1974): 360–79.

Smith, A. E. *Colonists in Bondage: White Servitude and Convict Labor in America, 1607–1776*. Chapel Hill: University of North Carolina Press, 1947.

Smith, Bruce. *Homosexual Desire in Renaissance England: A Cultural Poetics*. Chicago: University of Chicago Press, 1991.

Smith, E. "Disenfranchisement of Homeless Persons." *Journal of Urban and Contemporary Law* 31 (1987): 225–39.

Smith, Henry. *The Sermons of Mr. Henry Smith*. London: Thomas Orwin, 1592. STC 22718.

Smith, Walter. *The Twelve Merry Jests of the Widow Edith*. 1573. In *Shakespeare Jest-Books*. Ed. William Hazlitt. 3 vols. London: Willis and Sotheran, 1864. 3:27–108. (First published in 1525 as *The Widow Edith: Twelve Merry Jests of One Called Edith* [London: J. Rastell], STC 22869.7; 1573 edition [London: William Williamson], STC 22870.)

Souden, David. "'Rogues, Whores, and Vagabonds'? Indentured Servant Emigrants to North America." *Social History* 3 (1980): 23–41.

Spenser, Edmund. *The Faerie Queene*. Ed. A. C. Hamilton. London: Longman, 1977.

———. *The Yale Edition of the Shorter Poems of Edmund Spenser*. Ed. William A. Oram et al. New Haven, Conn.: Yale University Press, 1989.

Spierenburg, Pieter. *The Prison Experience: Disciplinary Institutions and Their Inmates in Early Modern Europe*. New Brunswick, N.J.: Rutgers University Press, 1991.

———. *The Spectacle of Suffering: Executions and the Evolution of Repression: From a Preindustrial Metropolis to the European Experience*. Cambridge: Cambridge University Press, 1984.

Splinter, Johan. *A Merry Jest and a True How Johan Splinter Made His Testament*. London: J. Notary, 1520[?]. STC 23102.

Statute of Artificers. 1563. In *Tudor Economic Documents*. Ed. R. H. Tawney and Eileen Power. 3 vols. London: Longmans, 1924. 1:338–49.

Starkey, Thomas. *A Dialogue between Reginald Pole and Thomas Lupset*. Ca. 1533–35. Ed. Kathleen M. Burton. London: Chatto and Windus, 1948.

Storer, Edward. "Introduction." In *The Facetiae of Poggio and Other Medieval Story-Tellers*. Ed. and trans. Edward Storer. London: Routledge, 1928. 1–32.

Stratton, Suzanne. "Rembrandt's Beggars: Satire and Sympathy." *Print Collector's Newsletter* 17 (1986): 77–82.

Stubbes, Phillip. *The Anatomy of Abuses in England*. 1583. Ed. Frederick J. Furnivall. London: N. Trübner, 1877–79.

Sullivan, Garrett A., Jr. *The Drama of Landscape: Land, Property, and Social Relations on the Early Modern Stage*. Stanford, Calif.: Stanford University Press, 1998.

Sumption, J. *Pilgrimage: An Image of Medieval Religion*. Totowa, N.J.: Rowman and Littlefield, 1975.

Supple, Barry. *Commercial Crisis and Change in England, 1600–1642.* Cambridge: Cambridge University Press, 1959.

A Supplication of the Poor Commons. 1546. Ed. J. Meadows Cowper. In Simon Fish. *A Supplication for the Beggars.* Ca. 1529. Ed. Frederick J. Furnivall. London: Early English Text Society, 1871. 59–92.

A Supplication to Our Most Sovereign Lord, King Henry the Eighth. 1544. Ed. J. Meadows Cowper. In Simon Fish. *A Supplication for the Beggars.* Ed. Frederick J. Furnivall. London: Early English Text Society, 1871. 19–58.

Surtz, Edward. "Richard Pace's Sketch of Thomas More." *Journal of English and Germanic Philology* 57 (1958): 36–50.

Swetnam, Joseph. *The Araignment of Lewde, Idle, Froward, and Unconstant Women; or, The Vanitie of Them, Choose You Whether.* London: Edward Allde, 1615. STC 23533.

Szittya, Penn R. *The Antifraternal Tradition in Medieval Literature.* Princeton, N.J.: Princeton University Press, 1986.

Tales and Quick Answers, Very Merry, and Pleasant to Read. 1532. In *Shakespeare Jest-Books.* Ed. William Hazlitt. 3 vols. London: Willis and Sotheran, 1864. 1:15–162. (1532 edition [London: Thomas Berthelet], STC 23665; reprinted in 1567 [London: H. Wykes], STC 23665.5; entered 1576, but no edition is extant from that date.)

Tarlton's Jests. London: Thomas Snodham, 1613. STC 23683.3. (There is evidence of a lost edition, pre-1592.)

Tarlton's News out of Purgatory. London: Robert Robinson, 1590. STC 23685.

Tawney, R. H. *The Agrarian Problem in the Sixteenth Century.* 1912. New York: Harper and Row, 1967.

——. *Religion and the Rise of Capitalism.* 1926. London: Penguin, 1966.

Tawney, R. H., and Eileen Power, eds. *Tudor Economic Documents.* 3 vols. London: Longmans, 1924.

Taylor, Archer. *Problems in German Literary History of the Fifteenth and Sixteenth Centuries.* New York: Modern Language Association, 1939.

Taylor, Barry. *Vagrant Writing: Social and Semiotic Disorders in the English Renaissance.* New York: Harvester, 1991.

Taylor, John (The Water Poet). "The Praise, Antiquity, and Commodity of Beggary, Beggars, and Begging." In *All the Works of John Taylor, the Water Poet.* 1621. London: James Boler, 1630. 95–102.

Thirsk, Joan. *Economic Policy and Projects: The Development of a Consumer Society in Early Modern England.* Oxford: Clarendon Press, 1978.

——. "England's Provinces: Did They Serve or Drive Material London?" In *Material London, ca. 1600.* Ed. Lena Cowen Orlin. Philadelphia: University of Pennsylvania Press, 2000. 97–109.

——. "Tudor Enclosures." In *The Tudors.* Ed. Joel Hurstfield. New York: St. Martin's Press, 1973. 104–27.

Thomas, D. B. "Preface." In *The Book of Vagabonds and Beggars with a Vocabulary of Their Language and a Preface by Martin Luther.* Ca. 1509. Ed. D. B. Thomas. Trans. J. C. Hotten. London: Penguin, 1932. xi–xiv.

Thomas, Keith. "Fateful Exposures." *Times Literary Supplement,* August 25, 1989, 913–14.

——. *Religion and the Decline of Magic.* Harmondsworth, England: Penguin, 1973.

Thompson, Stith. *Motif-Index of Folk-Literature.* Rev. ed. 6 vols. Bloomington: Indiana University Press, 1955.

Thomson, J. A. F. "Piety and Charity in Late Medieval London." *Journal of Ecclesiastical History* 16 (1965): 178–95.

Tierney, Brian. *Medieval Poor Law: A Sketch of Canonical Theory and Its Application in England.* Berkeley: University of California Press, 1959.

Tilney, Edmund. *A Brief and Pleasant Discourse of Duties in Marriage, Called the Flower of Friendship.* 1568. In *The Flower of Friendship: A Renaissance Dialogue Contesting Marriage.* Ed. Valerie Wayne. Ithaca, N.Y.: Cornell University Press, 1992.

Timpane, John Philip, Jr. "The Romance of the Rogue: The History of a Character in English Literature, 1497–1632." Ph.D. dissertation, Stanford University, 1980.

Todd, Margo. "Humanists, Puritans, and the Spiritualized Household." *Church History* 49 (1980): 18–34.

Toro, P. A., E. J. Trickett, D. D. Wall, and D. A. Salem. "Homelessness in the United States: An Ecological Perspective." *American Psychologist* 46 (1991): 1208–18.

Turner, John. "The Tragic Romances of Feudalism." In *Shakespeare: The Play of History.* Ed. Graham Holderness, Nick Potter, and John Turner. Iowa City: University of Iowa Press, 1987. 85–118.

Udall, Nicholas. *Respublica.* 1553. Ed. W. W. Greg. London: Oxford University Press, 1952.

Underdown, David. *Revel, Riot, and Rebellion: Popular Politics and Culture in England, 1603–1660.* Oxford: Clarendon Press, 1985.

U.S. Congress. House. Subcommittee on Housing and Community Development. *Home-lessness in America—The Need for Permanent Housing: Hearings before the Subcommittee on Housing and Community Development.* 101st Cong., 2d sess., March 15, 1989.

Utterson, Edward Vernon. *Select Pieces of Early Popular Poetry.* London: T. Davison, 1817.

Van Whitlock, Rod, Bernard Lubin, and Jean R. Sailors, comps. *Homelessness in America, 1983–1992: An Annotated Bibliography.* Westport, Conn.: Greenwood Press, 1994.

Vickers, Brian. *Appropriating Shakespeare: Contemporary Critical Quarrels.* New Haven, Conn.: Yale University Press, 1993.

———. *Occult and Scientific Mentalities in the Renaissance.* Cambridge: Cambridge University Press, 1984.

Vidler, Anthony. *The Architectural Uncanny.* Cambridge, Mass.: M.I.T. Press, 1992.

Vigarello, Georges. *Concepts of Cleanliness: Changing Attitudes in France since the Middle Ages.* Cambridge: Cambridge University Press, 1989.

Vitry, Jacques de. *The Exempla or Illustrative Stories from the Sermones Vulgares of Jacques de Vitry.* Ed. Thomas Frederick Crane. London: Folk-Lore Society, 1890.

Vives, Juan Luis. *Concerning the Relief of the Poor.* 1526. Trans. Margaret M. Sherwood. New York: New York School of Philanthropy, 1917.

———. *The Instruction of a Christian Woman.* Trans. Richard Hyrde. London: John Dant-er, 1592. STC 24863.

———. *The Office and Duty of a Husband.* Trans. T. Paynell. London: J. Cawood, 1553[?]. STC 24855.

Wager, Lewis. *The Life and Repentance of Mary Magdalene.* Ca. 1550–66. In *Reformation Biblical Drama in England.* Ed. Paul Whitfield. New York: Garland, 1992. 1–66.

Walker, Gilbert. *A Manifest Detection of the Most Vile and Detestable Use of Dice-Play.* 1555.

In *Rogues, Vagabonds, and Sturdy Beggars: A New Gallery of Tudor and Early Stuart Rogue Literature.* 1972. Ed. Arthur F. Kinney. 2d ed. Amherst: University of Massachusetts Press, 1990. (1555 edition [London: Abraham Vele], STC 24961.)

Wall, Wendy. *The Imprint of Gender: Authorship and Publication in the English Renaissance.* Ithaca, N.Y.: Cornell University Press, 1993.

———. "Renaissance National Husbandry: Gervase Markham and the Publication of England." *Sixteenth Century Journal* 27 (1996): 767–85.

Walter, John. "A 'Rising of the People'? The Oxfordshire Rising of 1596." *Past and Present* 107 (1989): 90–103.

Walter, John, and Keith Wrightson. "Dearth and the Social Order in Early Modern England." *Past and Present* 71 (1976): 22–42.

Walter, John, and Roger S. Schofield. *Famine, Disease, and the Social Order in Early Modern Society.* Cambridge: Cambridge University Press, 1989.

Ward, A. W. *Early Tudor Drama: Medwall, the Rastells, Heywood, and the More Circle.* London: Methuen, 1926.

Ward, Samuel. *Balm from Gilead to Recover Conscience.* London: Thomas Snodham, 1617. STC 25035.

Warneke, Sara. *Images of the Educational Traveller in Early Modern England.* Leiden: E. J. Brill, 1995.

Watt, Tessa. *Cheap Print and Popular Piety, 1550–1640.* Cambridge: Cambridge University Press, 1991.

Wear, Andrew. "Caring for the Sick Poor in St. Bartholomew's Exchange, 1580–1676." *Medical History,* suppl. 11 (1991): 41–60.

Webb, Henry J. "Elizabethan Soldiers: A Study in the Ideal and the Real." *Western Humanities Review* 4 (1950): 19–33, 141–54.

Webb, John, ed. *Poor Relief in Elizabethan Ipswich.* Suffolk, England: Suffolk Records Society, 1966.

Webb, Sidney, and Beatrice Webb. *English Poor Law History.* Part 1: *The Old Poor Law.* London: Longmans, Green, and Co., 1927.

Whately, William. *A Bride-Bush; or, A Direction for Married Persons.* 1616. London: B. Alsop, 1623. STC 25298.

Whigham, Frank. *Ambition and Privilege: The Social Tropes of Elizabethan Courtesy Theory.* Berkeley: University of California Press, 1984.

White, Richard Weddington. *Rude Awakenings: What the Homeless Crisis Tells Us.* San Francisco: ICS Press, 1992.

Whitford, Robert. *A Work for Householders; or, For Them That Have the Guiding or Governance of Any Company.* London: Robert Redman, 1530. STC 25421.8.

Whittinton, Robert. *Vulgaria.* 1520. Ed. Beatrice White. London: Early English Text Society 1932.

Wigley, Mark. "Untitled: The Housing of Gender." In *Sexuality and Space.* Ed. Beatriz Colomina. Princeton, N.J.: Princeton University School of Architecture, 1992. 327–89.

Willen, Diane. "Women in the Public Sphere in Early Modern England." *Sixteenth Century Journal* 19 (1988): 559–75.

Williams, Arnold. "Chaucer and the Friars." *Speculum* 28 (1953): 499–513.

———. "Two Notes on Chaucer's Friars." *Modern Philology* 54 (1956): 117–20.

Williams, C. H. *English Historical Documents, 1485–1558.* Gen. ed. David C. Douglas. New York: Oxford University Press, 1967.

Williams, Ethel Carleton. *Bess of Hardwick.* London: Longmans, Green, 1959.

Williams, Penry. *The Tudor Regime.* Oxford: Clarendon Press, 1979.

Williams, Raymond. *The Country and the City.* New York: Oxford University Press, 1973.

Wilson, F. P. "The English Jestbooks of the Sixteenth and Early Seventeenth Century." *Huntington Library Quarterly* 2 (1939): 121–58.

Wilson, Richard. *Will Power: Essays on Shakespearean Authority.* Detroit: Wayne State University Press, 1993.

Wilson, Robert H. "The Poggiana in Caxton's *Esope.*" *Philological Quarterly* 30 (1951): 348–52.

Wilson, Thomas. *The Art of Rhetoric.* 1553. Ed. Robert Hood Bowers. Gainesville, Fla.: Scholars' Facsimiles and Reprints, 1962.

Wily Beguiled. London: Humphrey Lownes, 1606. STC 25818.

The Wonderful Discovery of the Witchcrafts of Margaret and Phillip Flower. London: G. Eld, 1619. STC 11107.

Woodbridge, Linda. *The Scythe of Saturn: Shakespeare and Magical Thinking.* Urbana: University of Illinois Press, 1994.

———. *Women and the English Renaissance: Literature and the Nature of Womankind, 1540–1620.* Urbana: University of Illinois Press, 1984.

Woodward, Donald. "Wage Rates and Living Standards in Pre-Industrial England." *Past and Present* 91 (1981): 28–46.

Wordie, J. R. "The Chronology of English Enclosure, 1500–1914." *Economic History Review,* 2d ser., 36 (1983): 483–505.

Wotton, Henry. *The Elements of Architecture.* London: J. Bill, 1624. STC 26011.

Wright, S. J. *Parish, Church, and People: Local Studies in Lay Religion, 1350–1750.* London: Hutchinson, 1988.

Wright, Talmadge. *Out of Place: Homeless Mobilizations, Subcities, and Contested Landscapes.* Albany: State University of New York Press, 1997.

Wrightson, Keith. *English Society, 1580–1680.* New Brunswick, N.J.: Rutgers University Press, 1982.

Wrightson, Keith, and David Levine. *Poverty and Piety in an English Village: Terling, 1525–1700.* New York: Academic Press, 1979.

Wrigley, Edward Anthony, and Roger S. Schofield. *The Population History of England, 1541–1871.* London: Edward Arnold, 1981.

Wyther, George. *Abuses Stripped and Whipped.* London: G. Eld, 1613. STC 25891.

Xenophon. *Xenophon: Treatise of the Household.* Trans. Gentian Hervet. London: Thomas Berthelet, 1532.

Yarington, Robert. *Two Lamentable Tragedies.* London: R. Read, 1601. STC 26076.

Index

Protestant theologians: and demonization of beggary, 100; disempowering of vagrants by, 101; on monastics, 100; on poor relief, 95; and scapegoating of vagrancy, 17; on secular beggars, 100

Pullan, Brian, 274

punishment: in Poor Laws, 272–73; Slack on, 66; stripping as, 139; of theft by hanging, Starkey on, 120; of thieves, More on, 121–23; of vagrants, 43, 55–56, 73

Purgatory: Fish on, 82–83; More on, 83

Puritanism: defined, 107n.9; and linguistic anxiety, 259–60; work ethic in, 97

Puttenham, George, 71

Quast, Pieter, 36

Quintilianus, Marcus Fabius, 50

Rappaport, Steve, 151; on causes of poverty, 269; on political unrest, 278; on vagrants' migration, 267–68

Rastell, John, 129, 291

Reformation: beggary and clerical mendicancy in, 81; centralization in, 152, 175; confiscations of, 83, 93; and the discourse of vagrancy, 83, 100–101; as distraction from poverty, 105; as distraction from vagrancy, 105–6; effects on, of rogue literature, 92; Harman's experience of, 70; Henrician, 93; skepticism in, 54, 132; social costs of, 105; theologians, 28; and vagrancy as social issue, 85, 95

Rembrandt, 236n.11

repentance: Harman on, 69; as trope in vagrancy texts, 69

Richard II (Shakespeare), 218

riots, 7, 151, 235n.4

Ritson, Joseph, 291

rogue, the: connotations of, 29; defined, 29; etymology of, 76n.6; gallery of, 29; humorous conceptions of, 29; in *King Lear*, 228; as prejudicial term, 29

rogue literature: and anticlericalism, 89, 92; as anticourtesy literature, 193; authors of, 19; beggars' fakery in, 14, 16, 24; beliefs about vagrants in, 11; civility emphasized in, 192–93; as comic genre, 19, 28; and creation of vagrancy, 44; defined in *An Act for the Punishment of Vagabonds,* 41; and discourse of vagrancy, 28; evoked in *King Lear,* 221–23; fanciful nature of, 11; features of, 3; and harsh attitudes toward the

poor, 41; as historical source, 11; influence of, on legislation, 43, 92; and jest books, 6, 46, 92 101; *Liber Vagatorum* as, 90; as myth, 2; myths fostered in, 9; Othering of vagrants in, 160, 239; patriotism in, 157; posture of investigation in, 61–64; in prose jest genre, 47; as public warning, 91; readership of, 3; rhetoric of crime reporting in, 63; rogues' image in, 11; scapegoating in, 12; sexuality in, 3; and Shakespeare, 34; as term in *Caveat,* 43; vagrants in, 39; vagrant sexuality in, 9; women's role in, 77n.13

rogues: as convicts, 4; Cony-Catcher on, 2; defined, 3; Greene on, 2; image of, 11; literary representation of, 3;

Röhrich, Lutz, 132, 138, 142

Roper, William, 167, 197

Routh, Harold V., 136

Ruzzante, Il, 17

Rybczynski, Witold, 32, 257

salvation: and good works, 99

Sanudo, Marino, 21–22, 180

satire, religious, 86

Saunders, J. W., 57

Saxe, Leonard, 227

scam artist. *See* con artist

scapegoating: for crimes of society, 239; and easy identification of rogues, 251; in *King Lear,* 211–12; and Othering process, 100; in rogue literature, 12; social need for, 14, 15; of vagrants, 57, 212

scatology: as feature of jest books, 130–31; in *Howlglas,* 133; in Luther's work, 186; in monastic preaching, 186–87; in More's work, 185; as signifier of skepticism, in jest books, 131, 132–33; as weapon, 185–87

Schochet, Gordon J., 163

Schoenbaum, Samuel, 263

Schofield, John, 170

Schultz, Ernst, 290

Schuster, Louis A., 185

Scott, James C., 232

Scribner, R. W., 140, 186

security: preoccupation with, 31

sedition: defined, 7; of vagrants, 8, 151–52

Segni, Giovan Battista, 21, 223

Selden, Raman, 214

sexuality: and beliefs about vagrancy, 2, 14; and the clergy, 85–86, 100–101; criminals and, 11; misrepresentation of, among va-

grants, 9; in monasteries, 86–88; newly
privatized, 174; punishment of, 273; in
rogue literature, 3; in rogue society, 3;
among vagrants, Harmon on, 66; of vagrant women, 45
Shakespeare, William: *All's Well That Ends
Well*, 200; *Antony and Cleopatra*, 261; *As
You Like It*, 25, 143, 181, 192, 218, 261, 262;
comedies of, 18; and Copland, 34; *Coriolanus*, 35, 210; and the discourse of vagrancy, 34–35; *Hamlet*, 32; *1 Henry IV*, 34,
52, 136, 200; *2 Henry IV*, 143–44, 260, 264;
Henry V, 52–53, 200; *1 Henry VI*, 260; *2
Henry VI*, 24, 170, 181, 223, 242; home security in, 170–71; hospitality in, 260–61;
jesters in, 143–44; *King Lear*, 20, 34, 35,
144, 246, 205–34, 262, 264, 273; lodgings
of, 262–64; *Love's Labor's Lost*, 141; *Macbeth*, 34, 207, 260, 261; *Measure for Measure*, 170, 263; *Merchant of Venice*, 260;
The Merry Wives of Windsor, 142, 200; *A
Midsummer Night's Dream*, 199, 200, 249;
mobility in, 249; *Much Ado about Nothing*, 289; on parent-child relationship, 164;
soldiers' disabilities in, 52–53; *Richard II*,
218; *The Taming of the Shrew*, 199–200,
253; *Timon of Athens*, 116, 130, 207; *Twelfth
Night*, 18, 143; *The Winter's Tale*, 34, 159,
172, 189, 240. *See also specific works*
Sharpe, J. A., 3; on criminalization of the
poor, 37n.11; on economic crises, 24; and
fraternity of vagabonds, 4; on hangings,
272
Sherry, Richard, 71
Sidney, Sir Philip, 127
Siegel, Paul, 237n.18
skepticism: and *Howlglas*, 132–33, 139; humanist, in jest books, 130–32; in Reformation, 132
Slack, Paul, 152, 187, 270; on carnivalesque
depictions of poverty, 241; on charity, 99,
114; on creation of vagrant class, 44; on
criminalization of vagrants, 4; on culture
of poverty, 41; on disease, 271; on dissolution of monasteries, 94; on Elizabethan
crime and punishment, 66; on labeling,
227–28; on mortality crisis, 45; on power
of magistrates, 60; on prisons, 273; summary of vagrancy of, 268; on vagrant
idleness, 8; on vagrant threat, 7; on Wolsey's antiplague campaign, 179

slavery: and the vagrancy act, 5
Smith, Bruce, 107n.4
Smith, Henry, 8
Smith, Walter, 18, 19, 46, 80, 251; social ambi-
tions of, 197–98; *The Twelve Merry Jests of
the Widow Edith*, 125, 190, 192, 193–203,
204nn.9, 13. *See also* Widow Edith
society: instability of, 26; rogue infiltration
of, 251
sodomy, 107n.4
soldiers, 52
Soly, Hugo, 6, 95, 120, 277
spectacle: of death, 73; of poverty, 1, 121; of
public punishment, 154
Spenser, Edmund, 19, 127, 190, 203n.5,
266n.5, 289; *The Faerie Queene*, 184, 196
Spierenburg, Pieter, 36n.5, 37n.11, 107n.5, 154
Splinter, Johan, 101, 135
Starkey, Thomas, 109, 122, 156, 158, 159, 171; *A
Dialogue between Reginald Pole and
Thomas Lupset*, 119–21, 189–90; on disease, 181; on education, 119; on Elton,
176n.4; on idleness, 119, 136–37; on poverty, 120; on theft, 120
state, the: allegiance to, 254; centralized, 5;
and domesticity, 161; early modern, stability of, 2; identity, 158; modern, 32;
modern, creation of, 153; Tudor consolidation of, 149, 152–56; and vagrants, 32;
vagrant threat to, 7
statutes, Stuart, 1
stereotypes: of homelessness, 3
Stow, John, 42
Stratton, Suzanne, 17, 36n.7
stripping: as disclosure of deceit, in *The
Twelve Merry Jests of Widow Edith*, 196; as
expression of folk fear, 197; of the poor,
197; as punitive humiliation, 139
Stubbes, Philip, 1, 97, 146n.1
subculture: as imaginative creation, 6
subsistence: of vagrants, 6
subversion: state-manufactured, 5; and vagrants, 4
Sullivan, Garrett A., 52, 173
Supplication for the Beggars, A (Fish): va-
grancy and the Catholic Church in, 81
*Supplication to Our Most Sovereign Lord, King
Henry the Eighth, A* (anonymous), 216
Surly (character in *The Alchemist*), 65
Swetnam, Joseph, 244–45
Szittya, Penn R., 174

LINDA WOODBRIDGE, professor of English at The Pennsylvania State University, is the author of *Women and the English Renaissance: Literature and the Nature of Womankind, 1540–1620* (1984) and *The Scythe of Saturn: Shakespeare and Magical Thinking* (1994). She was a member of the faculty at the University of Alberta for twenty-four years, also serving as chair of the English department, and is a past president of the Shakespeare Association of America.

Typeset in 10.5/13 Minion
with Minion display
Composed by Barbara Evans
at the University of Illinois Press
Manufactured by Thomson-Shore, Inc.

University of Illinois Press
1325 South Oak Street
Champaign, IL 61820-6903
www.press.uillinois.edu